D0982529

The Early Works of John Dewey

1882 – 1898

John Dewey

The Early Works, 1882–1898

2: 1887

Psychology

Carbondale and Edwardsville

SOUTHERN ILLINOIS UNIVERSITY PRESS

FEFFER & SIMONS, INC.

London and Amsterdam

The Early Works of John Dewey, 1882–1898, *is the result of a co-operative research project at Southern Illinois University.*

Jo Ann Boydston is the General Editor. Fredson Bowers is Consulting Textual Editor.

The Editorial Advisory Board consists of Lewis E. Hahn, Chairman; Joe R. Burnett; S. Morris Eames; William R. McKenzie; and Francis T. Villemain.

Polly Dunn Williams is Staff Assistant.

CENTER FOR EDITIONS OF
AMERICAN AUTHORS
AN APPROVED TEXT
MODERN LANGUAGE
ASSOCIATION OF AMERICA
®

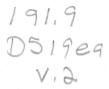

This is a photo-offset reprinting of the original edition. No changes have been made.

This reprinting has been made possible by a special subvention from the John Dewey Foundation.

Copyright © 1967 by Southern Illinois University Press
All rights reserved
First published, December 1967
Second printing, February 1975
Printed in the United States of America
Designed by Andor Braun
Frontispiece drawing of John Dewey by Herbert L. Fink
International Standard Book Number 0-8093-0282-9
Library of Congress Catalog Card Number 67-13938

Preface

WITH THE ASSISTANCE of many scholars and friends we began, in 1961, to collect and prepare for publication all of the extant published works of John Dewey. During the six years between 1961 and the issuance of the first volume in the series, the magnitude and difficulty of the undertaking confirmed the need for ready access by the public to this important philosopher's forty books and almost seven hundred articles published in some one hundred forty journals. Students had found it increasingly difficult to examine Dewey's thought, both because of the inaccessibility of materials and the size of the corpus of Dewey's writings. As work on the texts progressed and news of our project spread, we received numerous requests for copies of hard-to-locate materials, for identification of items, and for information about revisions. The varied sources of these requests indicated that the collected works will be useful to students in a number of specialized disciplines; and, of course, many readers will be interested in the reactions of a great mind to seventy years of tumultuous events. Americans will be able to follow Dewey's interpretation of and his growing concern with the global scene. Readers in other countries will have a basis for estimating the extent to which Dewey's thought transcends national boundaries and is viable for the twentieth century.

We decided that the extraordinary effort and expense of publishing the collected works would be best justified if we developed definitive texts. Therefore, in this edition we have applied the principles and techniques of modern textual criticism. This approach, developed primarily in connection with editing the works of such American literary figures as Hawthorne, has been used here for the first time in editing the writings of an American philosopher.

Those familiar with Dewey's essays will appreciate the reasons for our decision to print most of his works in approximately chronological order. (The exceptions are those in which Dewey's participation was limited or questionable—*Applied Psychology* [1889], *The Psychology of Number* [1895], the Chinese lectures, and a few other items—all scheduled for late volumes in the series.) Many of Dewey's insights were reflections upon the interrelations of such fields as philosophy, education, law, and the social sciences. To have identified a book or an article with only one particular discipline would have been to ignore its relevance to both the history and the continuing inquiries in other disciplines. It was decided that the disadvantages of a chronological order would be offset by two special features of the edition: 1] a complete analytical index; and   2] a guide to the works of John Dewey, presenting, in one volume, surveys by outstanding scholars of Dewey's contributions to such subjects as logic, psychology, and æsthetics. Included in that volume will be a listing of the works classified in each of the selected fields, with cross-references to major works in other fields.

The first five volumes, The Early Works, present most of the writings published in Dewey's "formative period," beginning in the year 1882 and ending in 1898. In addition to the articles, reviews, and other short pieces, the five volumes of The Early Works include the *Psychology*, *Leibniz's New Essays Concerning the Human Understanding*, *Outlines of a Critical Theory of Ethics*, and *The Study of Ethics*.

Each volume has the following parts: Preface, Textual Principles and Procedures, Table of Contents, Introduction to the Volume, Texts, Checklist of References, various kinds of textual apparatus—A Note on the Text(s), Emendations in the Copy-Text, Textual Notes, Special Emendations Lists—and an Index.

We are grateful to all those, and there were many, who helped in the work of preparing and publishing these volumes. Some of them are mentioned in the paragraphs that follow.

The administrative officers of Southern Illinois University most directly involved in our work were: Delyte W. Morris, President; Charles D. Tenney, Vice-President for Planning and Review; John E. Grinnell, formerly Vice-President for Operations, now retired; Robert W. MacVicar, Vice-President for Academic Affairs; John S. Rendleman, Vice-President for Business Affairs; William J. McKeefery, Dean of Academic Affairs; Elmer J. Clark, Dean, College of Education; Arthur E. Lean, former Dean of the College of Education; Ronald G. Hansen, Associate Dean of the Graduate School and Co-ordinator of Research and Projects; John O. Anderson, former Co-ordinator of Research and Projects; C. Richard Gruny, Legal Counsel; William E. Simeone, Dean of the Graduate School; Jacob O. Bach, former Chairman of the Department of Educational Administration and Supervision.

The Chairman of the Advisory Committee throughout the history of this undertaking was Willis Moore, Chairman of the Department of Philosophy, who deserves special thanks for his perceptive and able leadership. Members of the Advisory Committee not mentioned in other connections were: Henry Dan Piper, former Dean of the College of Liberal Arts and Sciences, and Robert D. Faner, Chairman of the Department of English. In the Office of Research and Projects, Webster Ballance and Wayne Stumph were of special help.

Many persons consulted with the Editorial Board on a variety of aspects of the work. We are indebted to all of them. Among those who helped with the design and advancement of the project were: John L. Childs, George S. Counts, George Dykhuizen, George R. Geiger, James Herrick Hall, Harry W. Laidler, Corliss Lamont, Richard P. McKeon, Charles Morris, Donald A. Piatt, George K. Plochmann, Paul A. Schilpp, Lloyd Suttell. In addition, the scholars involved in preparing an introduction to the works of John Dewey have made outstanding contributions: William W. Brickman, Max H. Fisch, Horace L. Friess, Gail Kennedy, Bertram Morris, Tsuin-Chen Ou, Darnell Rucker, and Herbert W. Schneider. Professor Schneider contributed to almost every aspect of our work.

We are profoundly indebted to M. Halsey Thomas, whose excellent bibliography[1] saved us years of work. For suggestions about materials and where to find them, we owe thanks to many of the persons mentioned in other connections as well as to Karl Andrén, James W. Merritt, Sidney Ratner, Paul G. Kuntz, R. D. Archambault, William S. Minor, Robert L. McCaul, Lewis S. Feuer, Charles A. Lee, the late Archibald W. Anderson, Erwin V. Johanningmeier, and for invaluable help on the Chinese materials, Robert W. Clopton and Cho-Yee To.

For the specialized help that only experienced and enthusiastic library personnel can give, we thank: Ralph W. McCoy, Director of Southern Illinois University Libraries; Ferris S. Randall, Director, Morris Library; Elizabeth O. Stone, former Assistant Director, Morris Library, now retired; Harold J. Rath and Maxine E. Walker in the Special Services Division; Ralph W. Bushee, Rare Book Librarian. Bill V. Isom and Thomas L. Kilpatrick, former and present staff members of the Education Library, and the Humanities Librarian, Alan M. Cohn, gave assistance far beyond the call of duty. Kenneth Duckett, University Archivist, contributed valuable insights and materials in the

[1] M. H. Thomas, *John Dewey: A Centennial Bibliography* (Chicago: The University of Chicago Press, 1962).

course of his work on the oral history aspect of this project.

We are grateful to Peter Draz, Robert H. Land, Joseph E. Hall, and Waldo H. Moore of the Library of Congress; Alice Bonnell, Carole Carlson, and Roland Baughman of Columbia University Library. Although we cannot acknowledge them by name, many other librarians in the United States, Formosa, Germany, England, and Hawaii co-operated in helping us obtain materials.

We are indebted in numerous ways to the textual consultants who worked with us in the initial stages to suggest procedures for our work: Matthew J. Bruccoli, Neal Smith, and Bruce Harkness.

For the outstanding role he played in this work in its beginning, and for his continued interest, our gratitude goes to Harold Taylor. Ernest Nagel, Mason W. Gross, and Agnes E. Meyer were also very helpful.

Eugene Exman, Vice-President of Harper and Row, gave willing and careful assistance in tracing the publishing history of *Psychology*. Mauck Brammer, Managing Editor of the American Book Company, co-operated wholeheartedly in the same task and made available priceless copies of the book.

The following, who were members of the project staff at various times, were instrumental in the successful launching of this publishing venture: Alimae Aiken Persons, Marilee Kuehn, Joan Lash, Kathleen Endsley, David L. Miller, and Edward F. McClain. For painstaking care and effort in all the textual work, our special thanks go to Polly V. Dunn.

The Editors

27 May 1967

Textual principles and procedures

THESE VOLUMES of The Early Works of John Dewey, 1882 – 1898, offer a definitive critical text of his writings arranged in a generally chronological order.

A text may be called "definitive," or "established," (a) when an editor has exhaustively determined the authority, in whole and in part, of all preserved documents containing the work under examination; (b) when the text is then based on the most authoritative documents produced in the work's publishing history; and (c) when the complete textual data of all appropriate documents are recorded, together with a full account of all divergences from the edition chosen as copy-text (the basis for the edited text) so that the student may recover the meaningful (substantive) readings of any document used in the preparation of the edited text.

A text may be called "critical" when an editor does not content himself with faithfully reprinting any single document without modification but instead intervenes to correct the faults or aberrations of the copy-text on his own authority or by reference to the corrections and revisions of some authoritative edition later than the edition or manuscript chosen as copy-text.[1]

The first step in the establishment of a critical text is the determination of the exact forms of the texts in the early editions and of the facts about their relationship one to another. An important distinction must be made immediately between an "edition" and a "printing" or "impression." Technically, an edition comprises a particular typesetting, without regard for the number of printings made at different times from this typesetting or its plates.[2]

[1] Various terms used here to describe textual principles and operations are discussed at length in Fredson Bowers, "Established Texts and Definitive Editions," *Philological Quarterly*, XLI (1962), 1 - 17; and in "Textual Criticism," *The Aims and Methods of Scholarship in Modern Languages and Literatures*, ed. James Thorpe (New York: The Modern Language Association of America, 1963), pp. 23 - 42.

[2] In the present edition the use of the bibliographical terms "edition," "impression" (or "printing"), "issue," and "state" follows that recommended in Fredson Bowers, *Principles of Bibliographical Description* (Princeton: Princeton University Press, 1949; offset by Russell & Russell, New York, 1962), pp. 379 - 426.

Textual variation is most commonly found when for one reason or another a publisher decides to make a new typesetting, since changes are inevitable in the process of transferring the words from the copy through the composing machines to the new form. Some of these changes may have authority if the writer himself took the opportunity presented by the new edition to correct or to revise his work; the remaining changes can have no authority since they emanate from publishers' readers or the compositors and may run the gamut from normal house-styling to positive though inadvertent error.

To establish texts for the present edition, all true editions up to Dewey's death in 1952 have been collated, their substantive variants recorded, and a decision made whether on the whole the new editions seem to contain authorial revision, or whether on the whole they represent no more variation than is normally to be anticipated in a series of unattended reprints. When new editions do give every evidence that they were revised by the author, an attempt is thereupon made to distinguish his corrections and revisions from the normal variation of publisher and printer that can have no authority.

Ordinarily, Dewey did not revise his work merely for stylistic felicity but instead to clarify, amplify, and sometimes even to alter his meaning. For this reason, that Dewey had himself revised a new edition is never in doubt, on the copious evidence.

On the other hand, alterations of various kinds can be made in the plates in preparation for running off more copies to form a new impression, or printing. Often these changes originate with the publisher, whose readers have seen misprints or other actual or fancied errors in the earlier printing and now take the opportunity to correct the plates. Although these corrections may prove to be so necessary or desirable that an editor will wish to accept them, they can have no basic authority, of course, when they were not ordered by Dewey himself. Moreover, it may happen that in the course of resetting a line to conform to the publisher's requested correction the printer may inadvertently make an error elsewhere that was not caught by the casual proofreading usually adopted for plate-changes. In addition, similar errors may be found when for purely mechanical reasons, such as damage to plates in storage between printings, or an attempt to refurbish excessive wear attacking a plate, the printer without the knowledge of the publisher or author may reset a page in whole or in part to make a new plate or extensively to modify an old one.

Corrections, as distinguished from revisions, made by a publisher's reader are almost impossible to separate from the corrections of an author unless they seem to bring variants into conformity with house-style, in which case their non-authoritative origin is manifest. On the other hand, meaningful revisions such as Dewey ordered made in the plates of both the 1889 and 1891 reprintings of *Psychology* are always recognizable owing to their particular nature or extent.

Not only every new edition but even every printing during an author's lifetime carries within itself the possibility for authorial correction or revision that an editor must take into account. Hence the first step in the establishment of the present text has been the collection of all known editions and impressions of each work, followed by the determination of their order and relationship from the examination of internal as well as external evidence. That is, publishers' markings may indicate the order of separate impressions, as found in the American Book Company's reprints of *Psychology*; but sometimes no external evidence is available, or else (like a failure to change the date on a title page) it is untrustworthy, and then internal evidence based on the wear and deterioration of the plates, combined with their repair, must be utilized to separate one otherwise indistinguishable impression from another and to determine its order in the printing history of the plates.

Such evidence has been gathered by the scrupulous examination of available copies of every known edition on the Hinman Collating Machine, which has also mechanically discovered for the editors the alterations made from time to time in the plates during their printing history, all of which have been recorded so that the evidence may be made available of the total body of facts from which the editors worked. This full stemma, then, of the total number of editions and impressions of any Dewey work, and their order, establishes the necessary physical base for proceeding to the investigation of the complete body of evidence about textual variation and its order of development, a matter that has a crucial bearing upon the determination of the authority of the variants in any given edition or impression.

Modern critics have come to a general agreement about the following propositions for the determination of authority in the process of editing a definitive edition that attempts to establish an author's text, in every respect. For overall authority, nothing can take the place of the manuscript that was used by the printer, because it stands in the closest relation to the author's intentions. In only one respect can the printed edition manufac-

tured from this manuscript exceed the manuscript in authority,
and that is in the specific alterations made in proof by the
author, which give us his final revised intentions. It is the
editor's task to isolate these from other variants such as errors
made by the compositor that were overlooked in the proofreading. The distinction between authorial revision in proof and
compositorial sophistication of a text is not always easy to make,
but informed critical and bibliographical investigation of the
corpus of substantive variants between manuscript and printed
text will ordinarily yield satisfactory results.

That is, when meaning is involved distinctions can be
made. But when meaning is not involved, as in the hundreds and
sometimes thousands of variations between manuscript and print
in respect to spelling, punctuation, capitalization, and word-
division, the inevitable assumption holds that the author has not
engaged himself to vast sums of overcharges for proof-
corrections, and that the ordinarily expected house-styling has
taken place, sometimes initiated by a publisher's reader, but
always concluded by the compositors.

A distinction develops, hence, between the words of a text—
the "substantives"—and the forms that these words take in respect to their spelling, punctuation, capitalization, or division,
what are known as the "accidentals" of a text.[3] Editorial criticism may attempt to assess the authority of the substantives,
but one must take it that, as against a printer's-copy manuscript,
no printed edition can have full authority in respect to the
accidentals.

On the other hand, some authors—and Dewey was often
among these—are extremely careless in the typing of the accidentals in their manuscripts since they are relatively indifferent
to anomalies and expect the printer to set all right for publication. Thus in some respects it is not uncommon to find that the
printed edition's accidentals may be superior to those of the
manuscript in matters of consistency and even of correctness.
Yet every author whether consciously or unconsciously, and
often whether consistently or inconsistently, does use the forms
of the accidentals of his text as a method for conveying meaning.
For example, Dewey frequently capitalized words he expected to
be taken as concepts, thus distinguishing them in meaning from

[3] The use of these terms, and the application to editorial principles
of the divided authority between both parts of an author's text, was
initiated by Sir Walter Greg in "The Rationale of Copy-Text," *Studies
in Bibliography*, III (1950-51), 19-36. For an extension and added
demonstration, see Fredson Bowers, "Current Theories of Copy-Text,"
Modern Philology, LXVIII (1950), 12-20.

non-capitalized forms of the same words. That he was not consistent does not alter the fact that he used such a device, which an editor must respect.

It follows that the words of the printed first edition have in general a superior, although not a unique, authority over those of the manuscript form of the text in view of the ever-present possibility that substantive variants in the print can represent authorial revision in proof. On the other hand, the author's accidentals, insofar as they are viable in correctness or consistency have a superior authority in manuscript from that in the printed form that has undergone the ministrations of copyreaders and compositors.

In these circumstances, a critical text—which is to say an eclectic text—will endeavor to join both authorities by printing each of the two major elements in the text from the form that is uniquely superior in its closeness to the author's own habits or intentions, although either element may be altered as necessary by editorial intervention to restore true authority, or purity.

This editorial principle can be extended logically to the situation when an author's manuscript has not been preserved, or is not available for use. In this circumstance the first edition, which is the only edition set directly from the author's manuscript, must necessarily take the place of the manuscript as the prime authority. If the author has not intervened to alter matters in any subsequent impression or edition, this first edition remains the single authority for both parts of the text and must therefore become the copy-text or basis for the definitive edition, although subject to editorial correction. Later impressions or editions may unauthoritatively alter, and even correct the text, but unless the author has himself ordered such alterations the changes have no authority and need only suggest possible corrections to an editor. Indeed, the usual history of a text in these circumstances is one of chronological degeneration into ever more corrupt readings.

On the other hand, when in a later impression or edition the author does indeed make his own revisions and corrections, these represent his altered intentions which must be accepted by an editor. The earlier readings should be recorded, because they have a historical importance in the development of the author's thought, but they obviously must be superseded by the author's final intentions. The substantive readings of a revised impression or edition, then, have a general authority superior to those in a preceding form.

Early editors were inclined to take as copy-text the last

edition of a work published in the author's lifetime, on the supposition that if he had corrected or revised it this edition would contain the maximum authority. This procedure is no longer current, for in relieving the editor of the necessity to demonstrate that any authorial revision had indeed taken place it usually resulted (in cases when no authoritative intervention had occurred) in an editorial reprint of the most corrupt edition of all. And even when somewhere in the publishing history authoritative revision had appeared, the naïve editorial acceptance of *all* substantive variants in the last edition as necessarily authorial produced an unscholarly mixture of true revisions side by side with the inevitable corruptions of a reprint.

No uncritical acceptance of *all* substantive readings in any edition, whether or not revised, therefore, meets modern standards of scholarly textual criticism. It is the duty of an editor to assess all the variants that have accumulated in a text during its history and to choose on critical and bibliographical evidence those that appear to be authorial while rejecting those that appear to be printers' corruptions.[4]

As suggested above, however, in cases when the manuscript is not available the accidentals of a first edition must necessarily be more authoritative, as a whole, than those of any later reprint. House-styled as in part these first-edition accidentals may be, the fact that they were set directly from the author's manuscript will often have influenced the compositors to adopt the manuscript forms; and in any event, they must necessarily represent a closer approximation of the manuscript accidentals than can any reprint, which is only one printed edition further house-styled and set from another printed edition. What changes in the accidentals may take place in a revised edition at the order of an author are often impossible to isolate but they must necessarily be fewer than the substantive alterations that were the chief reason for his intervention, especially with an author like Dewey.

On the modern textual principle of divided authority, therefore, the copy-text for this edition of Dewey remains stable as the earliest authority closest to the author, usually the first edition;[5] and hence the accidentals for Dewey's texts are es-

[4] As a case-history the first edition of Nathaniel Hawthorne's *House of the Seven Gables* may be cited. In this, scrupulous editorial investigation established that two-thirds of the substantive variants between the manuscript and first edition were unauthoritative in the print and were to be rejected. See the Centenary Edition of Hawthorne, Vol. II (Columbus: Ohio State University Press, 1965), pp. xlvii - lviii.

[5] Most Dewey manuscripts were not preserved, and among those extant some are in private hands and not available for re-editing. Those that have

tablished as those of the first editions printed from his manuscripts, when the manuscripts are not available. Whenever it is ascertained that no authorial revision or correction took place in any subsequent impression or edition, the first edition remains the final authority for the substantives as well. On the other hand, when substantive revisions were made in later impressions or editions, those that the editors believe are authorial are adopted in preference to the readings of the first edition, and thus an eclectic text is established that combines the highest authority in respect to the substantives drawn from revised forms of the text with the highest authority of the accidentals drawn from the edition closest to the manuscript source. In short, the copy-text remains the first edition, but into the texture of its accidentals are inserted the revised readings that have been selectively ascertained to represent Dewey's altered intentions.

In the process of editing, the principle has been adopted that each separate work is to be treated as an independent unit in respect to its accidentals. That is, each unit has its own problems of copy-text, with inevitable variation in the nature of the printer's copy and the house-styling given it, ranging from that found in all sorts of journals to that required by different book-publishers. Thus although an attempt has been made to secure uniformity of editorial result within each unit, certain features may vary between independent works within the present edition. For example, if the spelling or some other important feature of the accidentals differs within a given work, the editors attempt to reduce the variation to uniformity according to Dewey's own style as ascertained from his manuscripts. On

---

been studied or utilized suggest that the copy given to the printer might vary widely in legibility and in styling. According to his associates, Dewey usually composed on the typewriter with a margin-stop set at the left but seldom at the right, with the result that some words might be typed on the platen instead of on the paper. Customarily the machine was set for triple-spacing; revisions and additions were then typed in so that the final page might look as if it had been single-spaced. Handwritten comments might also be added, as well as handwritten revisions of the typed material.

Dewey was characteristically indifferent about his spelling; punctuation could be sporadic or altogether lacking. Colleagues have told of being asked by Dewey to work over a manuscript and put it into shape for the printer. One of Dewey's long-time editors in Henry Holt and Co. has stated ". . . I tried a number of times to 'improve' his style, but whenever I made a substantial change I found that I also had changed the sense and therefore had to reinstate the original. I did go over many passages with him and he improved them. He permitted us to use our house style, but I kept as close to the original as I could." (Letter from Charles A. Madison, 25 June 1964, preserved in Dewey Project Office, Southern Illinois University, Carbondale, Illinois.)

the other hand, if no variation is present in some such feature within an editorial unit, the copy-text form is retained even though it is known to be contrary to Dewey's own practice. That is, the editors have taken a narrow view of what constitutes authority and have declined to alter the copy-text in such respects except when variation itself is present that can be reduced to authoritative normality or when presumptive error requires correction.

Except for the small amount of silent alteration listed below, every editorial change in the chosen copy-text has been recorded, with its immediate source, and the original copy-text reading has been provided, whether in the substantives or the accidentals. The complete account will be found in the lists of emendations. The form is as follows. The page-line number is that of the present edition, followed by the reading adopted in the text. Following the square bracket is a notation of the immediate source of the emendation. If the responsibility of the editors, "W" will appear. Otherwise, the siglum will be that of the earliest printed edition or impression in which the adopted reading appears, followed by a notation of the choice of reading in all the collated impressions or editions that succeed. This notation is succeeded by a semicolon and thereafter appears the reading of the copy-text with a notation about the form of the reading in all impressions or editions, including any rejected intermediate revisions, up to the authority from which the emendation was drawn. With this information any student can trace the progress of Dewey's own revisions and changes of intention, or the editorial process in succeeding forms of the text that aided the process of its correction.

In most texts that have a reprinting history a certain number of variants will be positive errors or else unnecessary changes that are unauthoritative and have not been adopted by the present editors. All substantives of this kind have been recorded whether occurring in new impressions or in new editions. Likewise, all accidentals that in the history of the plates have been changed from the copy-text plating are also recorded so that the maximum information will be available to the student of the material on which the editors drew in making their estimates of the authority or non-authority of plate-variants.[6] However, when in a new edition the text is reset throughout, the number of accidentals changes would be too large to list. In

---

[6]   Changes made in the plates that correct errors that would otherwise have been silently made in the copy-text by editorial intervention (see below) are nevertheless recorded for the sake of completeness.

addition, since the editors will have adopted as emendations of the copy-text all such accidentals variants that seem to be either authoritative or advisable changes, no useful purpose would be served by listing the hundreds and hundreds of publishers' or printers' unauthoritative normalizings of the text on which they worked.

Since the number of rejected variants of the kind noted above that qualify for recording[7] is comparatively limited, no separate list has been made and this group of variants has been incorporated with the emendations lists.

In the lists of emendations an asterisk prefixed to the page-line number indicates that the emendation, or the refusal to emend, recorded in this item is discussed in the Textual Notes.

In special cases separate lists within the textual material may substitute for part of the Emendations List. For example, in the early articles as represented in Volume 1 the importance of capitalization to indicate concept meanings as distinct from non-concepts called for a certain amount of editorial emendation to correct the required sense from the inconsistent copy-text usage. The importance for meaning of these key words that have been emended is best called to the attention of the student in a separate list, whereas they might be overlooked if buried among a mass of material of other import in the general Emendations List. Similarly, some alterations or revisions in the system of headings in certain texts have seemed to warrant separate lists, as in the reworked headings system of *Psychology*.

The editors have made a number of silent alterations in the copy-text. These concern chiefly the mechanical presentation of the text and have nothing whatever to do with meaning, else they would have been recorded.

The most general class of these silent alterations has to do with Dewey's system of reference whether within the text, in footnotes, or in lists of authorities that he might append. Each of these references has been checked for accuracy, the titles have been expanded and made regular as necessary, and the details of capitalization, punctuation, and of bibliographical reference have been normalized for the reader's convenience. When a reference is within the text, its form may be condensed when the expanded information required by the reader to check the reference will be found in an appended list of authorities. Dewey's

[7]   Such rejected readings from editions later than the copy-text are to be distinguished from copy-text readings rejected in favor of subsequent revision or correction. These are recorded as emendations, of course.

footnotes, however, are kept in their original form and position, since their references are completed in the appended list.

All references in footnotes or within the text (and also in the rejected readings of the copy-text) that relate to points taken up within the work in question (whether by backward or by forward reference) have had the appropriate pages of the present edition substituted for their original page numbers applying to the copy-text itself.

A second large class of silent alterations concerns itself with the articles that Dewey published in England, wherein the English printer had styled in his own manner the American spellings, punctuation system, and other forms of the accidentals or presentation. Logically, on the principle of treating each separate text as an independent unit, the editors might have retained the English styling of these works; but for the convenience of American readers, and in some part as a means of automatically returning to certain undoubted features of the manuscripts that served as printer's copy, they have chosen instead silently to Americanize the elements in such copy-texts that were styled in the English manner when these run contrary to what can be established as Dewey's own usage. Thus words like "emphasise" have been altered silently to "emphasize", "colour" to "color"; and the position of punctuation in relation to quotation marks has been altered to American usage.

For the rest, the silent changes are mechanical and concern themselves with correcting typographical errors that could not be mistaken as true readings, making regular some anomalous typographical conventions or use of fonts, expanding most abbreviations, and so on. Typical examples are the removal of periods and dashes after headings, the expansion of "&c" to "etc.", changing syntactical punctuation after roman or italic words (or in italic passages) to follow a logical system, expanding titles such as "Professor" or "Governor", supplying accent marks in foreign words, on capital "E" in French titles, and normalizing German "ue" to "ü" whether in lower case or capitals. Roman numbers in chapter headings are silently altered to arabic, as are all references to them.

These remarks concern the general treatment of most texts in the present edition. When unusual features call for unusual treatment, special notice in the respective Notes on the Text(s) will be given of modifications or of additions. The intent of the editorial treatment both in large and in small matters, and in the recording of the textual information, has been to provide a clean reading text for the general user, with all the specialized material isolated for the convenience of the student who wishes to consult it.

The result has been to establish in the wording Dewey's final intentions in their most authoritative form divorced from verbal corruption whether in the copy-text or in subsequent printings or editions. To this crucial aim has been added the further attempt to present Dewey's final verbal intentions within a logically contrived system of accidentals that in their texture are as close as controlled editorial theory can establish to their most authoritative form according to the documentary evidence that has been preserved for each work.

Fredson Bowers

17 April 1966

Contents

Psychology

PART THREE: THE WILL

Introduction to Dewey's *Psychology*

DURING the years 1882 - 1886, John Dewey was appropriating the new philosophical method of George Sylvester Morris known as "the psychological standpoint." Following Morris's terminology, Dewey, in his articles in *Mind* (1886) had referred to the "universal" aspects of consciousness and had discussed "known objects" as "objective consciousness." This use of "consciousness" was attacked at once by Shadworth Hodgson in England as "illusory psychology." Dewey replied as best he could, but was evidently finding it difficult to make such language and method seem empirical and experimental.[1] He refers to this discussion on p. 17 of the *Psychology* and relates it to "one of the most disputed points . . . the relation of psychology to philosophy." In this connection he refers to current articles in the *Encyclopædia Britannica*, 9th edition, by Caird, Seth, and Ward, as well as to an article by Robertson in *Mind* for 1883, which shows his awareness of his relations to the British idealists. However, at the same time he adds a reference to his article in the *Andover Review* of 1884 on "The New Psychology", which he associates with those of G. Stanley Hall of Johns Hopkins, and puts in the context of "the more recent developments of psychology" and of "the bearings of the theory of evolution upon psychology". It would appear, therefore, that in his first major publication Dewey was attempting to incorporate the more recent physiological psychology represented by G. Stanley Hall into the philosophical system and ethics of Morris. The structure of the *Psychology* is dynamic idealism and psychological ethics, but the content embodies some of the latest experimental findings of the naturalists, especially in the 1891 revision.

This historical background may serve to give significance to the following lines from Dewey's "Preface" and explain why and how he took very seriously his aim to present psychology as

---

[1]   See the exchange in *Mind*: Shadworth Hodgson, "Illusory Psychology," XI (Oct. 1886), 478 - 94; Dewey, " 'Illusory Psychology,' " XII (Jan. 1887), 83 - 88; and Hodgson's reply, " 'Illusory Psychology'—a Rejoinder," XII (Apr. 1887), 314 - 18.

an introduction to philosophy, even though it "seems deserving of a treatment on its own account".

It is the custom of our colleges to make psychology the path by which to enter the fields of philosophy. . . . How shall we make our psychology scientific and up to the times, free from metaphysics . . . and at the same time make it an introduction to philosophy in general? . . . I am sure that there is a way of raising questions, and of looking at them, which is philosophic; a way which the beginner can find more easily in psychology than elsewhere.[2]

The language of the *Psychology* is that of voluntaristic idealism, but the actual analysis of the mind and of the "process of knowing" foreshadows much of Dewey's later philosophy. It is unnecessary to expound the doctrine here; the reader can readily discover for himself how the author succeeds in putting new wine into old bottles—an imprudent practice. The revisions of the *Psychology*, especially those for the "Third Revised Edition" (1891), indicate the gradual shift in Dewey's mind from the language of idealism to that of the "new" psychology.

It may be useful here to call the reader's attention to a few passages in the *Psychology* which are indicative of the later development. The revisions made for the second printing (1889) centered in an improved analysis of sensation, but even in these revisions there is evidence that the language of "universal intelligence" and "idealization" was giving him trouble. The more philosophical changes in the 1891 printing reveal that the author's thinking was already moving beyond the idealistic theory of self-realization to which his text was devoted. For example in the 1887 version, "Retention is the process by which external, actually-existing material is wrought over into the activities of self, and thus rendered internal or ideal." (p. 152) Compare the revision in the 1889 and 1891 printings:

> The idea is never a thing having an independent, separate existence; it is only a function of mind. . . . What is retained is the *effect* which the idea produces upon the mind. . . . The mind grows, not by keeping unchanged within itself faint or unconscious copies of its original experiences, but by assimilating something from each experience, so that the next time it acts it has a more definite mode of activity to bring to bear. (p. 134)

Here his criticism of the "reflex arc concept" is already foreshadowed.

His idealistic doctrine, first expressed in 1887 and continued through the revisions of *Psychology*, is summarized as follows:

[2]   *Psychology*, p. 4.

All products of the creative imagination are unconscious testimonies to the unity of spirit which binds man to man and man to nature in one organic whole . . . the free idealizing activity of mind working according to its own subjective interests, and having its end merely in this free play and self-satisfaction. . . . It dissolves this ideal element out of its hard concretion in the sphere of actual particular fact, and sets it before the mind as an independent element, with which the mind may freely work . . . in order to reach certain intellectual ends, [which] constitutes thinking. (pp. 174 - 75)

Every concrete act of knowledge involves an intuition of God; for it involves a unity of the real and the ideal, of the objective and the subjective. Stated in another way, every act of knowledge is a realization of intelligence. (p. 212)

Now note the contrasting doctrine of "feeling or interest," which first enters in the 1891 printing and becomes central in his later work.

Feeling, or the fact of interest, is . . . as wide as the whole realm of self, and self is as wide as the whole realm of experience. (p. 216) Every activity may . . . be regarded as one of *adjustment*. (p. 229) Feeling is an accompaniment of *activity*. It is the self finding . . . itself either hindered or furthered; either repressed or developed. . . . As no activity is entirely at random, but has certain connections and ends, feeling is an accompaniment of adjustment, of what in knowledge . . . [is] apperception. (p. 237) Feeling, so far as it is taken out of its isolation and put in relation to objects . . . is *interest*. . . . An interest attaches to an object. (p. 240) Every attempt to set up the ideal as *ultimate* has two evil effects. In the first place, it stifles the efforts of the individual, and substitutes for that spontaneous freedom of action which is the essence of æsthetic production a rigid obedience to externally imposed rules. In the second place, it ties the ideal down to what has already been accomplished, and thus destroys its ideal character. (p. 279)

G. Stanley Hall was correct in estimating Dewey's system to be primarily an ethics. The *Psychology* is continued in the *Ethics*. But it is also continued in Dewey's philosophy of education. The basic insights of *How We Think* (1910) are worked out in Chapters 8 and 18 - 20. The psychology of interest and of intelligent choice is developed in the context of a growing self, and Dewey is well aware of the practical pedagogical implications of his newer theory of self-realization. This fact is even more evident in the bibliographical notes at the end of each chapter, for they frequently close with references to the most recent German, post-Herbartian works on pedagogy. Especially impressive are the closing lines of "Appendix A" in which he gives the philosophical orientation of recent works on educational theory.

A few changes in the 1891 revision are indicative of new discoveries and new philosophical perspectives, but the main lines of his system are maintained, as they are also in the *Outlines of a Critical Theory of Ethics* (1891). All the changes made by Dewey in the text of *Psychology* are reproduced in this volume, either in the text itself or in the lists of emendations. Dewey's "Preface", with the "Note to the Second Edition" and "Note to the Third Edition", also included, indicate some of the sources of the changes and refer to the help especially of Professors Gardiner and Tufts. The influence of William James is also acknowledged, but at this time it related to certain technical changes in the theory of sensation and emotion, not as later to James's work on conception.

Dewey's interest and competence in psychology continued to develop throughout his life, and all his works reflect this development. But he abandoned the writing and amending of a textbook on psychology after 1891. The further developments in his ideas and applications in this field are associated with his work in ethics, education, logic, social and political theory, and philosophy of art.

During his Chicago years, especially from 1898 to 1904, he put this psychology in the context of Darwinian evolutionary theory and explained how the "mediation" of conflicting interests by ideas is a basic human "instrument" in biological adaptation to environment. But gradually his "genetic method" became a "social psychology" strongly influenced in this trend by George Mead and the anthropologists. He then emphasized the role of intelligent judgment not merely as an instrument of adaptation to the environment but also as an experimental process of reconstructing the social "sphere of action." Mind "in the concrete" must be understood as the critical and reconstructive process within customs and institutions which constitute the general framework of both human nature and human conduct. Thus his psychology became increasingly social and behavioral, approaching a culture analysis.

Herbert W. Schneider

29 April 1966

PSYCHOLOGY

BY

JOHN DEWEY, Ph.D.

PROFESSOR OF PHILOSOPHY IN MICHIGAN UNIVERSITY

Third Revised Edition

NEW YORK

HARPER & BROTHERS, FRANKLIN SQUARE

Preface

ANY BOOK, written as this one is, expressly for use in class-room instruction, must meet one question with which text-books outside the realm of philosophy are not harassed. What shall be its attitude towards philosophic principles? This is a question which may be suppressed, but cannot be avoided. The older works, indeed, were not so much troubled by it, for it is only recently that psychology has attained any independent standing. As long as psychology was largely a compound of logic, ethics, and metaphysics, the only thing possible was to serve this compound, mingled with extracts from the history of philosophy. And it must not be forgotten that such a course had one decided advantage: it made psychology a good introduction to the remaining studies of the philosophic curriculum. But at present, aside from the fact that there is already an abundance of text-books of this style, which it were idle to increase, psychology seems deserving of a treatment on its own account.

On the other hand, there are books which attempt to leave behind all purely philosophic considerations, and confine themselves to the facts of scientific psychology. Such books certainly have the advantage of abandoning—or, at least, of the opportunity of abandoning—a mass of material which has no part nor lot in psychology, and which should long ago have been relegated to the history of metaphysics. But one can hardly avoid raising the question whether such surrender of philosophic principles be possible. No writer can create nor recreate his material, and it is quite likely that the philosophic implications embedded in the very heart of psychology are not got rid of when they are kept out of sight. Some opinion regarding the nature of the mind and its relations to reality will show itself on almost every page, and the fact that this opinion is introduced without the conscious

3

intention of the writer may serve to confuse both the author and his reader.

But to me one other consideration seems decisive against such a course. It does not have due reference to the historic conditions of our instruction. One essential element in the situation is that it is the custom of our colleges to make psychology the path by which to enter the fields of philosophy.

How, then, shall we unite the advantages of each class of text-books? That is to say, how shall we make our psychology scientific and up to the times, free from metaphysics—which, however good in its place, is out of place in a psychology—and at the same time make it an introduction to philosophy in general? While I cannot hope to have succeeded in presenting a psychology which shall satisfactorily answer this question, it does appear to me an advantage to have kept this question in mind, and to have written with reference to it. I have accordingly endeavored to avoid all material not strictly psychological, and to reflect the investigations of scientific specialists in this branch; but I have also endeavored to arrange the material in such a way as to lead naturally and easily to the problems which the student will meet in his further studies, to suggest the principles along which they will find their solutions, and, above all, to develop the philosophic spirit. I am sure that there is a way of raising questions, and of looking at them, which is philosophic; a way which the beginner can find more easily in psychology than elsewhere, and which, when found, is the best possible introduction to all specific philosophic questions. The following pages are the author's attempt to help the student upon this way.

NOTE TO THE SECOND EDITION

The cordial reception given to a psychology written on a new basis, and which, as an innovation, might have found a shut door, has strengthened my conviction that, whatever the defects of the present attempt, its basis is the true one. I hope that the changes made in this edition will be found to make the book conform more nearly to the purpose as stated above. In thanking a number of correspondents for suggestions which I have utilized in preparing this edition, I cannot refrain from the particular expression of thanks to Professor Gardiner of Smith College, to whom my indebtedness is great. I am glad, also, to have an opportunity of saying that I shall be pleased to receive hints and suggestions from teachers using the book, and that I shall make use of them as far as possible.

NOTE TO THE THIRD EDITION

Many of the changes in this edition are in statement of particular facts where the science has advanced since the book was first written. In making them I have availed myself largely of the learning and aid of my friend and former colleague, Mr. J. H. Tufts, to whom are given my best thanks. Changes, tending to greater clearness or simplicity of statement, and amounting to a paragraph or more, will be found on pages 12 - 13, 29, 34 - 37, 43 - 47, 52, 53 - 55, 62, 75 - 76, 81, 85 - 88, 133 - 39 (except the references), 179 - 80, 190, 240, 241, 268 - 69, 270, 271 - 72. The only change involving an alteration of standpoint is in the general treatment of sensation. For the better theory, as it now seems to me, of the present edition I am indebted to the writings, on one side, of Mr. James Ward and Professor James, and, on the other, of Professor Watson. Finally, my hearty thanks are due to the teachers whose patience, energy, and learning have done so much to cover the deficiencies of this book and to make acceptable whatever of merit it has.

1

The Science and Method of Psychology

1] THE SUBJECT-MATTER OF PSYCHOLOGY

Definition of Psychology: Psychology is the Science of the Facts or Phenomena of Self

This definition cannot be expected to give, at the outset, a clear and complete notion of what the science deals with, for the reason that it is the business of psychology to clear up and develop what is meant by facts of self. Other words, however, may be used to bring out the meaning somewhat. *Ego* is a term used to express the fact that self has the power of recognizing itself as I, or a separate existence or personality. Mind is also a term used, and suggests especially the fact that self is *intelligent.* Soul is a term which calls to mind the distinction of the self from the body, and yet its connection with it. Psychical is an adjective used to designate the facts of self, and suggests the contrast with physical phenomena, namely, facts of nature. Subject is often used, and expresses the fact that the self *lies under* and holds together all feelings, purposes, and ideas; and serves to differentiate the self from the object—that which lies over against self. Spirit is a term used, especially in connection with the higher activities of self, and calls to mind its distinction from matter and mechanical modes of action.

Fundamental Characteristic of Self

This is the fact of *consciousness.* The self not only exists, but may know that it exists; psychical phenomena are not only facts, but they are facts of consciousness. A stick, a stone, exists and undergoes changes; that is, has experiences. But it is aware neither of its existence nor of these changes. It does not, in short, exist *for itself.* It exists only *for* some consciousness. Consequently the stone has no self. But the soul not only is, and changes, but it knows that it is, and what these experiences are which it passes through. *It exists for itself.* That is to say, it is a self. What distinguishes the facts of psychology from the facts of every other science is, accordingly, that they are *conscious* facts.

Consciousness

Consciousness can neither be defined nor described. We can define or describe anything only by the employment of consciousness. It is presupposed, accordingly, in all definition; and all attempts to define it must move in a circle. It cannot be defined by discriminating it from the unconscious, for this either is not known at all, or else is known only as it exists for consciousness. Consciousness is necessary for the definition of what in itself is unconscious. Psychology, accordingly, can study only the various *forms* of consciousness, showing the *conditions* under which they arise.

The Self as Individual

We have seen that the peculiar characteristic of the facts of self is that they are conscious, or exist for themselves. This implies further that the self is *individual*, and all the facts of self refer to the individual. They are unique in this. A fact of physics, or of chemistry, for the very reason that it does not exist for itself, exists for anybody or everybody who wishes to observe it. It is a fact which can be known as directly and immediately by one as by another. It is *universal*, in short. Now, a fact of psychology does not thus lie open to the observation of all. It is directly and immediately known only to the self which experiences it. It is a fact of *my* or *your* consciousness, and only of mine or yours.

Communication of an Individual State

It may be communicated to others, but the first step in this communication is changing it from a psychical fact to a physical fact. It must be expressed through non-conscious media—the appearance of the face, or the use of sounds. These are purely external. They are no longer *individual* facts. The next step in the communication is for some other individual to translate this expression, or these sounds, into his own consciousness. He must make them part of himself before he knows what they are. One individual never knows directly what is in the self of another; he knows it only so far as he is able to reproduce it in his own self. The fact of the existence of self or of consciousness is, accordingly, a unique individual fact. Psychology deals with the individual, or self, while all other sciences, as mathematics, chemistry, biology, etc., deal with facts which are universal, and are not facts of self, but facts presented *to* the selves or minds which know them.

Relation of Psychology to Other Sciences

Psychology holds, therefore, a twofold relation to all other sciences. On the one hand, it is co-ordinated with other sciences, as simply having a different and higher subject-matter than they. The student may begin with bodies most remote from himself, in the science of astronomy. He may then study the globe upon which he lives, in geography, geology, etc. He may then study the living beings upon it, botany, zoology, etc. Finally he may come to his own body, and study human physiology. Leaving his body, he may then study his own self. Such a study is psychology. Thus considered, psychology is evidently simply one science among others.

Psychology a Central Science

But this overlooks one aspect of the case. All the other sciences deal only with facts or events which are known; but the fact of *knowledge* thus involved in all of them no one of them has said anything about. It has treated the facts simply as *existent* facts, while they are also *known* facts. But knowledge implies reference to the self or mind. Knowing is an intellectual process, involving psychical laws. It is an activity which the self experiences. A certain *individual* activity has been accordingly presupposed in all the *universal* facts of physical science. These facts are all facts known by some mind, and hence fall, in some way, within the sphere of psychology. This science is accordingly something more than one science by the side of others; it is a central science, for its *subject-matter*, knowledge, is involved in them all.

The Universal Factor in Psychology

It will be seen, therefore, that psychology involves a *universal* element within it, as well as the individual factor previously mentioned. Its subject-matter, or its *content*, is involved in *all* the sciences. Furthermore, it is open to *all* intelligences. This may be illustrated in case of both knowledge and volition. For example: I know that there exists a table before me. This is a fact of *my* knowledge, of my consciousness, and hence is individual. But it is also a possible fact for all intelligences whatever. The thing known is just as requisite for knowledge as the knowing; but the thing known is such for all minds whatever. It is, therefore, universal in its nature. While knowledge, therefore, as to its *knower* is individual, as to *the known* it is universal. Knowledge may be defined as the process by which some universal element—that is, element which is in possible relation to all intelligences—is given individual form, or existence in a consciousness. Knowledge is not an individual possession. Any consciousness which in both form and content is individual, or peculiar to some one individual, is not knowledge. To obtain knowledge, the individual must get rid of the features which are peculiar to him, and conform to the conditions of universal intelligence. The realization of this process, however, must occur in an *individual*.

Illustration in Action

Volition, or action, also has these two sides. The content of every act that I can perform already *exists*, i.e., is universal. But it has no existence for consciousness, does not come within the range of psychology, until *I*, or some *self*, perform the act, and thus give it an individual existence. It makes no difference whether the act be to write a sentence or tell the truth. In one case the pen, the ink, the paper, the hand with its muscles, and the laws of physical action which control writing already exist, and all I can do is to give to these separate universal existences an *individual* existence by reproducing them in my consciousness through an act of my own. In the other case the essence of the truth already exists, and all the self can do is to make it its own. It can give it individual *form* by reproducing this universal exist-ence in consciousness or self.

Further Definition of Psychology

Our original definition of psychology may now be expanded. Psychology is the science of the reproduction of some uni-versal content or existence, whether of knowledge or of action, in the form of individual, unsharable consciousness. This individual consciousness, considered by itself, without relation to its content, always exists in the form of *feeling*; and hence it may be said that the reproduction always occurs in the medium of feeling. Our study of the self will, there-fore, fall under the three heads of Knowledge, Will, and Feeling. Something more about the nature of each of these and their relations to each other will be given in the next chapter.

2]   METHOD OF PSYCHOLOGY

Need of Method

The subject-matter of psychology is the facts of self, or the phenomena of consciousness. These facts, however, do not constitute science until they have been systematically col-lected and ordered with reference to principles, so that they may be comprehended in their relations to each other, that is to say, explained. The proper way of getting at, classifying, and explaining the facts introduces us to the consideration of the proper *method* of psychology.

Method of Introspection

In the first place, it is evident that, since the facts with which psychology has to do are those of consciousness, the study of consciousness itself must be the main source of knowledge of the facts. Just as the facts with which the physical sciences begin are those phenomena which are pres-ent to the senses—falling bodies, lightning, rocks, acids, trees, etc.—so psychical science must begin with the facts made known in consciousness. The study of conscious facts with a view to ascertaining their character is called *intro-spection*. This must not be considered a special power of the mind. It is only the general power of knowing which the mind has, directed reflectively and intentionally upon a certain set of facts. It is also called internal perception; the observation of the nature and course of ideas as they come and go, corresponding to external perception, or the observation of facts and events before the senses. This method of observation of facts of consciousness must *ultimately* be the sole source of the *material* of psychology.

Difficulties of Introspection

Some psychologists have gone still further and claimed that internal observation has a great advantage over external. It is said that while in examination of objects the mind may always be mistaken, in its introspection of itself it must always be correct, since the observer and observed are one. A man may be mistaken, for example, in holding that some substance is gold, it may be iron pyrites; but if he feels angry there is no danger of his mistaking anger for love. In reply to this, it may be stated, first, that the fact is not as thus reported. However it may be in anger, there are certainly many mixed and subtle emotional states, states of half-fear and half-hope, for example, which it is as difficult to identify as it is to identify a rare species of bird-life. Even as to anger, persons are not unknown who, the angrier they get, the more earnestly they assert themselves to be perfectly calm.

The experience is one thing; making that experience the object of reflection to find out what it is, is quite another. Psychological introspection is the latter act. A man unwonted to examining his experiences would have as much difficulty in correctly describing his own states of mind as would a layman in the accurate description of new chemical substances shown him.

Introspection a Scientific Process

Correctly to perceive a fact, in other words, is a work of analysis. To feel angry is one thing; to give a critical analysis of that feeling is quite another. They are so far from identity that, in this case, they are quite incompatible. When introspective analysis begins, the anger ceases. It is well understood that external observation is not a passive process—that it demands active attention and critical thought, and that its correctness will depend largely upon the ideas with which the object is approached. Plenty of objects are perceived wrongly every day because they are approached in the light of a wrong theory. To perceive with no ideas in the mind to which to relate the object is an impossibility. It is not otherwise with psychological observation. It is only recently that the great variety in the distinctness of mental images has been *observed*, although it must have been *experienced* millions of times. But the theory had been formed that all images are definite, and the theory rode rough-shod over the fact. To observe truly a mental fact demands a true hypothesis in the mind and proper material with which to correlate it. It is an act at once of analysis and of classification.

We shall see hereafter that there is no such thing as pure observation in the sense of a fact being known without assimilation and interpretation through ideas already in the mind. This is as true of the observation of the facts of consciousness as of perceiving physical facts.

Experimental

Amid these difficulties we can have recourse, first, to the *experimental* method. We cannot experiment directly with facts of consciousness, for the conditions of experimentation—arbitrary variation for the sake of reaching some end, or eliminating some factor, or introducing some other to test its effects, together with the possibility of measuring the cause eliminated or introduced and the result occasioned—are not possible. But we can experiment, indirectly, through the connection of the soul with the body. The physical connections of the soul—that is, its relation to sense organs and to the muscular system—are under our control, and can be experimented with, and thus, indirectly, changes may be introduced into consciousness. The method has two branches. One, *psycho-physics*, deals with the quantitative relations between psychical states and their bodily stimuli, while the other, *physiological psychology*, uses physiological processes for the sake of investigating psychical states.

Object of Physiological Psychology

Its object, as stated by Wundt, is to enable us to get results concerning the origin, composition, and temporal succession of psychical occurrences. Although this method has been employed but a short time, it has already yielded ample results in the spheres, especially, of the composition and relations of sensations, the nature of attention, and the time occupied by various mental processes. It will be noticed, therefore, that nerve and cerebral physiology cannot of themselves aid psychology directly; the mere knowledge of all the functions of the brain and nerves does not help the science, except so far as it occasions a more penetrating psychological analysis, and thus supplements the deficiencies of introspection.

Comparative Method

Even such results, however, are not complete. In the first place, the range of the application of this method is limited to those psychical events which have such connection with physical processes that they can be changed by changing the latter. And, in the second place, it does not enable us to get beyond the individual mind. There may be much in any one individual's consciousness which is more or less peculiar and eccentric. Psychology must concern itself rather with the *normal* mind—with consciousness in its universal nature. Again, the methods already mentioned give us little knowledge concerning the laws of mental *growth* or development, the laws by which the mind passes from imperfect stages to more complete. This important branch of the study, called *genetic* psychology, is, for the most part, untouched either by the introspective or experimental methods. Both of these deficiencies are supplemented by the *comparative* method.

Forms of the Comparative Method

Mind, as existing in the average human adult, may be compared with the consciousness (1) of animals, (2) of children in various stages, (3) of defective and disordered minds, (4) of mind as it appears in the various conditions of race, nationality, etc. The study of animal psychology is of use, especially in showing us the nature of the mechanical and automatic activities of intelligence, which are, in the human consciousness, apt to be kept out of sight by the more voluntary states. The instinctive side of mind has been studied mostly in animal life. The psychology of infants is of especial importance to us in connection with the origin and genetic connection of psychical activities. The study of minds which are defective through lack of some organ, as sight or hearing, serves to show us what elements of psychical life are due to these organs, while disordered or insane minds we may almost regard as psychical experiments performed by nature. The study of such cases shows the conditions of normal action, and the effects produced if some one of these conditions is altered or if the harmony of various elements is disturbed. The study of consciousness as it appears in various races, tribes, and nations extends that idea of mind to which we would be limited through the introspective study of our own minds, even if supplemented by observation of the manifestations of those about us.

Objective Method

The broadest and most fundamental method of correcting and extending the results of introspection, and of interpreting these results, so as to refer them to their laws, is the study of the objective manifestations of mind. Mind has not remained a passive spectator of the universe, but has produced and is producing certain results. These results are objective, can be studied as all objective historical facts may be, and are permanent. They are the most fixed, certain, and universal signs to us of the way in which mind works. Such objective manifestations of mind are, in the realm of intelligence, phenomena like language and science; in that of will, social and political institutions; in that of feeling, art; in that of the whole self, religion. Philology, the logic of science, history, sociology, etc., study these various departments as objective, and endeavor to trace the relations which connect their phenomena. But none of these sciences takes into account the fact that science, religion, art, etc., are all of them products of the mind or self, working itself out according to its own laws, and that, therefore, in studying them we are only studying the fundamental nature of the conscious self. It is in these wide departments of human knowledge, activity, and creation that we learn most about the self, and it is through their investigation that we find most clearly revealed the laws of its activities.

Interpretation in Self-consciousness

It must be borne in mind, however, that in studying psychological facts by any or all of these methods, the ultimate appeal is to self-consciousness. None of these facts mean anything until they are thus interpreted. As objective facts, they are not material of psychology, they are still universal, and must be interpreted into *individual* terms. What, for example, would language mean to an individual who did not have the power of himself reproducing the language? It would be simply a combination of uncouth sounds, and would teach him nothing regarding mind. The scowl of anger or the bent knees of devotion have no significance to one who is not himself capable of anger or of prayer. The psychical phenomena of infancy or of the insane would teach us nothing, because they would be nothing to us, if we did not have the power of putting ourselves into these states in imagination, and thus seeing what they are like.

So the phenomena made known in physiological psychology, would have no value whatever for the science of psychology, if they were not interpretable into facts of consciousness. As physiological facts they are of no avail, for they tell us only about certain objective processes. These various methods, accordingly, are not so much a departure from self-consciousness, as a method of extending self-consciousness and making it wider and more general. They are methods, in short, of elevating us above what is purely contingent and accidental in self-consciousness, and revealing to us what in it is permanent and essential; what, therefore, is the subject-matter of psychology. It is with the true and essential self that psychology deals in order to ascertain its facts and explain them by showing their connections with each other.

NOTES TO CHAPTER 1

One of the most disputed points is the relation of psychology to philosophy. Upon this point may be consulted, *Encyclopædia Britannica*, 9th edition, articles on "Metaphysic," by Caird; "Philosophy," by Seth; "Psychology," by Ward. See also *Mind*, Jan., 1883, "Psychology and Philosophy," by Robertson; April, 1883, "Psychological Principles," by Ward; Jan. and April, 1886, "The Psychological Standpoint," and "Psychology as Philosophic Method," by Dewey. See also psychological reviews in the same periodical, by Adamson (1884 and 1886).

Concerning the method of psychology, something may be found in almost every systematic treatise. See Lewes, *Study of Psychology*; Spencer, *Principles of Psychology*, vol. i, pt. 1, ch. vii; Sully, *Outlines of Psychology*, ch. i; Murray, *Handbook of Psychology*, ch. i; Hamilton, *Metaphysics*, lects. viii and ix; Porter, *Human Intellect*, introd., pp. i and iv; Volkmann, *Lehrbuch der Psychologie*, vol. i, pp. 1 - 54. Compare also the introduction to Waitz, *Lehrbuch der Psychologie*. For an excellent account of the various methods, see Wundt, *Logik*, vol. ii, pp. 478 - 502, with which compare *Philosophische Studien*, vol. i, p. 1.

Upon the special methods, psycho-physical, genetic, etc., see Appendix B. Accounts of some aspects of the more recent developments of psychology will be found, however, in articles upon "The New Psychology," in the *Andover Review* for 1884 and 1885, by J. Dewey and by G. Stanley Hall. A discussion of the bearings of the theory of evolution upon psychology will be found in Sully, *Sensation and Intuition*, ch. i.

There is no good history of psychology in either English or French. In German the student may consult Harms's *Geschichte der Psychologie*, and Siebeck's more extensive work with the same title, as yet (1886) brought down only through mediæval psychology. Much older, yet of value in some portions, is Carus's *Geschichte der Psychologie*. Volkmann (*op. cit.*) contains such complete historical accounts under each topic as to make it extremely valuable. Ribot has published accounts of contemporary English and German psychology, neither of which, however, is so thorough or accurate that it may be consulted instead of the original authorities. Höffding, *Outlines of Psychology*, pp. 1 - 28, has discussed the nature of psychology. See also James, *Psychology*, vol. i.

See also Bowne, *Introduction to Psychological Theory*, pp. 1 - 7; Ladd, *Elements of Physiological Psychology*, pp. 1 - 14; *Outlines*, pp. 1 - 10, for physiological psychology; and his *Introduction to Philosophy*, ch. iv, for relations of psychology to philosophy.

2

The Mind and its Modes of Activity

Introduction

Psychology has to do with the facts of consciousness, and
aims at a systematic investigation, classification, and explanation of these facts. We have to begin with a preliminary
division of consciousness into cognitive, emotional, and volitional, although the justification of the definition, like that of
psychology, cannot be seen until we have considered the
whole subject. By consciousness as cognitive, we mean as
giving knowledge or information, as appreciating or apprehending, whether it be appreciation of internal facts or of
external things and events. By consciousness as emotional,
we mean as existing in certain subjective states, characterized by either pleasurable or painful tone. Emotional consciousness does not, *per se*, give us information, but is a state
of feeling. It is the affection of the mind. By consciousness as
volitional, we mean as exerting itself for the attainment of
some end.

Cognitive Consciousness

Every activity or idea of the mind may be regarded as
telling us about something. The mind is not what it was
before this idea existed, but has added information about
something to its store. The consciousness may be the perception of a tree, the conception of government, the idea of the
law of gravitation, the news of the death of a friend, the idea
of a house which one is planning to build; it may, in short,
have reference to some object actually existing, to some
relation or law; it may be concerned with one's deepest
feelings, or with one's activities; but in any case, so far as it
tells about something that is, or has happened, or is planned,
it is knowledge—in short, it is the state of being aware of
something, and so far as any state of consciousness makes us
aware of something it constitutes knowledge.

Feeling

But the state of consciousness is not confined to giving us information about something. It may also express the value which this information has for the self. Every consciousness has reference, not only to the thing or event made known by it, but also to the mind knowing, and is, therefore, a state of feeling, an affection of self. And since every state of consciousness is a state of self, it has an emotional side. Our consciousness, in other words, is not indifferent or colorless, but it is regarded as having importance, having value, having *interest*. It is this peculiar fact of *interest* which constitutes the emotional side of consciousness, and it signifies that the idea which has this interest has some unique connection with the self, so that it is not only a fact, an item of knowledge, but also a way in which the self is affected. The fact of interest, or connection with the self, may express itself either as pleasurable or painful. No state of consciousness can be wholly indifferent or have no value whatever for the self; though the perception of a tree, the hearing of the death of a friend, or the plan of building a house will have very different values.

Will

A state of consciousness is also an expression of activity. As we shall see hereafter, there is no consciousness which does not depend upon the associating, and especially the attentive, activities of mind; and looked at in this way, every consciousness involves will, since in the perception of a tree, in the hearing of the death of a friend, or in the plan to build a house, the mind is engaged in action. It is never wholly passive in any consciousness. Yet it is evident that in the perception of the tree that factor of the consciousness is especially regarded which gives us information about something; in the death of a friend it is not with the fact of news nor with the mind's activity that we are concerned, but with the way in which the mind, the self, is affected; while in the plan and execution of the plan of building a house it is especially with the activity of the mind as devoted to realizing or bringing about a certain intention, purpose, or end that we have to do. The first would, ordinarily, be called an act of knowledge, the second, a mode of emotion, and to the third would be restricted the term volition or will. Any state of consciousness is really knowledge, since it makes us aware of something; feeling, since it has a certain peculiar reference to ourselves, and will, since it is dependent upon some activity of ours; but concretely each is named from the one aspect which predominates.

Relations to Each Other

Feeling, knowledge, and will are not to be regarded as three *kinds* of consciousness; nor are they three separable parts of the same consciousness. They are the three aspects which every consciousness presents, according to the light in which it is considered; whether as giving information, as affecting the self in a painful or pleasurable way, or as manifesting an activity of self. But there is still another connection. Just as in the organic body the process of digestion cannot go on without that of circulation, and both require respiration and nerve action, which in turn are dependent upon the other processes, so in the organic mind. Knowledge is not possible without feeling and will; and neither of these without the other two.

Dependence of Knowledge

Take, for example, the perception of a tree or the learning of a proposition in geometry. It may seem at first as if the perception of a tree were a purely spontaneous act, which we had only to open our eyes to perform, but we shall see that it is something which has been learned. Indeed, we have only to notice an infant to discover that the perception of an object is a psychical act which has to be learned as much as the truth of geometry. What, then, is necessary for the apprehension of either act? First, feeling is necessary, for unless the mind were affected in some way by the object or the truth, unless it had some interest in them, it would never direct itself to them, would not pay attention to them, and they would not come within its sphere of knowledge at all.

They might exist, but they would have no existence for the mind, unless there were something in them which excited the mind. Knowledge depends on feeling. But, again, the feeling results in knowledge only because it calls forth the attention of the mind, and directs the mind to the thing or truth to be known; and this direction of the attention is an act of will. In the case of first learning the proposition of geometry, it is easy to see that the directing, controlling, concentrating activity of will is constantly required, and the apprehension of the tree differs only in that there attention is automatically and spontaneously called forth, according to principles to be studied hereafter.

Dependence of Volition

An act of will involves knowledge. It may be a comparatively simple act, like writing, or a complex one, like directing some great business operation. In either case there is required a definite idea of the end to be reached, and of the various means which are requisite for reaching it; knowledge of the result aimed at and of the processes involved in bringing it about are necessary for the execution of any volition. But there is also a dependence upon feeling. Only that will be made an object of volition which is desired, and only that will be desired which stands in some relation to self. The purely uninteresting or colorless object, that which has not emotional connections, is never made an end of action. It is a mere truism to say that one never acts except for that which he believes to be of some importance, however slight, and this element of importance, of value, is always constituted by reference to self, by feeling.

Dependence of Feeling

Feeling, on the other hand, presupposes *volition*. Where there is no excitation, no stimulation, no action, there is no feeling. When we study feeling in detail we shall find that pleasurable feeling is always an accompaniment of healthy or of customary action, and unpleasant feeling the reverse. It is enough to notice now that feeling is the reference of any content of consciousness to self, and that the self is only as it *acts* or *reacts*. Without action or reaction there is, therefore, no feeling. If we inquire into the pleasure which arises from the acquisition of money, or the pain which comes from the loss of a friend, we shall find that one furthers and assists certain modes of activity which are in some way identified with the self, while the other hinders them, or wholly destroys them. One, in short, develops the self; the other reduces it. The activity of the self, either in raising or lowering the level of its activity, expresses itself in feeling.

All concrete, definite forms of feeling depend also upon the *intellectual* activities. We find our feelings clustering about objects and events; we find them associated with the forms of knowledge, and just in the degree in which they are thus associated do they cease to be vague and undefinable. Even in the lowest forms of emotional consciousness, as the pleasure of eating, or the pain of a bruise, we find some reference to an object. The feeling is not left floating, as it were, but is connected with some object as its cause, or is localized in some part of the organism. The higher and more developed the feeling, the more complete and definite is the connection with the intellectual sphere. The emotions connected with art, with morals, with scientific investigation, with religion, are incomprehensible without constant reference to the objects with which they are concerned.

Necessary Connection with Each Other

We have now seen that will, knowledge, and feeling are not three kinds of consciousness, but three aspects of the same consciousness. We have also seen that each of these aspects is the result of an artificial analysis, since, in any concrete case, each presupposes the other, and cannot exist without it. The necessity of this mutual connection may be realized by reverting to our definition of psychology, where it was said that psychology is the science of the reproduction of some universal content in the form of individual consciousness. Every consciousness, in other words, is the relation of a universal and an individual element, and cannot be understood without either. It will now be evident that the universal element is knowledge, the individual is feeling, while the relation which connects them into one concrete content is will. It will also be seen that knowledge and feeling are partial aspects of the self, and hence more or less abstract, while will is complete, comprehending both aspects. We will take up each of these points briefly.

Knowledge as Universal

We have already seen that the subject-matter of knowledge is universal; that is to say, it is common to all intelligences. What one knows every one else may know. In knowledge alone there is no ground for distinction between persons. Were individuals *knowing* individuals only, no one would recognize his unique distinctness as an individual. All know the same, and hence, merely as knowing, are the same. But feeling makes an inseparable barrier between one and other.

Two individuals might conceivably have feelings produced by the same cause, and of just the same quality and intensity, in short, exactly like each other, and yet they would not be the *same* feeling. They would be absolutely different feelings, for one would be referred to one self, another to another. It is for this reason, also, that as matter of fact we connect knowledge with ourselves as individuals. In any actual case knowledge has some emotional coloring, and hence is conceived as being one's *own* knowledge. Just in the degree in which this emotional coloring is absent, as in the perception of a tree or recognition of a truth of mathematics, the consciousness is separated from one's individual self, and projected into a universe common to all. Individuality of consciousness means feeling; universality of consciousness means knowledge.

Will as the Complete Activity

The concrete consciousness, on the other hand, including both the individual and the universal elements, is will. Will always manifests itself either by going out to some universal element and bringing it into relation to self, into individual form, or by taking some content which is individual and giving it existence recognizable by all intelligences. The knowledge of a tree or recognition of the truth of geometry illustrate the first form. Here material which exists as common material for all consciousness is brought into relation with the unique, unsharable consciousness of one. The activity of will starts from the interests of the self, goes out in the form of attention to the object, and translates it into the medium of *my* or *your* consciousness—into terms of self, or feeling. If we consider this activity in the value which it has as manifesting to us something of the nature of the universe, it is knowledge; if we consider it in the value which it has in the development of the self, it is feeling; if we consider it as an activity, including both the universal element which is its content, and the individual from which it starts and to which it returns, it is will. This we may call in-coming will, for its principal phase is that in which it takes some portion of the universe and brings it into individual consciousness, or into the realm of feeling.

Out-going Will

The other form of will is that which starts from some individual consciousness and gives it existence in the universe. The first stage is a desire, a plan, or a purpose; and these exist only in my or your consciousness, they are feelings. But the activity of self takes hold of these, and projects them into external existence, and makes them a part of the world of objects and events. If the desire be to eat, that is something which belongs wholly to the individual; the act of eating is potentially present to all intelligences; it is one of the events that happen in the world. If the purpose be to obtain riches, that, again, is a purely individual consciousness; but the activities which procure these riches are universal in nature, for they are as present to the intelligence of one as another. If the plan be to build a house, the plan formed is individual; the plan executed, the house built, is universal. This act of will resulting in rendering an individual content universal may be called *out-going* will, but its essence is the same as that of in-coming will. It connects the two elements which, taken in their separateness, we call feeling and knowledge.

The Subjective and Objective

Feeling is the subjective side of consciousness, knowledge its objective side. Will is the relation between the subjective and the objective. Every concrete consciousness is this connection between the individual as subjective, and the universe as objective. Suppose the consciousness to be that arising from a cut of a finger. The pain is purely subjective; it belongs to the self pained and can be shared by no other. The cut is an objective fact; something which may be present to the senses of all, and apprehended by their intelligences. It is one object amid the world of objects. Or, let the consciousness be that of the death of a friend. This has one side which connects it uniquely with the individual; it has a certain value for him as a person, without any reference to its bearings as an event which has happened objectively. It is subjective feeling. But it also is an event which has happened in the sphere of objects; something present in the same way to all. It is objective; material of information. Will always serves to connect the subjective and the objective sides, just as it connects the individual and the universal.

The student must, at the outset, learn to avoid regarding consciousness as something purely subjective or individual, which in some way deals with and reports a world of objects outside of consciousness. Speaking from the standpoint of psychology, consciousness is always both subjective and objective, both individual and universal. We may artificially analyze, and call one side feeling and the other knowledge, but this is an analysis *of consciousness*; it is not a separation of consciousness from something which is not in consciousness. For psychology no such separation can possibly exist.

Method of Treatment

In treating the material of psychology it is necessary, for purposes of presentation, to regard the separation of feeling from knowledge, and both from will, as more complete and rigid than it can be as matter of actual fact. Each will be considered separately, as if it were an independent, self-sufficient department of the mind. It might seem most logical to begin this treatment with feeling, as that is the most intimate, internal side of consciousness, but the dependence of the definite forms of feeling upon the definite forms of knowledge is so close that this is practically impossible. The dependence of knowledge upon feeling is, however, a general, not a specific one; so the subject of knowledge can be treated with only a general reference to feeling. Will, as presupposing both knowledge and feeling, will be treated last.

Material and Processes

In treating each of these heads we shall also, for purposes of clear presentation, subdivide the subject into three topics: (1) material, (2) processes, (3) results. That is to say, the object of the science of psychology is to take the concrete manifestations of mind, to analyze them and to explain them by connecting them with each other. We shall regard the existing states as the result of the action of certain processes upon a certain raw material. We shall consider, first, the raw material; second, the processes by which this raw material is worked up or elaborated; and third, the concrete forms of consciousness, the actual ideas, emotions, and volitions which result from this elaboration. The first two accordingly correspond to nothing which has separate independent existence, but are the result of scientific analysis. The actual existence is, in all cases, the third element only, that of result. Beginning, therefore, with knowledge, we shall define *sensation* as its raw material, consider the process of *apperception*, which elaborates this material into the successive stages of perception, memory, imagination, thinking, and intuition, finally recognizing that the concrete intellectual act is always one of intuition.

NOTES TO CHAPTER 2

Upon the questions of the relations of the various psychical factors to each other, and of the so-called faculties of the soul (questions which can hardly be separated), the following authorities may be consulted: Hamilton, *Metaphysics*, lects. x and xi; Porter, *Human Intellect*, introd., p. iii; Bain, *Senses and Intellect*, ch. i, pp. 321 - 27; Spencer, *Principles of Psychology*, vol. i, pt. 2, chs. ii and ix; Sully, *Psychology*, ch. ii; Lewes, *Problems of Life and Mind*, First Series, p. 146; Third Series, p. 240; Strümpell, *Grundriss der Psychologie*, pp. 1 - 14, 95 - 100; George, *Lehrbuch der Psychologie*, pp. 70 - 124; Ulrici, *Der Leib und die Seele*, vol. i, pt. 2, p. 161; Horwicz, *Psychologische Analysen*, vol. i, pp. 155 - 75; Volkmann, *Lehrbuch der Psychologie*, vol. i, pp. 54 - 216; Ward, *Encyclopædia Britannica*, article "Psychology." More directly upon the faculties of the soul, see

Wundt, *Grundzüge der physiologischen Psychologie*, vol. i, pp. 9 - 18; Herbart, *Lehrbuch zur Psychologie*, pt. 2, ch. i; Lotze, *Medicinische Psychologie*, §136 (this work of Lotze's is very rare, but a translation of the first part of it may be had in French, under the title, *Principes Généraux de Psychologie Physiologique*), and *Microcosmus* (Eng. transl.), vol. i, pp. 168 - 81; Drobisch, *Empirische Psychologie*, pp. 268 - 337; Steinthal, *Einleitung in die Psychologie und Sprachwissenschaft*, pp. 290 - 306; Volkmann (*op. cit.*), vol. i, pp. 22 - 34.

Upon the educational bearings of these topics, see Heine, *Die pädagogische Seelenlehre*, and Joly, *Notions de Pédagogie*, pp. 32 - 61.

PART ONE: KNOWLEDGE

3
Elements of Knowledge

1] SENSATION IN GENERAL

Sensation Identified

However great the difficulties connected with sensation, it is the easiest of all mental phenomena to *identify*. The feeling of warmth, of pressure, the hearing of a noise, the seeing of a color—such states as these are sensations. In reference to its bodily conditions, also, a sensation is easily defined: it is any psychical condition whose sole *characteristic* antecedent is a stimulation of some peripheral nerve structure. Thus, we refer the getting of sensations of warmth and pressure to some organs in the skin; noise to the ear; color to the eye, etc.

Treatment of Subject

A sensation is thus seen to involve two elements—a physical and a psychical. It is concerned, on the one hand, with the body; on the other with the soul. The physical factor may be considered with reference either to the stimulus which affects the nerve organ, or with relation to the nerve activity itself. We shall consider, accordingly, the following topics under the head of sensation: i. The physical stimulus in its broad sense, including subdivisions into the extra-organic stimulus and the physiological. ii. The psychical element, or sensation proper. iii. The relation between the physical and the psychical factors. iv. The function of sensation in intellectual life.

I.   The Physical Stimulus

1. EXTRA-ORGANIC STIMULUS

While a few of our sensations arise from operations
going on within our own body, the larger number, and those
most important in their cognitive aspect, originate in affections of the organism by something external to it. Things
just about us affect the organs of touch; bodies still more
remote impinge upon us through the sense of hearing, while
in vision almost no limit is put to the distance from which
bodies may affect us through light. But numerous as seem
the various ways in which external bodies may affect us, it is
found that these various modes are reducible to one—
motion. Whether a body is near or far, the only way in
which it affects the organism so as to occasion sensation is
through motion. The motion may be of the whole mass, as
when something hits us; it may be in the inner particles of
the thing, as when we taste or smell it; it may be a movement originated by the body and propagated to us through
vibrations of a medium, as when we hear or see. But some
form of motion there must be. An absolutely motionless
body would not give rise to any affection of the body such as
ultimately results in sensation.

Characteristics of Motion

Accordingly it is not the mere thing, but the thing with the
characteristic of motion, that is the extra-organic stimulus of
sensation. For psychological purposes, the world may be
here regarded, not as a world of things with an indefinite
number of qualities, but as a world of motions alone. The
world of motion, however, possesses within itself various
differences, to which the general properties of sensations
correspond. Movements are not all of the same *intensity*,
form, or *rapidity*. Put positively, motion possesses *amplitude*, *form*, and *velocity*. Amplitude is the extent to and fro,
up and down, of the movement. It is the length of its swing,
or the distance which the body moves from a point of rest.
The body may move through this distance in the thousandth

of a second, or in a second. This rate at which a body moves constitutes its velocity. Again, the motion may be regular or vibratory, or irregular. Amid the regular movements there may be further differences of form. It may be circular, elliptic, or parabolic. It may be a movement like that of a pendulum, a piston, or a trip-hammer.

Characteristics of Sensations

The differences which exist in sensations correspond to these differences in stimuli. To the amplitude of the motion agrees, in a general way, the intensity of the sensation. The wider the swing of the body the greater the force with which it will impinge upon the sense organ, and the stronger the resulting sensation. To differences of form correspond differences in quality. Stimuli which are irregular seem to occasion the vaguer, confused sensations, like those of taste and smell; the higher, of hearing and sight, being produced by regular vibrations. Within the sphere of sounds, the differences between noises and musical tones seem to correspond to this distinction of stimuli. Finally, vibrations of a low rate of velocity (below twenty per second) affect us through the sense of contact as a feeling of jar; from nineteen to about forty thousand per second we have affections of sound; to the various rates of which correspond those specific differences of sensation known as pitch. Above this rate the vibrations are too numerous to be responded to by the auditory apparatus, and we have a sharp feeling of whizzing. When the vibrations reach the enormous number of three hundred and ninety-two billions per second we begin to have color sensations, at this rate, of red; and these continue up to seven hundred and eighty-five billions, when violet finishes. Between these velocities lies the scale of colors. Above their highest rate the eye does not distinguish light, and we have the motions which produce the so-called actinic effects most largely.

Classes of Extra-organic Stimuli

These may be divided into general and special. Certain forms of motion, as mechanical pressure, heat, and electricity, affect all sensory organs alike. Any one of them, if

applied to the ear, occasions sound; to the eye, light, etc.
The motions which are termed special are peculiarly
adapted to some one sense organ, which alone is fitted to
respond to them. Waves of ether awaken no consciousness
within us except as they impinge upon the retina of the eye.
Waves of air find an especially responsive medium in the
ear, while certain chemical actions, not understood, have
special reference to the nerves of smell and taste.

2. THE PHYSIOLOGICAL STIMULUS

No sensation exists as yet. The external stimulus is but
the first prerequisite. It is a condition which in many cases
may be omitted, as when the stimulus arises within the body
itself. Its function is exhausted when the nerve is aroused to
activity. It must be transformed into a physiological motion
before any sensation arises. The mode of transformation has
given rise to a division of the senses into mechanical and
chemical. In some cases the physiological stimulus appears
as a continuation of the external. Thus the extra-organic
stimuli occasioning pressure undergo no decided alteration
upon affecting the organs of touch; it is highly probable that
the auditory nerve continues the stimulus without chemical
change. But in taste and smell there is evidently a chemical
transformation. The sapid or odorous substance sets up
some chemical process in the nerve endings, and the stimulus reaches the brain in a different form from that originally
affecting the sensory organ. In vision both mechanical and
chemical activities seem to be combined.

Stages of the Physiological Stimulus

Here three stages may be distinguished: first, the excitation
of the peripheral organ; second, the conduction of the excitement thus produced along the nerve fibre to the brain; and,
third, the reception of and reaction upon the transmitted
stimulus by the brain. There is change in the organ, change
in the nerve, change in the brain. Subject to a qualification
hereafter to be made, the integrity of each of these elements
is necessary for a sensation.

Specific Nerve Energy

Regarding the method of the reaction of the nerve organs upon the extra-organic stimulus which tranforms it into a physiological one, it may be said that each nerve organ responds to all stimuli, of whatever kind, in the same way. The mind, for example, always answers sound to all calls made upon the ear, whether these calls be made by way of pressure, electricity, or the more ordinary one of vibrations of air. In the same way the mind always reacts with a sensation of light to every excitation of the eye, whether made by etheric vibration or mechanical pressure and irritation. This is the fact known as specific nerve energy; whether it is due to the original structure of the nervous organism, or is the result of adaptation through constant use in one way, is disputed. Of the fact itself there is no doubt.

Vicarious Brain Action

It was mentioned that the statement regarding the necessity of integrity of brain, nerve, and sense organ for the production of a sensation would require qualification. It is found that when the connection between the sense organ and the brain has once been thoroughly formed the latter tends to have its structure altered in such a way that, in abnormal and unusual cases, nervous changes going on within it may take the place of that usually occurring in the organ and nerves. People who have become blind in adult life do not lose their power of imagining visual forms and color. Their appreciation of these is as real, though internal, as that of the person who has his eye affected by the physical stimulus of light.

Persons who have lost an arm or a leg still seem to feel in the amputated part. They continue to refer sensations to the absent member. In certain abnormal states, as in fevers, etc., sensations arise within the brain itself of such force and vividness as to occasion utterly erroneous ideas about the external world. When no affection of the nerve organ exists sounds are heard, lights appear, wonderful and strange scenes, to which nothing objective corresponds, pass before the vision. It is hardly possible to account for the phenomena of dreams, except upon the theory that every excitation of the brain is not due to an immediately antecedent excitation of a sense organ, but may spontaneously be called forth in the brain itself. These various facts lead to the supposition that the activity in the brain may be self-induced, under certain circumstances, having the same psychical result as would the more regular excitation through peripheral organs and sensory nerves, and that, consequently, the ultimate element with which the mind has to deal is the change in the brain alone.

II.   The Psychical Factor

Sensation as Consciousness

We have as yet no sensation. A sensation is psychical; it is a consciousness; it not only exists, but it exists for the self. The changes in the nervous system, including the brain, are purely physical; they are objective only, and have no conscious existence for themselves. They exist in consciousness only as brought into the mind of some spectator. The relations between the two processes, the objective stimulus of motion and the subjective response of consciousness, we shall study hereafter. At present we are concerned with finding out what are the essential traits of a sensation considered as an element in consciousness.

Erroneous Theory

When we first reflect upon our sensations, it is almost impossible to avoid the opinion that they are independent, separate mental states. A noise is wholly different from a color, a feeling of warmth from one of weight. More than this: every noise seems a unique event independent of every other noise. Thus we are easily led to a theory that sensations are a series of discrete mental states, numerically and qualitatively separate from one another—atoms out of which the mental life is built. But we are led astray here by a difficulty already spoken of (page 14). These separate ideas of color and sound, of the sounds of a piano and of a rattling cart, are developed states of adult life. Instead of being original conditions out of which more complex products are built up, they are themselves complex results of a long period of growth. If we compare sensations, for example, with the bricks out of which a house is made, we must remember that bricks are manufactured articles, for which we must go back to some original homogeneous bed of clay.

Sensation Continuum

This illustration is meant to point to the fact that there is a certain original continuous substratum of sensation out of which the various apparently distinct sensations have been slowly differentiated. The reasons for holding the existence of such an original continuum are fourfold: historical, physiological, experimental, and derived from psychological analysis.

1. HISTORICAL

If we accept the theory of evolution, we are inevitably committed to the doctrine of a single original continuous and homogeneous whole of sensation which is neither warmth nor taste nor sound, but from which these, and all other, sensory qualities have been gradually developed. As we go lower and lower in the animal scale, we find the distinctions of sense organs slowly obliterated, until we get to a point where there are no differentiated organs for sight, sound, and touch at all. At this point, sensation must be one palpitating homogeneous mass of consciousness, with no breach of continuity of kind or number, but simply expanding and contracting in intensity.

2. PHYSIOLOGICAL

The brain is both anatomically and functionally a single (or, at most, dual) organ. There is, of course, a great degree of specialization and even of localization of function within it. Centres of sight, hearing, and touch are more or less spatially as well as functionally distinct. But there is reason to believe that this specialization, like the corresponding division of labor in society, is acquired, not original, resting on the principle of economy, or the richest result with the greatest ease. Even with the most extreme localization, there is no *separation* of sensory centres. The centres for sight, for touch, for movement, etc., are all interwoven into one larger whole. With the movement of specialization, of differentiation, goes a movement of reunion, of interconnection. While, for example, the auditory centre may be constantly gaining in distinctness of localization, it is also gaining in multifariousness of connections with the other sensory centres. Physiological considerations, in fine, instead of pointing to original atomic sensations, point to a massive homogeneous sensation, gradually differentiated indeed, but, at the same time, with these different sensations bound into a whole.

3. EXPERIMENTAL

A few years ago it was discovered that some persons whenever they hear a certain sound see a certain color (photism), or when they see a color hear a sound (phonism). This integration of sensations usually distinct is so thorough-going that such persons are surprised upon finding that every one does not have the same experience. It is also known that large numbers of persons at least *associate* in a regular way different qualities of sensation, and that there are various grades shading off from loose association to almost actual sensation. Still later it was discovered that all sensations, no matter how apparently separate in quality, are so closely connected as greatly to influence one another. A tone from a tuning-fork, for example, may render visible a color not previously strong enough to be seen; or, if occurring simultaneously with a visible color, may perhaps render it invisible; or one may produce oscillations, as it were, in the intensity of the other—the phenomena being different in kind with different colors, sounds, and with different people, and yet uniformly showing *some* influence of all kinds of sensation upon one another.

4. PSYCHOLOGICAL

The evidence here is both general (or inferential) and specific. Generally speaking, the difficulties which we fall into, upon the basis of the atomic theory of sensation, in explaining the apparent unity of mental action and of mental products is an argument against the theory. The moment we start from the supposition of atomic units we are obliged also to have recourse to some special process for reconnecting these units. Some call the process "indissoluble association," others a *special* relating power of the mind. More particularly, examination shows that the discreteness and independence which we attribute to our sensations belong rather *to the objects to which we refer the sensory qualities*. A color, taken in itself, is simply one differentiation of a sensory continuum, and a sound, taken in itself, is another. They are no more two separate psychical states than a brook now falling over a rock and now reposing in a pool is two brooks. But the sound is referred, say, to a bell; the color to a table-cloth. We then fallaciously attribute the spatial independence and separateness of the objects to the sensations themselves. Or, if the color and the sound are both referred to the same object, as the bell, they are different qualities of the object, and we confuse the difference of objective meaning with difference of psychical condition.

III. The Relation of the Physical Factor to the Psychical

We are introduced at the outset to one of the most difficult problems of psychology. The general question is, What is the relation between the external world, including the organized body, and the mind or self? In this particular case the question takes the form, What is the connection between sensations or psychical states and the physical and neural changes which excite them?

Various Theories

We shall first consider two opposed and extreme theories, and then pass to what we conceive to be the true view of the matter. Of these two theories, one, which we may call the *materialistic* theory, regards sensations as facts of the same kind and order as the physical motions which occasion them, and reduces consciousness to one of the forms in which material motion appears. The other, or *dualistic* theory, denies any connection whatever between mind and

matter, between the sensation and the neural change which
appears to originate it. One theory, in short, absorbs mind in
matter, while the other holds that there is a chasm between
them over which no bridge can be built. Materialism identifies the sensation with its mechanical occasion. Dualism
holds to two opposed and unconnected sets of phenomena;
one physical, the other psychical.

1. DUALISM

This will be dealt with briefly, both because the most
extreme upholders of the general independence of mind and
matter rarely go so far as to deny the relative dependence of
sensation on nervous change, and because the fact of the
dependence is so evident upon examination. So far as we
know, positively, no sensation occurs without some accompanying change of nervous tissue. Negatively, the loss of an
organ, conducting nerve, or brain centre is found to be
accompanied by corresponding loss of sensation. Furthermore, whatever increases or diminishes the nervous activity
is found to increase or diminish the intensity of the corresponding sensation. We thus have about all the evidence we
could desire as to some connection between the conscious
sensation and the nervous change.

2. MATERIALISM

This holds that all the facts of the universe, mind
included, are to be reduced to changes of matter and motion.
It holds that the law of the conservation and correlation of
energy is the highest law of all phenomena, and that this is
as true of psychical phenomena, and of their relation to
physical, as it is of the facts of heat or of electricity. It holds,
that is to say, that all phenomena are reducible to forms of
motion which are convertible into each other without loss or
increase of energy or power of doing work. Thus, we know
that light is changeable into heat, heat into chemical energy,
this into electricity, while electricity completes the circuit
back into light.

Materialism holds that this generalization must be applied to the production of sensations. It says that we must
believe that when a wave of light reaches the retina the

energy involved in it is converted into an equal amount of energy known as nervous action, which is conveyed along the nerves to the brain, where it sets up another equal amount of energy, which results in the state we know as a sensation. It holds that along this line of changes there is no breach of continuity. Each process is the mechanical result of its antecedents. Sensations, as psychical states, are thus included among the material energies of the physical world, and are governed by the mechanical laws of this world. They are only one special class of the forms which energy, as convertible from one mode into another, takes.

Objections

To this view there are certain very serious objections, (1) one of which may be urged from the physical side itself, while the other (2) is psychological in its nature.

1. PHYSICAL. There is an unlikeness of *kind* which makes it impossible to apply the law of the transformation of energy to the relation existing between sensations and their stimuli. The law of the conservation of energy has been established regarding the phenomena of motion alone, and has meaning only with reference to motions. Sensations are not motions. The sensation of red may have a dependence upon a certain number of etheric vibrations, but as a sensation it is a unique psychical state, having no motion, no vibrations, no spatial length nor form. The motion is objective, existing in space, possessing relations of form, size, and number. The sensation is subjective, existing only in the mind, having no spatial nor numerical relations. The motion is an external fact which must be presented *to* the senses to be known. The sensation is internal, and is directly known to consciousness. Now these differences between the psychical and the physical constitute, it is said, a chasm which the law of the correlation of energy cannot bridge. The law holds only of motions; to apply it to sensations is to commit the absurdity of supposing that a sound or color is a movement occurring in space.

Materialism Does not Explain

Or the objection may be stated as follows: The only object of applying the law is to *explain* psychical phenomena. To explain consists, as logic tells us, in pointing out a relation of cause and effect existing between two phenomena. This relation can be found only where there is *quantitative identity* between the fact antecedent regarded as cause, and the consequent considered to be the effect. Where this identity is not found no causal relation exists. Now the attempt to make the mechanical and material phenomena of the world account for the psychical, through the law of the conservation of energy, fails, when looked at in this way, doubly: (1) it fails to explain sensation as a *general* fact; (2) it fails to explain any of the concrete *details* of sensation.

(1) There is no identity between the sensation as a state of consciousness and the mechanical motion which precedes it. The striking fact of the case is their difference: one exists as an objective spatial fact of movement, the other as the unique psychical fact of consciousness. No quantitative transformation can be made out, for the simple reason that the consciousness is not a quantity. So Mr. Huxley says: "How it is that anything so remarkable as a state of consciousness comes about by the result of irritating nervous tissue, is just as *unaccountable* as the appearance of the Djin when Aladdin rubbed his lamp." Mr. Tyndall remarks to the same effect that "the passage from the physics of the brain to the corresponding facts of consciousness is unthinkable." The German physiologist, Du Bois Reymond, says that "if we possessed an absolutely perfect knowledge of the body, including the brain and all changes in it, the psychical state known as sensation would be as *incomprehensible* as now. For the very highest knowledge we could get would reveal to us only matter in motion, and the connection between any motions of any atoms in my brain, and such unique, undeniable facts as that I feel pain, smell a rose, see red, is thoroughly *incomprehensible*." It is evident that if the connection be, as affirmed, unaccountable, unthinkable, incomprehensible, it is impossible to account for or

comprehend the sensation by it.

(2) Materialism fails to throw any light upon the specific facts of sensation. Were it supposed that we even knew all about the forms of motion which affect us, and knew the exact difference between one form and another, it would still remain incomprehensible why one mode of motion should give rise to that psychical fact which we know as color, and another to sound. So the knowledge of the difference of rates of rapidity in the musical scale does not enable us to explain why one rate should result in a low note and another, more rapid rate, in a higher. These are facts of consciousness only, and are as ultimate and unanalyzable in their differences from each other as they were when nothing whatever was known about the rates of motion. No identity between the conscious facts and the various forms of physical motion can be discovered which will enable us to explain one by the other.

2. PSYCHOLOGICAL OBJECTION. This objection cannot be fully presented here, as it presupposes a knowledge of the results of psychological study not yet attained. In brief, it is this: the material motions which are supposed to be the cause of psychical phenomena are never known in any independent existence. They are known to exist only through their relation to mind. Psychologically speaking, the fact of motion is a fact of knowledge which must be accounted for through a study of the elements and processes of the mind. It is not a fact which precedes knowledge and can be used to account for it, but it is a fact *in* knowledge which must be accounted for like all other facts of knowledge, by means of psychological laws. Motion cannot be used psychologically to account for mental phenomena, because it is itself a mental phenomenon, and, as such, depends upon psychological elements and processes. Materialism inverts the true order of facts by attempting to produce the subject from the object, knowledge from things, while the business of psychology is to deal with things as *known* things, and to show how the subject, as knowing, is involved in all those facts which the physical sciences treated merely as existing facts, overlooking that they are in reality facts *known* to exist, as

facts in relation to mind. Motion apart from mind is an abstraction and cannot be used to account for mind. We come now to what seems to be the correct theory in the matter.

3. NERVOUS CHANGES ACT AS STIMULI TO THE SOUL

It is evident from what was said under the first head that there is some positive connection between the material process and the psychical. It is evident from what has just been said that this connection is not of such a nature that the conscious sensation can be regarded as transformed molecular motion. Nothing is gained, however, by adopting a too customary evasion, and regarding the sensation as an impression made upon the soul by an external object, and consequently as a mere passive reception or copy of it. The sensation is a copy of neither the external nor the internal object and process. In the case of vision, for example, the external excitation is not color, and certainly the intra-organic one is not; the extra-organic process is simply certain undulations of ether which impinge upon the retina. The intra-organic process is the excitation and transference of molecular motion in and along the nerves and brain. What finally affects the mind, however it affects it, is only this brain molecular motion, and certainly color is not a mere passive reception of that.

Nervous Change not Cause but Stimulus

This molecular motion, accordingly, is conceived of as simply the stimulus or excitation necessary to call the soul into activity. The soul, when thus incited to action, responds to the stimulation with a characteristic production of its own, whose appearance, relatively to the physical phenomena, is a virtual creation; that is, cannot be in any way got out of them. The nervous change is not, properly speaking, the cause of the sensation, nor is the sensation the passive result of an impression. A sensation is not the simple affection of the soul by some bodily change, although the affection is a necessary prerequisite to sensation. The sensation is the state developed out of and by the soul itself upon occasion of this affection.

Distinction between Physical and Psychical Activity

This constitutes the great difference between physical and psychical action. Physical energy is always external; it never acts upon itself, but is transferred beyond itself. Such changes as external bodies undergo are never self-originated, but are initiated from an outside source. But the mind has the power of acting upon itself and of producing from within itself a new, original, and unique activity which we know as sensation. The appearance of physical causation which accompanies it is due to the fact that the nervous change is always necessary as a *stimulus* to the soul, and, furthermore, when this stimulus is once present, it is not left to the soul voluntarily to determine whether and how it will act, but, by a mechanism of its own, it responds to the stimulus in a definite and invariable way.

IV. Functions of Sensation

Having considered the relation of the physical to the psychical factor in sensation, we have now to say something about the position of sensation in the psychical life, or its function considered with reference to the mind as a whole.

(1) Sensation is the meeting-place, the point of coincidence of self and nature. It is in sensation that nature touches the soul in such a way that it becomes itself psychical, and that the soul touches nature so as to become itself natural. A sensation is, indeed, the transition of the physical into the psychical.

(2) Sensation is the *passive* or *receptive* aspect of mind. This does not mean that the mind is purely passive, or that it is like a wax tablet that merely receives impressions. On the contrary, sensation is the result of the *activity* of the psycho-physical organism, and is produced, not received. It is the passive *aspect*, not passive *side*, of mind. Sensation, compared with other psychical processes, indicates what is given to these processes. It is material which they must receive if they are to act. So far as perception, or memory, or

thinking is concerned, sensation is given, or a *datum*. It represents the contact of the individual with a realm larger than himself, and upon which he is dependent for the material of his mental operations.

(3) Sensation expresses the *excitation*, the stimulation of mind. It arouses the mind to put forth effort, either in new fields or for the more adequate apprehension of the familiar. As excitation it possesses intensity or degrees of vividness, and is allied to feeling. In fact, the widest definition of feeling is precisely psychical excitement. Sensation, as arousing the mind, leads it to act, and thus terminates in volition. As excitation, in short, it serves the function of inducing to knowledge and to volition, and is almost equivalent to feeling.

(4) Sensation *indicates the particular factor* in mental products. That is, it always refers the content in connection with which it is experienced to a *this* and a *now*. We can recollect or imagine or think about light, and the subject-matter under consideration by the mind will not vary essentially from that of a sensation of light, but the latter contains an index-finger that points to the immediate experience of light, while the other acts of mind at most tell of the conditions under which light *might* be experienced. In communicating with another in language we are obliged to make known the fact that we are talking about some definite object by saying "this" or "that," and pointing towards it. This function, thus performed by gesture, is performed in our internal experience by the intrinsic property of the sensation indicating a "this" and a "here."

(5) While sensation indicates existence, and this indication is particular, it *means* or *signifies quality*, and this meaning is *general*. Sensation possesses quality as well as intensity. This quality, if distinguished, or abstracted, from the particular *indication* of the sensation, becomes in itself general. A sensation of red indicates present particular existence, but the quality of redness has, *in itself*, no more connection with this existence than with any other. As redness, it is an abstract idea; that is, it is abstracted or drawn away from connection with this or that particular existence, and being freed from particular existence is itself universal.

This quality constitutes meaning, as the indicating property of sensation constitutes existence. The two factors which in union constitute the object of knowledge are therefore the particular and the general, the "this" and the "quality." The relating process which transforms sensations into knowledge consists in the explicit development of these two factors. On the one hand, there is an analytic activity which separates the quality from its particular manifestation; on the other, the synthetic, which unites it with other qualities, and refers it again to existence.

2] DEVELOPMENT OF SENSATION

The Original Sensation

Before proceeding to the details of our present sensations, let us consider the process by which the original sensation is differentiated, beginning with this supposed homogeneous sensation itself—a psychical existence related to our present sensory experiences much as the supposed original nebulous gas is related to existing solar systems and to the various bodies which make up these systems. We cannot, of course, accurately describe the nature of the homogeneous continuum which we suppose. But, by analogy, we can form some probable conception of its character. Imagine, for example, our organic or general sensation as it is now; the sensation of comfort or discomfort of the whole body, a feeling having no definite spatial outline nor any distinct quality which marks it off.

Or, let us imagine our various sense organs losing all their powers of giving distinct sense qualities, and being retracted into a sort of substratum of sensory stuff. Perhaps the nearest we get to such an experience is when we are falling asleep: our auditory sensations fall away; then we lose our sensations of color and of form; finally, our very feelings of contact, pressure, and temperature fade away into a dim, vague sense of nothing in particular. Or, again, consider an infant before it has gained use of its eyes or ears, when the senses of smell and taste are still dull, and when all that seems to appeal to it are the organic need of food, its satisfaction, actual pain, and changes of temperature—even these, it is probable, being fused into a general sense of well-being or the reverse, rather than distinctly apprehended. Consider these facts, remember that the sense organs are still present with their brain connections and with the inherited capacities and tendencies of generations, and we can form some idea of what a shapeless, vague, diffused state a sensation is to, say, an oyster or a jelly-fish.

(1) The development is from emotional to intellectual. Considering the process of differentiation itself, it is easy to see that the original sensation has a maximum of mere feeling or emotional quality, and a minimum of intellectual value. It is simply the condition, the inner affection of the organism itself; it tells or reports practically nothing. It gives us no qualities of objects. Going on from this point, we may classify our present sensations. Our feelings of hunger, thirst, fatigue; our feelings of uneasiness, well-being, etc., so far as they are not defined by connection with specific objects, are the residuum, as it were, of the original homogeneous feeling. At the other end of the scale lie our visual sensations, having in themselves a minimum of emotional tone, and, with their variety and distinctness of quality, the maximum of intellectual function.

(2) The development is from the vague to the definite. This is implied in what has already been said. The lack of intellectual value in the organic sensation is precisely its lack of defined character. It has no sharp, clear-cut limits in locality or in quality. Then we have contact and pressure sensations, which, while capable of great education and of reaching great acuteness of discrimination in reference to objects, yet have but comparatively few differences within themselves except of intensity. Such differences as exist are mainly of an emotional kind, as tickling, thrilling, etc. Apart from intentional discrimination, indeed, our contact sensations may be said to form a perfect jungle. Then we have smell and taste, with some differences of quality indeed, but yet, upon the whole, vague. The difficulty of discriminating various kinds of pure odors or tastes from one another, the tendency of one to pass into another without a sharp boundary line, their poor spatial localization—all illustrate this. In

great contrast are the auditory and visual sensations, with their sharp and clear limits in quality, their quick and accurate localization in space and time.

(3) The development involves increased differentiation and mobility of sense organs. Organic sensation has to wait passively, as it were, for the stimulus to come to it. But no special sense organ can be purely passive, even physically speaking, in sensation. It must adjust itself to the stimulus.

The mouth must secrete saliva and move the sapid substance about. We must sniff with the nostrils. The tympanum of the ear must be stretched; the eye-lenses must be accommodated, and the two eyes converged, and each must have muscular connections. But the connection of contact sensations with muscular sensations is still more intimate. Normally they are inextricably united. It is only in disease that we ever have one without the other. Thus the activities of our own body and those of external bodies are indissolubly associated from the first. The whole importance of this we shall learn hereafter. While the connection of touch with movement is most intimate, that of sight is most acute and varied. The eyes are constantly on the lookout for sensation. Instead of a mirror waiting for impressions, like the lower senses, they are a dark lantern rapidly moving and focusing here and there. The more mobile the sense organ, the more controllable the qualities had from it, and the more they can be reproduced at will.

Besides increase of mobility, we have increase of discriminating capacity. The lower organs receive the stimulus *en masse*. The higher ones are tools for breaking it up into different elements and receiving each separately. Consider, for example, the eye with its subsidiary mechanism for excluding most stimuli and thus narrowing them down to a single class, and then all the nerve structures for adaptation to different rates and intensities of vibration.

On account of the fundamental character of touch, we shall begin our special studies of sensation with it, and, following the order laid down under the general consideration of sensation, shall take up: 1. The physical stimulus; 2. The physiological stimulus; 3. The conscious sensation.

On account of the connection of contact sensations with muscular we shall consider this subject under the following heads: i. Passive touch, or touch proper, as separate from muscular activity; ii. Muscular sensations; iii. Active touch, the union of the two previous.

3] TOUCH

i. Passive Touch

1. THE PHYSICAL STIMULUS

This is mechanical pressure; consequently all bodies possessing weight, whether solids, liquids, or gases, are capable, under proper conditions, of exciting sensations of contact. Not all contact, however, with external bodies excites sensation. The pressure must reach a certain degree, known as its *threshold value*; for over this *threshold*, as it were, any stimulus must pass to enter into consciousness. This value varies with different parts of the body; the smallest amount appreciable is .002 grammes, by the cheek and back of hand. Upon the heel a pressure equal to one gram is required for feeling. Change of stimulus is also necessary, or at least contrast. If the hand be plunged into a liquid at rest no contact sensation is felt except at the margin; or if it be evenly compressed by a solid, as paraffine, only the boundary is felt.

2. PHYSIOLOGICAL STIMULUS, OR ORGAN

This is the skin of the whole body and the openings of the various membranes. Touch is classified as a special sense, because in the true skin, beneath the cuticle, exist certain peculiar endings of the nerves in raised organs, called papillæ, although their stimulation is not always necessary for the existence of any contact sensation. The tip of the tongue and the ends of the fingers, being especially well supplied with the papillæ, may be regarded as the specific organs of contact.

3. SENSATIONS OF TOUCH

These are (1) sensations of pressure, the objective cause being the weight of some body. A qualitative difference in pressure sensations constitutes what we may call (2) place sensations.

1. PRESSURE SENSATIONS. These are excited whenever any ponderable body is laid upon some portion of the skin at rest—a condition which is rarely perfectly fulfilled, as the muscles are generally brought into action to support and test the weight. It is a characteristic of pressure sensation that not every change of weight is felt. It is found that if a given weight affects the hand it must be increased by at least one thirteenth before the difference of pressure is felt, no matter how slight or strong be the intensity of the existing sensation. That is to say, if the objective stimulus be 1 gram, $\frac{1}{13}$ of a gram must be added for any new sensation to result; if it be 30 pounds, $2\frac{1}{3}$ pounds must be added, or no change of intensity in the feeling appears. This difference of stimulus, necessary to change of sensation, is called the *difference threshold*, and for pressure sensations is stated at 13:14.

Weber's Law

Anticipating the study of the other senses, it may be well to state here that some ratio, although quantitatively different, is believed to exist for every sense. That is to say, it is true of every sense that not every change in objective stimulus occasions a change in subjective sensation, but that every change in stimulus must bear a certain definite ratio (varying in the different senses) to the already existing stimulus before the intensity of the sensation, as a conscious state, changes. Differently stated, not absolute stimuli are felt, but only relative. This law is often called *Weber's* law, after its discoverer, and is stated as follows: *The intensity of one sensation changes from that of the preceding sensation, when the stimulus of the former changes in a fixed ratio to that of the latter.* This ratio of change is $\frac{1}{13}$ in the case of passive touch, as just seen; in active touch it is $\frac{1}{19}$; that is, the addition of a weight $\frac{1}{19}$ as great as the existing weight will change the sensation.

Methods of Research

The determination of this law evidently falls under the head of experimental psychology, and, as illustrating the methods of this, it may be well briefly to mention the ways in which Weber's law has been established.

   i. The Method of Right and Wrong Cases. Here two weights are used, one slightly heavier than the other, and the person experimented upon is required to tell from touch alone which is the heavier, and the process is repeated a large number of times with the same weights. It is evident that if the difference between the two weights is less than the real *difference threshold*, there will be no basis for judgment, and the number of right and wrong cases, or guesses, will be about evenly divided. Just in the degree in which the difference approaches the true ratio will the percentage of right cases increase, and when the ratio is made too large, about all the cases will be correctly judged.

   ii. Method of Just Perceptible Differences. A certain weight is laid on the hand. This is slightly increased. Probably no difference of sensation is felt. But more and more weight is added until the sensation does increase in intensity. This is repeated again and again, and the average difference taken as the basis for calculating the proper ratio.

   iii. Method of Average Error. A certain weight is put on the hand, and the person experimented upon is required to tell when another weight equals this. This is repeated a large number of times. Each time there will be a slight error, either positive or negative; that is, the weight supposed to be equal will, as matter of fact, be greater or less. The exact amount of error is noticed each time, and their average being taken will approach the normal perceptible difference.

Interpretations of the Law

The law has been interpreted physiologically, psychophysically, and psychologically.

i. Physiological Interpretation. This holds that the law is due to the nature of nerve-action. It holds that the sensation, as a conscious state, is directly proportional to the physiological stimulus, but that the physiological stimulus, owing to unknown causes, is not directly proportional to the physical stimulus, but increases more slowly than it.

ii. Psycho-physical. This holds that the law expresses the relations which exist between the physical nervous stimulus, and the psychical reaction to it, or the relations which exist between body and soul. Hence, Weber's law is often called the psycho-physical law. Fechner, who has made very careful and complete experiments, has adopted this view, and states the law in mathematical form as follows: The intensity of the sensation varies with the logarithm of the stimulus. This statement is called Fechner's law, but is not generally accepted.

iii. Psychological. This holds that the law expresses neither the relation which the physiological stimulus holds to the physical, nor that with which the psychical responds to the nervous stimulus, but a distinction between the sensation itself and our appreciation of it: that is, we appreciate any psychical state not by what it absolutely is, but what it is in reference to some other psychical state with which we compare it. We have no absolute measure for the intensity of a sensation, but measure it by comparing it with the sensation which immediately preceded it. The proper interpretation has not yet been finally decided upon, and a further discussion would lead us beyond our proper limits. We return from this digression to a study of

2. PLACE SENSATIONS. This expression must not be taken to mean that we have any sensations of place as such. The reference of a sensation to a given object or position is a further act of mind, to be studied under the head of perception. The phrase means simply that there exists a difference in the quality of the sensations corresponding to differences in the parts of the body whence they originate. What the exact nature of this difference is we do not know; we know, however, that it must exist, or there would be no basis for the mind to act upon in referring a sensation to one position

rather than to another. This difference is called the *local sign*. The local sign, in other words, is that peculiarity of the sensation which differentiates a sensation coming, say, from the extreme tip of the thumb of the left hand, from one of the same intensity and otherwise of the same quality coming from a similar part of the right hand. This peculiarity the mind uses as a sign of the part affected, and thus *learns* to localize impressions.

Discriminating Power

The sensation of pressure arises when certain definite portions, called "pressure spots," are stimulated. If the skin is touched by two objects, as blunted points of a compass, several pressure spots are stimulated by each point. Each group of spots so excited arouses a sensation with its own peculiar quality—its "local sign." If the two sensations thus called forth are sufficiently differentiated in quality, they are located as two distinct points. Otherwise only one point is reported. The distance by which the two compass points must be separated in order to be located as two depends partly on the *anatomy* of the portion (the distribution of spots) and partly on *exercise* in discrimination. The tongue and finger tip far exceed in discriminating power the back or upper leg with the greatest amount of practice; but practice and careful selection of pressure spots greatly increase the original fineness. Practice on one hand increases the power to define separate points on the other hand.

Mobility and Local Discrimination

It is found, as a general thing, that discriminative sensibility is a function of the mobility of the part. The finest differences are felt by those portions of the body most often in motion, while those parts which are relatively non-sensitive, like the middle of the back, are just those parts of the body which are most fixed. This introduces us to the subject of

II. Muscular Sensation

Meaning of Muscular Sensation

The nature of muscular sensation is one of the most disputed points in the psychology of sensation. As here used, it means all sensations that come from, or have to do with, the voluntary movements of the body. It does not necessarily mean sensations arising from the muscles in the same sense that visual sensations come from the retina, or touch sensations from pressure spots. Sensory nerves have been discovered ending in the muscles, and it is probable that we do have specific muscular sensations; but of their nature or importance very little is known. It is possible that under usual circumstances we are conscious of them only as fused into our organic sensations. It is certain that sensations of strain and effort such as we get when we have to lift a load are not wholly muscular sensations in the narrow sense.

The Innervation Theory

No voluntary movement can take place, of course, unless there is a current of nerve energy going out from the brain to the muscles in question. It is supposed by some that we have a feeling (called *innervation* feeling) of this outgoing current. A piano-player, for example, has constantly, just before he strikes the keys, a feeling of the amount of energy he is putting forth; of the amount of muscular effort to be used in a given movement of the piece as a whole, and of the delicate shadings required from passage to passage and note to note. The *innervationists* claim that this feeling of the activity required is a feeling of the output of cerebral energy through the motor nerves.

The Afferent Theory

The rival hypothesis holds that muscular sensations are, like all other sensations, passive. They are not feelings of action, but of the changes produced by action. They arise, not centrally from the putting forth of energy, but, like those of pressure and temperature, in the periphery, and are then reported by afferent nerves to the brain. They are not so much muscular sensations as sensations produced by the movement and tension of the muscles, joint surfaces, ligaments, etc., upon the ordinary organs of contact.

Illustration

This theory may be illustrated by a quotation from Ferrier, who, with James, is its chief upholder: "If the reader will extend his right arm and hold his forefinger in the position actually required for pulling the trigger of a pistol, he may, without actually moving his finger, but by simply making believe, experience a consciousness of energy put forth. If the reader will again perform the experiment and pay careful attention to the condition of his respiration, he will observe that his consciousness of effort coincides with a fixation of the muscles of his chest, and that in proportion to the amount of energy he feels he is putting forth he is keeping his glottis closed and actively contracting his respiratory muscles. Let him place his finger as before, and *continue breathing* all the time, and he will find that, however much he may direct his attention to his finger, he will experience not the slightest trace of consciousness of effort until he has actually moved the finger itself, and then it is referred locally to the muscles themselves." In other words, the consciousness of effort is really a consciousness of the pull and push of the muscles—either of the muscles of the chest connected with breathing or of the part actually moved. James lays great emphasis also upon the sensations produced at the joints by the rubbing of one surface against the other. As there is no direct introspective evidence for the innervation theory, as the afferent theory puts muscular sensation under the same principles as the rest of our sensations, and as it seems to account for all the facts of the case, we give it the preference.

Importance of Muscular Sensation

Remembering, then, that we mean by muscular sensations not wholly the sensations *of* the muscles, but also sensations produced by the movements of muscles, we may go on to note their importance. In the first place, they inform us of our own movements, and thus give us an extremely important information. Persons suffering in such a way that they lose these sensations cannot tell what they are doing excepting as they keep their eyes on their limbs as they move them. Consciousness of movement is also extremely important in differentiating our own body from other objects. It makes, also, the direct basis of volitional action. We are not conscious of our muscular structure, but we are conscious of how it *feels* to move a certain muscle, and this *feel* is our guide in performing the act. By this control of our movements we are enabled to control indirectly our other sensations. We can get the eye or the ear in position to receive sensations, instead of passively waiting for them.

III. Active Touch

In normal life sensations of contact proper are always accompanied by muscular sensations. It is only in disordered or abnormal conditions that they can be separated. This union has the following advantages:

(1) It greatly multiplies the number of impressions which can be had in a given time, thus abbreviating all touch processes. (2) It renders it possible to bring the object to be touched into contact with the most sensitive part of the organ, thus sharpening the sensation. (3) It occasions a rapid succession of impressions, thus heightening the contrast of those which are unlike, and rendering them more distinct. Active touch can thus discriminate differences of $\frac{1}{19}$, while passive touch is limited to $\frac{1}{13}$.

Ideas Got through Active Touch

The union of contact and muscular sensations, when interpreted by the mental processes, constitutes the basis of the following ideas. (1) The hardness or softness of a body. This is not given by mere weight sensations. It is discovered only by running the hand over the body, compressing, moulding it, etc. (2) The elasticity or inertia of the body. (3) The roughness, smoothness, etc., of the body. When the hand is moving and touches successive points, the body is judged coarse or rough. When the muscular sensations are united with continuous contact sensations it is judged to be fine or smooth. All these qualities as referred to bodies are not sensations proper, but judgments made on the basis of sensations.

The student will observe that a large number of sensations originating in the skin are not to be properly classed with touch feelings. Such are heat and cold, tingling, itching, numbness, etc.

4]   THE SENSE OF SMELL

I.   Physical Stimulus

Heat, so far as known, does not occasion this sensation. Whether electricity and mechanical pressure do so is disputed. The specific stimulus is what we call physical odor. Just what properties in a body make it odorous are not known. The substance, however, must be capable of assuming a gaseous form. Neither solids nor liquids, unless volatizable, excite sensation. Of some substances an exceedingly small amount suffices. Of musk, $\frac{1}{2000000}$ of a milligramme is enough.

II.   Organ

This is the ending of the olfactory nerve found in the mucous membrane of the upper and back parts of the nostrils. Touching the mode of excitation, nothing is known except that it is some mode of chemical action, and that no sensation results if the particles remain stationary.

III.   The Sensation Itself

The difference threshold, or the ratio of the discriminative sensibility of the sense, has never been satisfactorily determined. There is no satisfactory classification of odors. The same substance occasions various odors to different persons and to the same person at different times. Certain sensations, ordinarily called those of smell, may, however, be excluded; such are sharp, pungent sensations, originating from snuff, etc. These are properly feelings of mechanical irritation. So-called fresh and close smells are due rather to sensations excited in the lungs than to stimulation of the nostrils, and hence are organic in character. Disgust is an alimentary rather than olfactory sensation.

Connection with Organic Feelings

Odor sensations have a close connection with organic, and are related rather to the emotional side of our nature than to our cognitive. Psychologically, the best classification of odors is, therefore, into agreeable and disagreeable, as this frankly recognizes their subjective character. By reason of its organic connection, smell is of great importance in regulating animal life. As Bidder says, it is placed at the entrance of the respiratory organs, like a watchman. What is disagreeable in odor is rejected from the system; with the sense of taste it serves as a guardian over the digestive organs, preventing the entrance of whatever might be harmful.

Connection with Appetite

By reason of its connection with feeling the sense of smell awakens desire and repulsion for and against the substances which are odorous. Smells occasion all sorts of impulses and longings; some thirst, others hunger, others sexual. This fact appears more plainly in animals than in us; as in them smell is most closely connected with instinct. To them it serves as a means of preserving life by teaching to find friend, avoid foe, and discover food, and by directing to their mates. Hence in animals the centre in the brain for the sense of smell is often its predominating part, while in man it is reduced to insignificant proportions. In man this sense is overlaid by the intellectual processes; if a man wishes to find another man he uses none of his senses, but reflects upon the place where he is most likely to be found. The dog simply uses his sense of smell, and follows scent.

5]   TASTE

I.   Physical Stimulus

Both electricity and mechanical pressure occasion gustatory sensation. If the tongue be electrically stimulated a sour taste is felt at the anode and an alkaline at the cathode. If pressure be brought to bear upon the back of the tongue a bitter taste arises; if it be rapidly tapped, a sour. The specific stimulus, however, is that quality known as sapidity. Only bodies in a liquid condition are sapid. Solids can be tasted only in a crystallized, and hence soluble, form. The threshold value for taste varies with different substances. One part of sulphuric acid in a million parts of water can be tasted, while one eightieth of sugar is required.

II.   Organ

Taste has been ascribed to all portions of the mouth from the lips to the stomach, but is properly confined to those portions of the tongue and soft palate furnished with taste-buds. Experiments have been directed towards ascertaining whether certain tastes are confined or not to certain portions of the organ. The result is somewhat in doubt, but it is generally believed that bitter is best tasted on the soft palate and back of the tongue, and sweet and sour on the tip.

III.   The Sensation Itself

The classification of tastes is rendered difficult by the same causes operative in the case of smell—they can be reduced to four, however: sweet, sour, bitter, and salt. Pungent tastes must be excluded; as must also alkaline, astringent, and metallic tastes, which seem to be combinations of touch, taste, and smell. Many so-called tastes, like that of onions, are properly odors. Nausea is an organic sensation. The specific taste that distinguishes one body from another, as an apple from an orange, is not taste proper, but a combination of various sensory properties.

Organic Connection

Taste is rather an outpost of the whole system, for enabling it to assimilate the beneficial and reject the harmful, than a source of special cognitions. Psychologically, it hardly ranks as high as smell, for the associative power of the latter—as the odor of new-mown hay, or of a sniff of salt water—is very considerable. Odors in general seem to be associated with higher moods and states, of which fact the poets have availed themselves. Smell also can discriminate successive odors much better than taste. Taste, however, is capable of quite high specific cultivation, as is seen in epicures and professional wine and tea tasters, etc.

6] SENSE OF HEARING

I. Physical Stimulus

Electricity and mechanical pressure both act as stimuli: an example of the latter is found in the sensations of roaring, etc., due probably to unusual pressure of the blood-vessels. The specific stimuli are the vibrations of some elastic ponderable medium, generally air, known as physical sound. These vibrations must be within the limits of from, say, twenty to forty thousand per second. As to the lower limit of intensity, or threshold value, this sense seems to be most sensitive of all: a vibration of the amplitude of .00004 millimetre has sufficient energy to excite sensation. A difference of one third of a vibration will make a perceptible change in the sensation of a highly cultivated ear.

II. Organ

The organ is the ear, consisting of external, middle, and internal portions. The former two serve only as an apparatus for condensing and transmitting vibrations. The internal ear possesses the nerve-endings, exceedingly complex, for transforming the physical into the physiological stimulus. The apparatus especially fitted for this is generally said to be the *basilar layer of the organs of Corti*. This is thought to be a complicated series of minute stretched cords, like those of a harp; each of which possesses, like every vibrating medium, a certain definite rate of vibration, depending on its length and tension. Each of these is, accordingly, attuned to some mode of external vibration to which it responds. It thus forms an organ for all possible degrees of pitch. Whenever any external medium propagates vibrations of a certain rate that cord of this layer which has the same rate selects it, and responds to it. These vibrations are then conveyed to the brain by means of the auditory nerve.

III. The Sensation Itself

There are certain distinctions in the *sounds* which psychically result from these transmitted vibrations, which render possible a classified treatment of them. Sounds vary (1) in intensity; (2) in pitch; (3) in tone-color, or quality. Sounds, that is to say, are either loud or soft, high or low, noises or tones.

1. INTENSITY

The difference threshold for hearing is placed at one third—that is, it is found that an existing sound must be increased one third before difference of intensity is perceptible. The intensity of a sensation corresponds to the *amplitude* of the vibration which occasions it. A vibration is a periodic motion, or one which returns after equal intervals of time to the same phase or state of motion. It possesses, accordingly, breadth or amplitude; the moving particle swings a certain distance to and fro from its place of rest. The wider swing shows the greater energy of the vibrating particle, and, consequently, affects the nerve with greater force, and results in a more intense or louder sound. Hence the decrease of the loudness of sound with increase of distance from the sounding body. On the one hand, the waves extend in all directions in space, so that fewer of them reach the ear, and, on the other, these few are lessened in amplitude by the friction of resisting mediums.

2. PITCH

Vibrations, or periodic motions, possess *rate* as well as amplitude. That is, the period of vibration lasts a certain time; the vibrating particle will return from one phase of motion to the same again a certain number of times per second. The greater the rate, i.e., the more rapid the swing, the higher is the pitch of the resulting sensation. The lowest tone which one can hear is that due to eighteen vibrations per second, like the deepest tones of the organ. The highest comes from forty thousand per second, and then passes into a whizzing feeling. This limitation is, so far as we know, due merely to the structure of the nerve organ.

The Scale of Pitch

There is also a specific connection between certain *ratios* in the rates of vibration and certain peculiar sensations of tone, which occasions what we call the octave. Certain tones make the same emotional effect upon us; they feel alike, or harmonize, although differing in pitch. These tones, thus harmonizing with each other, are found to repeat themselves at various intervals through the series of pitch. This repetition of tones within the octave leads to classifying every octave as a *scale* of tones, and this scale is made the basis of musical composition, oral and instrumental. The tones within the scale may be variously divided—as by the Greeks, Arabians, and ourselves—but the existence of the scale is a unique psychological fact in no way conventional. The range of the mind in discriminating pitch seems to be about eleven octaves, though only seven are commonly employed in music.

Relation of the Octave to Physical Vibrations

Long after the peculiar psychological fact of the regular repetition of emotional quality of tones at certain intervals had been used in music, it was discovered that this repetition, or octave, bears a definite relation to certain properties of the rates of vibration. It was found that the recurrent interval constituting the octave corresponds to certain ratios in the physical vibrations, so that the tone at the upper end of the scale is produced by just twice as rapid a rate as the one at the lower end, and that the intermediate tones bear certain definite numerical relations to each other, expressed by such terms as thirds, fifths, etc.

3. TIMBRE, OR TONE-COLOR

Vibrations possess *form*, as well as rate and width. To this property of the stimulus corresponds that difference in the sensation which serves as the basis of the discrimination of the sound of one body from that of another, aside from its intensity or pitch—the difference of an organ from a violin, and both from the human voice. Such sensations are not simple, but composite, and are made up of a so-called *fundamental* tone, and other *partial* tones, which combine with it and give it its peculiar quality. The tone given by a tuning-fork is simple; all others are complex, and may be analyzed into one tone, corresponding to that of a tuning-fork, and others which bear certain relations to it—harmonious if it is music, unharmonious if it is noise. The subordinate tones are called partial, or under and over tones.

Musical Tones

When various simple tones combine in such a way that the various phases of their respective vibrations strengthen and weaken one another regularly, we have what is termed (from the German) a *clang*. What are ordinarily called musical notes are in reality such composite tones. Several "clangs" may now sound together, and the process of compounding of partials with a fundamental will be repeated, only in this case the several fundamentals will have to be adjusted to one another, as well as the partials to the fundamentals and to one another. If the adjustment succeeds, if there are regular coincidences and contrasts, we have a chord; a discord when the vibrations cut and chop one another up. Works on physics will give the principles of these combinations.

Noise and Musical Sound

Musical sound has already been spoken of as corresponding to an harmonious relation of partial tones to the fundamental, while noise corresponds to a non-harmonious. According to another theory, however, noise and musical sound are two different sorts of sensation, each being unique and occasioned through a different set of nerves. Evidence of this theory is thought to be found in the fact that capacity for appreciating musical discriminations and those of noises bear no relation to each other. It is probable that there is an element of truth in each theory, and that, in a general way, noise corresponds to irregularity, however produced, and musical tone to regularity.

Harmony

Certain tones, when heard together, give a pleasing result, forming a chord or consonance; others are displeasing, and are called dissonant. Psychologically this is a state of emotion, whose consideration falls under the head of æsthetic feeling. Yet there are found to exist certain physical and physiological processes constituting its basis. (1) Physical: Such vibrations as are in simple multiple ratios to each other occasion harmony of sound. Here the tones regularly strengthen and weaken each other; others come in conflict irregularly and interfere with each other. (2) Physiological: All irregular and interrupted nervous activity seems to occasion pain. For the best nervous action, it is believed that there must be regular alternations of rest and activity. Regular vibrations fulfil these conditions; irregular prevent them. The unpleasantness of discords would then correspond to the painful impression due to the affection of the visual organs by a flickering light.

7] SENSE OF SIGHT

1. Physical Stimulus

Electrical stimulus and mechanical pressure occasion sensations of light. The latter fact may be verified by simply pressing upon the eye-ball. To this principle are due the facts that we "see stars" when we hit the head a severe blow, and that the patient whose optic nerve is severed sees a flash of light. The specific stimuli, however, are the vibra-

tions of a hypothetical, imponderable, absolutely elastic medium, ether. Its vibrations occur within the limits of three
hundred and ninety-two billions per second, resulting in
sensations of red, and seven hundred and eighty-five billions,
in sensations of violet. Below they are felt as heat only;
above, they are known only indirectly.

II. Organ

The organ is the eye. This is an apparatus similar to a
camera obscura. The essential portion is found where the
optic nerve, entering, spreads itself as a fine network, called
the retina, over the back of the organ. The retina is composed of a series of nervous layers, of which the most important is that known as the layer of rods and cones. The
remainder of the eye consists of a set of subsidiary mecha-
nisms, some of which serve to protect the eye, while others
act as a system of lenses and refracting media to form an
inverted image upon the retina. There is also a mechanism
of accommodation which enables the eye to adjust itself to
varying distances of objects in such a way that their image
shall fall upon the retina, and neither behind nor before
it.

Blind Spot

The optic nerve is not itself sensitive to etheric stimulation,
consequently the point where it enters the eye leaves a blank
in the field of vision, known as the blind spot. Ordinarily this
blank is filled in by the restless movement of the eye, and by
the fact that the blank of one eye does not correspond to that
of the other. It may be rendered apparent, however, by the
simple expedient of closing one eye and holding the other
fixed upon some object. The optic nerve enters at one side of
the retina, and the centre of the retina, known from its color
as the yellow spot, is the point of most acute vision.

The Muscular Mechanism

The eyes are supplied with a set of very fine and powerful
muscles. These serve to turn the eye, so that the stimulus
shall fall upon the most sensitive point, the yellow spot.

They also serve to make the two eyes act as one organ, to move the eyes up and down, right and left, and to close them entirely. The result is that the eye is the most mobile organ of the body and is never at rest. The law of the movements of the muscles is that any given movement is always affected in the same way by the contraction of the same muscles to the same extent. It is this constancy of muscular movements which enables the muscular sensations, resulting therefrom, to be such an accurate and perfect basis for judgment of distance and direction. The connection, accordingly, between the visual sensations proper and the muscular ocular sensations is so important that we shall consider them together.

iii. The Sensations Themselves

We recognize two classes of optical sensations, the visual and the muscular.

1. VISUAL

There is no sense in which it is so necessary to discriminate between the simple sensuous element and the factor supplied by the activities of mind as in sight. Without consideration, it would seem as if the visual sensation were whatever we saw when we opened our eyes—the visible world of objects, of various kinds, at various distances. But, in reality, this is a complex psychical product, formed by judgments which are the interpretations of the sensuous material and not the material itself. Nor is the material of sensation the image found upon the retina. Physiology teaches us that this image is exceedingly small, is inverted, concave, and that the retinal elements stimulated are a mosaic-work. But, furthermore, psychology teaches us that this image is itself an external object, the knowledge of which is the result of the same processes that inform us of the existence and nature of any external object. In sensation there is no immediate knowledge of it whatever. We are aware of its existence only as the result of scientific investigation.

Light the Only Element of Sensation

It follows, accordingly, that the only element which can be
recognized as that of sensation proper is *light* with its various distinctions. These distinctions are of three kinds: (1)
of *intensity*, corresponding to the objective energy involved;
(2) of *hue* corresponding to the rate of objective vibration;
(3) of *tint*, corresponding to the purity, that is, the simple
or compound character of the vibrations.

1. INTENSITY OF LIGHT.   This does not refer to qualitative
differences, as shades of color, but simply to the force with
which any color or shade impinges upon us. It is the difference between the pitch darkness of midnight, the obscurity
of twilight, and the blaze of noonday. It depends simply
upon the amount of energy of the vibrations of ether which
affect the retina. The minimum amount of objective energy
necessary to occasion sensation (threshold value) is stated
at $\frac{1}{300}$ of the light of the full moon reflected from white
paper. The difference threshold varies with different colors.
For white light, it is about $\frac{1}{100}$, for red $\frac{1}{14}$, and the ratio
necessary decreases until it reaches the violet end of the
spectrum, where it is only $\frac{1}{268}$. The reason, accordingly,
that in the daytime we do not see the light of the stars in
addition to that of the sun is that they do not give $\frac{1}{100}$ of
the light of the sun.

2. HUE.   The hues are the various colors of the spectrum,
and these correspond to the various pitches of the musical
scale. These colors are such as white light decomposes into
when refracted through a prism—namely, violet, indigo,
blue, green, yellow, orange, red—given in the order of de-
creasing rapidity of vibration and amount of refraction; of
these, red, green, and violet are called the primary colors,
because from their proper mixture white light and the other
spectral colors may be formed. The physical basis of colors
is, therefore, various rates of vibration of the ether.

3. TINTS OR SHADES.   We recognize more than the above
seven colors—at least forty thousand have been distin-

guished. This is due to the fact that, not only is the spectrum itself a perfect continuum of colors, but each of these spectral colors is, in turn, a continuum of shades. These are due to the degree of purity, or, as it is technically called, *saturation* of light. When rays corresponding to one prismatic color fall upon the retina unaccompanied by any other kind of stimulation, the resulting sensation is pure, or saturated, color. Just in the degree it is mixed with sensations of other kinds it is non-saturated, and *shades* of the color are produced.

Color-curve

In general two kinds of shades are recognized, whitish and purplish. This is due to the following fact: Certain sets of colors, as red and blue-green, yellow and indigo-blue, unite to form white light. Such sets are called *complementary* colors. Now if we arrange the spectral colors on a line, and select from this line such as are nearer together than the complementary colors, and mix them, the result is a whitish tint of the intermediate color. If, however, we take those that are farther apart, it results in a purplish tinge. The spectral line thus takes the form of a curve, with green at the apex, red and violet at the bases, while purple connects these two, and the surface included by these lines represents all possible tints, perfect white being found at one point, whitish shades above it, and purplish tints below.

2. MUSCULAR SENSATIONS

These serve two purposes: (1) they aid the visual sensations; (2) they add a new and different element to them.

(1) They increase wonderfully the fineness and accuracy of color distinctions. As already said, the yellow spot is the most finely discriminating portion of the retina. Two points can here be discriminated as two when they are separated by only .005 millimetre. Sight thus makes two hundred times finer spatial discrimination than the tip of the tongue, the most sensitive of the organs of touch. This fineness decreases very rapidly as we go towards the periphery of the retina—at forty degrees difference it is not more

than $\frac{1}{100}$ as great as at the centre, and it decreases at a still more rapid rate nearer the limits. Were it not for the power of moving the eyes rapidly, only that comparatively small part of the field of vision which falls upon the centre would be distinctly seen; all else would be vague and blurred. The muscular connections of the eye also allow us to multiply and contrast color sensations almost indefinitely. Vision, in fact, is even more dependent upon motor activity than touch, for with a slight muscular contraction the eyes close and vision ceases, or the eyes are turned and the sensation changes in quality and intensity.

(2) The motor activity *complements* the visual by adding new sensations. Each movement of the eye is accompanied by a distinct muscular sensation. It requires less muscular contraction of the eye muscles to occasion change of sensation than any other portion of the system—a change of $\frac{1}{50}$ produces a new sensation. There is always a tendency to move the eyes so that they shall fixate the object whose image falls on the point of most acute vision. Thus there comes to be a fixed connection between the visual sensation of any part of the eye distant from the centre and the muscular sensation which accompanies the change of the position of the eye, so as to bring the image upon the yellow spot. Thus, by a process to be studied under the head of perception, each muscular sensation gets to be a permanent and accurate sign of a certain spatial distance and direction.

8]   TEMPERATURE SENSE

By the diffusion of the organs of this sense over the skin, and by the emotional and vague character of its sensations, this sense is specially well fitted to make the transition from specific to organic sensation. It will be found practically impossible to separate what is to be said about this sense under the three heads which we have formerly used.

1.   Organ

Recent investigations have shown that not the whole skin is sensitive to differences of heat and cold. The skin, in fact, may be divided into points of three kinds: neutral, which are barely sensitive of temperature distinctions; heat spots; and cold spots. The two latter respond only to stimuli of one kind. That is to say, if a cold body be put upon a heat spot, no sensation of cold results; but if it be mechanically stimulated by a body of any temperature whatever, heat results.

ii. Nature of the Organ

Just what the nerve ending is which functions for the temperature sense is not known. It is believed, however, to exist only in the true skin, and some of the mucous membranes of the body, as the mouth, œsophagus, and probably the stomach. It is destroyed by wounds, burns, scalds, etc., but is regenerated with the healing of the wound. It is distinct from the organ which mediates contact sensations, for the parts which are most sensitive to pressure are not those most responsive to temperature differences, which are the cheek and the back of the hand. Again the heat and cold spots do not coincide with the tactile corpuscles. In clinical cases it has been noticed that one sense may be in abeyance while the other is vigorous. The organ is also distinct from that of pain. By the use of cocaine it is possible to produce local insensibility to pain, or anæsthesia, while the part remains as sensitive to differences of heat and cold as ever.

iii. The Sensations

Temperature sensations are specifically different from others, therefore, and have organs of their own. Feelings of heat and cold are not two degrees of the same sensation, but are specifically different, having separate organs. The threshold difference is stated at one third. There are some points connected with sensations of this class which remain unsettled. Why, for example, do we generally perceive only differences of temperature, and not temperature itself? The body seems to have the power of adjusting itself, within certain limits, to the degree of temperature which surrounds it, and this normal temperature we do not feel, but only departures from it. This has its analogue in other senses, and may be due partly to an actual change in the sensory organ, and partly to the fact that we do not pay attention to whatever is customary. Another fact is that a body of luke-warm temperature will appear hot to a cold hand, while it seems cold to a hot hand, showing the influence of contrast upon our perceptions.

9]   GENERAL SENSATION

General, or organic, sensations have been already de-fined. They are such as arise incidentally in the nerve organ whose main function is the regulation of some animal proc-ess. They are differentiated from specific sensations as much by their own character as by the way in which they origi-nate. They are extremely vague and changeable; they pass into each other by imperceptible gradations. It is almost impossible to localize them. They do not have that connec-tion with muscular sensation which characterizes specific sensations. It follows that they serve as the basis of knowl-edge only to a very slight degree, whether knowledge of extra-organic bodies or of the organism itself. They are more closely allied with feeling.

Classification

They may be divided into (1) those arising from the state of a body as a whole, or serving to regulate it; (2) those connected with some one set of bodily organs; (3) those arising indifferently in any part of the body.

1. *SENSATIONS OF THE ORGANISM, AS A WHOLE*
These may be subdivided into (1) coenæsthesia, and (2) systemic feelings.

1. COENÆSTHESIA, or as it is otherwise called, *com-mon* feeling, which seems to arise from the summation and cumulation of all the sensations of all the sensitive parts of the body. Any one, taken by itself, is very minute, and might be imperceptible. Taken together they constitute the sense of life, of vitality, and of general *bien aise*, or *malaise*. They

seem also to make up the underlying emotional temperament of the individual as distinct from his varying moods and dispositions. They also serve as the sensuous basis, which, when interpreted, goes to determine the feeling which each has of his own individuality. Any sudden or abnormal alteration of it is quite likely to result in some disorder of individuality, as seen in insane persons, who imagine themselves to be Job, Queen Victoria, Julius Cæsar, etc. These feelings, constituting the report in consciousness of one's body, as a whole, are certainly intimately connected with self. They are constant, continuous, and relatively permanent. They form the background on which all other feelings display themselves. It is not strange that their disorder should be accompanied with results otherwise startling.

2. SYSTEMIC FEELINGS. These are such as regulate the animal activities of the organism. They are especially the feelings of hunger, thirst, and sex, and get their name from their connection with the system as a whole. Some have attempted to localize these sensations; to refer hunger, for example, to the stomach, as its organ; but there is no doubt that they are properly feelings of the whole organism. Not the stomach, but the system, wants food; and so of thirst and sexual feeling.

2. SENSATIONS OF ORGANS

The nerve endings of the stomach, for example, have as their proper business the regulation of the processes of digestion. Usually such feelings as accompany this process are lost in the coenæsthetic feeling, adding to our sense of vitality and well-being. They may appear, however, as especial feelings of relish and disgust, nausea. In case of disease, they obtrude themselves very distinctly. Sensations accompanying indigestion are characterized equally by their painful feeling, and by the influence which they exert upon the emotional mood. Besides the sensation of digestion may be mentioned those accompanying respiration, the pulmonary sensations; and, in abnormal cases, those accompanying the action of the heart. Each organ of the body, however, has its special report in feeling, and the hypochondriac often gains great skill in recognizing them.

3. SENSATIONS WHICH MAY ARISE IN ANY ORGAN

These are pain and fatigue. Disease or overwork of any portion of the body, or of the body as a whole, makes itself known in peculiar sensations. These sensations are evidently wholly emotional in their natures, and hence take us beyond our present subject.

NOTES TO CHAPTER 3

[Sensation in General] Upon the general nature of sensation the following references will give an idea of the various opinions held. Hartley, *Conjecturæ quædam de Sensu, Motu et Idearum Generatione*; Spencer, *Principles of Psychology*, vol. i, pt. 2, chs. i and ii; Morell, *Elements of Psychology*, pp. 85 - 118; Sully, *Sensation and Intuition*, and *Psychology*, ch. v; Lewes, *Problems of Life and Mind*, Third Series, pt. 2, pp. 36 - 50; Bain, *Senses and Intellect*, p. 117; Brown, *Philosophy of Mind*, vol. i, pp. 417 - 99; Murray, *Handbook of Psychology*, pp. 18 - 31; Carpenter, *Mental Physiology*, ch. iv; Maudsley, *Physiology of Mind*, ch. iv; Guillaume, *Nouveau Traité des Sensations*; Lotze, *Outlines of Psychology* (transl.), pp. 5 - 27, and *Metaphysic* (transl.), pp. 445 - 56; Wundt, *Grundzüge der physiologischen Psychologie*, vol. i, pp. 271 - 320; Volkmann, *Lehrbuch der Psychologie*, vol. i, pp. 216 - 49; Waitz, *Grundlegung der Psychologie*, p. 42; Horwicz, *Psychologische Analysen*, vol. i, pp. 175 - 85; George, *Lehrbuch der Psychologie*, pp. 55 - 69, and *Die Fünf Sinne*; Rosenkranz, *Psychologie*, pp. 75 - 93; Michelet, *Anthropologie und Psychologie*, pp. 240 - 67; Schneider, *Die Unterscheidung*, pp. 1 - 23; Bergmann, *Grundlinien einer Theorie des Bewusstseins*, pp. 31 - 53; Helmholtz, *Wissenschaftliche Abhandlungen*, vol. ii, pp. 591 - 609; Stricker, *Studien über das Bewusstsein*, pp. 15 - 29.

For the educational aspect of the question, see Perez, *L'Éducation dès le Berceau*, pp. 1 - 34; Pape-Carpantier, *L'Éducation des Sens*; Delon, *Méthode Intuitive*; Jahn, *Psychologie*, pp. 5 - 13; Delhez, *Gymnastik der Sinne*; Beneke, *Erziehungs- und Unterrichtslehre*, pp. 71 - 86.

[Touch] Foster, *Text-book of Physiology*, pp. 589 - 98; Bain (*op. cit.*), pp. 175 - 205; Bernstein, *Five Senses of Man*, pp. 10 - 43; Taine, *Intelligence*, bk. iii, ch. ii, §4; Murray (*op. cit.*), pp. 40 - 46; Hermann, *Handbuch der Physiologie der Sinnesorgane*, pt. 2, pp. 289 - 358; Wundt (*op. cit.*), vol. i, pp. 365 - 81; Preyer, *Die Seele des Kindes*, pp. 70 - 84; and especially Weber, "Tastsinn und Gemeingefühl" in Wagner's *Handwörterbuch der Physiologie*. Upon local signs in particular, see Ribot, *Contemporary German Psychol-*

ogy, ch. iv; *Revue Philosophique*, vol. iv, by Lotze; *ibid.*, vol. vi, by Wundt; Lotze, *Metaphysic*, pp. 485 - 505; Stumpf, *Psychologische Ursprung der Raumvorstellung*, pp. 86 - 101. Additional upon muscular sensation are Mach, *Die Lehre von den Bewegungsempfindungen*; Bastian, *Brain as Organ of Mind*, in Appendix; Ferrier, *Functions of Brain*, pp. 266 - 71; Lewes (*op. cit.*), Third Series, pt. 2, pp. 312 - 29; Bain (*op. cit.*), pp. 87 - 106; and (especially) James, *Feeling of Effort*; Jeanmaire, *La Personnalité*, pp. 247 - 340; Bertrand, *L'Aperception du Corps Humain par la Conscience*; Hermann (*op. cit.*), pt. 2, pp. 359 - 74; Donaldson and Hall, *Mind*, vol. x, p. 557. For optical muscular sensations in particular, see Bernstein (*op. cit.*), pp. 123 - 36, and Helmholtz, *Optique Physiologique* (French transl.), pp. 595 - 680.

[The Sense of Smell] Murray (*op. cit.*), pp. 36 - 40; Bain (*op. cit.*), pp. 163 - 75; Bernstein (*op. cit.*), pp. 285 - 94; Preyer (*op. cit.*), pp. 95 - 102; Hermann (*op. cit.*), pt. 2, pp. 270 - 88. For an odd collection of facts and fancies regarding the sense of smell, see Jäger, *Die Entdeckung der Seele*.

[Taste] Murray (*op. cit.*), pp. 32 - 36; Bain (*op. cit.*), pp. 152 - 63; Wundt, *Grundzüge der physiologischen Psychologie*, vol. i, pp. 382 - 85; Preyer (*op. cit.*), pp. 85 - 94; Ulrici, *Der Leib und die Seele*, vol. i, pp. 332 - 35; Taine (*op. cit.*), bk. iii, ch. ii, §3; and especially Bernstein (*op. cit.*), pp. 295 - 301; and Hermann (*op. cit.*), pt. 2, pp. 192 - 225.

[Sense of Hearing] Upon this sense Helmholtz's *Tone Sensations* is the principal authority, along with articles in his *Wissenschaftliche Abhandlungen*, vol. i, pp. 233 - 426, and vol. ii, pp. 503 - 88; and his *Popular Scientific Lectures*, pp. 61 - 106. Next in importance come, perhaps, Stumpf, *Tonpsychologie*, and Hermann (*op. cit.*), pt. 1, pp. 1 - 126. See, also, Bernstein (*op. cit.*), pp. 164 - 284; Sully, *Sensation and Intuition*, pp. 163 - 85; Wundt (*op. cit.*), vol. i, pp. 386 - 409; vol. ii, pp. 34 - 60; *Philosophische Studien*, vol. i, pp. 463 and 495; Riemann, *Über das musikalische Hören*; Hostinský, *Die Lehre von den musikalischen Klängen*; Czermak, *Über das Ohr und das Hören*.

[Sense of Sight] There is considerable literature upon the historical development of this sense. See, besides discussions in periodical literature by Gladstone and Max Müller, Allen, *Colour-Sense*; and Magnus, Marty, and Hochegger upon *Die geschichtliche Entwickelung des Farbensinnes*. Compare also Graber, *Der Helligkeits- und Farbensinn der Thiere*. The chief authority upon the sense is Helmholtz, *Optique Physiologique* (French edition), pp. 204 - 444, and *Popular Scientific Lectures*, pp. 229 - 70; see also Volkmann, article "Sehen," in Wagner's *Handwörterbuch der Physiologie*. For various theories upon color, see Goethe, *Theory of Colors*, and Schopenhauer, *Über das Sehen und die Farben*, which, though antiquated, are still interesting. For the sense in general, see Jeffries, *Color Blindness* (contains a valuable bibliography);

Bernstein (*op. cit.*), pp. 48 - 122; Hermann (*op. cit.*), pt. 1, pp. 139 - 234; Wundt (*op. cit.*), vol. i, pp. 410 - 64; Foster (*op. cit.*), pp. 510 - 51; Bain (*op. cit.*), pp. 222 - 50; Preyer (*op. cit.*), p. 451. For remarkable associations of color and tone sensations, see Bleuler and Lehmann, *Zwangsmässige Lichtempfindungen.*

[Temperature Sense] Hermann (*op. cit.*), pt. 2, pp. 415 - 39, and Donaldson, *Mind*, vol. x, p. 399, with the bibliography there given.

[General Sensation] References upon organic sensations will be found included, for the most part, in the foregoing. In addition may be consulted, Preyer (*op. cit.*), pp. 103 - 28; Horwicz (*op. cit.*), vol. i, pp. 185 - 91, 337 - 40; Murray (*op. cit.*), pp. 60 - 71.

On the senses, see Ladd, *Elements of Physiological Psychology*, pt. 2, chs. iii - v. Experiments throwing light on the interconnection of the various sense qualities and going to show that photisms and phonisms may be only extreme exaggerations of normal processes may be found in Pflüger's *Archiv*, Bd. xlii, p. 154. For an extremely useful compendium of experiments, etc., regarding the senses, see Sanford, in *American Journal of Psychology*, April, 1891.

4

Processes of Knowledge

1] THE NATURE OF THE PROBLEM

Sensations are not Knowledge

But these elements which we have been studying do not constitute knowledge or knowing. Knowing does not consist in having feelings of heat, of contact, of color, and of sound. The world which is known is not a disorderly, passing assemblage of these feelings. We have now to discover the processes by which these sensations are elaborated, on the one hand, into the objects known, and on the other into the subject knowing. The best way of approaching this study will be to ascertain what some of the general characteristics of the known world and knowing self are, and by comparing these characteristics with those of sensations, find out what gap it is which the processes are to bridge over. We shall begin, in short, by pointing out the necessity of these processes, and the function which they fulfil in the psychical life.

I. The Nature of the Known World

(1) Actual knowledge is concerned with a world of related objects—that is to say, with a universe of things and events arranged in space and time. By an object we mean (1) something having a certain permanence, (2) existing, therefore, aside from the mere occurrence of a sensation, and (3) capable of being presented to any normal mind. What we need to explain, then, is how we become conscious of a sensation, instead of merely feeling it; how the *quality* of a sensation becomes consciously distinguished from the mere *event* or occurrence of the sensation. As an event, sensation is limited to some one mind, and to some one

moment. It lasts only as long as it is felt. But the world of objects is not a series of unconnected, unrelated objects. Each is joined to every other in space and in time. We never experience any breach of continuity. We pass naturally, by some connecting link, from one to another. We live, in short, in an ordered, harmonious world, or cosmos; not in a chaos. All objects and events are considered as members of one system; they constitute a *uni-verse*, one world, in which order, connection, is the universal rule.

(2) Actual knowledge is concerned with relations. We are not limited to particular objects or events alone. Science opens to us the realm of relations, or laws — uniformities which connect phenomena with each other, and are hence universal. Science deals only incidentally with *this* apple, or *that* rose; this particular cat or jelly-fish. It deals with them only to discover exemplified in them certain common features which it expects to find in all members of the class; that is, certain relations universally present. These relations, accordingly, are not mere objects or events. They are permanent connections which hold objects and events together, and make a unity of them. As just pointed out, the objects and events which we know are connected with each other, but in ordinary perception we pay no particular attention to these relations. We are absorbed with the individual existence. Science takes a step in advance and discovers what these relations are which connect things and occurrences together so that they all constitute a harmonious whole.

Nature of Science

Scientific knowledge, in other words, differs from ordinary knowledge in being unified, systematic, connected knowledge. Science is not content with knowing that objects are connected in time and space; it endeavors to find out just what the relations of succession and coexistence are which do thus connect them. It reduces many separate facts to their unity in one law. It finds one form, or a uniformity, in many facts apparently unconnected. The ultimate aim of science is to unify all facts and events whatever, so that it may not only *feel* that they are members of one system, but may actually realize their systematic unity. It is evident that the original, fleeting, subjective affections, known as sensations, will have to be still further transformed, in order to account for that form of knowledge which we call science.

(3) Actual knowledge is concerned with ideal elements. The epic of Homer, the tragedy of Sophocles, the statue of Phidias, the symphony of Beethoven are *creations*. Although having a correspondence with actual existences, they do not reproduce them. They are virtual additions to the world's riches; they are ideal. Such creations are not confined to art, nor are they remote from our daily existence. When shall we *see* justice? Who has touched righteousness? What sense or combination of senses gives us the idea of the state or church; of history, as the development of man; of God, or the source and end of all our strivings? What a meagre life were left us, were the ideal elements removed! It would be, as has been well said, a world in which the home would be four walls and a roof to keep out cold and wet; the table a mess for animals, and the grave a hole in the ground.

A world in which everything is regarded simply as a fact presented to the senses would hardly be a world in which we should care to live. The processes we are about to study must, therefore, be capable of transmuting sensations into these ideals which make life rich, worthy, and dignified.

II. The Nature of the Knowing Self

Along with the transformation of sensations into this world of objects, relations, and ideals, goes their transformation into the self which knows and idealizes. The man not only knows more than the child, but he is a man instead of a child. He not only knows more, but he is more. This difference is not a physical one of bulk, or stature, or age; any more than it is difference of color of hair, or texture of the skin. These are of any importance only because they are connected with a psychical difference, the difference in the degree of development of the knowing self. The processes which we are to study must therefore be such as to enable us to account for this growth of self.

The Processes

These processes are ultimately reducible to two, one of which is principally concerned with the formation of the world of known objects and relations out of the elementary sensations, while the other is concerned with the formation of the knowing self. To these two processes the names of apperception and retention may be given. Apperception may be defined, at the outset, as *the reaction of mind by means of its organized structure upon the sensuous material presented to it*. Retention is *the reaction of the apperceived content upon the organized structure of the mind*. Apperception organizes the world of knowledge by bringing the self to bear upon it; retention organizes the self by bringing the things known to bear upon it. Each process, accordingly, involves the other. We begin with the subject of

2]　APPERCEPTION

1.　The Problem of Apperception

In general, this is the fact that there is such a thing as knowledge; that we not only have sensations, but have an intelligent life and intelligible experiences. Whatever appeals to the investigation of intelligence, offers it material upon which to exert its activities, whatever responds to the inquiry by producing some fruit for intelligence, we call *significant*, or possessing *meaning*. It is the characteristic, then, of the subject-matter of our psychical life that it has meaning. Whatever is meaningless has no point of contact with intelligence or the apperceiving activity of mind. The main-spring of our cognitive experiences is the more or less conscious feeling that things have meaning.

Significance and Relations

If we inquire under what circumstances any object or event enters into our intellectual life as significant, we find that it is when it is connected in an orderly way with the rest of our experience. The meaningless is that which is out of harmony, which has no connection with other elements. To have meaning, the fact or event must be related to some other fact or event. The isolated, the separate, is never the object of knowledge. Were not sensations capable of being connected so that the mind could go from one to another naturally, they never could become even materials of knowledge. To be significant is to be a sign; that is, to point to something beyond its own existence to which it is related. Whatever has its meaning exhausted in itself, and consequently has no connection with anything beyond itself, has no meaning. Relationship is the essence of meaning.

Two Kinds of Relations

Looking at the matter in a very general way, we find that psychical life has meaning because its elements are connected in two ways: (1) They are combined; (2) They are continuous. That is to say, all the cognitive elements occurring at any one time are combined into a whole, and all these combinations, made at various times, are connected into an orderly, continuous whole. Our ideas are significant because they are related in two ways: any given idea is related to all ideas existing at the same time, and is related to all ideas which occur at different times. These two kinds of relations evidently cover the whole of our psychical life. Such relations are, however, external, and we shall find certain internal relations, those of identity and difference, more essential. Yet by relations our mental life has meaning.

Illustration

This may be shown in a simple way by asking what is involved in the apperception of, say, an orange. The sensations of sight, touch, taste, and smell are its constituent elements. They give the material which enters into the cognition. As sensations alone, these are unrelated and unconnected. Each is transitory, complete in itself, therefore isolated and pointing to nothing beyond itself. Hence they are meaningless. They are not the idea of an orange; they are half a dozen separate elements of weight, color, flavor, etc. These elements must, accordingly, be combined. They must be brought into connection with each other, and made members of a whole—only then do they get meaning, and appeal to intelligence. But this combination does not give us knowledge of an orange. This means more than that we do not know that its *name* is "orange." We do not yet know the *thing*. When we know a thing we recognize it, but we cannot recognize anything unless we can connect it with our previous experience, and recognize it as like some of our past ideas, and unlike others. In short, it must be given a place in the connected series of ideas which make up our experience before it is known.

First Objection

An examination of the objections which might be brought against this assertion will tend to make the matter clearer. In the first place, it may be objected, that we do know things which we have never experienced before, and that if we did not, there would be no such thing as learning or new knowledge. For example, we may be given a strange fruit, perhaps a guava, and by "trying" it, we find out almost everything about it. But, if we inquire what we mean by finding out about it, we see that the objection confirms rather than refutes the original assertion. In the first place, we shall find out that it is a fruit, and this we can do only as we recognize its identity with some of our previous experiences, and thus connect them together. Then we may discover that it is edible, but this is only because its odor, flavor, etc., have been formerly associated with objects that are edible. So far, in short, as the guava is known, it is known by discovering points of likeness between it and what has been previously known. Knowledge is extensive and accurate just in the degree in which we have had experiences in the past, similar to the present one, with which we can connect it. Were it absolutely unfamiliar it would be absolutely non-significant. This condition, however, can never be fulfilled, for we shall at least be able to recognize it as a thing or object, as having existence, etc.

Second Objection

But it may be said that there was a time when we experienced something absolutely unfamiliar, that intelligent life had a beginning, so that there was in infancy a time when the thing was first known, and could not be known by connecting it with other knowledge. But this objection overlooks the fact that the baby's knowledge is not a thing which occurs all at once, but is a matter of gradual growth. The first years of childhood are spent, not so much in knowing things, as in getting experiences which may be brought to bear in the future, and thus enable him to know. The infant has all the *sensations* that we have, yet no one would say that he has the knowledge. The reason for this fact is that he does not have the past store of experience with which he may connect the present, and thus render it significant. The child spends his early years in *learning* to know. Knowledge is an acquired product, due to the possibility of connecting present experiences with past.

Summary

The characteristic of our intelligent life, both as a whole, and in its parts, is that it is significant. Significant means ordered, connected; and connected in two ways, simultaneously and successively. Accordingly, in studying apperception, or the activity of mind which renders psychical life intelligent, we are studying the means by which the sensuous elements of our knowledge gain significance through the union of all elements occurring together, and by the mutual reference to each other of those occurring at different times. We now turn to a study of the definite ways in which this is accomplished.

II. Kinds of Apperception

Apperception is that activity of mind in which the *significance* of mental *events* is brought out, through becoming explicitly conscious of the relations involved in them. It is the *appropriation* of the intellectual, or qualitative, value of an experience merely momentarily felt. In our study of it we shall recognize three stages: (1) Association; (2) Dissociation; (3) Attention.

Three Stages

These are not to be understood as three kinds of apperception, but only as three degrees in the development of the
apperceiving activity. The basis of the division is the relative
simplicity of the processes, and the relative *activity* of the
mind in performing them. Association is comparatively simple, dealing with the original sensuous forms, and combining them into comparatively non-complex wholes. Attention
begins with these wholes, already prepared for it. Its results
are the highest and most complex creations of our intellectual life.

Relative Activity

The mind is, of course, active in all processes, but in association the activity appears to be externally occasioned and
directed. The mind is active in combining sensations, but
the combining activity follows mechanically upon the presence of the sensations, and the direction which it takes is
dependent upon them. In attention, the activity is not produced by the mere presence of the ideas, but is due to the
interests and aims of the mind itself. The mind *associates*
whatever is given to it; it *attends* only to that which it
selects. So the special direction which the attention takes is
determined not by the character of the sensations themselves, but by the end which the mind wishes to reach for
purposes of its own. The activity, in one case, is externally
determined; in the other case, it is self-determined. Dissociation occupies an intermediate place. It frees the mind from
the mechanical pressure which association exerts upon it,
and disengages the various ends towards which attention
may direct itself. Each of these later stages grows naturally
out of the previous one; and we shall find that the emotional
side of the mind, or its interests, is the active factor in
occasioning the growth of the mind in intellectual freedom.

3]   ASSOCIATION

I.

The law of association, stated most generally, is that *the activity of mind never leaves sensuous elements isolated, but connects them into larger wholes.* We begin with a study of its conditions, positive and negative.

1. POSITIVE CONDITIONS

These are: (1) The presence of sensuous elements; (2) That state of mind which we call being awake. It is evident, on the one hand, that if there be no sensuous elements present, there will be nothing for the apperceiving activity to combine, and also nothing to stimulate it into activity. The mind, in spite of its tendency to act, would remain an undeveloped blank, were it not for the presence of sensations to call forth its processes. In the case of a person who had lost all senses excepting hearing, it was only found necessary to close his ears to induce sleep. On the other hand, no matter how strong and numerous are the sensations presented, if the mind is not in that state of readiness which we call being awake, no association results. Mere sensations are not enough to keep the mind awake, although it will not be awake without them. Constant stimulation seems to fatigue the mind, and, finally, bring it to a state where it is no longer able to respond. In just the degree in which this awakeness ceases, fails also the combining activity of self. It must be remembered, however, that in the state of dreaming the mind is still partially awake.

2. NEGATIVE CONDITIONS

The conditions just mentioned are equally conditions of *any* activity of mind. To differentiate association from the higher activities, it is necessary to mention some negative conditions. These, as already suggested (page 82), are relative passivity of the mind, and relative simplicity of the sensory elements. By *passivity* is not meant that the mind is wholly passive, and that the sensory elements impress themselves upon it, but that its activity is determined rather by the stimuli themselves than by a conscious end or interest of the mind. The process is much like that already studied in sensation (page 43). In the latter the nervous change in the brain serves as a stimulus to the *sensitive* activity of the mind, and the latter responds mechanically with the sensation. In association this sensation acts as a stimulus to the *apperceiving* activity of self, and it responds mechanically by combining it with others.

Simplicity

The stimuli which affect the mind must be of *like* character. This does not require that they should be of the same sense; it only requires that there should be no striking incongruity or incompatibility between them. There must be no such conflict between them as would compete for the apperceiving activity, so that the latter must make a distinction between them. All ideas of any degree of complexity do have, however, factors that appear non-harmonious, so that the only elements which can fulfil this condition are extremely simple ones—either original sensations, or ideas where the quality of likeness predominates over that of difference.

Transition to Higher Forms

In its higher forms, however, the associating activity passes insensibly into dissociation, for it is impossible to emphasize the predominating quality of likeness without, partially at least, discriminating the unlike. If, for example, we associate in our minds a whale with a bear because of some fundamental identity between them, as that both are mammals, it is because we can sift out all unlike qualities and disregard them. The difference between association and dissociation is not so much in the modes of activity as in the elements upon which stress is laid. Association emphasizes the like element; dissociation accentuates, rather, the unlike, and while one results in combination, the other results, rather, in separation. They might almost be treated, therefore, as two sides of the same activity. We shall draw the line simply when the *selective* activity of intelligence grows more apparent.

II. Forms of Associating Activity

We now inquire what are the various forms or modes in which this activity manifests itself. The mind binds together all actual sensory elements into a total experience: this is *Presentative* Association. It also binds together former experiences with new ones which suggest the former: this is *Representative* Association. The two together constitute the ordinary train of ideas.

Law of Presentative

The mind connects all sensations as far as possible into one total maximum experience. If, for example, the eye sees a rod striking a surface at certain intervals, and, at the same periods, the ear hears a noise, the two will go together into one idea, whether or not they have a common source. Just so two events occurring at about the same time, say a rain storm and a certain phase of the moon, will tend to be united. The tendency to shun isolated elements and to force connections wherever possible is perhaps the fundamental law of mental action.

Importance of Law

This law economizes mental force. Ten elements united into one idea are grasped and carried almost as easily as any one of the ten separately. Moreover, through this tendency to connect the mind realizes for itself the maximum of significance; it gets the fullest possible experience; or, if we use the word sensation in its broadest sense, gets the completest and richest sensation. The mind's instinct for a full unity often leads it astray, but it is the secret also of all its successes. The discovery of laws, the classification of facts, the formation of a unified mental world, are all outgrowths of the mind's hunger for the fullest experience possible at the least cost.

Law Illustrated

Watch a young child at play with a ball. First, perhaps, he spies it with his eyes, getting a sensation of color. This sensation, while isolated, irritates him. He must get the ball into his hands. This done, he pokes and punches it; he squeezes and throws it. He does everything to get the maximum of sensation out of it. Before this, probably, he has put it to his mouth to get, if possible, sensations of taste. In throwing it, he has heard noises as it struck. He keeps up this process until he has exhausted the sensations coming from this object. If we do not go through this same process in adult life, it is partly from acquired self-restraint, and partly because one sensation now symbolizes the others to us. But the sign in art galleries that canes and umbrellas must be left outside testifies that this same instinct still endures. The continuous union of the varied sensations into one whole constitutes presentative—or, as it is sometimes called, simultaneous—association.

Fusion or Integration

If we represent the isolated sensations of sight by A, of touch by B, of muscular sensation by C, of taste by D, and so on, the outcome is not to be designated by $A + B + C + D + E$, etc. Presentation is not a mechanical mosaic of independent sensations. By the touch sensation the color is modified into a B; muscular sensation changes this into a b C'; taste sensations modify this to a' β c D'; sound sensations transform this to a'' β' γ d E', and so on. We have, that is to say, a continuous whole of sensation constantly undergoing modification and constantly expanding, but never parting with its unity. This process may be termed *fusion* or *integration*, to indicate the fact that the various elements are continually entering into a whole in which they lose their independent existence. Professor James illustrates this intimate union by the taste of lemonade. This does not retain unchanged the tastes of sugar and of lemon, but is itself a new sensation into which the old ones have passed as elements. What association gives us, in other words, is not a loosely connected aggregate of separable parts, but a new total experience.

Transition to Representation

This process alone would give us a series of presentations. As the same elements would often be stimulated, there would often be a repetition of some former experience. The child, for example, who played with a ball yesterday might play with another to-day. This repeated activity of the same elements undoubtedly gives a sense of familiarity to the presentation. Some new sensations may be had and thus the presentation further expanded. But there would be as yet no *re*-presentation. The object known is still actually present. Suppose, however, that while the ball played with yesterday was black and hard, the ball handled to-day is soft and red. We have a certain core of identity in both experiences. Now, this identity will strive to complete itself by the addition of all connected factors. This core of identity, the "ball," is only a fragment, and the other fragments, the blackness and the hardness, must be supplied in order that the maximum of meaning, the whole idea, may be experienced. Thus the idea of the hard black ball will be formed. But there is also going on an integration of sensations of red and soft with the "ball." These elements, moreover, being occasioned by an actual peripheral stimulus of the sense organs, will surpass in intensity the centrally excited images of black and hard. The presentation of the red soft ball, in other words, will displace the idea of the black hard ball. The latter, however, is not destroyed. It is simply degraded from the position of an actual presentation. It becomes a *representation*. Or, as we term the primary process of association by which actual sensory elements are fused *integration*, we may term this extension of present sensory elements by distinct revival of past elements *redintegration*.

The Train of Experiences

Representative association is thus only a further development of our original principle—the tendency of the mind to work towards a unified totality. The totality of presentation is that of elements actually experienced at the time. In representation the mind enlarges its grasp. It enriches its present experience by supplying the results of previous experiences. Were there no incongruity or opposition between the present and the past, the former would undoubtedly simply be absorbed in the present, adding to its meaning. But the opposition of elements, as of red to black and of soft to hard, prevents this direct absorption. The unlike elements are forced into independent consciousness, and, being weaker, take the form of representation. By this extension of our experience to the reproduction of former presentations the train of ideas is formed. This is the succession of our experiences with the relative proportion of presentations and representations ever waxing and waning. This train does not differ in principle from dissociation and attention, to be studied later, but only in the degree in which it is controlled by some idea or end.

Forms of Redintegration

All redintegration rests on *identity* of present activity with some past activity. This identity, however, may be a comparatively *external* one, of place or time of occurrence, or it may be an *internal* one, of likeness of quality or content. The former is generally called association by *contiguity*; the latter, association by *similarity*. An example will illustrate their difference. At some time, I have seen in the post-office a certain person; these two elements, being involved in the same act of apperception, thus became members of one whole idea. To-day I go into the post-office again, and although the individual is not sensuously present, the idea of him immediately occurs to my mind. This is evidently redintegration by spatial contiguity. The idea which occurs to me upon entering the post-office may, however, not be that of any one ever seen there. It may be the image of a post-office in some other town. This is redintegration by similarity.

External and Internal Association

It is evident the former is external and the latter internal. There is no reason internally involved in the idea either of the man or the post-office, why one should suggest the other. It merely happened to be so. It was an affair of circumstance. In the other case the connection is intrinsic. It is the internal identity of the significance of the two ideas which connects them. The same *idea* is conveyed by both to the mind. It is the principle of identity which is working in both associations, but in that by contiguity it is mere identity of place or time of happening. There is no need that they should be identical. In the other case the identity is necessary; it is involved in the very existence of the idea. In all cases of association by similarity, some partial identity of internal significance may be detected.

The subject of connective association will be treated under the following heads: (1) Redintegration by contiguity; (2) By similarity, together with their laws and sub-varieties.

1. ASSOCIATION BY CONTIGUITY

Its law is as follows: *If various sensory elements, or even ideas, contiguous in place or time, are associated simultaneously in one activity, they become integral portions of it and recur with it.* Three points are to be taken up in connection with it; (1) The original union of elements in one activity; (2) The re-presentation of an element not sensuously present; (3) Two kinds of contiguous association, spatial and temporal.

1. The student must carefully avoid identifying an idea with some one of the factors into which it may be analyzed. The neglect of this caution has led to needless discussion as to the number of ideas which may be present in the mind at once, some holding that only one idea can exist at a time; others, that a much larger number may be present. The truth is that there can be but one idea present in the mind at a time, but this one idea may have an indefinite number of subordinate ideas coexisting within it. There can be but one idea, for the associating activity necessarily combines into one all that is presented to it at once.

Illustration

When I open my eyes upon a room full of people, it is not to be supposed that I have as many ideas as there are people and things in the room, and then make these into one idea by a process of patchwork. The very apperception consists simply in uniting these various elements in one whole; it does not exist until they have been united. The separation of this whole into its constituent elements is a later act. The same holds true of successive elements. When I listen to a

spoken sentence I do not apperceive separately each sound,
and then piece them together. I take in the idea of the whole
sentence. The analytic recognition of separate elements is a
later process. Psychologically, the synthesis precedes analysis.

2. RE-PRESENTATION.   The understanding of this fact
is necessary to any comprehension of redintegration by contiguity. Were the ideas which are recalled originally separated and isolated atoms, nothing less than a miracle could
explain the possibility of their recurrence. We should have
to suppose that, in some way, these ideas were preserved in a
storehouse of the mind, and that when some other idea
occurred which dwelt next to some one of them, it had the
power of compelling its neighbor to appear in consciousness
also. But there is no ground for supposing the existence of
any such limbo of ideas, or of any process of resurrection.
Nor is the supposition necessary to account for the representation of an experience.

Explanation of Re-presentation

Recognizing that ideas were once organic members of the
same activity of mind, it is not difficult to see how they
recur. The *activity* will recur whenever the mind acts in the
same way again. The elements occur because they are portions, members, of this one activity. If we draw one end of a
stick towards us, it is not surprising that the other end
comes too; or if we spur one flank of a horse, it requires no
miracle to explain why the other flank moves too. There is
but one rod, and one horse. So there is but one idea. Getting
hold of any part of it, it is necessary that the other parts
should follow. If the perception of a flower recalls the spot
where I picked it, it is because the flower and the place are
members of the same whole; they are organically united in
the same activity of apperception; one has no mental existence without the other. The difficulty, accordingly, is not in
explaining why redintegration sometimes takes place, but in
explaining why it does not always occur. This will be explained under the head of dissociation.

3. FORMS OF CONTIGUOUS ASSOCIATION. Elements are thus redintegrated which have been contiguous with the presented element either in space or in time.

i. Spatial Association. It is through this kind of suggestion that upon seeing a building we form a mental image of the street in which it is, or of the whole town. Through it we form such connections as the suggestion of a lecture, or of the man who delivered it, upon seeing the lecture-hall. It covers all cases where one element recalls some other which has been coexistent with it in space. It is an important mode of connection, both because of the ease with which it is cultivated, and because of the results which it has in psychical life. Its ease of cultivation is due to the fact that we get the larger number of our ideas through sight, and sight is pre-eminently the spatial sense. To *see* a thing is synonymous with clear knowledge of it. That principle of modern pedagogy that wholes shall be presented to the child before parts, and the other one, that the child shall see the objects about which he learns, are based, in their usefulness, upon this law of association.

Spatial Association in Language

The fact that words denoting spiritual and ideal processes were originally words which signified material things existing in space, serves still further to illustrate the importance of this kind of association. In the early history of the race the occurrence of a psychical process was so closely connected with its physical accompaniment or embodiment that the two were confounded. The soul was breath, to comprehend was to grasp together, etc. The process is still more clearly illustrated in the names given to material objects. These were almost always some quality of them which appealed to sight, and hence was capable of spatial association. So the moon was the measurer; the earth was the ploughed; wheat was the white, etc. The race, as the individual, begins its life in captivity to external associations, and it is only by slow processes that the mind is freed from them and learns to grasp the ideal, the internal significance. The naturalness of the association of spiritual states and the ideal with spatial things is illustrated by the poet, who reverses the process just mentioned, and embodies these in, or finds them illustrated by, natural objects. The personification of objects, and the attributing of aspirations, sympathies, and moods to nature, are due largely to spatial association.

ii. Temporal Contiguity. A simple illustration of this kind of association is seen in illustrating the alphabet, where the sound of *a* calls up *b*, *b* suggests *c*, etc. It is important to notice that temporal association affects, as a rule, only the order of the connection; *a* will call up *b*, but *b* fails to redintegrate *a*. The reason for this seems, however, to be rather in the frequency with which the same act has been repeated than in the nature of the association. Had *a* been associated with *b* but once, *b* would probably suggest *a* as easily as it now calls up *c*. Repetition in the same order has made this order a part of the activity, and hence one of the elements recalled. The fact that the words of a sentence, if repeated but once, suggest each other in a certain order, and not in the reverse, is due to the aiding of one association by the sense of the passage. In fact, it is in forming the proper *order* that the cultivation of temporal association consists.

Illustrations

It will be noticed that hearing is the sense of temporal associations as sight is of spatial. Speech, music, etc., are dependent for their existence upon the formation of regular associations in time. The "learning to speak" by a child consists, for one thing, in forming a consecutive series of associations, so that one sound calls up another. The association of the name with the object is, however, a case of spatial association. Sight, by virtue of its muscular connections, plays a large rôle in forming temporal associations, as, for example, in reading.

Composite Associations

The majority of associations are complex, involving spatial and temporal associations together with simultaneous fusion. This may be illustrated in such well-defined associations as walking, speaking, playing a musical instrument, etc. Learning to walk consists first in the formation of a temporal association, so that each muscular grouping does not have to be thought of and willed separately, but the appearance of one of the series serves to redintegrate each of the others. There is also involved spatial association, for no movement can be performed by one muscle alone. The commencement of contraction by some one muscle must immediately call forth the activities of other muscles, some of which reinforce this, while others counteract it and preserve the equilibrium of the body. Fusion also comes in inseparably to weld these associations together.

Speech

Language involves a threefold association at least. The sound must be associated with the presented object, through a tactual or visual sensation generally; it must be associated with the idea of the object, so that it shall convey meaning even when the object is not present; and it must be associated with the muscular sensation which corresponds to the tension, etc., necessary to produce the sound. If any one of the elements is lacking, a corresponding defect of speech occurs. In educated persons, two further associations are added. There is an association with the visual sensation of the printed or written appearance of the word so that it may be read; and there is association with the muscular sensation which is required to write it. The student may develop for himself the associations involved in playing a musical instrument by note.

2. REDINTEGRATION BY SIMILARITY

The law of association by similarity is as follows: *If any activity has frequently recurred, any element often occurring gains in redintegrating power at the expense of those occurring less often, and will finally gain the power of acting independently, so as itself to redintegrate ideas by the law of contiguity.* An example will serve to bring out the meaning of this law. Let us take again the association of the man with the post-office. Were we always to see the same man in the same post-office, and only him, association by contiguity would never pass into association by similarity.

But this is not the case. We see other men and things in the post-office. We see this man in other places. Thus there arise associations with the post-office which are unlike each other in most elements. The only thoroughly constant element is that of the post-office itself. It is evident that the less necessary, the more accidental, are the elements involved, the more they will vary, and hence tend to crowd each other out, while the internal element, in this case, the very idea of the post-office, will remain constant. Thus it is that external redintegration, or that of contiguity, passes into internal, that of similarity. We take up: (1) conditions of association by similarity; (2) its forms.

1. CONDITIONS.   These are: (*i.*) Varying concomitants; (*ii.*) Analogy of feeling.

   i. Varying Concomitants.   This corresponds to the process just spoken of as constituting the transition from contiguous to similar association, and its law may be stated as follows: If one given element has been associated at various times with various elements unlike each other, the tendency towards the redintegration of any one of these will be checked by an equal tendency towards the redintegration of each of the others, so that the one permanent element will be set free from its varying accompaniments. Thus, if *abcd* have been at one time associated in the activity *x*; at another time, *aefg* in the activity *y*; and, again, *ahij* in the activity of *z*, and now *a* recurs again, the tendency towards the redintegration of any given element will be equally assisted and equally checked in every instance; while *a* itself will stand out with triple emphasis.

Illustration

The varying concomitants being thus eliminated, the permanent element of similar character will redintegrate other elements by the subordinate action of the law of contiguity. For example, I see a portrait and there immediately comes before me the idea of its original in a position where I saw him at some given time. By the action of the pure law of contiguity the portrait might have called up something entirely different; but the various tendencies in different directions check each other, while the likeness of each of the parts of the face, eye, ear, mouth, etc., with the face of the original strengthen each other, and tend towards that definite form of redintegration.

Further Illustration

Or, again, I see a St. Bernard dog from my window. This perception may call up the place where first I saw him, or the idea of the man whom he generally accompanies. This is evidently by the law of contiguity purely. Or it may redintegrate the idea of another St. Bernard dog which I once saw somewhere else. The first step is the exclusion of all associations depending upon the varying circumstances, times, and places of previous perceptions of St. Bernard dogs, and the emphasizing of the identical element—the idea of a St. Bernard dog itself. Then this element operates by the law of contiguity and calls up the surroundings of place and time with which the idea of *a* St. Bernard dog, although not *this* one, was once associated.

ii. Analogy of Feeling. Its law may be stated as follows: At any given time only those ideas will be redintegrated which are of like emotional tone with the mood then present. Ideas quite dissimilar in intellectual content may thus serve to call up each other. The train of ideas in a cheerful mood differs from that which goes on in a melancholy state. A mood may indeed become so dominant as to entirely govern the course of images and ideas. A present sorrow may so darken the mind that it can find no joyous experiences in the past. A present happiness may effectually exclude all recollection of past sorrows. In all cases we are able to call up experiences of past events most effectually when we can assume a mood congruous to that in which the events occurred.

Importance of Feeling in Association

Feeling, in all cases, seems to serve as a matrix in which ideas are embedded, and by which they are held together. There is no more permanent tie between ideas than this identity of emotion. The power of a flag to awaken patriotic ideas and resolves, of a cross to arouse religious meditation or devout action, is due to the tie of feeling rather than to that of intellectual process. The same fact governs the higher flights of oratory and the processes of poetic production. In oratory, indignation, enthusiasm, some passion, brings the whole resource of the mind to bear upon the point at issue. The intensity of feeling shuts out from the discourse all inharmonious images and irrelevant ideas far more effectually than any direct purpose of attention could bring about. The contingent and accidental detail that usually accompanies the course of our ideas vanishes, and they follow each other in an original and vital unity, a unity which reflective thought may imitate, but only overmastering emotion produce.

In Poetry

The poet not only detects subtler analogies than other men, and perceives the subtle link of identity where others see confusion and difference, but the form of his expression, his language, images, etc., are controlled also by deeper unities. These unities are unities of feeling. The objects, the ideas, connected are perhaps remote from each other to intellect, but feeling fuses them. Unity of feeling gives artistic unity, wholeness of effect, to the composition. When unity is wanting there is no poetry; where the unity is one of reflection, purpose, or argument, we instinctively feel that the composition approaches prose. It is the analogy of feeling, the identity of noble or impassioned emotion, which creates unity of substance and unity of form, insuring apt transition, appropriate images and metaphors, harmonious setting in style of metre, rhyme, etc.

Analogies of Sensation

There are various associations among sensations which would be inexplicable were it not for this associating effect of feeling. We regard tones as high and low, although they have no spatial quality; colors are soft, although they offer no pressure to touch; and contact may be sweet, although it cannot be tasted. We express our likes and dislikes by the terms delicious and disgusting. "Taste" is the arbiter of æsthetic productions. Men are upright and base; hearts are hollow and firm; characters are white and black. In some cases the association extends so far that persons, on seeing certain colors, hear certain sounds (phonisms), or, more often, on hearing sounds, see colors (photisms).

2. FORMS. Three forms of redintegration by similarity may be noticed: (*i.*) by resemblance; (*ii.*) by contrast; (*iii.*) by assimilation.

i. Association by Resemblance. It has been already noticed that association by similarity is a higher kind than that by contiguity. It depends upon likeness of meaning or internal content, not upon accident of time or place. The intellectual power of mind is accordingly largely determined by the relative predominance of either kind over the other. One individual never gets beyond outer connection; he is taken up with accidental circumstances and contingent events. Another mind pierces through this external husk, and connects objects by some fundamental relation of likeness. The former remembers an historical event by placing it on a chart, or associating it with some position on the page of a book which relates it; the latter remembers it by its causal connection with other events. To the peasant the falling apple redintegrates only spatial associations of its pleasant taste; to Sir Isaac Newton its resemblance to all falling bodies suggested the law of gravitation.

Place in Mental Life

The connection of each with the very structure of psychical life is no less important. Facts or events connected by local association burden the mind, for they have no necessary or intrinsic connection with each other. They are so much material which the mind must carry by main force. If the accidental association of place or time is let go, all is gone. The connection by similarity is internal, and involved in the very nature of the ideas. They would not be what they are except for this property of likeness to some other ideas. The tie between them is natural, and it broadens the mind therefore, and does not burden it. Such a connection, instead of requiring to be carried by the mind, forms part of its carrying power. It is one of the links forming the chain of memory which holds ideas together. The difference between the two kinds of association, in their effect upon mental life, has been aptly illustrated by comparing one to food carried in a bundle strapped upon the back, and the other to food eaten, digested, and wrought over into the bones and muscles which hold the body firm and solid. One uses up the power of the mind, the other adds to it.

Two Classes of Minds

Even those minds which use especially association by resemblance may be divided into two classes. There are those which simply *use* the bond of resemblance in passing from one idea to another, and there are those which *notice* the tie. The former are the persons of artistic temperament, those of quick and keen intuitive power. The latter are those of a scientific turn of mind, of reflective and deliberative power. The former pass over the path of resemblance, but are so taken up with the goal that they pay no attention to the road that takes them thither. They proceed by analogy, the striking simile, and the quick metaphor. They express in a single sentence what years of reflective study may not exhaust, the subtle and hidden connections, the points of identity with the whole framework of truth are so many and deep. Such minds are the world's artists and teachers. The others wish to know every step of the road, the way in which each part of it is connected with every other, and how all conduct to the goal. They are the world's investigators and formulators.

    ii. Association by Contrast. It is a striking extension of the law of similarity that opposites tend to recall each other as well as those which resemble each other. A mouse may suggest an elephant; sorrow call up joy; a dwarf, a giant; vice, virtue, etc. When connected with contiguous association its operation is still more marked. The sight of a mountain in juxtaposition to a valley, the occurrence of an act of great generosity after one of striking meanness of nature, constitute associations of great force and tenacity. But it introduces us to no new principle. Contrast involves similarity. We contrast the extremes of something fundamentally like in nature. The dwarf and giant are connected by the common element of size; generosity and meanness by their relation to moral action. Black and white are but the extremes of the common quality, color. Such cases only emphasize the common feature at bottom by manifesting it in diverse forms.

iii. Assimilation. This is, in reality, a complex form of association, uniting the two principles of contiguity and similarity, and in its results like that of simultaneous association or fusion. In association by fusion some one element always stands out more prominently than others. It serves to represent the others, or acts as their bearer or carrier. They are more or less absorbed in it. In sound, for example, the partial tones are lost in the fundamental. They have a very important part in determining the character of the fused product, yet they have lost independent existence. So in flavors, the touch and odor sensations are lost in the taste. In all perceptions where visual sensations are involved the latter stand out most prominently. The result is that this more prominent element gains greatly in associative power, and, when occurring at any time, redintegrates all these elements formerly fused with it, which are immediately assimilated to it.

201893

Illustration

This may be illustrated by the visual perception of an orange. Here the only presented sensation is that of color. This color, however, by virtue of its predominance in all former perceptions, has just the same independent redintegrating power as the identical element in association by similarity, and proceeds to call up the elements of taste, size, weight, odor, etc., which had been formerly fused with it. These, however, do not get a separate existence as in the other forms of successive association which we have studied, but are assimilated to the color sensation, so that there results but one complex idea. All perceptions of things illustrate the same process. In result, therefore, it does not differ from simultaneous association. As a process, it approaches association by similarity.

III.   The Function of Association in Psychical Life

Having studied the nature and kinds of association, we turn to a consideration of the part which it plays in building up psychical life. What end does it serve; what are its effects and its purpose? In general the function of association in the psychical life is the formation of a mechanism. It serves to connect the various elements of our mental life together by such firm bands that they may be used as a foundation upon which to erect more complex mental structures. It takes isolated sensations and consolidates them. It takes chaotic material and it gives it definite form, consisting of a number of specialized modes of activity. The state of the mind without associations may be compared to a fluid; that on which the associative powers have been at work to this fluid crystallized, thus made into solid forms of positive shape and definite relation to each other.

Habit

More specifically, all that we call routine or habit, all that is mechanical in the life of the soul, is the result of associative activities. The way in which habits are formed will throw considerable light upon the matter. By habit, whether intellectual or volitional, we mean nothing else than such a connection of ideas or acts that, if one be presented, the rest of the series follow without the intervention of consciousness or the will. It is, in short, a form of successive association where one element redintegrates the next, and so on. It differs from ordinary association in the fact that in the latter the number of varying elements is large, and consequently the precise channel which the suggestion of ideas will follow cannot be told, while in habit the activity has been so repeatedly performed in one way that a definite groove of succession has been occasioned.

Illustration

The law of the formation of habit is that all successive associations constantly recurring in the same form tend to become simultaneous. It may be illustrated in the case of walking. This is a true habit, because given the initial act, all the other acts necessary to locomotion follow naturally, without the intervention of consciousness, and even while consciousness is occupied with something entirely different. The formation of the habit consisted, in the first place, in the formation of a series of successive associations. In this series the presence of any act was a sign to consciousness that the next act ought to be performed; each redintegrated the next. The child cannot walk at first, not for the reason that his muscles will not contract, but because no association has been formed such that any one contraction leads to the next of the series. This is only serial association however; not yet habit. This arises when the association has been so often performed that one act not only serves as a sign to consciousness that the next must be performed, but when the sign has become fused with the act signified. It is like the rapid rotation of a point of light. Each becomes fused with the next, and the successive series appears as a coexistent circle. So in the formation of the habit of walking, the various acts necessary for its performance no longer form separate successive members of a series, but the end of one is the beginning of another.

Habit as Automatic and Mechanical

The habitual act thus occurs automatically and mechanically. When we say that it occurs automatically, we mean that it takes place, as it were, of itself, spontaneously, without the intervention of will. By saying that it is mechanical we mean that there exists no consciousness of the process involved, nor of the relation of the means, the various muscular adjustments, to the end, locomotion. The various steps of the process follow each other as unconsciously as the motions of a loom in weaving. The tendency of habit is thus to the formation of a mechanism which the mind may employ and direct, but which, once started, goes of itself. This constitutes the special function of habit, or of association.

The Twofold End of Habit

Habit (1) thus forms a self-executing mechanism whereby the mind apprehends readily and expeditiously those elements in its cognitive life which are regularly recurring, and adjusts itself in its actions to the permanent demands of its surroundings; and thereby (2) enables conscious intelligence to devote itself to the apprehension of variable elements, and the will to apply itself to the mastery of novel and changing acts. The object of habit is thus, on the one hand, to create a mechanism which shall attend to the familiar and permanent elements of experience, and, on the other, to leave the conscious activity of mind free to control new and variable factors.

(1) There are certain elements in our surroundings and in our wants which are comparatively permanent. Both in relation to ordinary psychical life, and as the basis of higher activities, these constant factors are all-important. Such elements are to the child, his parents, his nurse, the room in which he lives, his playthings, etc. If there were no power of forming habits, if the sight of the child's food, of his nurse, etc., appealed to him in no different way the second and third time than the first; if associations did not cluster about his playthings with every time that they are employed; if the muscular adjustments which he makes in dressing himself did not grow fused into a series by repetition—it is evident that the child would remain ignorant in mind, empty of feeling, and helpless in action.

Extension of Range

As years advance the range of things and events with which the mind comes in contact increases, but there remains a certain set of objects which appeals to it, and constitutes its familiar and important environment, as others do not. About this permanent environment cluster the interests of the individual, and group the activities of psychical life. It is the centre of gravity of the spiritual world. It is constituted, on the one hand, by the simple facts of family, business, church, and social life; on the other, by the objects which present themselves most regularly, varying with the man of affairs, the artist, and the man of science. But, in all cases, it is of the highest importance that the individual's response to these permanent surroundings should not be dependent upon conscious reflection nor careful deliberation. It is necessary that his response should be automatic and mechanical, that it may be prompt, speedy, effectual, and invariable. The person must be instinctively linked to the world about him, both the social world and the physical world. The individual is thus constituted an organic, integral part of the world of nature and of society, and the latter becomes a whole, capable of combined deliberation and action, possessing one will and a common conscience.

(2) But the other side is no less important. If existence depends upon adjustment to permanent elements, growth depends no less upon right relation to changing factors. A life of complete routine, a condition of fossilized habit, though it be one in which every act corresponds quickly and accurately to some familiar feature of the environment, is not one that we desire. We want change, variety, growth. Only as we familiarize ourselves with things and acts once strange, only as we build upon the foundation of habits the superstructure of varying activities, is psychical life rich and manifold and progressive. The point which we are to notice here is, that this power of adaptation to new circumstance, the ability to grow, requires the conscious effort of intelligence and the active direction of will, and that this can be given only upon condition that the automatic mechanism of the soul attends to all other demands made. There would be no chance of learning a new fact or mastering a new action, were it not that the automatic action of habit takes care of all old and familiar experiences, and thus leaves conscious and purposive action free.

The Unconscious in Psychical Life

It has been noticed that the formation of habit, when once it has become automatic and mechanical, results in the relegation of ideas which once were conscious to the sphere of unconscious action. They become absorbed or lost. The extent to which this may go is disputed. None, however, deny that it may cover such actions as walking, talking, writing, playing a musical instrument, etc. Such acts are called secondarily automatic, because they imitate so closely automatic actions, like the beating of the heart, with which consciousness has no concern. It will be noticed that this

relegation to unconscious action means that the act is performed by the body, consciousness intervening only to start
the process, not to direct each of its stages.

Other Examples

Other examples of action becoming so habitual that it is
performed for the mind by the brain or body are probably
found in re-presentation. It is thought that every representation is accompanied by an action of those parts of
the brain which were originally active at the time of presentation, and that a sensation, similar to that produced by the
original excitation of the nerve organ, but weaker, results.
(See page 33.) This brain excitation may, however, in
certain cases, be so intense that it is as vivid as the original
external stimulus, and the individual will consequently con-
found the internally-excited image with some objective reality. This is the state known as hallucination.

Unconscious Cerebration

Others claim that the vicarious action of the nervous system
for the mind, due to activities so often repeated that they
have become psychically unconscious, extends to higher
processes, like thinking out complicated problems, laying
plans, producing artistic creations, etc. To these phenomena
they give the name of unconscious cerebrations. The extent
to which such facts actually exist is a matter of some question, but it can hardly be doubted that phenomena of this
kind occur which it would be impossible to account for
without the principle laid down, that all associations, often
repeated, tend to become simultaneous, and hence unconscious. It is no more impossible that such associations should
result in forming automatic connections of one part of the
brain with another, than that they should result in connections of one part of the muscular system with another, such
as we certainly find in acts like locomotion, the playing of a
musical instrument, etc.

4]   DISSOCIATION

Dissociation will be considered under the following heads: i. Relation to association; ii. Conditions; iii. Function in psychical life.

i.

The law of dissociation, stated in its most general form, is as follows: *In associating sensuous elements, the mind never gives all the elements equal value, but emphasizes some, and neglects others.* The statement of this law shows that dissociation always presupposes association, and is rather one aspect of it, hitherto overlooked, than something fundamentally different. We shall take up, accordingly, (1) the points of connection between association and dissociation; and, (2) the points of difference, the phase hitherto passed over.

1. CONNECTION OF LIKENESS

Regarding this, in a general way, not much need be said. Only those elements can be dissociated or disconnected which were originally associated or connected. Analysis presupposes synthesis (page 90). Only that can be disintegrated which was once a whole. We dissociate the idea of a man from that of a post-office only when they have been at some time combined. We separate the taste of an apple from that of its color, because once they were parts of the same fused product. Dissociation, in short, is not absolute separation, but, as defined, is giving some element *in an association* predominance over others. This prominence causes it to stand forth with relative independence, while the unemphasized elements fall into the background. The result is that they appear in consciousness as freed from their combination into one and the same whole.

Illustration in Special Forms of Association

Dissociation is, then, not a process which follows after association in time, but one which accompanies it. While asso-

ciation is at work in combining elements into a whole, dissociation is active in emphasizing some one of these combined
elements, and thus giving it a certain independence in consciousness of the other elements. In order to bring out this
factor, which was overlooked in the discussion of association, we shall hastily run over the two forms of simultaneous
and successive association.

1. SIMULTANEOUS ASSOCIATION. In fusion there is something more than a mere conglomeration or consolidation of
sensuous elements. In the integrated totality (page 86),
some one element stands out so as to serve as a bearer or
representative of the others. They are subordinated to it.
Generally it is the visual sensation which is most prominent,
while the muscular sensations are so much absorbed that we
rarely notice them unless they are the result of great fatigue.
Now this prominence of one element of the sensation over
another in fusion makes this prominent element stand forth
more distinctly in consciousness, while the others are thrust
into the background. It thus partially dissevers them from
each other and gives them relatively independent existences.
Just in the degree to which this process of relative stress and
neglect is carried, will the absolute fixity of association be
broken up, till finally some element may appear in consciousness alone.

2. SUCCESSIVE ASSOCIATION. Dissociation is involved here
to a greater extent than in simultaneous. In *contiguous* association, for example, not every element which was originally
contiguous to the one now presented is re-presented with
equal force and vividness, or even re-presented at all. There
is in every occurrence almost an infinity of detail, and it is
out of the question that it should be all redintegrated. Were
it, the result would be utter confusion of mind, for each of
these elements is, in turn, connected with an immense number of other elements, each of which would be redintegrated,
and so on indefinitely. The mind would be thus kept in what
has well been termed the tread-mill of concrete reminis-
cence. It would be in bondage to its past experiences; still
more it would be as much enslaved by one element of experi-

ence as by another. The minutest detail would exercise the same overmastering force as the most momentous factor, or, rather, there would be no distinction between minute and important. There would be no perspective, no background nor foreground, in psychical life. But, as matter of fact, not all elements do thus have equal value. In associating some are slurred and others accentuated. This is still more clearly seen in association by similarity, where the entire emphasis is thrown upon the emphasized identical element. In fact, association by similarity forms the natural transition to dissociation, for it requires the disconnection of the like element from the unlike.

2. THE POINTS OF OPPOSITION BETWEEN ASSOCIATION AND DISSOCIATION

These are ultimately reducible to two. (1) Dissociation requires a number of factors in the elements presented so dissimilar as to compete with each other, and requires, therefore, (2) a selecting activity of the mind which shall neglect some and emphasize others at their expense. Hence the process of dissociation is more complex and less passive than that of association. Instead of combining the elements presented at their face value, it weighs them with each other, and stamps one as worth more than another. It distinguishes, or makes a difference. Its energy is varied; it is directed in at least two directions. It looks beyond the immediate presence of the elements, and unconsciously tests them by some standard, the value which they have for mental life, and selects accordingly. In dissociation the mind, therefore, is actively related to the elements concerned. Instead of having the direction of its activities determined mechanically, it directs them according to its own ends and interests. This brings us to a study of

II. The Conditions of Dissociation

These, in a general way, we have just seen to be competing or incongruous elements in the presentations, together with selecting activity of the mind. We have now to discover what features render the presentations incongruous, and what it is that gives one such value that the mind selects it to the exclusion of others. We have to recognize that the meaning of psychical life is determined largely by the differences of *value* that its elements possess. This difference of value is not due to their existence as data, for as existences each is worth as much as every other; it is due to their relation to the mind, that is, to the *interest* which the self takes in them. The interests of the self are the factor which is influential in breaking up the hard rigidity of a psychical life governed wholly by the principle of association, and introducing flexibility and perspective into it. In studying the conditions of dissociation, we have to discover what features render one datum more *interesting* than another: the features which attract the mind. For convenience of classification these attractive features will be considered under two heads: (1) Natural value, or the attraction which the presentation has for the mind spontaneously, independent of its association with other members of consciousness; (2) Acquired value, or the attraction which it has by virtue of its connection with other factors of experience.

1. NATURAL VALUE

Those features of the presentation which interest the mind through their intrinsic characteristics are two in number, *quantity* and *tone*.

1. QUANTITY. Other things being equal, stimuli attract the mind in proportion to their quantity. If, for example, there are presented in succession or simultaneously, two sounds, one feeble, the other loud, or two colors, one obscure, the other bright, the mind, if not otherwise led by some acquired interest, will direct its activity to the stronger and neglect the weaker, thus partially at least dissociating them. Quantity includes intensity, duration, and multiplication of stimuli. A low noise, if constantly repeated, may possess more quantity and hence more attractive power than a loud noise coming at less frequent intervals. As motion multiplies greatly the intensity of a sensation, the well-known fact that moving objects attract the mind more than those at rest comes under this head.

2. TONE. Every sensation, by virtue of its quality, possesses an agreeable or disagreeable property, called tone, which serves to interest the mind naturally in it, either by way of attraction or repulsion. At first, the child's life is almost wholly one of organic sensations, hunger, thirst, satisfaction, fatigue. These have the largest natural emotional accompaniment. At first, they absorb about all psychical activity. Gradually taste with accompanying smell attracts consciousness to the sapid qualities of objects. Meantime there is going on a constant overflow of muscular activity in various directions, and the pleasure taken in this free, unrestrained movement results in calling the mind to those features of objects which are connected with grasping and touching. Then the peculiar charm of sweet sounds and beautiful colors will make itself felt, and the audible and visible properties of bodies begin to stand forth; when this point is reached quality exercises more attractive force than mere quantity.

Transition to Acquired Interest

Advance in psychical life depends largely upon the power of advancing from natural values to acquired. The tendency of those elements which spontaneously attract the mind is to keep it absorbed in them, and hence prevent it going out beyond them to connect them with others and render them significant. Acquired interest, on the other hand, necessarily leads the mind beyond what is actually present to other elements in our experience which give what is present its attractive power. The mental life of an animal always remains upon a low plane, because it is taken up with the interesting features of the *sensations* as such, and, therefore, is never led beyond them to relate them to each other in a meaning way.

Criterion of Sensations

The criterion of the intellectual value of any sensation is the readiness with which it lends itself to the acquirement of interest. Those which prominently assert their own value as mere sensations can never have any great worth for knowledge. It is the superior capacity of the visual and auditory sensations in clustering interests about themselves through associations with the rest of our experience that gives them their supreme importance in the cognitive life, as it is the inability of thirst and hunger sensations to do aught but thrust their own sensational quality into consciousness, which debars them from any high place. Whatever tends to absorb the mind with *purely sensuous* interest detracts just so much from the possibility of intelligent interest. Refusal to let appetites and passions run riot is as much the requirement of a sound intellect as of a right conscience.

2. ACQUIRED VALUE

The interest which any presentation has, not merely on account of the fact that it is a sensation, but in virtue of what it brings with it from out past experience, is *acquired value*. But since it is *order* which connects our past and our present experience, acquired value is evidently dependent upon certain relations of order existing between ideas. To say that a present experience is connected with a past, is to say that it is related to the *self* in a definite way, and this relation to self is what we mean by interest, and since the form it takes depends upon the experience of the self, it is acquired interest. The connection of order among our ideas thus necessarily insures acquired interest to every idea as it arises. The new experience will harmonize with some past experiences, and be incongruous with others. There will be on one hand a feeling of fitness, of satisfaction, which will lead the mind to be content with the connection, and on the other hand a feeling of unrest which will lead the mind to investigate the relations of the two. In either case, this feeling will serve to emphasize those elements which are especially like, and especially unlike, previous experiences, and thus dissociate them. The two sources of acquired interest in inducing the activity of dissociation are, consequently, familiarity or likeness of connection, and novelty, or unlikeness of connection.

1. INTEREST OF FAMILIARITY.   These may be analyzed into two factors: (*i.*) Repetition, or frequency; (*ii.*) Recentness.

i. Repetition. Our interest clusters about those elements in our experience which are constantly repeated. The multiplication of any occurrence marks it off from those occurring rarely, and invests it with attractive force. This principle is of especial importance in the early life of children. Originally all experiences, aside from the emphasis of quantity and quality already mentioned, are on the same level. The child's experience has no perspective, no recognition of varying importance. The equal value of all is the same as lack of value in each. But finally, from the mere force of repetition, this background and foreground of psychical life is created. Some objects—the sight of the cradle, of the nurse, of utensils of food preparation, etc.—are constantly recurring. This breaks up the monotony of intellectual life. Distinctions arise; these familiar objects are dissociated from their surroundings, and stand forth prominently. Distinctness of impression is thus seen to be due to the relative accentuating by the mind, from its own interest, of some elements above others.

Further Importance of Repetition

The action of the principle of frequency is not confined to childhood. In *learning* anything we voluntarily set ourselves to repeating an act so many times that this act gradually separates itself from the background of ever-varying acts, and thus obtains a superior hold upon consciousness. The familiar in all cases arouses the mind and absorbs consciousness. Every man has established, through his experience, certain lines or grooves in which consciousness tends to run whenever stimuli demanding immediate action or thought are not present. This plexus of consciousness determines largely one's intellectual character. In a certain way each of us has the whole universe open to himself for investigation, yet few of us ever get beyond a certain limited range of interests, because the constant repetition of certain elements has given these great prominence. Yet it must not be forgotten that a certain amount of such limitation to definite lines is necessary to the creation of any perspective in mental life.

Apperceptive Organs

Familiarity not only determines what the dominant conceptions of mental life are, but it also determines what the attitude of the apperceiving activity will be towards new conceptions. This is illustrated by the fact that a man in a foreign country may pay no attention to the words that he hears as long as they are uttered in a strange language, but if he hears a few words of his own language he is immediately all interest. Our past experiences decide along what lines the present activities of intelligence shall be directed. Occupations and special pursuits establish *apperceptive organs* or ways in which we tend to interpret presentations. We see with what we have seen. The artist interprets his new experiences in harmony with his æsthetic tastes; in the same object, the scientific man finds illustration of some law; while the moralist finds that with which to teach a lesson. General education consists in so familiarizing ourselves through repetition with certain objects, events, and processes that we form apperceptive organs, for the ready and quick apprehension of whatever presents points of connection with these, while technical education forms more particular organs of apperception.

ii. Recentness. Any element which has been *recently* in consciousness possesses an emphasis which dissociates it from more remote experiences, by virtue of its superior vividness and distinctness. Remoteness dulls the intensity of an impression, and causes it to sink back into a dull and unbroken level, from which recentness of occurrence lifts it. Recent impressions are thus more likely to be recalled than others; are more dwelt upon, and serve to force the mind from the bondage of too frequent repetition. The principle of recentness, while acting in the same way with that of familiarity in laying special stress on certain elements, yet partially counteracts it, by freeing the mind from the tendency to dwell in certain oft-repeated realms of experience.

2. NOVELTY. The principle of *novelty*, however, is that which especially counteracts this tendency. Familiarity may be carried to a point where the familiar element no longer

attracts the mind. It is matter of common observation that the continued ticking of a clock ceases to come in consciousness, while change, such as its stopping, is immediately noticed. Those who live near the roar of a cataract, or in a mill amid the clash of machinery, have similar experiences. In such cases it is the new, the unfamiliar, that attracts notice, and that is especially emphasized in consciousness. The presence of a few foreign words in our own language will arrest the mind almost as soon as the occurrence of known words in a strange tongue. A shock of surprise is one of the most effectual methods of arousing attention. The unexpected in the midst of routine is the accentuated. The very contrast between the two rivets attention, and more effectually dissociates each from the other. Thus variety and mobility of psychical life are secured.

Mutual Relations of the Two Principles

The way in which the two principles of familiarity and novelty limit each other must be noticed. Strictly speaking, they are two phases of the same activity. Neither the absolutely customary, nor the entirely novel, attracts the mind; it is the old amid the new, the novel in the wonted that appeal. Only to the extent in which the old and permanent element is found in the new and varying can the mind deal with the latter. Points of identity between the present experience and the past are necessary for any comprehension of the former. On the other hand, without the new element there would be no change, no expansion, no growth. The novel is the source of development. Without the interest of novelty there would be complete stagnation, as without the element of familiarity there would be complete meaninglessness. The psychical life of an infant begins when his tendency to go from one stimulus to another is checked by action of the interest of familiarity emphasizing some one at the expense of others; but it is developed only when the interest of novelty leads the child to consider some old and familiar fact in a new light, and thus expand it.

Relations of Identity and Difference

The interest of familiarity is thus what leads us to *identify* the present experience with some past one; while that of novelty leads us to *differentiate* the past, by introducing something new into it. And these relations of identity and difference always go together. We should never think of hunting after likeness between two peas or two cents. It is the likeness of the pea-blossom to the bean-blossom, *despite* their differences, which is the interesting fact. So, too, we do not search for differences between an elephant and the conception of righteousness. It is the difference between a whale and a porpoise, in spite of their apparent likeness, that attracts the mind. In short, the activity of intelligence consists in identifying the apparently unlike, and in discriminating the apparently like; and it is through the relation of identity that the present experience is comprehended, and through the element of difference that past experience grows into richer forms. Each relation is, therefore, indispensable to intelligence.

Illustration

Both relations are involved in any act of knowledge, but we may illustrate by the apperception of an unknown species of plant by a botanist. The botanist will apprehend it only so far as he is attracted to it by certain familiar elements in it, which stand out above others; and through the relations of identity involved in this familiarity he will recognize it, and refer it to its proper sub-kingdom, class, order, etc. On the other hand, the presence of novel features in this plant will necessitate a certain revision of old knowledge. He may be compelled to acknowledge a new genus of plants in his classification, or he may be obliged to make over his old classification, so that some order may include the properties of the new member. In either case the relation of difference serves to develop the old knowledge.

III. Function of Dissociation in Psychical Life

We have already anticipated this in what has just been said. But, looked at from a somewhat different standpoint, it may be said that the emphasizing of some elements and their consequent prominence over others serves two purposes, one negative, the other positive. The negative function consists in breaking up the mechanism which the activity of association, if left to itself, would result in, and the disintegration of those bonds which would tie the mind down to objective data, without allowing it free play according to its own interests. The perfection of the principle of association would be reached when the mind was governed by purely mechanical principles, and its activity controlled by external considerations. The negative function of dissociation is to break up this control.

Positive Function

This consists, accordingly, in setting the mind or self free from its subjection to purely objective influences, and causing it to act for *ends of its own*, that is, for *ideal or internal ends*. In short, dissociation paves the way for *attention*, which is simply this mental activity for self-regulated ends. The essential influence in freeing the mind is the fact of interest. The existence of interest as a factor in psychical life means that not all data are on the same level to the mind, but that they have more or less intimate connection with the self, expressed by some pleasurable or disagreeable quality in them. It is this emotional, subjective motive to which the existence of perspective or difference in value in psychical life is due. Its result is to bring into consciousness the *ends* towards which attention, as the internally initiated activity of mind, may direct itself. These ends are of two kinds, general and special.

1. GENERAL

This consists in the fact that *self*, as a whole, is set free to act for its own ends. In association the activities of the self are governed by external considerations; in attention, they are directed towards the ends of the self; dissociation is the intermediate process which renders the self independent of the external influences, so that it may act for its own ends. The infant, for example, is originally at the mercy of the external world in his cognitive life. One fact is of as much value for it as another. Quantity and quality of sensations are the first differentiating factors. But soon the child learns that not the loudest sound is of most importance for it. The voice of the mother or nurse is the most *interesting* to it, for this has the most connection with its pleasures and pains, with the satisfaction of hunger, and the rest after fatigue, etc. Here the child begins to discriminate with reference to *self*; reference to *self* becomes the motive of discriminating activity. From this time on, action for *self* is the essential feature even of its intellectual life.

2. SPECIAL

But dissociation does more than free the self so that it may act with reference to itself. It also sets free or analyzes out the various *special ends* which are included in the general welfare of the self. The emphasis which the fact of interest puts upon certain elements in cognition makes them ends for knowing, as other elements are not. These ends will be almost infinite in number, varying with the stage of development of the person, with his prevailing pursuits and occupations, etc.; but, as to their form, they may be reduced to two—the relations of difference and of identity; and so it may be said that the special ends of the mind in knowing are to discover these relations or to identify and to discriminate. This activity, to which we are now introduced, and which unites and separates with conscious reference to the value which such uniting and separating have for knowledge, is *attention*. In association the sequence of our ideas is unconsciously governed by these relations; in dissociation these relations are set free from all their accompanying contingent associations; in attention the train of ideas is directed with conscious reference to them.

5]   ATTENTION

Consciousness and Attention

In a broad sense every act of knowledge may be regarded as due to attention, for every consciousness involves the activity of the mind. Nothing can be in consciousness which consciousness does not put there. Consciousness is an active process. The mind, as originally defined (page 23), presupposes some relation between the universal content and the individual. Attention, in a general sense, is precisely this connection which exists in every act of knowledge, between that which knows and that which is known. It is the active connection of the individual and the universal. As there is no consciousness without this relation, consciousness and attention, as so defined, are identical. But this active connection may be called forth either from without or from within, and it is found better to limit the term attention so that it shall not apply to every activity of the mind, but only to that which starts from within.

Attention and Association

Attention might, accordingly, be defined as active association, while association could be regarded as passive attention. In the latter the motives to activity are external, due to the sensations, or the way in which they present themselves; in the former the motives are internal, due to some interest which the mind takes in reaching an end of its own. In dissociation, also, the activity is still in some sense mechanical, for the mind does not consciously recognize that itself and its interests are the basis of the process. Dissociation results, however, in making the self stand clearly forth separated from the multiplicity of its associations, and holds before it the distinct ends in which it is interested; and attention begins just here, where dissociation leaves off. Hence association, dissociation, and attention are only stages in the same active process.

Definition of Attention

Attention may be defined as follows: *Attention is that activity of the self which connects all elements presented to it into one whole, with reference to their ideal significance; that is, with reference to the relation which they bear to some intellectual end.* The essential characteristic of attention is, therefore, activity directed towards some end. Ultimately this end is the self. The various activities of attention are based in the interests of the self, and directed towards ends which will satisfy the self, by fulfilling these interests. Its process is such a direction of its own contents that these ends will be reached. Starting-point, goal, and way are all found in the self, therefore. Attention is thus a process of self-development. In studying attention we are studying the activities by which the mind develops or realizes itself. Various aspects in this process may be noted, and hence we may distinguish attention as an activity—i. Selecting; ii. Adjusting; iii. Relating.

i.   Attention as a Selecting Activity

The mind actively attends to and thus directs the sequence of ideas, instead of surrendering itself passively to them. It manipulates its presentations; some it selects, while it neglects others. Thus considered, it is merely a higher form of dissociation, with its relative emphasis and slurring of elements. The difference is that in dissociation the stress is laid because of the immediate interest which the element possesses, while in attention it is due to the active interest which the mind takes. One is interest of the presentation for the mind; the other is interest of the mind in the presentation.

Distinction from Dissociation

In dissociation the selection takes place with reference to *past* experiences. Novelty and familiarity determine the accent. In attention the selection occurs with reference to the *future*. The interests previously studied would allow the mind to see things only in the light of the past; the interests which determine the direction of attention have reference to coming experiences, which the mind is endeavoring to gain. Attention has always an end in view, with express consideration of which it selects. The mind at-tends; it is stretched out towards something. Attention has been called "asking questions of the future," and it selects only such material as seems fitted to furnish the answer.

Nature of Attention

The activity of attention has been compared to that of the eye. When we wish to see anything distinctly we turn the eyes upon it, so as to bring its image directly upon the yellow spot, the point of most acute vision, while all peripheral images become blurred. So in attending, we fixate the mental content in the centre of the mind's activity, and allow all else to become dim and indistinct. In attention we focus the mind, as the lens takes all the light coming to it, and instead of allowing it to distribute itself evenly concentrates it in a point of great light and heat. So the mind, instead of diffusing consciousness over all the elements presented to it, brings it all to bear upon some one selected point, which stands out with unusual brilliancy and distinctness.

Kinds of Selection

The point to be borne in mind is that attention always selects with reference to some end which the mind has in view, some difficulty to be cleared up, some problem to be solved, some idea to be gained, or plan to be formed. There will be as many kinds of selection, therefore, as there are ends before the mind. The sensuous elements presented to a farmer, a botanist, and an artist, in a flower, are the same, but the first will direct his mind only to those elements which are serviceable to him, which will enable him to decide whether the plant is a weed or an article of food. The botanist will select whatever enables him properly to classify the plant, while both useful and scientific considerations will be neglected by the artist, who will select æsthetic factors. In a certain sense no two of the three apperceive the same flower. One sees, that is selects, one thing, while this is invisible to another; that is, is neglected by him.

Permanent Ends of Selection

Besides these variable interests, which lead to differing kinds of selection, there are, however, certain permanent ends, which are the same to all minds. Such a permanent and universal element is the self. If there is anything necessarily involved in every activity of self this will be an end to all individuals, and to the same individual at all times. Now, one factor which is necessary to the very being of the mind is knowledge. The mind *is* not, except as it knows. Interest in *knowledge* must, therefore, be universal in all minds, and must, in some way, control every action of the same mind; that is, be a permanent end. A brief study of this universal interest in knowledge will serve to show both the importance of the selecting activity of intelligence and the way in which it works.

Law of Selection

The mind neglects the sensuous presentation of everything which cannot be regarded as a sign of something, and selects only those elements which can be interpreted as pointing to something beyond themselves. Otherwise stated, sensations, *as such*, never enter into our knowledge. Knowledge always consists of *interpreted* sensations: elements which have gained meaning by their connections with other elements, of which they serve as signs. Experience, accordingly, or the world of known objects, is not a colorless copy of what actually exists, stereotyped or impressed upon us, but is an experience produced by the mind acting according to the interests of self in interpreting sensuous data.

Illustration by Muscular Sensations

These, as already seen, are of the greatest importance in our psychical life, yet ordinarily we are not conscious of their existence. We neglect them because of their place in the intellectual life. They are signs to us of various qualities in objects, and when they are thus objectively interpreted they entirely lose their sensuous existence. They are symbols of objective things and properties; they are no longer subjective states. We are not conscious, for example, of the muscular sensations involved in the sweep of the arm through the air, because they are immediately interpreted as so much space passed through. We neglect their sensuous existence, and select their ideal significance. *Meaning* always takes us beyond the bare presentation, to its connections and relations to the rest of experience. We select not what a thing *is*, but what it points to.

Illustration by "Subjective Sensations"

We have already seen that sensations may arise when there is no extra-organic stimulus present, by affection of the nerve organ, or nerve centre itself. Sensations thus produced are termed "subjective," although, strictly speaking, all sensations are subjective. Ordinarily such sensations are not observed, because they are not regarded as signs of objects. Such are the so-called entoptic phenomena, the constant play of internally-initiated colors, the existence of after-images, such as continue after looking at a bright object and withdrawing the head, etc. Just as soon, however, as these sensations are attended to they are objectified and projected into space. Our interest in significance is so great that we perforce regard sensations as signs of objects, whether the objects be actually present or not. This constitutes the psychological basis of hallucinations, dreams, etc.

Further Illustrations

We do not ordinarily perceive over-tones. We interpret them as signs of the musical instrument—piano, violin, human voice, etc.—whence they proceed, and thus entirely neglect their sensuous existence. When we do pay attention to them it is because of their *intellectual* value; it is because they will add to our knowledge of the theory of tones. In vision, also, we habitually neglect the fact of double vision. We have two visual sensations of all objects, owing to the doubleness of the organ, yet we perceive but one object. This is because the existence of the sensations, whether one, two, or fifty, is of no benefit to us, except as signs of objects. We neglect the sensation, therefore, for what it points to—the single object. Such illustrations might be increased, but enough have been given to exemplify the principle.

Knowledge as Idealization

This study of the necessity of the selecting activity of intelligence for knowledge leads us to recognize that all knowledge is a process of idealization. Sensations, *per se*, never enter into knowledge. Knowledge is constituted by interpretation of sensations, that is, by their idealization. The sensations furnish the data, but these data must be neglected, selected, and manipulated by the self before they become knowledge. The process is properly called one of *idealization* because it goes beyond the sensuous *existence*, which is actually *present*, and gives this present datum meaning by connecting it with the self, and thus putting into it significance, which as bare existence it does not have. Meaning, in short, is connection, is relation, is going beyond the mere presentation to something beyond. This element must be supplied by the self or mind, and hence is *ideal*. Just the process by which this ideal element is supplied we have yet to study.

II.　Attention as Adjusting Activity

It has already been pointed out that attention is always directed towards the future, since it is concerned with reaching some end, or realizing some interest of the self. We have just studied the selection of the proper material for attaining the end; we have now to study the way in which this selected material is utilized, or brought to bear so as to reach the desired end. In short, we have seen that material is always selected with reference to its ideal or intellectual significance. We have now to see how it gets this ideal meaning. It is by the process of *adjustment*, or *that activity of intelligence whereby the whole organized self is brought to bear upon the presented and selected elements, so as to read itself into them and give them meaning.*

Adjustment Requires Ability to Anticipate

Adjustment is, accordingly, the active application of the mind with all its contents upon presentations, so as to shape these presentations towards the intellectual end sought. Now this process of adjustment will be able to occur only in the degree in which the mind is conscious of the end, and of the steps necessary to reach it. If the idea of the end is definite the self will know just how to bring itself to bear; how to direct itself. If it is vague the process must largely be a tentative one, the mind feeling around, as it were, adopting now this expedient and now that. The process of adjustment, in short, will be performed imperfectly and with difficulty. If, however, there is a clear anticipation of the end, that is, of the approaching psychical experience, the mind will not only be ready for it, in a general way, but will be able to employ just those activities and apperceptive organs which are most fitted to render the act of apprehension speedy and complete. The perfection of an intellectual act depends, therefore, upon the definiteness and completeness with which an act of adjustment can be performed, and this depends upon the extent that the mind can anticipate what is coming.

Illustration

The nature of the mental life may be illustrated as follows: Suppose an individual in a dark room, with which he is wholly unacquainted, and which is lighted up at brief intervals by an electric spark; at the first spark the individual will perceive next to nothing, and that little indistinctly. At the next spark he has, however, this vague basis of expectation upon which to work, and the result is that he apperceives somewhat more. This apperception now enables him to form a more perfect anticipation of what is coming, and thus enables him to adjust his mind more perfectly. This process of apperception through anticipation, and reaction of the apperceived content upon the completeness of the anticipation, continues, until, during some flash, he has a pretty definite and perfect idea of the scene before him, although the spark lasts no longer than the first, and there is no more material sensuously present. The sole difference is in the adjusting power of the mind, due to its ability to anticipate.

Necessity of Past Experience

This illustration brings out the additional point that ability
to perform adjustment depends upon past experiences. Our
capacity of anticipation will be decided by what we have got
out of previous experiences. These, the sparks of light of the
illustration, have formed some idea of the world, the dark
room in which the mind is placed, and through these the
new experiences are apprehended. In all knowing we are
thus forming organs for future knowing; we are deciding
our future adjustments. In the presence of the world to be
known, the man differs from the child; not only in sensations, but in the fact that the latter has not had enough
experience in the past to bring to bear upon the interpretation of these presented sensations, while the man comes to
them with definite organs of adjustment due to his past life.

Experimental Evidence

The truth that ready and distinct apperception depends
upon the degree to which the mind can prepare itself for the
coming experience, and adjust itself to it, is shown by certain experiments. By methods not necessary to detail here it
has been found that the average time for the apperception of
a simple sense stimulus is from $\frac{1}{8}$ to $\frac{1}{5}$ of a second. That is
to say, it takes that length of time for an individual to
apprehend a flash of light, for example; to interpret the
stimulus, discriminate it from others, and recognize it as
light. But if a signal is given beforehand, so that the mind
can prepare itself, the time is reduced as low as $\frac{1}{13}$ of a
second. If the stimuli follow each other at perfectly regular
intervals, so that the mind can perform a constant series of
similar adjustments, the time may be reduced to nothing.
The mind, because of its ability to accurately anticipate
what is coming, is perfectly adjusted, and requires no time.

Evidence Continued

On the other hand, it is found that everything that tends to
make the process of adjustment less easy or complete retards
apperception. If the mind is unaware of the time or of the
intensity of the awaited stimulus the time is greatly length-

ened. If the mind is expecting a loud sound, and a soft one occurs, the time is almost doubled. If in a series, which have been occurring at regular intervals, one is put in at a shorter interval, or the time is delayed, either the time is greatly increased or the apperception does not occur at all. If the mind cannot anticipate the quality of the stimulus, that is, tell whether it is to be light or sound, the time is also lengthened. If various stimuli occur together the time of the apperception of any one is retarded, because the mind has to choose to which it shall adjust itself. Hence we can lay down the rule that just in the degree in which the mind has a definite idea of the end towards which attention is directed, and is thereby enabled to adjust itself to this end, is apperception speedy, distinct, and complete.

The Process of Idealization

We saw under the head of "selection" that idealization of sensations is necessary for knowledge. We now see how this idealization comes about. We apperceive the sensation, or interpret it, by adjusting the mind to it; and this adjustment is bringing past experiences to bear upon the present. We know with what we have known. In adjustment the mind reads out of itself and into the sensation ideal elements which transform the sensation and make it a part of knowledge. Former acquirements serve as the means of giving significance to the new. The same object may awaken only a look of stolid surprise in the savage, or the comprehension of a new law of the action of bodies. The hog reads into the apple simply that it is good to eat; Sir Isaac Newton that it exemplifies the law of all falling bodies. Each puts self into the same sensation, and the result is a world-wide difference. All knowledge consists in thus putting self into presented data of sensation.

Meaning is Reference to Self

The sensation gets significance, accordingly, just in the degree in which the mind puts itself into it. As it puts itself into the sensation it makes it a *sign* of its past experiences. Adjustment is the process by which the self so connects itself with the presented datum that this becomes a sign, or

symbolic—points to something beyond its own new existence, and hence has meaning. The fact known is not a bare
fact, that is, an existence implying no constructive activity of
intelligence, but is idealized fact, existence upon which the
constructive intelligence has been at work. That which is
not thus idealized by the mind has no existence for intelligence. All knowledge is thus, in a certain sense, self-
knowledge. Knowing is not the process by which ready-
made objects impress themselves upon the mind, but is the
process by which self renders sensations significant by reading itself into them.

III.   Attention as Relating Activity

We have seen that in order to reach the end which the
mind in attention always has before it, it is necessary to
neglect much of the sensuous data and select certain portions of it with reference to this end; and, also, that this
selected material gets significance by the adjusting activity
of intelligence, which brings past experiences to bear upon
it. Just what this adjusting consists in, or how past experiences are brought to bear upon the interpretation of present
data, we have not studied. This occurs through the process
of *relating*. This may be termed the act of *comparison*.

Two Kinds of Relations

The relations which connect mental contents are those of
identity and of difference. Comparison is an act of mind
which considers various cognitions in their relations to each
other, so as to discover in what points they are alike, and
hence may be unified, and in what they are unlike, and
hence must be distinguished. The function of attention as a
relating activity is therefore to introduce unity and distinctness into psychical life. In attention, mental contents are
held before the mind simultaneously, and yet are held apart,
so that they do not fuse. In association, if two elements are
presented simultaneously, they are fused; or if elements are
not fused, they can come before the mind only successively.
But attention can hold contents together and apart at the
same time. It necessarily unifies and discriminates in one

and the same act. There are not two acts, therefore, but two phases of the same act of attention; and as such they must be studied.

1. IDENTITY, OR UNIFICATION

The unity which is the result of attention must be distinguished from the unity which is the result of fusion. In the latter the various associated elements lose their distinct existence, and are absorbed in the result. The unifying activity of attention is always accompanied by the discriminating, and hence this actual fusion does not occur. The unity is an ideal one; that is, it is of a *relation* which connects them, not of an actual thing. It is identity of *meaning*, not of *existence*. Thus when the botanist compares a rose with an apple-blossom, and unifies the two perceptions in a common class, he does not cease to have two things before him. The unification is an intellectual one, consisting in the recognition of an ideal element of meaning in both. They both signify or point to the same *law* or relation. The process of unifying always consists in the discovery of an identity of meaning in objects apparently unlike.

Importance in Knowledge

Without this discovery of identity of meaning between presentations, which, as existences, are separate from each other, there could be no knowledge. Knowledge always consists in going out beyond the present sensation, and connecting it with others by finding that both *mean* the same; that is, that both point to the same psychical experience. Without this ideal identification of one sensation with another, knowledge would be impossible, and psychical life would consist of a series of transitory and shifting sensations, no one of which would be recognized nor referred to an object. Growth in knowledge consists in discovering more and more fundamental unities, and thus in reducing to ideal unity facts, events, and relations before separate. Knowledge can reach its goal only in a perfectly harmonious system of all truths. Its aim is everywhere to see every fact as dependent upon every other fact, or all as members of one organic unity.

Growth of Attention

It is the constant tendency towards unification of ideas which allows the mind to take in larger and larger wholes in the same act, and thus economize mental power. The unifying of attention is simply the unity of end or likeness of meaning found amid various facts, and it requires no more energy of mind to grasp a thousand facts in their *unity* than it does ten. Some have announced as a principle of attention, *Pluribus intentus, minor est ad singula sensus*; holding that the wider the grasp of attention, the less perfect will it be in its details. But this overlooks the fact that the movement of attention is always towards the discovery of identity, and the grasping of all objects possessing this identity of significance in one act of thought. The effect of attention is necessarily as much to render it possible for the mind to apprehend more and more at the same time, as it is to make details more definite and precise.

2. DIFFERENCE OR DISCRIMINATION

But identification is only one side of the process of comparison. We never compare things exactly alike; we compare only where there is some element of difference. The apperception of distinction must go hand in hand with that of unity. We can discover identity of meaning amid diversity of fact only as we can exclude all that is unlike. Mental contents are held apart when they are related to each other; they are not indistinguishably fused into one. This is because of the relations of difference. Without this differentiating act of attention mental life would be a chaos. There would be no meaning in it, because there would be no distinction of one object or event from another. We are able to refer one object to another, to connect one element of experience with another, because we can distinguish them from each other.

Distinction and Consciousness

What we do not distinguish or differentiate has no existence in consciousness. It remains absorbed in some other element, or is neglected. The act of bringing anything into consciousness consists in separating it out from other elements through this distinguishing activity of attention. The soldier excited in battle does not know of his wound. The orator afflicted with a disease ordinarily most painful, is unconscious of suffering during the delivery of his speech. The same fact is illustrated without leaving the most usual consciousness. There are constantly flowing in upon us stimuli from all our organs—ear, eye, and skin especially—yet we are ordinarily conscious of but few of these. The pressure of clothing, of our position, of most objects about us, sounds in which we are not interested—these do not come into consciousness at all, for they are not discriminated, and thus lifted into relief. On the other hand, paying constant attention to any element of experience gives that element great distinctness. This is illustrated in persons of special attainments, as well as in all monomaniacs, hypochondriacs, etc.

Distinctness and Intensity

The distinctness of mental content must be separated from its intensity. Intensity is the amount of consciousness which it occupies, or the *force* with which it thrusts itself into consciousness. Distinctness is always relative, and implies the points of difference which separate two compared contents from each other, or one part of a content from another. The perception of the sun is exceedingly intense, but very indistinct. So the flavor of a fruit may be exceedingly strong, but if it has never been experienced before it will not be distinct, for its relations to other flavors will not be recognized. Distinctness, in short, always implies the distinguishing activity of intelligence. When I say that my memory of a certain event is indistinct, what I mean is not necessarily that my image of it is very dim, but that I cannot discriminate it clearly from other events occurring at about the same time, or from similar events occurring at different times. It is not differenced, and thus made definite. Definition is always the recognition of this relation of difference.

The Nature of Attention

We saw that a sensuous presentation gets meaning by its connection with past experiences given by the mind reading itself into the sensation. We now see that this connection is twofold. The process of adjustment consists in bringing the past experiences to bear upon the present so as to unify it with those ideal elements which resemble it, and separate it from those which are unlike. These two processes necessarily accompany each other, so that, while the goal of knowledge is complete unity, or a perfectly harmonious relation of all facts and events to each other, this unity shall be one which shall contain the greatest possible amount of specification, or distinction within itself. A relation necessarily unifies and separates at the same time. *It unifies because it enables us to see the facts related in a common light, as possessed of a common significance; it separates because the two facts are not fused into one existence, but are rendered more definite than they were before by the possession of a distinct property.* The final fact which we learn about attention, therefore, is that it is a relating activity, and that, since there is no knowledge without relation, there is none without attention. Attention cannot cease until all relations have been perfectly developed; that is, until all objects, events, and minor relations stand out clearly defined in a final unity, and are recognized as members of one whole—the self. The self constitutes the ultimate unity of all. We end, therefore, as we began, with the statement that attention is a self-developing activity.

6]   RETENTION

Retention is thoroughly bound up with the apperceptive activities, and, as the latter have been treated at length, may be passed over with briefer notice. As apperception is the reaction of the self with the character given it by past experiences upon sensory presentations, so retention is the reaction of the content thus apperceived upon the self. Apperception gives character to the material apprehended. Retention gives character to the self. The apperceived content is not mechanically held in the mind, but reacts upon it so as to alter its nature. It becomes organically one with self. We shall consider retention under three heads: I. Implied in apperception; II. Apperception as involved in it; III. The function of retention.

I. The Implication of Retention in Apperception

No apperception, whether of association, dissociation, or attention, occurs except upon the basis of past experiences. The mind is an activity which connects every fact, event, and relation with others. None remains isolated. The significance or meaning which is supplied by the apperceptive activity is this connection between various factors of experience, so that one becomes symbolic of another, or both point to the same idea. Such a connection evidently presupposes that past experiences still have an ideal existence; they are not utterly lost, but still exist preserved in some way in the self. Were they not thus retained, all relation between parts of experience would be impossible, and apperception would not exist; i.e., nothing would have meaning for us. This has been presupposed in all our previous exposition, which renders needless present dwelling upon it. Idealization we found to be the process by which the self, *acting upon the basis of its past experiences*, interprets sensations.

II. Apperception as Necessary to Retention

The mind becomes organized, gets definite character, only through its apperceptive activities. Without organized mind there is, indeed, no apperception; but without apperception, no organization. The mind can retain or preserve as an organic part of itself only what it has experienced. Without these experiences it would remain a mere capacity. The infant comes into the world with no *definite* tendencies and abilities except some inherited ones, which are instinctive. These he uses to gain experiences with, but these experiences once got, immediately react upon the mind and develop it. They organize it in some particular direction. The mind of the child which has apperceived his nurse is not the same that it was before; he has formed an organ in his mind for the performing of like apperceptions in the future.

Illustration in Association and Attention

That retention requires apperception may be seen from both association and attention. We found that the result of association was the formation of a psychical mechanism, the existence of certain habits, or automatic ways of acting and apperceiving. This mechanism is evidently what we mean by the organization of self; it is what the self has *retained* from its experiences and made organic members of self. In attention, as soon as the mind is brought to bear upon the sensation so as to read itself into it and give it meaning, the apperceived content becomes a condition which determines how the mind shall act in the future. Every element thus apprehended and absorbed into the mind gets an ideal existence, and becomes the means by which future idealizations, that is, acts of attention, are executed. Attention forms *apperceptive organs*, in short.

III. Nature of Retention

The student must avoid regarding retention as a mechanical process. Retention does not mean that the mind retains as so many particular existences in itself all past experiences, as grains of wheat, for example, are held in a basket. Our past experiences have no more *actual* existence. They are gone with the time in which they occurred. They have, however, *ideal* existence, existence as wrought into the character of the self, and as fixing its definite nature, and this is what we mean by retention. The mind is not a storehouse, nor does it have compartments furnished with past experiences. It is not a chest, in the drawers and pigeon-holes of which the factors of its life are packed away, classified and labelled.

Metaphors from Organic Processes

The only illustrations of its nature can be drawn from vital phenomena. It corresponds to the reception, digestion, and elaboration of food by the living organism. As the tree is not merely passively affected by the elements of its environment—the substances of the earth, the surrounding moisture and gases—as it does not receive and keep them unaltered in itself, but reacts upon them and works them over into its living tissue—its wood, leaves, etc.—and thus grows, so the mind deals with its experiences. And as the substances thus organized into the living structure of the tree then act in the reception and elaboration of new material, thus insuring constant growth, so the factors taken into the mind consti- tute the ways by which the mind grows in apperceiving power. But even this analogy is defective as concerns the higher activities of the mind. To make it complete we should have to suppose that the tree knew what it was thus assimi- lating, and *why* it did so, and that it selected and manipu- lated its nutriment with special reference to its own develop- ment along certain lines. The mind in retention not only forms its own structure, but is conscious of, and can direct, the processes by which it does so.

Organization

The metaphor explains why the term organization has been so often employed. Retention organizes the mind in certain directions; that is, it gives it organs for certain kinds of activity. If we suppose that the mind at first is merely indefinite capacities, every experience realizes these capaci- ties in some direction and makes them definite, or really efficient. The final result is the formation of organs which apperceive rapidly, distinctly, and adequately whatever is presented to them. Retention must, therefore, be distin- guished from memory. Memory, or the power of referring experiences to the past, and of connecting them with others in the train of ideas, is one of the forms in which psychical factors are related to each other; it is one mode of appercep- tion. Retention, on the other hand, is the growth or develop- ment of the *mind* itself, and is necessary to memory and to every other form of apperception.

Retention is not of Copies of Ideas

It is not, therefore, the ideas as wholes that are retained. There is another theory which, admitting that ideas cease to exist as ideas when they pass out of consciousness, holds that "traces" or "residua" of these ideas persist, and that this persistence constitutes retention. But there is no more evidence of the retention of ideas in faint, partial, or mutilated form than there is of them in their totality. Such a conception rests upon a mechanical and spatial analogy which has no place. In the first place, the idea is never a thing having an independent, separate existence; it is only a function of mind; that is, the mind considered in a certain mode of activity. When the mind passes on into a new mode of action, the idea, as such, ceases to exist. In the second place, since it is not an independent thing, the idea can leave no separate "trace" behind it, if by trace be meant a remnant or enfeebled copy of the original idea. If, however, the word is used to denote the fact that the idea does not pass away without leaving behind it some witness to its existence, there is no objection to its use.

Various Synonyms for Retention

What is retained is the *effect* which the idea produces upon the mind. The idea is not written in water, but gives the soul a certain set or bent in some direction. Various terms have been used to denote the nature of this effect. It has been called a "disposition," that is, a tendency, towards the production of a similar content in the future. The term functional arrangement has also been employed as suggesting that the retention consists in an alteration in the structure of the mind which affects the way in which it functions. Some psychologists use the expression "dynamical association" for the same fact, implying that the result of any idea is not a mere statical existence *in* mind, but an active tendency *of* mind to operate along certain lines. But all terms signify the same fact, namely, that the mind grows, not by keeping unchanged within itself faint or unconscious copies of its original experiences, but by assimilating something from each experience, so that the next time it acts it has a more definite mode of activity to bring to bear, one which supplies a greater content to whatever is acted upon. This is the psychological side, just as we must suppose the physiological side to be, not preservation of copies of the original molecular motions, but such a change in the structure of the nervous system that, in responding to future stimuli, it acts in a more complex way, containing elements due to the former motions.

NOTES TO CHAPTER 4

The literature of the association of ideas is exceedingly voluminous, the theory having been the foundation of one school of British Psychology since the time of Hume, of Hartley, and, in another and different form, of German Psychology following Herbart. The following references will serve as a clew to the treatment of the subject: Brown, *Philosophy of Mind*, vol. ii, pp. 211 - 325; Hamilton, *Metaphysics*, lects. xxxi and xxxii; Porter, *Human Intellect*, pp. 269 - 99; Bain, *Senses and Intellect*, *passim*, but especially pp. 355 - 69, 463 - 98, 559 - 623; Sully, *Psychology*, pp. 233 - 75; Spencer, *Principles of Psychology*, vol. i, pp. 228 - 71; Robertson, *Encyclopædia Britannica*, 9th edition; Bradley, *Principles of Logic*, pp. 273 - 321 (critical and constructive, very valuable); Murray, *Handbook of Psychology*, pp. 75 - 104; Hodgson, *Philosophy of Reflection*, vol. i, pp. 273 - 87, and upon redintegration in particular, his *Time and Space*, pp. 256 - 95; compare also the valuable articles by James, *Popular Science Monthly*, on "Association of Ideas," and in *Journal of Speculative Philosophy*, on "Brute and Human Intellect." For a general account of the theory, see Ferri, *La Psychologie de l'Association*. For the Herbartian theory, see Herbart, *Lehrbuch zur Psychologie*, pt. 1, ch. iii; Volkmann, *Lehrbuch der Psychologie*, vol. i, pp. 338 - 71; Drobisch, *Mathematische Psychologie*, and *Empirische Psychologie*, pp. 82 - 133; Schilling, *Psychologie*, §22 ff.; Steinthal, *Einleitung in die Psychologie und Sprachwissenschaft*, pp. 115 - 63. For other German views, see Lotze, *Microcosmus* (transl.), pp. 193 - 219; *Outlines of Psychology* (transl.), pp. 28 - 39; and *Metaphysic* (transl.), pp. 456 - 70; Ulrici, *Der Leib und die Seele*, vol. ii, pt. 2, pp. 232 - 69; Horwicz, *Psychologische Analysen*, vol. i, pp. 315 - 31; Glogau, *Grundriss der Psychologie*, pt. 3. For experimental researches and conclusions therefrom, see Galton, *Human Faculty*; Wundt, *Grundzüge der physiologischen Psychologie*, vol. ii, pp. 291 - 317; *Logik*, vol. i, pp. 11 - 23; and *Philosophische Studien*, vol. i, p. 213 ff.; Stricker, *Studien über die Association der Vorstellungen*. Something about habit will be found in many of the foregoing references; additional are Murphy, *Habit and Intelligence*; Radestock, *Habit in Education*, together with Horwicz (*op. cit.*), vol. i, pp. 357 - 68; and Rosenkranz, *Psychologie*, pp. 157 - 63.

Upon attention and the relating activity consult Hamilton (*op. cit.*), lect. xiv; Sully (*op. cit.*), ch. iv; Sully, on "Comparison," *Mind*, vol. x, p. 489; Murray (*op. cit.*), pp. 105 - 8; Carpenter, *Mental Physiology*, ch. iii; Ferrier, *Functions of Brain*, pp. 284 - 88 (for probable physiological basis); Maudsley, *Physiology of Mind*, pp. 312 - 21; Wundt, *Grundzüge der physiologischen Psychologie*,

136   THE EARLY WORKS OF JOHN DEWEY

vol. ii, pp. 205 - 12; Lotze, *Medicinische Psychologie*, p. 506 ff.; *Outlines of Psychology*, pp. 40 - 46; and *Metaphysic*, pp. 470 - 80; Schneider, a monograph on *Die Unterscheidung*, for the distinguishing activity of attention; Horwicz (*op. cit.*), vol. i, pp. 226 - 34; Ulrici (*op. cit.*), vol. i, pt. 2, pp. 15 - 42; see also Bradley, *Mind*, July, 1886.

For the nature of apperception as a whole, see in particular, Staude, "Der Begriff der Apperception in der neueren Psychologie," in *Philosophische Studien*, vol. i, p. 149; Volkmann (*op. cit.*), vol. ii, pp. 175 - 211; Wundt (*op. cit.*), vol. ii, pp. 219 - 90, and *Logik*, vol. i, pp. 30 - 65; Lazarus, *Das Leben der Seele*, vol. ii, pp. 41 - 58, 251 - 75, and *passim*; and Steinthal (*op. cit.*), pp. 166 - 262. Special studies upon apperception in its temporal relations will be found by Friedrich, Tchisch, Cattell, and others, in Wundt's *Philosophische Studien*.

Concerning the pedagogical aspects of these questions, consult Lange, *Über Apperzeption*; Walsemann, *Das Interesse*; Ziller, *Allgemeine Pädagogik* (simple apperception, pp. 212 - 43; complex, pp. 243 - 66; involuntary attention, pp. 266 - 89; voluntary, pp. 290 - 314); De Guimps, *L'Éducation*, pp. 101 - 18; Thring, *Theory and Practice of Teaching*, pp. 165 - 76; Perez, *First Three Years of Childhood* (attention, pp. 110 - 20; association, pp. 131 - 46); Fröhlich, *Wissenschaftliche Pädagogik*, pp. 87 - 128; Beneke, *Erziehungslehre*, pp. 86 -118; Radestock (*op. cit.*); and Lederer's *Methodik der Gewöhnung*.

5
Stages of Knowledge: Perception

1] KNOWLEDGE AS SELF-DEVELOPMENT

We have finished our study of the material and of the process of knowledge, and we come now to the concrete facts—the result of the processes upon the material. These facts may be arranged by either of two methods, the psychological or the chronological. The latter begins with the earliest psychical manifestations of the infant, and follows the order of upward growth. The former rests upon an investigation of the principles involved, and arranges the facts according to the relative simplicity or complexity of principles involved. These methods by no means exclude each other. The order in which intelligence actually grows corresponds, in the main, to the complexity of the underlying principles involved. To follow, however, exactly the temporal order introduces needless confusion and repetition. We follow, therefore, the internal, psychological order.

The Psychological Order

This may be stated in various ways. We may say that intelligence begins with the external and least representative state, and advances to the *internal* and most *symbolic*. That is to say, there is a stage in which sensations are but little transformed, in which they stand for comparatively little besides their own existence. At the other end of the scale there is a stage in which the actual existence of sensations is of small value compared with what they stand for or represent. This additional symbolism always gives additional meaning; it is introduced by a process of idealization. We may say, therefore, that the development of knowledge is a process of increasing *idealization* from the less to the more significant. Since significance consists in relations, we may say that the growth of knowledge is measured by the *extent*

of relations concerned. Each advancing stage is characterized by the development of a new and wider-reaching sphere
of relations. These three modes of statement may be
summed up by saying that intelligence is a process of realization of itself, and that it occurs as new relations are
developed and new meaning given to its products.

Knowledge a Progressive Process

There will be, therefore, various stages in the process. The
individual is not born a realized self, but his psychical existence is the process of realization. Various forms of knowledge will, therefore, be recognized according to the stage of
universality or realization of intelligence reached. These are
the so-called faculties of knowledge, which, therefore, are
not various powers of the mind, but mark various stadia of
its development. These "faculties" are Perception, Memory,
Imagination, Thinking, Intuition or self-consciousness.

Relation of Perception to Other Stages

There has been a theory in psychology that individual objects are impressed upon the mind as wholes without any
constructive activity of the mind, and that this process,
perception, gives us knowledge of reality. The activity of
mind from this point on was supposed to consist in combining and separating these wholes, so that the results are more
or less artificial in nature, and constitute a departure from
the simple realities made known to us in perception. But this
theory falls into a double error. In the first place, perception
or knowledge of particular things is not a passive operation
of impression, but involves the active integration of various
experiences. It is a process of reaching out after the fullest
and richest experience possible. In illustration, consider the
process of scientific observation. The mind does not wait for
sensations to be forced upon it, but goes out in search of
them, supplying by experiment all possible conditions in
order to get new sensations and to modify the old by them.
Secondly, such processes as imagination and thinking are
not mechanically working *upon* percepts, but are their transformation and enrichment in accordance with the same law
of a demand for the unified maximum of meaning. Thinking

transforms perception by bringing out elements latent in it, thereby completing it.

2] PERCEPTION

Definition

The original and least developed, that is, most particular, form of knowledge is perception. Perception may be defined as *knowledge of actually present particular things or events*. The object of the perceiving activity of mind is, in ordinary phrase, "the world of the senses." It is the stage of knowledge least advanced in the interpretation of sensations, the world of things seen, heard, touched, tasted, etc. Before explaining the process we shall analyze out the main characteristics of this perceived world, in order to see more definitely what the problem is which we have to explain.

1. Problem of Perception

The world of perceived objects has the following characteristics: (1) it is *not ourselves*; (2) it is made up of *particular* separate things and events; (3) which, when perceived, are *existing in space*.

(1) The world of perception, with all the things that constitute it, is set over against the self. The world appears to be there *independent* of the intelligence; the latter has only to open its sensory organs and let the world report itself in consciousness. It is an *external* world, while the mind appears to be wholly *internal*. The train of ideas which seems to constitute the mind comes and goes, but this effects no change in the objects. All existences and all changes in this world are due to *physical* laws, independent of the mind. To perceive is opposed to thinking. The latter is *subjective*, depending upon intelligence for its existence. The former is *objective*, and is there whether intelligence exists or not. Such is the apparent relation which the perceived world bears to the perceiving self. In perception not-self is entirely discriminated from self.

(2) The world thus set over against self is constituted by particular concrete things. As I open my eyes I perceive a

room; in this room are chairs, tables, books, pictures, etc. These are all distinct things. Extend this perception and we have the whole world before us. Each object appears to be just itself, separated from every other object, and without any necessary relation to it. One may be in another, as the table is in the room; or by another, as the chair is near the table; but this is purely accidental. The table would be just as much a table if it were in the open air and near a tree.

(3) The perceived world is a *present* world; that is, one existing in *space*. This distinguishes it from the remembered world, which is equally set over against the self, and equally composed of particular elements, but which is a *past* world, or one existing in *time*. Every perceived object has spatial relations, both as a whole to other objects, and of its various constituent parts to each other.

II.   Solution of the Problem

Psychology, accordingly, has to explain how the sensations, the elementary, raw constituents of knowledge, are transformed into this spatial world of definite things through the processes of apperception and retention. Before coming to the positive solution, we shall discuss certain ways in which the problem cannot be solved.

Incorrect Solutions

It cannot be solved from the mere existence of the external world. The world exists undoubtedly absolutely without any dependence upon the individual minds which know it, but which are merely born into it. But the perceived world is more than an *existent* world; it is a world existent for the consciousness of the individual, a *known* world; and knowledge is a process of intelligence, not of existing things. The fact to be explained is that of knowledge, and the mere existence of objects does not suffice for this. But it may be supposed that the affections which these objects occasion in the mind, the sensations, will suffice to explain the knowledge. This is also an error. The sensations are mere subjective states of consciousness, and do not go beyond themselves. They tell us nothing of self or not-self, objects or space. The sensations, in short, must be construed, must be interpreted, by intelligence.

Positive Solution

The presence to the mind of the world as perceived must be explained from the process of knowing. It is due to the activity of the mind, which not only has sensations, but which takes them and projects them. It relates itself actively to them by associating and attending to them. We have now to study the means by which the *apperceiving* activity of mind transforms the data of sensation into (1) concrete definite objects (2) existing in space and (3) external to ourselves.

1.

This may be passed over rapidly, as it has often been treated. Take, for example, the visual perception of a tree. The actual presented data are sensations of light, and muscular sensations due to the moving of the eye from one point to another. These sensations must first be joined together, or fused, by simultaneous association, so that they may become capable of reference to one object. These sensations must also redintegrate all previous elements involved in the perception of a tree, whether visual, tactual, or got through whatever sense, and these must be assimilated to those actually present. But it is not yet the perception of a *tree*; it is only various consolidated sensations. The interpreting, discriminating, unifying activity of attention must come in and translate these sensations into the definite meaning of a tree.

The Perceived Object

The characteristics of the perceived object, viz., that it is a *particular* and a *definite* object, are due to the unifying and discriminating activities of intelligence. Perception may be defined as the act in which the *presented* sensuous data are made symbols or signs of all other sensations which *might* be experienced from the same object, and thus are given meaning, while they are *unified* by being connected in one wholeness of meaning, and made *definite* by being discriminated from all mental contents possessing different meaning.

The unity of a perceived object expresses the fact that it has been grasped together in one act of mind; its particular character expresses the fact that this same act has separated it from all other acts of mind. An object, in short, is the objectified interpreting activity of intelligence.

2. SPATIAL RELATIONS

All objects, as perceived, are projected in space, and given definite position. This is seen most clearly in the case of sensations of touch and sight, which form the especial data of space perception. There are two reasons for this: they are the two sensitive organs which have their endings extended, and hence can receive simultaneous impressions; and they are also the organs which have the most intimate connection with muscular associations. The mere presence of simultaneous sensations, however, is not identical with perception of spatial coexistence. The mind must recognize their distinction, and construe them spatially. The "local signs" (page 52) serve to prevent their fusion, and intelligence then interprets these local signs, through their association with muscular sensations, into spatial order.

Importance of Muscular Sensations

The sensory organs which are not mobile furnish no perceptions, but only feelings. Just in the degree in which the organ is mobile, perception is ready and accurate. Hence it is that the general sensations, smell and hearing, give us comparatively little knowledge of space relations, while sight and touch are all-important. So, too, the finest discriminative organs of touch are the tip of finger and tongue, which are the most mobile. It may be said, therefore, that the perception of space relations is due to the association of muscular sensations with others, interpreted by the apperceptive activity of mind. In the explanation of this association there are two points to be considered: first, the process by which the muscular sensations which accompany movement give definiteness to the sensations of touch and sight; second, the process by which these latter sensations become symbolic of the former, so that finally the definite perception takes place, although no movement occurs.

Tactual Perception

If an adult lays his hand upon something he has a vague perception of space relations, while it requires movement to explore the outlines and make it definite. Infants, however, have not even such a vague perception. It is, therefore, the result of a process by which tactual sensations have become symbolic of motor. Originally the child will have muscular sensations as he moves his hands, and also sensations of contact proper. It is the element of "local sign," the element which differentiates every sensation of touch from every other, with which we are especially concerned; and the problem is to see how, from the union of motor and local sensations, the perceptions of size, form, direction, and distance arise.

Association of Motor and Local Elements

The infant, as his hand is at rest upon some object, receives simultaneously a large number of sensations, each of which is kept from fusion with others by its characteristic local sign. Thus there is constituted a series of sensations qualitatively different from one another, not a perception of related points. It is not even a perception of isolated points, for a point can be perceived only by locating it with reference to other points, giving it relation. With the movement of the hand there arise certain fixed associations. It requires a certain amount of movement, and thus occasions a certain amount of muscular sensation to pass, say, from the local sign of the thumb to that of the little finger. This muscular sensation will evidently vary with the distance between any two local signs, and also with the direction which they are from each other. It will not give the same kind of sensation to go from the little finger to the thumb as from the latter to the wrist. Thus the muscular sensations begin to connect the isolated local signs with each other, and to serve as signs of distance and direction. All the points of the hand, and, indeed, of the body, come to be definitely placed or ordered with reference to each other through the medium of the amount of muscular sensation necessary to change any one local sign into another.

Perception without Movement

The associations thus formed between the motor sensations and the local signs are so fixed and strong that, as in all associations, one element of it becomes capable of symbolizing the other. The actual presence of one redintegrates the ideal presence of the other. Finally, the hand may be entirely at rest, and only tactual sensations be actually given to the mind. Each of these will suggest, however, the muscular sensation which has in previous experiences been associated with it, and hence symbolize to the mind its distance and direction from all other points.

Visual Perception

Here we have to consider two points: the process by which tactual sensations are symbolized through visual; and the process by which visual sensations become simultaneously symbolic of each other, and thus become the signs of spatial relations.

Ultimately visual perception rests on tactual. The visual perception of space, in its definite forms at least, is representative, and embodies for the mind the results of tactual perceptions. To say that an object is seen to be at such a distance, means that so much muscular sensation must be had before it can be touched; to say that it is of such an outline, is to say that certain muscular and local sensations would be had if the hand were passed about it, etc. According to this theory, originally propounded by Bishop Berkeley, spatial relations are not originally perceived by the eye, but are the result of the association of visual sensations with previous muscular and tactual experiences. These latter having become, through the process already described, the signs of space relations, are transferred to the ocular sensations constantly associated with them, so that the latter redintegrate them when they are not actually present. Thus the adult comes to *see* all that he could touch if he tried. The visual sensations immediately and instantaneously call up all the tactual perceptions which have been associated with them, so that the individual has all the benefit of his previous experiences without being obliged to repeat them, or in this case actually to touch the objects.

Evidence of the Theory

The proofs of this theory of the acquired nature of sight perception of space are found in the observations made upon infants, and upon the congenital blind, when given sight. The child grasping for the moon, and crying because he cannot get it, illustrates the defective nature of visual space perception, when not associated with muscular sensations. The blind, when first made to see, have no idea of the distance, form, and size of objects, unless they can walk to them and touch them. Some describe all things seen as touching their eyes, as touched things do their skin. Pictures are not regarded as copies of actual spatial relations, but as planes painted various colors. When the patients finally do realize the perspective significance of paintings, they expect, upon touching one, to find the foreground actually projecting. On the other hand, after they learn that seen objects do not actually touch the eyes, they consider them all on a level, and are surprised, for example, to find when they touch the face that the eyes are sunken, and the nose projected. They cannot tell a cube from a globe, a dog from a cat, by sight alone. Hence it is concluded that the perception of spatial distinctions, by means of sight alone, is the result of the connections brought about by means of past experiences between visual and tactual sensations, so that the former finally symbolize all that the latter convey. However, it is hardly to be denied that sight by itself gives a vague rudimentary perception of space as a whole, though this is rendered definite only by association.

Visual Perception Proper

This association with tactual perception we will now suppose to be accomplished, and proceed to inquire how the various optical sensations are connected so as to symbolize spatial distinctions. Here we shall take up: (1) Direction; (2) Distance; (3) Size and form.

1. DIRECTION.   For a time it was thought that direction was an element involved in the sensation itself, and that the

retina unconsciously projected, as it were, every excitation
along the line of the ray of light which occasioned it. It is
better, however, to regard the element of direction as the
result of the activity of the mind in interpreting the sensations. The latter are, first, the sensations which inform us of
the position of the head, and of the eye in the head. Everything is placed relatively to the position of the body thus
fixed. Then, secondly, we have the sensations of the movements of the head and eye, which are necessary to bring the
image of the object upon the point of most acute vision. The
muscular sensations which accompany the turning of the eye
up or down, right or left, become signs of the variation of
the direction of the object looked at, from a direction perpen-
dicular to the plane of the body.

Law of Perception of Direction

This association between muscular sensation and direction
being once firmly fixed, it is no longer necessary to move the
eyes in order to know the direction of objects. A sensation of
any part of the retina symbolizes, through past associations,
the amount of movement necessary to bring the sensation
upon the yellow spot, and thus symbolizes, without movement, the direction. The law is, therefore, that all bodies are
seen according to the direction in which it is *customary* to
receive sensations of light—not always in the direction in
which it actually comes. Thus if by some artificial means
light stimulates the retina from one side instead of through
the pupil, as ordinarily, the sensation is still projected as if
the object were in front, and the stimulus had entered in its
usual way. This is evidently because through past experience there has been an association formed between this
direction and a sensation on this part of the retina. The same
law accounts for the fact that objects are seen erect, and not
inverted, like the retinal image. The position of the sensation has nothing to do with the perception, except through
the associations that have been formed; and in this case a
sensation on the upper part of the retina is associated with
an object in the lower part of the field of vision, as made
known through touch.

2. DISTANCE. This includes both distance of the object, as a whole, from the eye, and relative distance of one part of the object from another—depth or geometrical solidity. We begin with a study of the object as made known to a single eye at rest. Such perceptions of distance are limited and inaccurate. Such signs as we do have, apart from movement, are five in number. First, the dimness or distinctness of the retinal image serves as a sign of nearness or remoteness. The farther away the object the less the light that reaches the eye, and the more vague the image. Anything that tends to increase the intensity of the sensation, such as clear air, etc., decreases the apparent distance. The strain of the accommodation muscle of the eye is another sign of distance. The less distant the object the more tense will be the muscle, and the stronger the resulting sensation. The fact that objects which are nearer than others cover them, is a third means of estimating distance. The so-called parallax of motion constitutes a fourth; when we are moving, near objects seem to move by more remote ones; the nearer the object the more rapid the apparent movement. If the absolute size of an object is known, its *apparent* size aids in deciding upon distance. If we see a speck which we know none the less to be a man, we know it to be remote. Thus the telescope, by enlarging the image, seems to lessen distance.

The Eyes in Motion

All these means together give only an inadequate perception. The movement of the eyes is necessary for a complete and adequate perception of distance. It is particularly the combined movements of the two eyes that are serviceable here. The difficulty of judging with one eye may be realized by attempting to thread a needle with one eye closed. Monocular vision is also open to deceit in the judgment of solidity, as in the perception of reliefs, and even of paintings. Nor is perception of distance instantaneous with one eye. Movements have to be executed to and fro, right and left, and put together piecemeal into a final perception. But with binocular vision the perception of the third dimension of space is accurate, minute, and instantaneous, as is witnessed by the fact that solidity may be perceived during a flash of lightning.

Cause of Superiority

The superiority of binocular vision is primarily due to the fact that the muscular sensations which result from the convergence of the two eyes upon any object is a sign of its distance. The greater the distance the less will be the convergence and the intensity of the sensations, while at a great distance the eyes become parallel. The varying degrees of convergence thus become signs of the varying distances of objects. We judge an object to have three dimensions when we have to converge the eyes more and less upon looking at different points of it, while we consider it plane when, upon the fixation of various points within it, the muscular sensations of convergence remain the same.

Instantaneous Perception

But this does not account for the fact that we can perceive differences of distance or geometrical solidity without converging the eyes at different points, or in one and the same act. This is due to previous associations between these muscular sensations and the purely visual sensations, whereby the latter become capable of taking the place of the former. If an object fixated by the two eyes has three dimensions, the images in the two eyes are unlike; more of the right side of the object is seen by the right eye, more of its left side by the left eye. But if the object is a plane surface, the images upon the two eyes will not differ. It is this differential element which enables us to judge solidity without testing by various degrees of convergence. This is shown by the fact that if a body, as the moon, be so far away that it produces the same image in both eyes, it appears flat, while a near object, spherical on a much smaller scale, as the lamp globe, is perceived to be a curved surface.

Direct Proof

The dependence of the perception of depth upon difference in retinal sensations is more directly proved by the stereoscope. In stereoscopic vision we have two pictures which are not exactly alike, but which are taken from two cameras, and hence represent the object from somewhat unlike points of view. If by an arrangement of lenses, or otherwise, one of these pictures is seen only by one eye, and the other by the other, the two eyes being converged upon the same point, we have all the conditions of the ordinary perception of solidity fulfilled, and the result is a marvellous confirmation of our theory. The objects in the picture appear no longer on a flat surface, but projected into space. No more sufficient proof that the perception of depth is due to variation in the two retinal images could be desired.

The Field of Vision

In the perception of the spatial field as a whole, all distances are fixed primarily with reference to the position of the body, and, secondarily, with reference to each other. It is, in fact, the mutual reference of objects to each other that makes perception accurate and complete. The elements of size, direction, and distribution of light and shade come into this mutual reference as deciding factors. An object can be placed in the field of vision without these factors very imperfectly, even if all the signs previously mentioned are present. This is seen, for example, by observing the approach of the head-light of a locomotive in the midst of surrounding darkness. It will be found almost impossible to judge of its distance, or its place with reference to other objects. But if surrounding objects be lighted up in some way, the locomotive will be immediately placed properly and accurately. All spatial perception is relative. We place one object only when we connect it with others.

3. SIZE. The principal datum for determining size is the amount of sensation. The larger an object, the greater will be the portion of the retina stimulated. This holds good, however, only when objects are at the same distance. A pin-head near by will stimulate more of the retina than a tree farther away. The amount of sensation is useful as a sign of size only when the distance of the object is already known. Hence whatever affects our judgments of distance affects the perception of magnitude. A man seen in a fog may appear of

great size because the fog occasions indistinctness of image,
and consequent perception of apparent greater distance, and
this, since the amount of retinal stimulation remains the
same, the judgment of increased size. Many other illusions
of size are to be accounted for in the same way. All judgments of size are inaccurate where there is no opportunity of
comparison. Perception of *form* goes with that of size; it is
outline of magnitude.

3. OBJECTS AS NOT OURSELVES

Having explained the perception of particular concrete
objects in their space relations, we have now to explain the
fact that they are contrasted with and set over against self.
Virtually this is included in what has already been said. The
sensations in being unified and objectified by their projection
in space are by these very acts made not-self. Space is
externality, and all that exists in space is hence recognized
as external to self. Why it is, however, that we perceive
objects external to ourselves, that is, as in space, has not
been explained. We have just shown upon the basis of
what sensations the perception of spatial relations is formed,
but this does not touch the question why perception should
take upon itself the form of space as externality. This is
equivalent to the question why intelligence should distinguish between self and not-self.

Perception as Distinction

In answer to this question, it may be said that the separation
of objects in space from self is the fundamental form in
which the universal activity of mind, as a *distinguishing*
activity, manifests itself. In perception this discriminating
factor predominates over the unifying. The action of the
unifying function of mind is witnessed in the fact that particular objects are identified as such and such, and that all
objects are regarded as constituting *one* world, while all
ideas about them are referred to *one* self. The predominance, however, of the distinguishing function is witnessed
by the fact that each of these objects is distinct from every
other, and all from the self. This is manifested in the existence of space. Every part of space is regarded as outside of

every other point, while space, as a whole, is regarded as wholly external to and independent of mind. It is the extreme form of the differentiating activity of intelligence, which in perception thus results in complete self-externalization. This opposition of self to not-self in perception is, therefore, one of the stages in which *relation*, constituting the essence of all knowledge, appears.

The Will as Distinguishing Power

The principal agent in bringing about this separation of objects from self is the will. It has already been pointed out that perception of spatial relations occurs only in conjunction with muscular sensations; but muscular sensations are ultimately occasioned by the activity of the will in bringing about movements. Involuntary muscles have no connection with any perception of space. Furthermore, it is to be noticed that it is the connection of muscular sensations with those of sight and touch which we employ to decide whether any sensation is subjective, or is to be referred to an object. Whenever the muscular sensation cannot be dissociated from the other, we do not refer the sensation to a thing, that is, do not objectify it; otherwise we do. If, for example, I wish to decide whether a spot of red which I seem to see on the wall is really there, or is only an organic affection, I move my head and eyes. If the "spot" then changes with change of muscular sensation, we say that it is "in one's eyes." If it remains permanent, and is dissociated from the muscular sensation, it is referred to the object. Were there no will to originate these movements, there is no reason to believe that we should ever come to distinguish sensations as objective or referred to things, or as subjective, referred to the organism. It is by an active process of experimentation, directed by the will, that the infant comes to distinguish between self and not-self.

Nature of Perception

Perception, as a whole, is that stage or phase of knowledge in which the function of discrimination or differentiation predominates over that of identification or unification. Since the end of knowledge is the complete unity of perfectly discriminated or definite elements, it follows that perception is not a final stage of knowledge. There are relations of identity which connect objects with each other, and with the self, which are enveloped or absorbed in perception, and which must be developed or brought into consciousness. The next stage, in which this is partially done, is memory, where the relations which connect objects with each other in a series, and with the self as permanent, are given explicit existence in consciousness. The relations of time, that is to say, which connect events with each other, and with the self, are developed.

NOTES TO CHAPTER 5

We begin with some references to the general subject of perception, and then pass on to the special discussion of space perception, where the literature, from a psychological point of view at least, is much more abundant and valuable. Ward, *Encyclopædia Britannica*, article "Psychology"; Hamilton, *Metaphysics*, lects. xxi - xxvi; Porter, *Human Intellect*, pp. 119 - 247; Morell, *Elements of Psychology*, pp. 124 - 66; Sully, *Psychology*, ch. vi; Bain, *Senses and Intellect*, pp. 369 - 402; Jardine, *The Elements of the Psychology of Cognition*, pp. 17 - 148; Spencer, *Principles of Psycholgy*, vol. ii, pp. 131 - 77; Helmholtz, *Die Thatsachen in der Wahrnehmung*; Von Stein, *Über Wahrnehmung*; Sergi, *Teoria Fisiologica della Percezione*.

Visual perception is worthy of most careful and detailed study, because physiological and experimental psychology have gone further in dealing with it than with any other question; because it is so closely connected with space perception, and because so many questions of wide psychological and even philosophical bearing centre in its treatment. It is undoubtedly the most important *special* subject in psychology at present. Our references are, therefore, fuller than usual. Berkeley, "Essay Towards a New Theory of Vision"; Mill, *Dissertations and Discussions*, vol. ii, p. 162 ff.; Brown, *Philosophy of Mind*, vol. ii, pp. 96 - 121; Abbott, *Sight and Touch*; Monck, *Space and Vision*; Le Conte, *Sight*; Clarke, *Visions* (illusions of sight); Carpenter, *Mental Physiology*, pp. 176 - 209; Foster, *Textbook of Physiology*, pp. 552 - 71; Bernstein, *Five Senses of Man*, pp. 137 - 63; Sully, in *Mind*, vol. iii, pp. 1 and 167; Helmholtz, *Optique Physiologique* (general theory, pp. 561 - 94; monocular, pp. 681 - 876; binocular, pp. 877 - 963), and *Wissenschaftliche Abhandlungen*, vol. ii, pp. 229 - 500; Wundt, *Beiträge zur Theorie der Sinneswahrnehmung*, pp. 1 - 65, 145 - 70; *Vorlesungen*, vol. i, p. 234 ff.; and *Grundzüge der physiologischen Psychologie*, vol. ii, pp. 61 -

160; Hermann, *Handbuch der Physiologie der Sinnesorgane*, pt. 1, pp. 343 - 600; Lipps, *Psychologische Studien* (first three essays); Überhorst, *Die Entstehung der Gesichtswahrnehmung*; Classen, *Physiologie des Gesichtssinnes*, and *Das Schlussverfahren des Sehactes*; Nagel, *Das Sehen mit zwei Augen*; Cornelius, *Die Theorie des Sehens*; Panum, *Über das Sehen*; Schleiden, *Theorie des Erkennens durch den Gesichtssinn*; and especially Hering, *Beiträge zur Physiologie* (for views opposed to Helmholtz).

Most of the foregoing contain something upon spatial perception, but further, see as follows: Hamilton (*op. cit.*), lect. xxviii; Mill, *Examination of Hamilton*, ch. xiii; Hall, on "Muscular Perception of Space," in *Mind*, vol. iii, p. 433; Montgomery, on "Space and Touch," in *Mind*, vol. x, pp. 227, 377, and 512; Ribot, *Contemporary German Psychology*, ch. v; Helmholtz, *Optique Physiologique*, pp. 999 - 1028; Lotze, *Revue Philosophique*, vol. iv (on local signs); *Metaphysic*, pp. 481 - 505; and *Outlines of Psychology*, pp. 47 - 65; Sully, *Psychology*, pp. 173 - 94; Murray, *Handbook of Psychology*, pp. 159 - 82; Spencer (*op. cit.*), vol. ii, pp. 178 - 206; Mahaffy, *Kant's Critical Philosophy*, vol. i, ch. iv; *Journal of Speculative Philosophy*, vol. xiii, pp. 64 and 199, articles by James and Cabot; Herbart, *Werke*, vol. vi, p. 114 ff.; Volkmann, *Lehrbuch der Psychologie*, vol. ii, pp. 36 - 117; Strümpell, *Grundriss der Psychologie*, pp. 219 - 33; Preyer, *Die Seele des Kindes*, Appendix C; Wundt (*op. cit.*), vol. ii, pp. 4 - 33, 161 - 78, and *Revue Philosophique*, vol. vi (criticism of Lotze on local signs); Weber, "Raumsinn"; and for a historical and critical discussion of the whole subject, see Stumpf, *Über den psychologischen Ursprung der Raumvorstellung*.

For the pedagogy of perception, see any of the numerous treatises in German upon "Erziehungslehre," and in addition, Perez, *First Three Years of Childhood*, pp. 32 - 43; Jahn, *Psychologie*, pp. 20 - 30; Schnell, *Die Anschauung*; and Treuge, *Der Anschauungsunterricht*.

6

Stages of Knowledge: Memory

Definition of Memory

The next higher stage of knowledge is memory, which may be defined as *knowledge of particular things or events once present, but no longer so.* Memory consequently removes one limitation from knowledge as it exists in the stage of perception: the limitation to the *present.* The world of strict perception has no past nor future. Perception is narrowly confined to what is immediately before it. What has existed and what may exist it has nothing to do with. Memory extends the range of knowledge beyond the present. The world of knowledge as it exists for memory is a world of events which *have* happened, of things which have existed. In short, while the characteristic of perception is *space* relations, that of memory is *time* relations. Knowledge, however, is still limited to individual things or events which have had an existence in some particular place, and at some particular time.

I.   General Problem of Memory

The fact which the psychologist has to account for is how our knowledge can be extended beyond the realm of the immediate present to take in that no longer existing, namely, the past. We begin by stating how the problem cannot be solved: (1) It cannot be solved by the mere fact that we have had past experiences which are called into the light of consciousness when wanted; even if there is added to this supposition (2) the laws of association of ideas.

1.

The case is analogous to that of perception. Just as we found that knowledge of present existent objects cannot be explained from the mere fact of their existence, but that knowledge of them requires a constructive activity of mind, so the knowledge of objects existent in the past cannot be explained from the mere fact that we have once had experience of them. Memory is not a passive process in which past experiences thrust themselves upon the mind, any more than perception is one where present experiences impress themselves. It is a process of construction. In fact it involves more of constructive activity than perception. In perception the objects, at all events, do exist before the perception construes them. In memory they do not. Our past experiences are gone just as much as the time in which they occurred. They have no existence until the mind reconstructs them.

Objects of Memory are wholly Ideal

Their existence is wholly mental. Thus the object of memory does not exist as a *thing* in space, but only as a mental image. The table which I perceive is one really there in space. The table which I remember exists only in the form of an image in my mind. The perceived table is solid and resists. The remembered table has no physical properties of this kind. The memory of the color red is not itself red, nor is the memory of the odor of a rose fragrant. It is evident, accordingly, that in memory the idealizing activity which is involved in all knowledge is carried a point further than it is in perception. The experiences with which memory deals are, *per se*, wholly ideal. They exist only as results of the constructive activity of intelligence.

Misleading Metaphors

This fact makes many metaphors regarding memory entirely misleading. For example: Memory is compared to a scar left by a cut. Every experience, that is, is thought to leave some permanent trace of itself on the mind, and the mere presence of this trace at any time is thought to constitute memory. But the characteristic of the scar is that it is really present; it still exists as a thing, but has no ideal existence; that is, no conscious existence for itself. The remembered experience, on the other hand, has real existence no longer. The knife which made the cut does not exist in memory as it does in perception, as a thing really there. It may still exist, but that means that it *could be* perceived; not that *it is* remembered. Again, the remembered experience has an ideal existence. It exists for itself in consciousness. The essential characteristic of memory is thus seen to be the ideal presence of an object or event no longer really present; and the mere fact that it was once really present is of no avail to account for its new ideal presence, though, of course, the latter could not occur had it not been for the former.

2.

While this is generally admitted, it is often thought that the laws of the association of ideas, conjoined with the past experience, are enough to account for the facts of memory. We have had experiences; these exist stored up, in some unexplained way, in the mind, and when some experience occurs which is like some one of these, or has been previously contiguous with it in time or space, it calls this other up, and that constitutes memory. This, at most, solves but one half the problem. The association of ideas only accounts for the *presence* of the object or event. The other half is the reference of its present image to some past reality. In *memory* we *re-cognize* its presence; i.e., we know that it *has been* a previous element of our experience. We place the image in the train of our *past* experiences, we give it some *temporal* relation; we refer it to some real object once perceived. No idea, however it comes into the mind, certifies of itself that it has ever been experienced before, or under what circumstances it has been experienced. The mind must actively take hold of the idea and project it into time, just as in perceiving it takes hold of the sensation and projects it into space. Were it not for this projecting activity of the mind all would be a fleeting present; the range of intelligence would not extend into a past world.

3. POSITIVE SOLUTION OF PROBLEMS

Memory, therefore, like perception, is an active construction by the mind of certain data. It differs from perception only in the fact that the interpreting process which is involved in both is carried in memory a stage further. In perception the sensation is interpreted only as the sign of something present, which could be experienced by actually bringing all the senses into relation with it. In memory it is interpreted as the sign of some experience which we once had, and which we might have again, could we accurately reproduce all its conditions. If I perceive the President of the United States, certain visual sensations *represent* to me all the sensations which my other senses *could present* to me, and also symbolize certain past experiences which I have had, which enable me to interpret the visual sensations as a man, and as this particular man. If I remember this perception, certain ideas now present serve as data (as the sensations do in the perception), and represent to me, not the experiences which I could now have by trying, but the experiences which I once had.

Memory as Involved in Perception

Memory is thus a natural outgrowth of perception. Past experiences are really *involved* in perception, and memory does nothing more than evolve them, and give them a distinct place in consciousness. We perceive only by bringing past experiences to bear upon the present, so as to interpret it; but in perception these past experiences are wholly absorbed or lost in the present. When we see a man we do not recognize that there are involved in this perception all the other men which we have seen, and that it is only through the ideal presence of these experiences in the present data that the latter signify to us a man. But such is the fact. What memory does is (1) simply to disengage some one of these experiences from its absorption in the perception, giving it an independent ideal existence; (2) at the same time interpreting it in such a way that it stands for or symbolizes certain relations of time, and (3) gets its place in the course of experience, or in the train of ideas taken as a whole.

II.   Elements of Problem of Memory

It is thus evident that there are three elements in the problem of memory, as there are in the problem of perception. The first (1) corresponds to the existence of particular objects, but takes the form of the presence in the mind of the *image* or *idea*—an ideal presence, instead of an actual one; the second (2) is the reference of this image to some past reality, or its projection in time, corresponding to the spatial relations of perception; while, corresponding to the distinction between self and not-self, we have (3) the distinction between the present self and the course of experience, or train of ideas, taken as a whole. That is, just as the spatial world, the world of perceptual experience, appears set over against the self, so the temporal world, the world of our experiences as presented in memory, is distinguished from the present self, as existing at every point of time, or permanently.

1. THE PRESENCE OF THE MEMORY IMAGE IN THE MIND

The laws of association evidently account for this. Nothing is ever remembered which does not have some point of association with what is actually present in the mind. However far the train of images may go, therefore, it will always be found ultimately to rest upon some perception. This perception, getting its meaning through its idealization, on the basis of past experience, involves, *ideally*, these past experiences within itself. There are involved in my perception, for example, of this book all the perceptions which I have had of similar books, and of objects which have been *contiguous* to these formerly perceived books. For the independent existence of a memory-image it is only necessary that some one of these involved former perceptions be disengaged or dissociated.

Process of Disengagement

This may occur in two ways, one of which was mentioned (page 94) when studying successive association. It is quite probable that some of the factors involved in the former perception of a book are wholly incongruous with those involved in the present perception. Its size, its color, its subject-matter, above all, its original spatially contiguous surroundings are so different from those of the present perception that only with the greatest difficulty can it lose its identity in being absorbed by the present perception; while the similarity of nature of both will necessitate its coming into consciousness along with this perception.

Result an Image

The result of this incongruity is its disengagement from the perception, and consequent existence as an *image* or *idea*. Were it absorbed in the perception, it would be referred to some present thing, and hence have no more existence ideally, i.e., as a mental image. The very fact that it is not thus referred to the real object makes it manifest itself as it exists, i.e., in the mind alone, or as an image. It follows, from what has been said, that every perception will tend to call up an indefinite number of images, as many as there have been experiences of a similar nature before, which are incompatible in some particular. This is undoubtedly the case. Besides the image which comes into distinct consciousness, careful introspection will always reveal a large number of nascent or rising images, which are only suppressed by the attention paid to some one selected. This introduces us to the second way in which the image is given an ideal existence, or separated from its absorption in the perception.

Recollection

It is not always left to the laws of association, acting in the way just described, to produce the image. The mind may have an especial *interest* in the appearance of one idea over another, and voluntarily direct itself to securing its appearance. In short, the *attentive* activities are concerned with memory as well as the associative. For example, suppose that I remember vaguely having obtained a certain idea upon psychology yesterday, and I wish to recall it definitely. It is not enough to let the laws of association passively bring it back, for they are as likely, by themselves, to bring up anything else. Neither is it possible to direct the will immediately upon it, and bring it forth; for just what it is the mind does not know. So the emphasis is laid upon those elements which are known to be associated with it, and the associative lines, having been led in this direction, finally call it up of themselves.

To take a simpler case, suppose I wish to recall the name of a man I met yesterday. I cannot call it up by an immediate act of the will, for what it is I do not know. The associative activity, if left to itself, might expend itself in some other channel; so what I do is to fix my attention on all circumstances connected with the man, the place where I saw him, the man who introduced him, etc.; and thus, intensifying these elements, I increase their associative power at the expense of others, until, by their own action, they call up the name desired. This direction of the mechanical action of association into some given channel, to make it work towards a desired end, is called *recollection*. It is evidently a form of memory in which attentive activities are involved as well as associative. The presence of the latter alone results in reverie, day-dreaming, etc. One of the principal characteristics of dreams, indeed, is that attention is in abeyance, and the train of ideas is governed by the mechanical principles of association alone. It will also be noticed that the associative activities in memory are *successive*, while in perception they are simultaneous fusion and assimilation.

2. THE ELEMENT OF TIME RELATION

But no true memory exists until this image, which has, by its disengagement, got independent existence, is projected in time; that is, referred to some point in past experience. Time relations may be reduced to two—succession and duration, change and extent. There is no reason to suppose that, at first, the child has any idea of succession or duration in time, any more than he has of direction in space. He can have no idea of it until he connects successive experiences with each other, and regards them as members of a whole. It is, of course, a fact that every mental state occupies a certain time; comes after another, and precedes a third; but this does not constitute the recognition of succession. The recognition of succession implies not only the coursing of one idea after another, but the recognition of the relation of precedence and consequence, before and after. It is not enough that there be change in the ideas. There must also be connection. The past idea and the present idea must be held together before the mind in spite of their succession; otherwise the succession may exist, but it will not be known. The recognition of succession requires a *permanent relating* activity of the mind itself.

Hearing and Time Perception

The general nature of the perception of time may be best brought out by considering its perception through the sense of hearing, as typical of the whole process. As the visual sensations are fitted, by their coexistent character and by their association with simultaneous muscular sensations, to become symbols of space relations, so auditory sensations, by virtue of their successive character and their association with successive muscular sensations, are fitted to serve as signs of temporal relations. One hundred and thirty-two beats per second may be recognized as distinct to a well-trained ear, while upon the eye forty consecutive impressions seem as one continuous light. This characteristic of hearing forms the basis of very fine time discriminations; but it is only the basis. For the recognition of such differences are requisite the combination and mutual reference of tone sensations in the peculiar way known as rhythm.

Fundamental Character of Rhythm

The importance of rhythm in the psychical life can hardly be overestimated. It plays the same part there that periodicity does in the physical universe. It is a native form under which the soul tends to apperceive all with which it comes in contact. And it is also a form in which it tends to express its own most intimate states. It is the language of the manifestation of emotion. All the early traditions of the race are expressed by its means. Poetry is everywhere an earlier and more natural mode of expression than prose. Prose still retains traces of its origin; there has been intellectual rhythm substituted for sensuous. The sentence has its beginning, middle, and end. It is divided by semicolons and commas. Its parts are balanced and antithetical. Each part is arranged so as at once to continue the thought of some other, and to make a transition from it. In music, rhythm gave rise to the earliest and most widely diffused of the arts, while the accompanying dancing was one of the earliest modes of physical activity, and may, in some way, be considered more natural than walking, which is, after all, but a more regular dance.

Nature of Rhythm

Considered very generally, rhythm is simply the tendency of the mind everywhere to reduce variety to unity, or break up unity into variety. In its broadest sense, rhythm is identical with the apperceiving activity of the mind. If we listen to regular and even beats, like those of a pendulum or of an engine, we immediately emphasize some one and slur another, so as to introduce rhythm. The clock no longer says tick, tick, but tick, tack. The strokes of the engine go through a regular alternation of weak and strong. Variety is introduced by the mind into the monotony. On the other hand, if we listen to the ticking of two clocks, we are not content to take the irregular combination of beats as they come, but we endeavor to combine them into some regular system, to introduce rhythm into them. We endeavor to reduce their variety to some underlying unity. These simple illustrations serve as types of the character of intelligence as universally manifested. It always combines in this rhythmical way.

Relation of Rhythm to Time

It is now necessary to see how this introduction of rhythm facilitates time perception through hearing. Rhythm may here be defined as change in the intensity of sound at regular intervals. A sound of the same quality may be now stronger, now weaker; and if these risings and fallings of stress occur at regular periods we have rhythm. It is evident that this is the very means of the recognition of succession. If there were absolutely no regularity in the sounds they would be wholly disconnected; each sound would be an independent existence, and would not carry the mind beyond itself. On the other hand, if the sound were absolutely continuous, it would give us no ground whatever for distinguishing time intervals. The same thing without difference would be constantly *present*. But in rhythm every sound points, by its very structure, both to the past and future. Every part of the sound is at once a continuation of the old sound, thus combining the two, and a transition from it, thus separating them. The accented portion, being a repetition of the former stress, refers itself immediately to it, and thus supplies the element of permanence. But alternations of stress are also necessary for rhythm, and thus there is supplied the element of change. Rhythm, accordingly, meets the requirement of perception of succession in time; permanence amid change.

Rhythm not Confined to Art

The importance of rhythm is most plainly seen in music and poetry, whose very existence depends so largely upon the organic connection of elements into a whole through this reference of one element to every other by the medium of time. The connection of successive parts into a whole is increased by various other contrivances—melody and tonicity in music; rhyme and assonance in poetry; in both, by the fact that measures are united into periods, etc. Each of these carries the mind backwards and forwards at once; and this, amid the succession, preserves the idea that the successive parts are members of one whole. It is only because of this that time relations are perceived. But the process is not confined to art. Time itself is divided into centuries; centuries into years; years into weeks, days, hours, minutes, seconds, etc. Each of these divisions is an artificial, yet natural, result of the tendency of the mind towards rhythm. Were it not for these rhythmical intervals our perception of time would be exceedingly inaccurate and indefinite. Through these beats, into which we instinctively divide time, any event may be accurately placed and dated.

Origin of Time Perception

Time will be perceived, accordingly, when some event is recognized as being changed from some previous event, and still connected with it. The child, perhaps, will first perceive succession in connection with taking food. Hunger and satisfaction are the two most intense states of consciousness, and they are very intimately connected together. They form the arsis and thesis of the life of the child. They are exceedingly different from each other, and yet one succeeds the other. They may, accordingly, form the rudiments of the perception of succession and duration. The very tendency of the child, while hungry, to recall his previous satisfaction, and to anticipate the coming one, is the beginning of the recognition of time. It grows more definite and accurate just in the degree in which all experiences are related to each other as members of one whole. Every time any event of psychical life is connected with and referred to some other, a time relation is discriminated.

Growth of Time Perception

It was remarked, under space perception, that the starting-point is the position of the body, and that the perception of any spatial position depends upon the ability to place the object definitely with reference to other objects. An isolated object can hardly be placed at all. The same is true of the projection of ideas in time. The mental image is always referred *from* the present point of psychical life, and *with reference to* other experiences. When we are unable to refer an image definitely to any time, it simply means that we cannot place it with reference to other experiences. We know that it has come in our past experiences, but *where* it came we do not know. Ability to put events in their proper time relation depends, accordingly, upon ability to connect our various experiences with each other. Events are always dated relatively to other events; never absolutely. And, apart from this unification of events as members of one series, there is, accordingly, no reference of images to any given time, and hence, strictly speaking, no memory.

3. MEMORY AS INVOLVING DISTINCTION OF TRAIN OF IDEAS FROM PERMANENT SELF

As perception involved the distinction of self and notself, that is, the activity of the mind in taking its sensations and objectifying them by setting them over as unified objects against itself, so memory involves the distinction of self, as permanent, from the ever-changing course of its experiences. In memory the activity of the mind takes its ideas and combines them into a connected whole, standing in relations of time to each other, and sets these over against itself in such a way that the latter is regarded as always *present*, while the former are past. Memory involves, therefore, the distinguishing activity of mind. Were it not for this distinction, if the mind could not take its ideas and project them always from itself and thus regard them as not members of its present self, no such thing as memory would exist.

Memory requires a now and a then — the recognized difference between past and present; and this is not possible without the recognition of the difference between a self which is present both now and then, permanently present, and the idea which changes, and consequently *was then*, but is not now. Memory exists, accordingly, only where there is a permanent self amid changing experiences. Were there changing experiences alone there would be succession, but no possibility of the recognition of succession; hence no distinction between past and present, and no memory. Were there only a permanent self all would be forever present, and hence no memory.

Identifying Activity in Memory

Thus it is evident that memory implies the uniting, identifying activity of mind, as well as its discriminating, separating activity. The self *recognizes* this experience as similar with, or contiguous to, some previous experience. This recognition implies, of course, their conscious identification. This is what is meant by saying that memory involves a permanent self; it is the activity of the self in uniting the various elements of its experience, and making a connected whole of them. Memory carries, therefore, the identifying activity of mind one step further than perception does. The perceived world appears to be a world wholly distinct from the self; the world of memory is recognized as a world which the self has once experienced. It is still regarded, however, as separate from the present self. It is yet an incomplete stage of knowledge.

Time as Involving Unity and Difference

The relations of time, which we have seen to be characteristic of memory, repeat the evidence of the existence of both the identifying and the discriminating activities of intelligence. All *times* are regarded as constituting one time; any point of time has no existence, except as in relations of before and after to other points. It exists only by virtue of its relations to them. It is the continuing of the previous time and the passing into the next time. Time, in short, is one or continuous. But we must recognize, also, that time is discrete. Each point of time is outside of, external to, every other point. The essential trait of any given period of time is, in fact, that it is not any other period. We discriminate events as particular by referring them to some time, as we do objects by referring them to some place. Time as a whole appears, also, external to, and unconnected with, the self. The self in memory appears identical with itself and permanent, while time is always changing. But that time has less of the element of externality than space is evident from the fact that the mind regards its own experiences as happening in time, while it never thinks of supposing that they occur in space. Time presupposes, in fact, a certain degree of internality, or intimate connection with self.

NOTES TO CHAPTER 6

Hamilton, *Metaphysics*, lect. xxx; Morell, *Elements of Psychology*, pp. 166 - 204; Porter, *Human Intellect*, pp. 248 - 68, and 300 - 24; Spencer, *Principles of Psychology*, vol. i, pp. 434 - 53; Carpenter, *Mental Physiology*, ch. x; Calderwood, *Relations of Mind and Brain*, ch. ix; Maudsley, *Physiology of Mind*, p. 512 ff.; Butler, *Unconscious Memory* (compare relevant portions of Von Hartmann's *Philosophy of the Unconscious*); Galton, *Mind*, vol. v, p. 301, and *Human Faculty*; Ribot, *Diseases of Memory*; Ulrici, *Der Leib und die Seele*, vol. ii, pp. 207 - 31; George, *Lehrbuch der Psychologie*, pp. 281 - 321; Erdmann, *Psychologische Briefe*, ch. xvi; Horwicz, *Psychologische Analysen*, vol. i, pp. 266 - 314; Wundt, *Grundzüge der physiologischen Psychologie*, vol. ii, pp. 318 - 26. See also monographs by Autenrieth, Hering, Hensen, and Ebbinghaus, *Über das Gedächtniss.*

Concerning the development of time relations, see Romanes, "Consciousness of Time," *Mind*, vol. iii, p. 297; Spencer (*op. cit.*), vol. ii, pp. 207 - 15; Volkmann, *Lehrbuch der Psychologie*, vol. ii, pp. 12 - 36; Sigwart, *Logik*, vol. ii, pp. 77 - 83; Horwicz (*op. cit.*), vol. i, pp. 129 - 43; Strümpell, *Grundriss der Psychologie*, pp. 207 - 18; Wundt (*op. cit.*), vol. ii, pp. 34 - 60 (tone perception); and for experimental researches, see *Mind* for Jan., 1886, by Hall; *Philosophische Studien*, vol. i, p. 78; vol. ii, pp. 37 and 546, by Kollert, Estel, and Mehner; and Vierordt, *Zeitsinn.*

For the pedagogy of memory, see Thring, *Theory and Practice of Teaching*, pp. 177 - 86; Perez, *First Three Years of Childhood*, pp. 121 - 30; Ziller, *Allgemeine Pädagogik*, p. 314 ff.; Beneke, *Erziehungslehre*, pp. 91 - 99; Schnell, *Der Lernakt*; Dörpfeld, *Beiträge zur pädagogischen Psychologie*, vol. i; Schumann, *Kleinere Schriften*, vol. ii, p. 69 ff.; Joly, *Notions de Pédagogie*, pp. 62 - 79; Miquel, *Lehre vom Gedächtniss*; Huber, *Das Gedächtniss*; and Fortlage, *Acht psychologische Vorträge.*

7

Stages of Knowledge: Imagination

Nature of Imagination

Imagination may be defined as *that operation of the intellect which embodies an idea in a particular form or image.* From this definition we discover both its resemblance to the two previous operations of the intellect and its differences from them. It is like them in that its product is always *particular*; it is an idea of this or that object, person, event. It is one distinct existence. It is unlike them in that this particular mental existence is not necessarily referred to some one place or time as existing there. It is, in short, an idea; not an object or event. It is, however, an idea of some object or event. Othello, as a product of the imagination of Shakespeare, is like Julius Cæsar as an object of perception or memory, in that he is one particular individual, with personal traits and acts. He is unlike Cæsar in that the idea is not referred to some existence in space or time. Othello is, indeed, given a local and temporal habitation, but it is recognized that this is done purely from motives of the mind itself, and not from constraint of external fact.

Imagination Involved in Perception

The first step towards explaining how the intellect advances beyond its interpretation of a sensation as referred to a thing or event, to its interpretation as ideal, or an image, is to recall that imagination is involved in perception. In the perception of an object, as an apple, there are actually present, it will be remembered, only a few sensations. All the rest of the perception is supplied by the mind. The mind supplies sensations coming from other senses besides those in use; it extends and supplements them; it adds the emphasis of its attention, and the comment of its emotions; it interprets them. Now all this supplied material may fairly be said to be the work of the imagination. The mind ideal-izes—that is, fills in with its own images—the vacuous and chaotic sensations present.

Imagination as Involved in Memory

In perception these images are implicitly present, but they are not recognized. They are swallowed up in the product, so that the object of perception appears to be a mere thing, which exists without any ideal connections. In memory some of the images—those supplied from previous experi-ences—are set free from this absorption, and given an inde-pendent existence. The memory of Niagara Falls is very different from its perception. The latter is a thing which is really there; the former is an idea in the mind. Yet, even in this case, the idea is not considered as ideal, but is referred to an object in existence. The image has not yet received an independent, free existence, severed from connection with some facts actually existing, or some event which has really occurred. The presence of imagination is still implied rather than explicit. Yet it is implied so completely that memory is often treated as one mode of imagination.

The Development of Imagination

Imagination, as the recognition of an idea in a concrete form, will exist just as soon as the ideal element involved in both perception and memory is freed from its reference to some existence, and treated freely; that is, as an image, not as tied down to some thing or event. This is no new opera-tion; it is only the more complete development of one already at work. It is bringing into consciousness what was pre-viously in unconsciousness. The factors which are engaged in this development are, especially, dissociation and atten-tion, while association reigns especially in perception and memory. Dissociation disengages the image, and prepares it for free recombination; attention transforms into novel and unexperienced products.

Dissociation

The first step of dissociation is to recognize that an image may have an ideal existence, and need not be referred to an actual thing. Children are often spoken of as possessed of great imagination, when the fact really is that they have not learned as yet to make this distinction, and consequently every idea or image which occurs to them is taken for reality. Imagination proper appears only with the ability to distinguish between the ideal and the real. This distinction originates largely through the dissociation of some element from its varying concomitants, according to the process already treated (page 94). It is found that the same idea, say of a man, occurs under so many different circumstances, that it is freed from its detail of space and time circumstances, and thus gets an independent and ideal existence.

Mechanical Imagination

Along with this isolation of various elements of our perception goes a recombination of them. A tree is separated from its position along with others, and is set in lonely grandeur on a mountain. A house is imagined greatly enlarged in size, and filled with all beautiful objects. It is made a palace of things that delight. It is this double process of separating and adding that constitutes the lowest stage of imagination. It deals with real material—things and events previously experienced—and confines its activity to forming abstractions, and producing combinations not experienced. Only the form is new. Imagination of this sort, proceeding for the most part by the laws of association and dissociation, may be called mechanical imagination.

Fancy

The next higher stage is known as fancy, or fantasy. Here the formation and connection of images is controlled by an exceedingly vivacious and receptive emotional disposition. The web of fancy throws itself about all things, and connects them together, through the medium of feeling. It is characterized by the predominance of similes, of metaphors, of images in the poetical sense, of subtle analogies. In its higher forms it is seen in such a wonderful production as "Midsummer Night's Dream." Its home is romance. Yet even here there is no creation; there is only unwonted connection—connection rendered harmonious and congruous through the oneness of emotional tone which characterizes it all. Fancy is not revealing in its nature; it is only stimulating. It affords keen delight rather than serves as an organ of penetration.

Creative Imagination

The highest form of imagination, however, is precisely an organ of penetration into the hidden meaning of things — meaning not visible to perception or memory, nor reflectively attained by the processes of thinking. It may be defined as the direct perception of meaning — of ideal worth in sensuous forms; or as the spontaneous discovery of the sensuous forms which are most significant, most ideal, and which, therefore, reveal most to the intellect and appeal most to the emotions. In its highest form, imagination is not confined to isolation and combination of experiences already had, even when these processes occur under the influence of sensitive and lively emotion. It is virtually creative. It makes its object new by setting it in a new light. It separates and combines, indeed; but its separations and combinations are not the result of mechanical processes, nor of the feeling of the moment. They are filled with a direct and spontaneous sense of the relative values of detail in reference to the whole. All is left out that does not aid in developing the image of this whole; all is put in that will round out the meaning of the details and elevate them into universal and permanent significance.

Idealizing Action of Imagination

Creative imagination, in short, is only the free action of that idealizing activity which is involved in all knowledge whatever. Perception is idealization of sensations so that they become symbolic of some present reality; memory is such an extension of this idealization that past experiences are represented. Imagination takes the idealized element by itself, and treats it with reference to its own value, without regard to the actual existence of the things symbolized. There is an ideal element in both perception and memory, but it is tied down to some particular thing. Creative imagination develops this ideal element, and frees it from its connection with petty and contingent circumstances. Perception and memory both have their worth because of the *meaning* of the perceived or remembered thing, but this meaning is subordinate to the existence of the thing. Imagination reverses the process; existence is subordinate to meaning. We perceive a man because we read into the sensations all that is required to give them this significance; creative imagination instinctively seizes upon this significance, this *idea* of man, and embodies it in some concrete manifestation.

Universalizing Activity of Imagination

Creative imagination is not to be considered as the production of unreal or fantastic forms, nor as the idle play of capricious mind working in an arbitrary way. It is a *universalizing* activity; that is to say, it sets the idea of memory or perception free from its particular accidental accompaniments, and reveals it in its universal nature, the nature which it possesses independent of these varying concomitants. It is thus that Aristotle said that poetry is truer than history, meaning by history the mere record of succession of facts. The latter only tells us that certain things happened; poetry presents to us the permanent passions, aspirations, and deeds of men which are behind all history, and which make it. Keats expresses the same thought when he says:

> *What care though owl did fly*
> *About the great Athenian admiral's mast;*
> *What care, though striding Alexander pass'd*
> *The Indus with his Macedonian numbers?*
>   *Juliet leaning*
> *Amid her window-flowers, sighing, weaning*
> *Tenderly her fancy from its maiden snow*
> *Doth more avail than these; the silver flow*
> *Of Hero's tears, the swoon of Imogen,*
> *Fair Pastorella in the bandit's den,*
> *Are things to brood on with more ardency*
> *Than the death-day of empires.*

Of course, this universalizing activity is not to be confined to the relation of poetry to annals; the function of the creative imagination everywhere is to seize upon the permanent meaning of facts, and embody them in such congruous, sensuous forms as shall enkindle feeling, and awaken a like organ of penetration in whoever may come upon the embodiment.

Imagination and Interest

It will be noticed that imagination presents a stage in the development of knowledge where the self and its interests are explicitly freed from slavery to the results of the action of mechanical association (pages 115 - 16), and are made an end in themselves. Imagination has no external end, but its end is the free play of the various activities of the self, so as to satisfy its interests. Imagination, in short, takes its rise in feeling, and is directed by feeling much more explicitly than either perception or memory. Imagination represents the subjective side of self acting in its freedom. Its forms are as various and numerous as the subjects who exercise it, and as their interests. For this reason it is impossible to lay down rules for the working of the imagination. Its very essence is spontaneous, unfettered play, controlled only by the interests, the emotions and aspirations, of the self.

Individual and Universal Interests

The interests, however, which direct the creative play of the imagination, may be peculiar or general in their nature, and the freedom of its activity may be somewhat arbitrary, or it may express the universal aspect of mankind. Fancy, for example, is directed for the most part by feelings which one individual possesses rather than another, and the same individual, in various ways, at different times of his life. So most poetry of fancy is ephemeral. To a generation other than that in which it is produced it seems unreal and forced. The product of the imagination may also be the result of morbid and unhealthy feeling. It then falls into what Ruskin has well named the "pathetic fallacy"; as when the poet, for example, finds his own particular mood reflected in the workings of nature. Ruskin finds an example of this in Tennyson's "Maud," where the hero attributes his own feelings to the rose and the lily. But there are interests which are universal, common to all persons; and the art

which is the result of these interests is the permanent, enduring art. The poem of Homer, the art of Michael Angelo,
and the drama of Shakespeare are true to the universal side
of humanity, not to the individual and peculiar tastes and
experiences of their authors.

Basis of the Universal Interests

It must be observed that the sole basis of such action of
imagination as is controlled by the universal feelings is a
fundamental unity between man and man and between man
and nature. Were there not such a thing as the unified life of
humanity, with common interests, in spite of separation of
time and space, all workings of the imagination would be
unreal and fantastic. But, more, there must be an organic
connection between man and nature. Man must find himself
in some way in nature. It is not all identification of humanity
with nature that comes under the head of the pathetic fallacy; it is only the identification of temporary, unhealthy, or
fleeting aspects of either. We find joy in any scene of nature
just in the degree in which we find ourselves therein, and are
able to identify the workings of our spirit with those of
nature. The art which deals with nature is perfect and
enduring just in the degree in which it reveals the fundamental unities which exist between man and nature. In
Wordsworth's poetry of nature, for example, we do not find
ourselves in a strange, unfamiliar land; we find Wordsworth
penetrating into those revelations of spirit, of meaning in
nature, of which we ourselves had already some dumb feeling, and this the poetry makes articulate. All products of the
creative imagination are unconscious testimonies to the unity
of spirit which binds man to man and man to nature in one
organic whole.

Practical and Theoretical Imagination

We have spoken so far of imagination as controlled by the
æsthetic interest, the feeling for the beautiful. But it may
also be directed by practical or theoretic interests. All inven-
tions are the result of the creative imagination realizing
some idea in behalf of the practical needs of men. The
discoveries of Wolf or of Niebuhr in history, of Cuvier and

Agassiz in science, are evidence of the constructive power of the imagination in theoretic realms. The sciences of historical geology and astronomy are almost entirely fruits of the constructive imagination. Science, as it advances, makes greater and greater demands upon the imagination, for it recedes further from the sphere of that which is sensuously present to the realm of hidden, ideal significance and meaning, while it is constantly necessary to body these ideas in concrete forms.

Place of Imagination in Knowledge

Imagination, considered in itself, manifests, as we have seen, the free idealizing activity of mind working according to its own subjective interests, and having its end merely in this free play and self-satisfaction. But it has also an aspect as a *stage of knowledge*. As such, it is the transition from the particular stage to the universal. Memory and perception deal with the particular object as such. Thinking, which we shall now take up, is concerned with the universal as such. Imagination deals with the universal in its particular manifestation, or with the particular as embodying some ideal meaning, some universal element. It dissolves this ideal element out of its hard concretion in the sphere of actual particular fact, and sets it before the mind as an independent element, with which the mind may freely work. Such free working of the mind with the universal elements, rendered fluid by imagination, in order to reach certain intellectual ends, constitutes thinking.

NOTES TO CHAPTER 7

Hamilton, *Metaphysics*, lect. xxxiii; Porter, *Human Intellect*, pp. 325 - 76; Carpenter, *Mental Physiology*, ch. xii; Maudsley, *Physiology of Mind*, pp. 522 - 33; Sully, *Psychology*, ch. viii; Day, *Elements of Psychology*, pp. 103 - 31; Lewes, *Problems of Life and Mind*, Third Series, pt. 2, pp. 445 - 63; George, *Lehrbuch der Psychologie*, pp. 274 - 80; Rosenkranz, *Psychologie*, p. 258 ff.; Volkmann, *Lehrbuch der Psychologie*, vol. i, p. 480 ff.; Ulrici, *Der Leib und die Seele*, vol. ii, pp. 270 - 300; Michelet, *Anthropologie und Psychologie*, pp. 284 - 309; Fortlage, essay in *Acht psychologische Vorträge*; Frohschammer, *Die Phantasie*, pp. 73 - 141; and monographs as follows: Michaut and Joly, *L'Imagination;* Rubinstein,

Psychologisch-ästhetische Essays; Cohen, *Die dichterische Phantasie*.

Educational references are to Märkel, *Die Einbildungskraft*; Dörpfeld, *Beiträge zur pädagogischen Psychologie*, vol. i, p. 87 ff.; Grube, *Von der sittlichen Bildung der Jugend*, p. 258 ff.; Perez, *First Three Years of Childhood*, pp. 147 - 63, and *L'Éducation dès le Berceau*, pp. 73 - 110.

Dreams may be most conveniently referred to here: Murray, *Handbook of Psychology*, pp. 250 - 62; Maudsley, *Pathology of Mind*, ch. i; Carpenter, *Mental Physiology*, ch. xv; Sully, in *Encyclopædia Britannica*, and *Illusions*, ch. vii; Cobbe, *Darwinism, and other Essays*; Wundt, *Grundzüge der physiologischen Psychologie*, vol. ii, pp. 359 - 70; and monographs as follows: Scherner, *Das Leben des Traums*; Binz, *Über den Traum*; Spitta, *Die Schlafzustände*; Strümpell, *Die Natur und Entstehung der Träume*; Frensberg, *Schlaf und Traum*; Radestock, same title; Delbœuf, *Le Sommeil et les Rêves*.

8

Stages of Knowledge: Thinking

1] DEFINITION AND DIVISION

Thinking is the next stage in the development of knowledge. Thinking may be defined as *knowledge of universal elements; that is, of ideas as such, or of relations*. In thinking, the mind is not confined, as in perception or memory, to the particular object or event, whether present or past. It has to do, not with this man whom I see, or the one I saw yesterday, but with the idea of man; an idea which cannot be referred to any definite place or time; which is, therefore, general or universal in its nature. Its closest connection is with imagination, which deals with the general element in the form of a particular concrete image, but in imagination the emphasis is upon this particular form, while in thinking the particular form is neglected in behalf of the universal content. We do not imagine man in general; we imagine some characteristic man, Othello, King Arthur, etc. We cannot think a particular man; we think man in general; that is, those universal qualities common to all men—the *class* qualities.

The Ideal Element in Thinking

It is worth noticing that the universal element which is always the object of thought is *ideal*. The phase of *fact* is always particular. It exists now or then; in this or that form. But fact, as we have so often seen, is intelligible only because of its meaning—of the ideal element contained. This ideal element cannot be particular. Meaning is always universal. A fact means, at one time or place, just what it means at another. If the meaning is changed the fact is not the same. Indeed, what we understand by identity, or sameness of fact, is oneness of meaning. It is this element of meaning common to all facts, in so far as they are the same, which thinking seizes upon, to the neglect of the limitation which may be given it by its especial reference to this or that time. Thinking endeavors to discover the *meaning* of facts universally. To think man is to apprehend that universal element of ideal significance which constitutes a man wherever and whenever he is found.

Element of Relation

It is also worth noticing that this universal element of idea or significance which thinking apprehends, without reference to its special embodiment, is always a *relation*. The universal meaning of man is what every man has in common with every other; it is the relation of manhood, whatever that be. It is not the final object of the botanist to perceive or to remember or to imagine vegetable forms, although he must do all this. His final object is to *think* vegetable life; that is, to apprehend the universal essential meaning of these forms. More particularly, it is to discover what growth is, without reference to this or that growing thing in its separateness; to apprehend the nature of a rose, without considering the peculiarities of this, that, or the other rose. It is evident that this object-matter of vegetable life, of growth, of rose, is the relation which all forms of vegetable life possess; which makes them vegetable as opposed to inorganic or animal; it is the relation of growth common to all growing things, and which characterizes them as such; it is the common property, the link, the relation which binds all roses together as members of one class. In short, if things had nothing in common, if each was absolutely distinct from every other, no thinking would be possible. Since every thing *is* distinct from every other in its existence in this or that time or place, the common element is one of meaning or idea. Thinking is possible because there exists in things thought an ideal, universal element. The discovery of this element constitutes thinking; when discovered it is always expressed in the form of a relation.

Aspects of Thinking

There are three aspects of thinking as more or less complete stages of it. These are, conception, judgment, and reasoning. They are not to be considered three distinct acts; not even three successive stages. No one of them could occur without each of the others. Conception, however, is the least, and reasoning the most, developed.

2] CONCEPTION

1. NATURE OF CONCEPTION

Every mental state is, *as an existence*, an image. There are not different kinds of mental existences, one a percept, the other a concept. Their distinction is not in the state of the mind, but in the *function* of this state. A percept is an image referring to some object present in space; a fantasy is an image referring to any object which satisfies an emotional or practical interest, whether or not that object was ever present in space. A concept is an image having the function of symbolizing some law or principle in accordance with which a thing or number of things may be constructed. The number of things constructed on the basis of this single principle is a class, kind, or genus. Thus we solve the old controversy about "universal ideas." Many psychologists have denied that there are general ideas, since every mental state must be particular. An idea of a triangle, for example, must be of an object of a certain size and definite form. It cannot be an idea of all possible sizes and varieties at once. This is true; *as to its existence*, every idea must be particular and have more or less sensuous detail. But it is not the existence that we mean by concept. The concept is the power, capacity, or function of the image or train of images to stand for some mode of mental action, and it is *the mode of action which is general*.

Conception is a Form of the Movement of Intelligence

In a *mere* image of a triangle, what is actually present is the meaning; the particular three lines enclosing a particular space. In the concept of triangle the meaning is *the process by which the three lines are put together* so as to enclose a space. The concept is not the thing, nor the image of the thing. It is the *way* in which lines are made and then combined. And this process, this way of constructing, *is* general. All possible triangles must be made in this same *way.* And anything whatever *made in this way* is a triangle, and thus belongs to the class. A concept, in other words, does not mean a mental state; it is not static. It means a mode of mental movement; a form of mental action; this action involving, as we shall see, isolation or analysis, and putting together or synthesis. So a class does not mean a static group; it means a number of objects having as a basis a common principle of production.

2. *DEVELOPMENT OF CONCEPTION*

Conception, as the apperception of the universal, the grasping of it in a single act of thought, therefore, is not a new kind of knowledge, distinct from perception. It is the more complete development of the element which gives meaning to the percept, and which renders the act of perception possible. When we perceive a book, in the very act of perception we classify it; we bring it under the concept "book." Perception is, as we have repeatedly seen, the idealizing of sensations. The mere existence of sensations does not constitute knowledge of a particular object. Sensations must be interpreted; they must be brought into relation with each other, and with the past experience of the self. Perception is not passive reception; it is the active outgoing construction of mind. In perception, however, these elements of idealization, of relation, of mind activity, are not consciously present; they are absorbed, swallowed up, in the product. In conception they are definitely brought out. *Conception is the apperception of the apperceptive process.* The self here makes its own idealizing, relating activity its object of knowledge; it grasps this activity, and the product is the concept. Conception is, in short, but the development of the idealizing activity involved in all knowledge to the point where it gains distinct conscious recognition, freed from its sensuous, particular detail.

Processes of Conception

1. ABSTRACTION. It is in conception that the stage of apperception called attention, or the active direction of the mind to an end, begins to get the upper hand of the associative

activities predominant in perception and memory, and of the dissociative activity of imagination. It is the selective activity of attention which is most apparent. The mind seizes upon some one aspect of the infinite detail of the perception or the image present to it; in technical language, it abstracts or prescinds it. This very seizure of some one element generalizes the one abstracted. In the perception this quality which attention lays hold on exists absorbed in the object; attention, in drawing it forth, makes it a distinct content of consciousness, and thus universalizes it; it is considered no longer in its connection with the particular object, but on its own account; that is, as an idea, or what it signifies to the mind; and significance is always universal. The other process of attention involved is comparison.

2. COMPARISON. This has already been discussed (page 126), and its essence shown to be the holding of unlike mental contents before the mind with a view to discovering their points of identity, or likeness of significance. This process always goes on along with the emphasizing activity of abstraction just spoken of. When any one element or aspect of an image has been isolated the mind does not stop short with the bare abstract universal thus reached, but immediately proceeds to impose this upon its other images, or to find it in them. Thus a child, when he has got from some salient object, say a plate, the idea of roundness, will find this idea in as many other of his experiences as possible. He goes from the isolated idea to the idea as connected with other objects. This requires the process of comparison; at first unconscious, afterwards purposive.

3. COMPLETE PROCESS OF CONCEPTION. There are thus revealed two processes in conception; one of analysis, the other of synthesis. The first step is one of analysis, of abstraction, of isolation. Its result is a purely abstract universal; as when a child, upon perceiving a red apple, emphasizes, and thus separates, the idea of redness or of edibility. Such an idea is called an *abstract* idea. But the mind never stops here. It immediately connects this idea of redness with as many concrete objects as possible. It enriches each of them by

recognizing that it possesses this quality. It performs an act of synthesis. Only when the reference of the abstract idea to objects is performed is the act of conception completed. A true concept, in other words, is an *organic unity*, containing within its unity synthetic connection with all the diversity of objects to which it refers.

Example

Let us consider again the action of the botanist who is forming his concept of vegetable life. At first, we will say that some salient aspect of vegetable life—growth, assimilation, reproduction, decay—forces itself upon him from some instance. This will remain a purely abstract, and therefore useless, idea, until he compares; that is, until he recognizes the presence of this element in other plants. But every time he does recognize its presence his idea becomes less vague, less abstract, more definite. He recognizes new qualities, which must be included in the idea; every time he perceives a new plant his concept must be somewhat enriched. His concept, with growing experience, becomes, therefore, at once more universal (for it refers to more and more objects) and more definite, for he knows more and more elements which go to make up the conception of vegetable life. It is the same with the growth of every concept. It grows at once in *wideness* of reference and in *depth* of significance. More and more objects are unified by being referred to the conception; more and more diversity is included within it. The concept, in short, is a union of the two elements of unity and difference. It is the recognition of a one comprehending many differences.

Extension and Intension

The logicians distinguish between the extension of a concept and its intension. Extension is the *width* of its symbolism, the number of objects to which it refers; intension is the *depth* of its significance, the number of qualities to which it refers. The logicians further say that the wider the extension the less the intension, and *vice versa*. That is to say, the larger the number of objects included under a concept, the fewer qualities will be contained in the conception of the class. However this may be in formal logic, it has no application to psychological processes. We have already seen that the widening of the grasp of attention does not mean that less attention is paid to the *different* objects included in the grasp, but that these differences are reduced to a more fundamental unity (page 128), and conception only illustrates this same truth.

With all increase of abstract analysis, or widening of extension, goes increase of synthetic connection, or deepening of intension. Were this not so, we would be compelled to say that the more the botanist studies vegetable life the less he knows about it. If the concept were simply the abstract idea of what is *common* to all the objects of the class, each new item, each new plant known, would strike out something of the definiteness of the idea. When the idea had reached reference to all objects of a class, or complete extension, its meaning, or intension, would reach its lowest degree. The more objects known the thinner and poorer the idea of them. The absurdity of this makes us recognize that a true concept is, as was said, an organic unity, growing more *definite* by connection with the diversity of objects, at the same time that it grows more *universal* by reference to the similarities of objects.

Growth of Knowledge

This is a convenient place to refer to a common theory regarding the nature of growth of knowledge. It is too often said that knowledge proceeds from the concrete to the abstract, or from the particular to the general. The fact is that knowledge proceeds from the individual to the individual. The individual with which it begins may be regarded indifferently as exceedingly indefinite or generalized, or as very particular, i.e., non-universal, in its reference. The typical example of this is found in a child's recognition of men. The child first calls his father papa; at the same time he calls all men papa. His idea is very vague; he refers it to the whole class. In this sense, he begins with general knowledge, and his knowledge advances by becoming definite or distinct. He learns to distinguish between his father and other men; between one man and another.

Increase in Universality

But, at the same time, his knowledge is increasing in universality. This vagueness does not constitute true universality, for the child has no recognition of what constitutes a man. He has simply a particular idea which he refers to every individual whom he sees. At the same time that his knowledge becomes more definite, in that he distinguishes between one man and another, it becomes more universal, for he learns what constitutes a man. He no longer calls all men papa, for he recognizes the relation of paternity necessary for this idea; but in calling individuals men, he knows more and more what is *meant* by the term, and meaning is always universal.

Real State of Case

When one says that knowledge begins with the concrete or particular, he overlooks the fact that it is an extremely indefinite or vague particular, and that knowledge advances by making it more definite and distinct, that is, more concrete. When one says that it goes to the general or abstract, he overlooks the fact that this abstract idea is only one phase of conception; that, as matter of fact, the general idea is always immediately referred to some object, and that it is through this reference of universality to the object that the latter gets its definite meaning. The state of the case is that knowledge begins with a vague individual, and advances towards a definite individual, through the medium of relation to other ideas, or of the universalizing of the original idea. The general idea which is the result of analytic abstraction is never left floating in the air, but is synthetically returned upon the individual objects, to their lasting enrichment and growth in meaning or universality. At the same time the universal idea which is thus referred to the diversity of objects included under it becomes more definite. Put concretely, perception grows through the medium of conception; conception grows through its synthetic reference to perceptions.

3. CONCEPTION AND LANGUAGE

It is especially through the medium of language that the universal element of conception gets its reference to particular objects and is made definite. Language is the constant activity of mind seizing upon particular objects and universalizing them by reference to the conception, and seizing upon the conception and particularizing it by connecting it with objects. Every *name* is universal in its nature. When I say "man," I do not say any particular man, this man or that man; I say man "in general," that is, the ideal quality, the significance of man. Language can never get hold of existence; it can only get hold of meaning. Language needs some sensuous pointing index-finger, as the term "this" or "that," connected with gesture, to become particular in its reference.

Language in Existence Particular

Yet we must avoid falling into a common error. It is sometimes said that the idea is always particular, as of this or that man, and becomes general by being brought under the name "man," which is the only universal element. The fact is that the name "man" as an existence is purely sensuous or particular in its nature. It is so much breath, put forth at a certain time, by a certain person, and as *existence* that is all it is. It becomes general only because, by embodying the *idea* in itself, it stands for, represents, symbolizes, all objects possessing this idea or significance. Language has, therefore, a double function. On the one hand, it is purely general in its reference. Without language our capacity for general ideas, or the recognition of relations, of common meaning in different objects, would be almost null. But, on the other hand, language, as purely sensuous and particular in its existence, serves to make abstract ideas concrete or definite, by necessarily connecting them with some object.

Twofold Activity of Mind

It is all-important, in this connection, to recognize that language is not an excrescence of mind or graft upon it; but that it is an essential mode of the expression of its activity.

Conception, as the apprehending of a universal element of meaning, is, as we have seen, the grasping by the mind of its own activity; it is the apperception of the apperceptive process. In conceiving, the mind gets hold of what it has itself put into presentations, namely, meaning. Universalizing is, therefore, one form of the activity of mind. But if this activity of mind remained without a name it would be shapeless; it would be abstract beyond recognition. The mind takes this idea, its own universalizing activity, and particularizes it; it renders it sensuous, concrete, by bodying it forth in language. The abstract idea is projected into real existence through the medium of language.

Language and Mind

It is generally said that animals do not have language because they cannot form general ideas. This is true, but what is generally overlooked is just as true. They are also lacking in the particularizing activity of intelligence. Their ideas are too *abstract*—not lacking in abstractness. They have not the power of rendering them definite, hence they lack language. Language is objective testimony to the twofold activity of mind; in its *meaning*, its *symbolism*, its ideal quality, it is universal; in its *existence*, its real quality, it is particular. Mind is at once a universalizing or ideal activity, and a particularizing or real activity.

3] JUDGMENT

A concept, we have seen, involves reference of the universal element contained in it to a particular definite object; it involves connection of its ideal significance with reality. Judgment is the express affirmation of this connection. It develops and asserts what is contained in the concept. Judgment may be defined as *the express reference of the idea or universal element to reality, the particular element.* In judgment we not only think man, but we affirm that man exists; that this man is a European, is an American; that man has a brain; that he is rational, etc. Judgment takes the concept and says something about it; it makes it definite.

Elements of Judgment

A judgment expressed in language takes the form of a proposition, and includes two elements, the subject and the predicate. All judgments involve both intension and extension, but one of these aspects may be more apparent than the other. For example, when I say that "a lion is a quadruped," the judgment states one element of the meaning of lion, the idea of fourfootedness, and it also includes the lion in the class or number of objects called quadrupeds. When we consider the aspect of intension or meaning, we refer the predicate as the idea to the subject as reality; when we consider the aspect of extension or reference to objects, we refer the subject as the ideal element to the predicate as reality. For example, when I say that "man exists," I may mean to assert either that the quality of existence belongs to the object man, or, more likely, I mean that, among the objects constituting reality, the idea of man is to be also found. The judgment, in short, may either idealize a real thing, by stating its meaning, or it may, so to say, realize an idea by asserting that it is one of the universe of objects. As matter of fact, it always does both.

Judgment the Typical Act

It follows that judgment is the typical act of intelligence. When we were studying the processes of knowledge, we found that apperception consists in giving a presentation meaning by interpreting it or idealizing it. When we studied the material of knowledge, we found that the basis of knowledge is sensation, and that without this basis an idea cannot exist. Apperception idealizes sensation, sensation realizes apperception. In studying the concrete forms—perception, memory, imagination—we have discovered in all cases this dual relation of sensation as real basis, and apperception as ideal interpretation; the elements of meaning and existence. Judgment is not, therefore, a new and hitherto unheard-of act of mind; it is simply the conscious recognition of the essence of every act of mind—the mutual connection of the ideal element with the real. Perception is a judgment of place; memory, a judgment of time; imagination, a judgment of ideal worth.

Judgment and Conception

The relation of judgment and conception is a twofold one. The judgment is an amplification of the conception; and it is also an enrichment of it. All the possible judgments that I can form about gold are, in one sense, so many developments of the conception. When I say that its atomic weight is 197; that it is malleable, soluble in aqua regia, etc., I am only stating so many elements already involved in the conception of gold. But, on the other hand, without these judgments I should never have discovered that these elements were involved in the conception of gold. Each new judgment that I form enables me to include something in the conception of gold not included before. The conception, in this sense, is only a concentration of judgments; it is the result of them; while, on the other hand, judgment is a result of conception. Each presupposes the other.

Analytic and Synthetic Judgments

The judgment, so far as it unfolds something involved in the conception, is analytic; so far as it enriches the conception by some new meaning, or refers it to some reality to which it had not been previously referred, it is synthetic. These are not, therefore, two kinds of judgments; they are two aspects of one and the same judgment. Judgment is at one time synthetic, at another, analytic. This may be put in another way by saying that every judgment affirms both identity and difference.

Examples

If I say that a hog is a pachyderm, it is evident that I identify both ideas; I form a connection or synthesis. What is not so evident is that I also differentiate them, or distinguish between them. That this is so may be seen from the fact that there can be no judgment where there is only one idea. A judgment involves duality. No one, except a formal logician, ever makes an identical judgment only. When we say "a man's a man," we still imply difference. We mean that, in spite of all differences of rank, wealth, education,

etc., every man *is distinguished* by the possession of manhood. We assert distinction as well as unity, though the
latter affirmation is generally more apparent, except in negative judgments. Since every act of intelligence implies both
unification and differentiation, and judgment affirms this
implication, it is evident, from another point of view, that
judgment is the typical act of intelligence.

Falsity and Truth of Judgments

In one sense psychology is not concerned with the distinction
between false and true judgments, as both are equally psychological processes. But, even from a purely psychical
standpoint, a difference is recognized, for the mind regards
some of its judgments as untrue, and proceeds to correct
them, while others it does not change. The psychological
question is simply, therefore, as to the *conditions* under
which the mind regards any judgment as true or false. It is
to be noted, in the first place, that judgment is the act of
mind to which this distinction clings. Both in perception and
in memory the sensuous element is always true, and the act
of the mind is always true. To speak more correctly, they are
facts which exist, and to which the distinction of falsity or truth does not apply. The element of truth comes in
only when one is referred to the other; that is, in the judgment.

Examples

If, for example, one perceives a ghost, the sensuous element
is really there, and is just what it is. The act of mind also
takes place. Each of these is a fact, and cannot be called true
or false. At most it may be called normal or abnormal. The
element of truth comes in when one is connected with the
other; that is to say, when the sensuous presentation is
interpreted by the act of mind, as an existing ghost. This is
the reference of the ideal element to reality, or the judgment. Only a judgment, accordingly, can be true or false.
From a psychological standpoint a judgment is called true
when it harmonizes with all other judgments; false when it
is in contradiction to some other. Suppose, for example, an
individual interprets a distant cloud as a mountain. The

judgment is false, because it does not agree with other judgments which he would be forced to make about the presentation with growing knowledge of it. If I interpret a shadowy form, seen in dim moonlight, as a tree, and the judgment is true, it is so because all other judgments which I can make about it will be in harmony with this one. Truth, in short, from a psychological standpoint, is agreement of relations; falsity, disagreement of relations.

Test of Truth

It follows from what has just been said that the mind always tests the truth of any supposed fact by comparing it to the acquired system of truth. When a novel proposition is brought before the mind, intelligence views it in the light of what it already regards as true, or in the light of relations previously laid down. If the new relation coincides with the former, still more if the new one expands them, or *vice versa*, it is judged to be true; if there is irreconcilable conflict, one or the other must be false.

It must not be thought from this that the mind has any ready-made test existing within it by whose application it can decide upon the falsity or truth of any judgment. There is no simple criterion or rule for determining truth which can be applied immediately to every judgment; the only criterion is relation to the whole body of acquired knowledge, or the acquired system of relations, so far as it is realized. The worth of the criterion will evidently depend upon the degree in which the intelligence has been realized and knowledge acquired.

Belief

This introduces us naturally to the subject of belief. Belief is, perhaps, emotional in character, while its test is volition, but its content is always fixed by knowledge. It is the subjective side of knowledge. To believe a thing is to regard it as true. The most important point regarding the psychology of belief is the recognition that it is not a separate state of mind over and beyond the judgment, but is a necessary accompaniment of it. Every act of intelligence, every assertion, that is, of a relation, is believed to be true. Intelligence must recognize its own existence, its own workings; and this recognition is belief. Intelligence must believe in itself, and must therefore accompany every judgment, so far as it is considered as an exercise of intelligence, with belief in its truth.

Doubt

But the mind learns, in growing experience, that not every judgment does agree with the conditions of universal intelligence; that is, it discovers that some of its judgments contradict others. It thus arrives at a state of suspense; it is not sure whether *this particular* judgment agrees or not with itself, with the whole system of knowledge. It learns that a great many, perhaps most of its judgments, have to be corrected with growing experience, and thus it learns to assume a state of suspended judgment. It no longer assumes truth, as the child's mind does; it waits for evidence; and by evidence is meant simply token of the connection of the relation under consideration with the whole body of relations which constitute intelligence.

Unbelief

When the evidence points to the particular given relation not standing in harmonious relation with the entire body of known truth, the mind assumes an attitude of unbelief. But it must be noted that unbelief is only a particular act of mind; it cannot be universal. Universal unbelief would be unbelief of intelligence in intelligence, and this is self-contradictory. More concretely, every definite unbelief presupposes belief. We disbelieve *this* or *that* particular judgment because we believe, first, in the general workings of intelligence; and, secondly, because we believe some other judgment is true which contradicts this one. We disbelieve *this*, in short, because we believe *that*; unbelief is only a special case of belief. Denial must be because of some affirmation.

4]   REASONING

The whole previous discussion has been such as to make us recognize that there is no such thing as purely *immediate* knowledge. Any cognition is dependent; that is, it is *because of* some other cognition. The act which is apparently most immediate is perception. But perception, as when I say this is a book, is still *mediated*. The sensation which I have, the direct presentation, does not tell me that this is a book. I know that this is a book when I can refer these present sensations to my past experience and interpret them thereby. Were it not for this act of reference the sensations would have no meaning, and would not be interpreted as a book, or as anything else. All knowledge implies, in short, a going beyond what is sensuously present to its connection with something else, and it is this act of going beyond the present which constitutes the mediate factor.

Definition of Reasoning

In perception, in memory, in judgment, however, this mediate element is absorbed in the result. We do not recognize when we say, "This is a book," "Snow is white," "Columbus discovered America in 1492," "I once saw General Grant," that there is a *reason* for each of these psychical acts, outside of itself, and that the whole meaning of each depends on its relation to this something beyond. We perform the act and get the result because, indeed, of something else; but we do not recognize the because. All meaning is *through* relation to something else, but in the results so far studied we have neglected that *through* which each result is, and have considered it only as a result. Reasoning is the explicit recognition of this mediate element involved in all knowledge. It is consciously knowing that a thing is so *because* of, or through, its relations, its reference to something beyond its own existence. It is, therefore, no new act of knowledge, but the development of the act upon which all knowledge depends. Reasoning may accordingly be defined as *that act of mind which recognizes those relations of any content of consciousness through which it has the meaning which it* has, or is what it is.

Implicit Reasoning

Ordinarily the relation is recognized through a particular case. We say, "This is snow," *because* it is like the snow we experienced last winter. We conclude from one particular instance to another. So the child says, "This fire will burn," because he has seen some other fire that burned. He throws iron into the water to see it sink, because some other heavy body has sunk. If all bodies which he had thrown in had sunk he would conclude that a piece of cotton would sink likewise. Such reasoning, in short, simply goes from the likeness of one case to another without recognizing in what the likeness consists. This is called *implicit* reasoning. Every perception, every remembrance, is a case of implicit reasoning. If the child interprets certain sensations and says that he sees a man, it is because of the likeness, unconsciously recognized, of this experience to others.

Explicit Reasoning

The mind may, however, consciously recognize the element of identity which connects the two cases; it may know *why* it calls this substance snow, and why it expects that fire will burn. It will recognize in the present object those properties which constitute snow—water, reduced to a certain temperature and crystallized in a certain way. It will perceive in the burning of fire an exemplification of a general law of molecular action. It will not merely proceed from the likeness of one case to make some assertion about another, but it will recognize that it does so, and also in what the identity consists. This is *explicit* reasoning, and to it the term reasoning is generally confined.

Universal Element in Reasoning

Reasoning, whether implicit or explicit, is dependent upon the presence of a relation, that is, of a universal factor. When we reason from one particular case to another and say, "This drug will cure your disorder because it cured mine," the basis of the conclusion is still a universal element. The person identifies one disorder with another, and reasons that what a drug does once it will always do. The trouble with such reasoning is not that it is too particular, but that it is too general. It overlooks any differences that may exist between the disorders which will cause the drug to act differently in the two cases, and lumps them both under the vague and general ideas—disorder, cure. Explicit reasoning discovers the universal element, the relation of identity, which is at work in implicit reasoning. It says that this drug will cure the disorder because of a certain relation existing between the two. Its advantage over implicit reasoning is that it does not perform the identification at a jump, but looks to see where the relation, the universal element, really is.

Particular Element in Reasoning

It follows, from what has been said, that reasoning involves the particular element as well as the universal. Reasoning always connects the universal and the particular; judgment does this also, as when one says that wood floats. Here we may say that the universal idea of wood is made more definite and particular by attributing to it the possession of a certain quality; or we may say that the particular idea of wood is brought under the wider and more general idea of floating, according as we regard it as a judgment of intension or of extension. In either case it expresses the relation of a particular with a universal element; and what reasoning does is to *develop the ground or reason* of this relation. *This* piece of wood floats because it possesses a characteristic of wood in general—a certain specific gravity. Here reasoning universalizes the particular, for it finds the reason for a particular fact in a universal relation or law. Or we say wood *floats*, because the general idea of wood is *distinguished* by the possession of this quality. Here reasoning particularizes the universal. It finds the connection of a universal relation with a particular definite case.

A Priori and A Posteriori Reasoning

This enables us to understand a distinction sometimes made between empirical and rational thought, or knowledge *a posteriori*, the result of experience, and knowledge *a priori*, the result of reason. These are often treated as if they were two kinds of knowledge, instead of being, as they really are, two stages in the development of knowledge. Empirical knowledge goes from one particular to another by means of the universal element which connects them, but is not conscious of the universal element. Reason recognizes the universal element, the relation, and uses it to connect one particular, one fact, with another. All knowledge is, as we have seen, the recognition of reason; for it is the recognition of relation, and reasoning is the act of relating. Perception is the recognition that an object is such or such, *because* it has the same *meaning* as some past experience; that is, is identical with it in significance, though not in existence. As recognition of *meaning*, it is recognition of reason, for meaning is the connection of sensuous presentations with past experiences, and reasoning is the act of connecting. *A posteriori* knowledge is simply the *unconscious* recognition of the universal element, or relation, the ideal significance; *a priori* knowledge is the conscious recognition of it. For example, if one simply notices that a loud noise accompanies an explosion, such knowledge is rightly called empirical. But if one discovers an identity of internal connection between the two facts the knowledge is rational. The known fact is no longer a mere coincidence, but depends upon a necessary relation. Knowledge, in one case, is *a posteriori*, for it follows the occurrence; in the other, it is *a priori*, for the relation is the condition of the event.

Inductive and Deductive Reasoning

All reasoning, accordingly, connects a universal and a particular element. Its procedure may, however, be in either direction. It may consist in making the particular universal, by bringing it under the head of some law, and thus giving it the properties of a class. This act of bringing a particular under a universal, or of imposing a universal upon a particular, is called *deduction*. It may be illustrated as follows: This substance has a less specific gravity than water; all such substances float; therefore this substance floats. The reason for a particular fact is found in the general relation. If the mind, however, starts from the particular facts, and discovers in them the universal, the law, the process is one of *induction*. A scientific man, for example, investigates some oxygen, and finds its atomic weight to be 16. He immediately says that the atomic weight of oxygen is 16; not of *this* oxygen examined alone, but of oxygen, the substance, generally. He regards the particular as an instance of a class, and finds in the part the law of the whole. He isolates some one relation from the complex whole. This act constitutes induction. The universal is discovered *in* the particular.

Synthesis and Analysis

We have seen from our study of the mind that it is always active in the discovery of relations of identity and of difference; that it unites and separates. Deduction and induction are not new, previously unexperienced activities of the mind. They are the reappearance of the identifying and distinguishing activities. They are highly developed forms of the process of attention. Deduction is synthetic. It connects the universal relation with this or that special case; it finds that the apple falls to the ground because of the law of gravitation. It enriches the particular by adding a new element, a new quality, a new significance, to it. Induction is analytic. It examines some particular so as to discover its law. It concentrates attention upon the meaning of the fact and neglects all else. It neglects all the diverse and particular elements in the fact so as to separate out its universal element, and thus discover the law, the *idea* of the object.

Effect of Each

Induction, or analytic reasoning, sees the law in the light of the fact; deductive, or synthetic, sees the fact in the light of the law. Induction is more abstract than deduction, for it ends in the discovery of a general relation only, while deduction goes back to the fact with this law, and adds it to the meaning of the fact, thereby making it concrete. The ultimate effect of deduction is, therefore, greater distinctness or definiteness. The fact which has been connected with a law by way of deduction is more definite than it was before; it is transfigured by the possession of a new *property*. Induction, on the other hand, tends towards identification. It makes us lose sight of the differences that exist between this and that stone, the stone and the bullet, each and the earth, the earth and all planets, in the fact that all are falling bodies and come under the same law. It identifies them.

Each Involves the Other

We saw, when studying attention, that the distinguishing and identifying activities are not two kinds of action, but different aspects of the same self-developing activity of mind. The same is true of induction and deduction. In the first place, each leads to the other. Deduction is a synthetic activity, yet it ends in rendering its object more distinct, more defined, i.e., more separated. Induction is an analytic activity, yet it ends in rendering its object more unified, more identified with other objects, i.e., more connected with them.

This is because induction never stops with itself, but immediately leads to deduction. The scientific man is not content with the general statement that the atomic weight of oxygen is 16, but he returns with this general law to every specific chemical fact which he knows, thereby enriching them. But deduction as surely implies induction. The fact which has been made more specific through deduction has also been made more universal. It does not possess this definite property as an isolated object, but as one of a class, as having a common relation or law. The universal is detected in the particular, and this is induction. Induction and deduction are aspects of the same act, and each occurs *through* the other.

Example

We may take, to illustrate this point, mathematics; say geometry. This is ordinarily taken as the type of a deductive or synthetic science, because it advances from certain highly general axioms and definitions, by a process of construction, to highly specific and definite assertions about definite relations, or particular forms of space, each new step being derived or deduced from the preceding. Yet it is evident that the process has been, at the same time, one of analysis. The idea of space, with which we began, was a thoroughly vague, undefined notion; the development of the science of geometry has been to split it up into definite specific relations. We know a great deal more about the *particulars* of space than we did before. We have also been discovering, in every element of space treated, the triangle, the circle, certain general laws or relations exemplified; and this is the essence of induction.

Physics, on the contrary, is generally called an inductive science, because it starts from the investigation of certain facts, and ends in the discovery of certain laws; it analyzes the facts and finds certain relations in them. Yet it is also a process of synthesis, for we not only know the laws, but we know immensely more about the facts than we did before. Each fact is more distinct, because it is seen exemplifying the action of certain laws, or involving certain relations, and this perception of a fact in the light of a law is the essence of deduction. Deduction and induction are, in truth, two aspects of the same process; and any given method will be called one or the other from the aspect that predominates.

Fact and Law

It follows that the two elements of law and fact cannot be separated from each other. Law is the *meaning* of fact; it is its universal aspect; the side that gives it relation. It is necessary to fact, for only that is a fact to intelligence which has meaning, which signifies something or points beyond itself. Sensation, as mere psychical existence, does not constitute fact. A sensation, as such, never enters into knowledge; it must be transformed, that is, *related*. In perception and memory we do not, it is true, recognize the presence of the relation or universal element; we do not see what it is that is pointed towards; while in reasoning we do bring this element of significance into conscious recognition, and see that what is pointed towards is a relation, a law. Every new relation or law that is discovered adds so much to the meaning of the fact; it makes it so much more of a fact for us.

Law, on the other hand, has no existence for us except in connection with some fact. When out of all connection with fact, it is absolutely meaningless to us; it is pure abstraction; and just in the degree in which it is brought into connection with fact it becomes definite, and hence significant. In other words, fact and law are abstract ways of looking at the same mental content. When we abstract its particular aspect, its definite side, we regard it as fact; when we abstract its universal side, its relation of identity, we regard it as meaning or law. But every concrete mental content, every actuality for psychology, is a union of universal and particular, of identity and difference, of fact and meaning, of reality and ideal significance. It is not a mechanical unity, so that we can separate out each, but a living one.

Process of Mind in Knowledge

Fact and law are not, therefore, to be opposed to the activity of mind as something set over against it. Each is rather the result of one function of the mind's activity. Fact and law cannot be regarded as anything except two ways of looking at the same content, because one is the expression of the differentiating activity of mind and the other of its identifying activity, and these two modes of activity cannot be separated from each other. When we look at the aspect of fact, we are considering the result of the *distinguishing* function of mind; we are considering the content as rendered definite by the possession of certain particular properties. When we look at the aspect of law, we are considering the result of the *identifying* function of mind; we are considering the content as rendered universal by the possession of a mental significance or *idea*. Each of these functions is an abstraction; in actual knowledge we always identify and distinguish. In other words, all actual knowledge proceeds from the individual to the individual.

Conception, Judgment, Reasoning

Judgment, we have already seen, stands in a twofold relation to conception. In one aspect, its analytic, it is based on the concept and develops it; in the other, its synthetic, it returns into the concept and enriches it, by connecting some new element with it. Reasoning, it is now seen, stands in a like relation to judgment, and therefore to conception. It is based on judgment, for it takes two or more judgments, that is, affirmations of relations, and analyzes them to discover the common or identical relation which unites them. And it expresses this in the form of a new judgment. Thus, Sir Isaac Newton took two judgments, one regarding the revolution of the moon, and another regarding a falling body, and, analyzing them, arrived at a relation common to both: he reduced both judgments to one in the new judgment of the law of gravitation. But this does not remain an isolated judgment. It is carried back to the judgments from which it was analyzed out, and combined with them, so that, as soon as we know the law of gravitation, we know more about the revolution of the moon and the falling of bodies than we did before. In short, the process of reasoning has resulted in the enrichment of the judgment; it is more definite and concrete than it was before.

The Individual the End of Knowledge

All knowledge is therefore of an individual. There are two elements which cannot of themselves be, by any possibility, the object of knowledge; one is the isolated particular, the other is the isolated universal. The isolated particular is that which has no relation to anything beyond itself; it is not universalized by any relation. It is the result of the distinguishing activity of mind, supposing that this could go on alone. The isolated universal is that which is simply a relation; it is not made definite by its synthetic reference to that which is related. What is actually known is always a combination of the universal and the particular, of law and fact; in other words, an individual. The individual known is becoming constantly a richer object of knowledge, by virtue of the two processes of universalization and definition. The individual known is always becoming more universal because it is being identified with other individuals under some common relation or idea. It is becoming more definite, for these various relations which are thus recognized are taken into it, and become part of its content; they enlarge its significance and serve to distinguish it. A completely universalized or related individual, which is at the same time perfectly definite or distinct in all its relations, is, therefore, the end of knowledge. Each special act of knowledge is the recognition of an individual which is yet in process of identification and distinction. This we learned is the process of attention (page 126).

5] SYSTEMATIZATION

Final Presupposition

It is now evident that the very tendency towards knowledge, or the activity of intelligence, is based upon relation. It presupposes that there is no such thing as an isolated fact in the universe, but that all are connected with each other as members of a common whole. The final presupposition is that every fact is dependent or mediated. It is not what it is by its own independent existence. Considered as such it has no meaning whatever, and hence is no possible object of intelligence. Each is what it is, because of its connection with and dependence upon others. Reasoning is the act of mind which recognizes this dependence, and develops the modes of connection. But reasoning confines itself to the special relations which connect facts. It does not deal with the truth that all these relations are also related to each other, and are factors of one harmonious whole.

Process of Systematization

This higher development of reasoning, which not only develops relations of dependence between one fact and another, but which also consciously recognizes that there is no such thing as an isolated relation, but that all constitute a system, is called systematization. It is in result what we call "science" and "philosophy," which are not only knowledge, but co-ordinated knowledge arranged in connected form. Each special branch of science is one form of this attempt at harmonious system. Philosophy is the attempt to systematize or arrange in their organic unity all special branches of science. No isolated science fulfils the end of knowledge or is complete system, because in it the analytic activity predominates over the synthetic. Science in its completeness, including the synthetic function, is philosophy.

Scientific and Ordinary Knowledge

Science is the attempt to reduce the world to a unity, by seeing all the factors of the world as members of one common system. Its various subordinate unities are expressed in the form of *laws*, but science is not complete with the formulation of analytic laws. These laws must not remain isolated, but must be referred, as far as possible, to some more comprehensive law, and thus connected with each other as factors of one whole. The highest form of knowledge previously studied—reasoning—develops, as we saw, what had been implied in all previous knowledge—namely, the dependence of every fact of knowledge upon its relations to other facts. This presupposition of all knowing whatever, that all facts are related to each other as members of one system, science more consciously develops, explicitly setting forth the relations.

Philosophic Knowledge

Philosophy, as complete science, aims to do this fully. It is, therefore, no new kind of knowledge, but is the conscious development of what is unconsciously at the heart of all knowledge—the presence of unity in variety. It is the attempt to find a true *universe*; a world which, in spite of its difference, or rather *through* its difference, is one. It is the attempt to fulfil the conditions of all knowledge, and to recognize the world as one; in other words, to reach an individual object of knowledge which is at the same time thoroughly universal. The details of philosophy as well as of science we are not concerned with in psychology. We have only to recognize them as exemplifications of the law of all knowledge, and thus show their psychological origin and position.

NOTES TO CHAPTER 8

Hamilton, *Metaphysics*, lects. xxxiv - xxxvii; Porter, *Human Intellect*, pp. 376 - 491; Morell, *Elements of Psychology*, pp. 204 - 58; Lewes, *Problems of Life and Mind*, Third Series, pt. 2, p. 463; Bain, *Senses and Intellect*, pp. 524 - 38; Sully, *Psychology*, chs. ix and x; Murray, *Handbook of Psychology*, pp. 185 - 219; Spencer,

Principles of Psychology, vol. i, pp. 453 - 72; vol. ii, pp. 6 - 17, 521 - 38; Taine, *Intelligence*, pt. 1, bk. i, chs. ii and iii; Laurie, *Metaphysica*, pp. 27 - 34, 53 - 83; Bradley, *Principles of Logic*, pp. 1 - 39 (judgment); pp. 235 - 49, 396 - 411, 430 - 50 (reasoning); pp. 412 - 29 (analysis and synthesis); George, *Lehrbuch der Psychologie*, pp. 400 - 53; Bergmann, *Grundlinien einer Theorie des Bewusstseins*, pp. 129 - 54; Herbart, *Lehrbuch zur Psychologie*, pt. 3, §2, ch. ii; Strümpell, *Grundriss der Psychologie*, pp. 252 - 65; Horwicz, *Psychologische Analysen*, vol. ii, pt. 1, pp. 9 - 55; Wundt, *Logik*, vol. i, pp. 37 - 131 (concepts); pp. 134 - 54 (judgment); pp. 270 - 90 (reasoning); Sigwart, *Logik*, vol. ii, pp. 156 - 76 (concepts); Lotze, *Logik*, pp. 14 - 57 (concepts); *Philosophische Studien*, vol. ii, p. 161.

References to the psychology of language may also be conveniently made here as follows: Calderwood, *Relations of Mind and Brain*, ch. x; Maudsley, *Pathology of Mind*, pp. 475 - 81; Ferrier, *Functions of Brain*, pp. 269 - 80; Lotze, *Microcosmus*, pp. 601 - 39; Taine, in *Mind*, vol. ii, p. 252; Perez, *First Three Years of Childhood*, pp. 236 - 64; George (*op. cit.*), pp. 331 - 41; Rosenkranz, *Psychologie*, pp. 283 - 95; Michelet, *Anthropologie und Psychologie*, pp. 368 - 407; Steinthal, *Einleitung in die Psychologie und Sprachwissenschaft*, pp. 44 - 71, 359 - 487; Lazarus, *Das Leben der Seele*, vol. ii, pp. 87 - 345; Wundt, *Grundzüge der physiologischen Psychologie*, vol. ii, pp. 428 - 40; Preyer, *Die Seele des Kindes*, pp. 259 - 391; Gerber, *Die Sprache und das Erkennen*; Geiger, *Ursprung und Entwickelung der menschlichen Sprache und Vernunft*; Kussmaul, *Störungen der Sprache*; Stricker, *Studien über die Sprachvorstellungen*. Lazarus and Steinthal are the best authorities upon the purely psychological aspects of language.

Upon the pedagogy of thinking, see De Guimps, *L'Éducation*, pp. 264 - 334; Joly, *Notions de Pédagogie*, pp. 80 - 113; Thring, *Theory and Practice of Teaching*, pp. 155 - 64; Perez (*op. cit.*), pp. 164 - 235; Beneke, *Erziehungs- und Unterrichtslehre*, pp. 122 - 41.

9

Stages of Knowledge: Intuition

Mutual Implication of Stages of Knowledge

The general law of knowledge, that *knowledge is a process of recognition of the individual through the functions of analysis and of synthesis*, is applicable, of course, to the stages of knowledge themselves, or rather these are so many manifestations of the law. If we begin, as we have done in this book, with perception and ascend to systematization, it is evident that we follow the analytic, identifying, or universalizing function. But attention has been frequently called to the fact that each of these more general processes returns upon the lower and enriches it. It has been shown that perception is as impossible without conception, or the presence of the universal element, as conception is without perception as the definite element.

Two Scales in Knowing

In short, every higher analytic stage immediately influences the lower process, rendering it more definite. It is synthetically combined with it. Every process of reasoning expands a judgment; every judgment enlarges a concept; every concept adds new meaning to a percept. As we universalize, we also see the particular more in the light of the universal, and thus make it more significant and more definite. Without the process of mediation or reasoning there is no perception; the more the element of reasoning is involved, the more does the percept mean, or tell us of the object. There is a complete implication of every stage of self-development in every other. The scale from perception to systematization looks at the development as an analytic process of growing universality; the scale from systematization back, looks at it as a synthetic process of growing definiteness. As matter of actual psychological fact, there is no separation of ascending and descending movements, but every concrete act of mind is an act both of perception and reasoning, and each because of and through the other. This is but another way of saying that all knowledge involves both the identifying and the distinguishing activities.

Intuition

It follows, in a word, that every concrete, actually-performed psychological result is an *intuition*, or knowledge of an individual. The acts previously studied are abstractions. It is necessary to perform these abstractions in order that the various elements involved in knowledge may be brought into consciousness, and our comprehension of the nature of knowledge become more definite. What we call perception is a concrete act of mind involving both the universalizing and the distinguishing activities; but all the weight, the emphasis of attention, is thrown upon the latter function. In reasoning, attention isolates especially the universalizing function; but, as matter of fact, neither of these can exist without the other, and their union constitutes knowledge of an individual. The phase of reasoning makes this individual more and more universal or related in character; the phase of perception makes it more definite. The union of perception and reasoning involved in every act constitutes *intuition*.

Nature of Intuition

Intuition is often conceived to mean a purely *immediate* act, or one taking place without the recognition of any relation of dependence. Intuition is defined in a way which opposes it to reasoning and excludes the latter. It is thought to be an act of mind in which the mind is wholly taken up with the *presented* content, and does not advance at all beyond what is thus given; it is opposed to all *mediation*. Something perceived by intuition is supposed to be just what it is by virtue of its own independent existence. We are in a position to recognize that there cannot possibly be intuition of such a kind. Every act of mind involves relation; it involves dependence; it involves *mediation*. A thing as known gets its meaning by its symbolism; by what it points to beyond itself.

Intuition must be defined to include this factor.

Ultimate Knowledge

When, however, we come to know ultimate reality, it is evident that this cannot be related to anything beyond itself; it can symbolize only itself. All dependence, all mediation, must be *within* itself. Intuition is most properly confined to those acts of knowledge, therefore, in which we know ultimate wholes; that which is related to self instead of being only externally related. It is needful to recognize that such wholes exist only by virtue of the distinctions, the relations, which are comprehended *within* themselves. The analytic act, the development of relations of identity, has been completely performed, and these relations are now reflected back into the object, and, synthetically connected with it, serve completely to distinguish it, or make it definite. In the act of intuition we grasp that which is self-related.

Stages of Intuition

Every act of knowledge is, in some sense or other, the recognition of something self-related, or an individual, for it involves the synthetic return of the relation into the content known. Perception, memory, imagination, conception, etc.—each of these is an act of intuition, and consequently the recognition of something self-related. But the recognition of self-relation may be more or less complete. The botanist's knowledge of a tree is more intuitive than that of an ordinary man, because he sees in it more of those relations to the universe which constitute the real life of the tree. Recognizing more relations, more laws, he is able to combine more into the knowledge of the object, and thus his knowledge of it includes more of self-relation than that of any one else. So of all objects; the more universality is recognized, the more truly self-related does the object known become. We again arrive at the conclusion that, while every concrete act of knowledge is one of intuition, the term may be most appropriately applied to the most developed acts of knowledge; those, that is to say, in which the greatest amount of individualized or synthetic universality is recognized. These may be spoken of under three heads: 1.

Intuition of the world; ii. Intuition of self; iii. Intuition of God.

i.   Intuition of the World

We are concerned here with our knowledge of nature as a whole. After what has been said so many times, there is no need of repeating that since unity is presupposed in every act of intelligence, every act of knowledge of the external world is an intuition. The *wholeness* of the world, the truth that all things and events are in unison with each other, is implied in the simplest perception, and the further acts of knowledge consist only in developing this unity and rendering it explicit and definite. The intuition of which we are to speak, the recognition of nature as a system, is not, therefore, a new act of knowledge, but simply the more complete development of perception, memory, etc., which are also acts of intuition. We shall speak first of the process of this more complete development.

Growth of Intuition of Nature

It begins with the recognition of *things*. The first intuition is that of *existence* or *reality*. We recognize that we not only have sensations, but that these sensations are objectified, and constitute a world. The first stage of intuition may be said to be that there is such a thing as an *object*, a *world* at all, giving rise to the *conception of substance*. But the mind immediately advances beyond this highly general intuition to a recognition that the plurality of objects and events which are real, or exist, are in space and time. The intuition of space, as the condition of the coexistence of objects, and the intuition of time as the condition of the sequence of events, constitute the more perfect definition of the intuition of reality.

Second Stage

There comes, then, the intuition of force or motion. We recognize that objects are not only separated in space and time, but that they are in dynamic relations with each other; that they are constantly exchanging places in space, and passing into each other in time. We have an intuition not only of space and time, but of that spatial change which we call *motion*, and of that temporal change which we call *force*. From these intuitions the mind forms the *conception* of *cause and effect*.

Third Stage

The mind advances beyond the recognition of change to the recognition of the regularity, the constancy, of change. It *perceives* that all spatial changes are connected with temporal changes—that is, manifestations of force—and it further recognizes that these manifestations are connected with each other in an orderly, permanent way. It thus gets the intuition of order, or relation. From this intuition the mind forms the *conception* of *law*. It is evident that each stage of intuition grasps something more of the wholeness of the world, and renders that wholeness more definite. In the intuition of thing, or reality, each appears separate from every other, though we know that their unity is implied. In the intuition of space and time we recognize space and time as one, indeed, but we do not recognize the necessary unity of each with the objects and events existing and occurring in it. The intuitions of force and motion enable us to make this unification, and see nature more as a whole; and if we add the intuition of relation, we see all parts interconnected.

Final Stage

This originates the final stage of intuition. Here we have the intuition of reality as a whole, defined and particularized indeed by its existence in space and time, but yet universalized by its connections of order and permanence, expressed in the laws which constitute its unity. Here every fact is seen as dependent upon and necessitated by its relations to every fact. The aim is to see in every part of nature the law of the whole; to see exemplified in any fact the relations of the whole system. It finds a poetical expression in the following lines of Tennyson:

> *Flower in the crannied wall,*
> *I pluck you out of the crannies;—*

> *Hold you here, root and all, in my hand,*
> *Little flower—but if I could understand*
> *What you are, root and all, all in all,*
> *I should know what God and man is.*

It must be remembered that this is truly an intuition, for we *see* in the part the whole. This constitutes its difference from systematization. For *complete* intuition, that activity of the mind implied in science and philosophy is doubtless necessary, but systematization is not intuition. It is only the highest means by which the original intuition, knowledge of an individual thing, becomes complete intuition, or knowledge of the universe as an individual. It is only necessary to add that from this intuition of completeness of interdependence, the mind forms the *conception* of *necessity*.

Transition to Intuition of Self

It must be noticed that, as the growth of intuition of nature towards completeness occurs, we approach nearer and nearer to the self. Each new stage comprehends within itself a more universal relation than the preceding, and hence leads more nearly to the recognition of the action of intelligence. In the intuition of *things*, and even of space and time, what is perceived seems opposed to intelligence (page 141); when we perceive order, we are, in truth, perceiving the ordering action of intelligence; when we perceive the world as an interdependent whole, every part of which is in orderly connection with every other, we are perceiving objectified intelligence; for this unification of relations is precisely the work of intelligence. Or, put in a more psychological way, this intuition of the whole in a part is the recognition of *all* that the part *means*, and meaning is put into fact from the activity of the self (pages 125 - 26). We are thus led to

II. The Intuition of Self

We are concerned here especially with what is called self-consciousness, or the knowledge of the self as a universal, permanent activity. We must, however, very carefully avoid supposing that self-consciousness is a new and particu-

lar kind of knowledge. The self which is the object of
intuition is not an object existing ready made, and needing
only to have consciousness turned to it, as towards other
objects, to be known like them as a separate object. The
recognition of self is only the perception of what is involved
in every act of knowledge. The self which is known is, as we
saw in our study of apperception and retention, the *whole*
body of knowledge as returned to and organized into the
mind knowing. The self which is known is, in short, the
ideal side of that mode of intuition of which we just spoke—it
is their meaning in its unity. It is, also, a more complete
stage of intuition, for, while in the final stage of intuition of
nature we perceive it as a whole of interdependent relations,
or as self-related, we have yet to recognize that we leave out
of account the intelligence from which these relations proceed. In short, its true existence is in its relation to mind;
and in self-consciousness we advance to the perception of
mind.

Stages of Growth of Intuition of Self

The self is a connecting, relating activity, and hence is a real
unity, one which unites into a whole all the various elements
and members of our knowledge. In association and in attention it is the activity of mind which associates and which
attends, and thus only does our mental life become significant in its products (page 78). The self is consequently the
bond of unity. There is no member of our psychical life, no
object of knowledge, which is not such because the self has
acted upon it, and made it what it is. All knowledge is
knowledge of and through self. In knowing anything whatever we know some activity of self, and therefore all knowledge is an intuition of self, just as it is an intuition of the
world. But in the first stages of knowledge this is not recognized. We recognize only *meaning* or *significance*, without
recognizing where it comes from—the mind. The first intuition may be called that of *ideality*, as opposed to reality in
the intuition of the world; it is *meaning* as opposed to *thing*.
The mind, on the basis of it, forms the *conception* of *unity
and universality*.

Final Stage

The development of the intuition of self consists simply in *recognizing* more and more of what is implied in the simplest acts of knowledge. The activity of self is involved in perception. In memory some of this activity, that by which elements are related in time, is re-cognized. We re-know what we knew before, and in so doing develop some factor of which we were previously unconscious. There is no need to follow the process through in detail, but it is evident that every higher "faculty" in re-knowing the lower, brings out more and more of the activity of the self implied in it, until we get to complete self-consciousness, which is the recognition of the whole of self in any special act of self. From the intuition of self we form the *conception* of *freedom*, as we recognize that the process is one which goes on through self alone.

Transition to Intuition of God

There is no knowledge which does not include both the particular and the universal factor. There is no knowledge which does not include both the real and the ideal element. In the two previous intuitions we have treated each as if it could exist independent of the other, though we saw that intuition of the world, as a unity of interdependent relations, implies the self. We know, also, that knowledge of the self would be entirely without content were it not for the acts of apperception which it is always performing, and which, when performed, are *retained* or *organized* into the self (page 133), and thus make it real. In short, we know the world because we idealize it; we know the self because we realize it. Every concrete act of knowledge must involve both factors. This brings us to the complete stage of intuition.

III. Intuition of God

Neither the world nor the knowing self can be called truly self-related. The world gets its existence as known only because of its relations to the activity of the intelligence knowing; the intelligence knowing becomes a definite actuality only through the relations which it puts forth in construing the world. The true self-related must be the organic unity of the self and the world, of the ideal and the real, and this is what we know as God. It must be remembered that this intuition is one like in kind to the other intuitions, and involves the process of mediation as much as they. It is not a unity which has no relations, but a unity which is self-related. It must be remembered, also, that we are speaking wholly here of an *intellectual* intuition, which is simply perfectly realized intelligence or truth.

Development of Intuition

Every concrete act of knowledge involves an intuition of God; for it involves a unity of the real and the ideal, of the objective and the subjective. Stated in another way, every act of knowledge is a realization of intelligence; an attainment of some relation which constitutes truth. The development of this intuition is the recognition of complete truth, the perfect unification of intelligence. The steps of the process are precisely the process of intelligence itself in knowledge; and as that is just what we have been studying in this psychology, it need not be repeated here. It needs only to be recognized that every act of knowledge is an intuition of truth, and that the goal of all knowledge is the complete intuition of truth, and that this truth is the complete manifestation of the unifying and distinguishing activities of the intelligence. All failure to grasp truth, or statement that ultimate reality is unknowable, consists simply in laying emphasis upon one of these processes to the exclusion of the other. It is the intuition of God as perfectly realized intelligence that forms the cognitive side of the religious consciousness. It is the most concrete and developed form of knowledge; but it is, at the same time, implied or involved in every act of knowledge whatever. There is more truth, in short, implied in the simplest form of knowledge than can be brought out by our completest science or philosophy. These latter are processes of systematization, and find their function in enriching the primal and the ultimate intuition.

NOTES TO CHAPTER 9

Upon intuition and self-consciousness, see Spencer, *Principles of Psychology*, vol. ii, pp. 454 - 88; Wundt, *Grundzüge der physiologischen Psychologie*, vol. ii, pp. 216 - 18; Strümpell, *Grundriss der Psychologie*, pp. 294 - 309; Erdmann, *Psychologische Briefe*, ch. ii; Horwicz, *Psychologische Analysen*, vol. ii, pt. 1, pp. 122 - 29; Ulrici, *Der Leib und die Seele*, vol. ii, pp. 43 - 66; George, *Lehrbuch der Psychologie*, pp. 341 - 51; Bergmann, *Grundlinien einer Theorie des Bewusstseins*, pp. 54 - 91; Ribot, *Maladies de la Personnalité*; Jeanmaire, *L'Idée de la Personnalité dans la Psychologie Moderne*.

10
Introduction to Feeling

Nature of Feeling

Feeling, it is to be remembered, signifies not a special class of psychical facts, like memory or conception, but *one side of all mental phenomena.* It is not a particular group of psychical experiences, occurring now and then in our mental life; it is coextensive with mental life; it is its *internal* aspect. All knowledge occurs in the medium of feeling, for in knowing we render internal, or make belong to our consciousness, something which exists in the universe. In knowledge we do not pay attention, indeed, to this internal factor, but to the information that we get about something existing. The very fact, however, that we regard this knowledge as *our* knowledge, that we refer it to ourselves as subjects, shows that it is also feeling. There is no consciousness which exists as *wholly* objectified, that is, without connection with some individual. There is, in other words, no consciousness which is not feeling.

Feeling and the Individual Self

Every consciousness is felt as *my* consciousness. This is feeling. It is feeling that constitutes the essential difference between me and thee. We cannot define the "*ego*" as that which is at once subject and object, for this is true of every *ego*. It gives us the universal form of selfhood, but does not give any ground for distinction between myself and thyself. Knowledge affords no ground for this distinction, for knowledge is of the object, and is universal. Knowledge is, indeed, regarded as my knowledge or as your knowledge, but this is because of the existence of the self. It cannot constitute that self. Feeling is, however, unique and unsharable. Feeling expresses the fact that all is not purely objective and universal, but that it also exists in individual and subjective form. Feeling cannot be defined. For the very good reason that it is individual and particular, it can only be felt. But it may be characterized again by saying that feeling is the *interesting side* of all consciousness; consciousness in its unique personal reference to me or thee.

Feeling and Activity of Self

Feeling, or the fact of interest, is therefore as wide as the whole realm of self, and self is as wide as the whole realm of experience. *To determine the forms and conditions of feeling we must know something about self.* Self is, as we have so often seen, *activity.* It is not something *which* acts; it is activity. All feeling must be an accompaniment, therefore, of activity. Through its activity, the soul is; and feeling is the becoming conscious of its own being. *The soul exists for itself; it takes an interest in itself, and itself is constituted by activities.* This is all that can be said in a general way about feeling. But the activity may be in two directions, and there may be consequently two kinds of interest. The activity may further or develop the self; it may hinder or retard it. The interest may be one of *pleasure* or of *pain.* Between these poles all feeling moves.

The Source of Qualitative Feelings

Pleasurable feeling is the rendering manifest to the soul its own activity in a direction tending to increase of well-being, or self-realization; painful feeling, the reverse. We have seen before that self is not a mere *formal* existence, that is, one having no necessary connection with the material with which it deals, and with the results which it produces; but it is a real activity, that is to say, one with a *content.* The various spheres of experience are only so many differentiations or developments of the real nature of the self. The self, through its retentive activity, is constantly organizing itself in certain definite, explicit forms, and only as it does thus organize itself is it anything more than mere capacity. It follows, therefore, that there is no such thing as pain or pleasure *in general*, any more than there is such a thing as color in general. Every feeling has a definite content which distinguishes it from every other feeling, over and above the mere fact of pleasure and pain; just as red is distinguished from blue by a quality over and above the mere fact that both are colors. Every activity of the self, in other words, has a definite filling or quality quite distinct from every other; and feeling, as the accompaniment of this activity, or rather as its immediate presence in consciousness, must be differentiated also.

Treatment of Feelings

All feeling is the individual side of the activity of self. The activity of self develops itself in an infinity of directions, and with an infinity of contents. These are the facts upon which we have to base our discussion. None the less, the activities may be reduced to a few general heads, and thus a basis of treatment discovered. The quality or content of feeling is evidently determined by the degree of the development or realization of self, and we may recognize as many classes of feeling as we distinguish degrees of activity of self-realization in the soul. The self, taken in its lowest terms, is the organic body, fitted out with a nervous system, and capable of responding to physical stimuli, through its connection with soul, in the form of sensations. 1. The first class of feelings will be those accompanying this organic activity of self, or sensuous feelings. The mind also appears as associative activity, or as mechanically combining the various elements of its experience, as well as an attentive activity which idealizes them, and gives them their especial significance. The next two classes of feeling might, with great propriety, be made to conform to these two kinds of feeling, but it is more convenient to adopt a cross division. In both associative and attentive activities there are feelings which are due to the relations which the activities bear to each other, and there are those which are due more especially to the contents with which they are concerned. This gives rise to II. Formal feelings, and III. Qualitative feelings, of which we shall consider (1) the æsthetic, (2) the intellectual, and (3) the personal and moral.

11
Sensuous Feeling

Nature

The first and simplest form in which the soul puts forth its activity is through the physical organism. Feeling is the internal or individual side of all activity, and here it appears as rendering internal the organic processes. For physiology the organism is an external body, existing with each part distinct from every other in space. In feeling, this externality and separation are overcome. If the eye sees, the whole organism feels the experience; if the hand is bruised, or if the digestive apparatus does not work normally, through feeling the entire man is made conscious of it. Each action and reaction has a unique reference to the whole self. We have now to analyze the forms of this class of feeling.

Sensation as Feeling

Every sensation, considered in itself, is a feeling. We have previously considered sensations as stimuli to the apperceptive activity, and hence as resulting in knowledge; and they are rightly so considered. But a sensation is none the less itself an intrinsic affection of the soul, possessing a peculiar emotive quality of its own. An infant, we may suppose, has sensations long before he has knowledge; there are affections of his eye and ear, etc., before he recognizes colored or sounding objects. Such sensations have an existence very similar, we may suppose, to our own digestive sensations. They are feelings. When these sensations become objectified, they do not cease to be feelings; and their characteristics are found to depend (1) on intensity, and (2) upon quality.

1. DEPENDENCE OF FEELING ON INTENSITY

Pleasure and pain have certain quantitative aspects. Any sensation intensified beyond a certain point becomes

218

painful. Almost all sensations lowered below a certain point become painful. Between these limits a sensation is agreeable, and at a given point it seems to reach a maximum of agreeableness. An obscurity which is neither light nor dark—one which calls forth a slight sensation, and yet one which cannot be defined—is painful. Exceedingly strong light, as that of the sun, is also painful. Yet, between these limits, light is grateful and pleasing. A feeble whisper or rustle is irritating; a loud bang is offensive. Between these limits sound delights the soul and is sought for. There is pleasure in mere seeing and hearing, independent of what is seen or heard, when the stimulus is of a certain intensity. In tactual impressions, varying from tickling to abrasion, the same law is illustrated. In the temperature sense it is illustrated in the progression from cold through genial warmth to extreme heat.

The Place of the Limits

The position of the limits is fixed by the fact that a stimulus which occasions pain is either too slight to allow the sense to respond normally, or is so great that it calls forth so much activity of the organism that it exhausts the latter or actually destroys some part of it. The moderate stimulus which gives pleasure lies within the bounds of possible easy adjustment without excess of activity. The stimulus calls forth a ready response, and one which does not make too much demand on the organism. A very slight stimulus leaves the soul in a divided state. It calls the mind out towards itself, and yet it does not offer sufficient inducement to be actually responded to. A very strong stimulus calls forth the reserve strength of the organism to meet it, and, making excessive demands, drains the system. Exceedingly irregular stimuli call forth futile attempts at adjustment, and energy is wasted. All such forms occasion pain, while freer moderate play is pleasurable. This is what we should expect from the theory. Normal or healthy activity furthers the organism; other, destroys or retards it. It should be noticed, also, that the greatest amount of pleasure seems to be given at that point of the intensity of the sensation which is most conducive to clear discrimination, thus affording a basis in feeling for the best workings of the differentiating function of intelligence.

Duration of Sensation

Connected with the intensity of a sensation may be considered its *duration*. There seems to be a natural rhythm or ebb and flow of feeling, independent of all the processes operating upon it. Physical activity seems to discharge itself in alternating pulses. Very short and rapid stimuli interfere with this regular recovery and loss, and are unpleasant; while the same sensation, long prolonged without change, whether of pleasure or pain, becomes deadened. A stimulus enduring just long enough for the mind to respond adequately to it, and then giving away, without too abrupt change, to another, seems to afford the maximum amount of pleasure.

2. DEPENDENCE OF FEELING ON QUALITY

Feeling is, however, much more than a matter of bare pleasure or pain. Feelings differ qualitatively or in their content according to the quality of the sensation. The organic sensations, as we saw when studying them, have much greater value for the emotional life than for the cognitive; and in general it may be said that the more value a sensation has for knowledge, the less it has for feeling *directly*. Thus sensations of sight seem to possess, as mere sensation, the least degree of emotional quality. The student must be careful, however, to distinguish between the emotional value of a sensation considered by itself, and its value when idealized by the higher processes. The less emotive power a sensation possesses *per se*, the more it seems capable of taking on in complex forms. Thus the organic sensations enter very slightly into the more developed forms of feeling, while those of sight and hearing are all-important.

Organic Feelings

Sensations of the organism serve for the most part simply to give us a feeling of general well-being. The feeling of health, of being alive, is due to the summation of the various minute feelings which the sensations proceeding from each organ possess. Feelings of this character are well termed voluminous or massive; they are so pervasive that they seem almost to possess spatial characteristics. This feeling is much keener in childhood than afterwards. Whether this is due to an actual falling-off of emotional quality, or to the fact that the adult consciousness is much more occupied with more complex feelings, it would be difficult to say; but there can be no doubt that the sense of "being alive" is much more vivid in childhood than afterwards. Leigh Hunt says that when he was a child the sight of certain palings painted red gave him keener pleasure than any experience of manhood. Making allowances for exaggeration, this expresses a common experience.

Characteristics

This vital sensation remains at all periods, however, the substructure of every feeling; it is the most permanent and enduring of all feelings, and any interference with it is sure to produce the most disastrous psychical effect. It is the summation of the feelings of the workings of the entire organism that appears to form the basis of the temperaments, and which, interwoven with more complex states of emotion, constitute mood or emotional tone. While it seems impossible that we should have feeling and not be conscious of it, it yet appears to be a fact that while the healthy workings of the organism give us our most fundamental feeling, and that other feelings are, in a sense, only differentiations of it, we are not reflectively conscious of it. In truth, however, there is no contradiction, for it is one thing to possess a feeling, and another to make it an object of recognition. The healthier the feeling, the more we are absorbed in it, and the less we recognize it, even as a feeling. It is only when the feeling ceases to be healthy, when it is due to some abnormal action, that we are reflexly conscious of its existence.

Taste and Smell

It has already been noticed that in taste and smell the emotional side preponderates over the cognitive. The latter is more apparent than in the organic sensations, however, for the properties of the latter we never think of referring beyond the organism, while we do speak of the taste of sugar or the smell of cologne. Nevertheless both tastes and smells are more easily classified as agreeable or disagreeable than from any objective standard. Taste has the more immediate capacity for giving pleasure and pain, and the feelings arising from it and the organic sensations seem to constitute most of the psychical life of an infant. Smell is more elusive and subtle in its effects, and, by reason of its less degree of grossness, enters more readily into higher associations.

It must be noticed that the organic sensations and taste are personal in the narrowest sense, a sense in which "person" is identified with our own organism, distinct from others in space and time. It is only one's own bodily processes which occasion organic feeling; and a substance must be actually taken into the organism through the mouth before it can be tasted. Such feelings tend to divide one individual from another, for their enjoyment by one is either not shared with another, or is actually incompatible with such sharing. In smell, feeling becomes a whit more objective and universal. The odorous object, as a whole, is not dissolved in the organism. A number may get and enjoy similar feelings from one object.

Touch

In touch we see an emotional side manifested in the fact that we speak of *feeling* something when we come in contact with it. The object which stimulates sensations of contact is extra-organic, and the feeling is more universal in its nature than any yet studied. The tactual qualities which give pleasure are smoothness and softness—especially when combined, as in velvet, the human skin, etc. Roughness and hardness, on the other hand, are highly disagreeable, especially when combined in the form of harshness. The physiological basis of this fact seems to be that a smooth, soft surface allows a continuous, uninterrupted nervous discharge, while jagged and uneven surfaces occasion an intermittent, irregular activity. The feeling occasioned by running the fingers over sand-paper is not unlike that experienced by hearing the filing of a saw.

Muscular Feelings

The feelings originating from muscular sensation occupy a peculiar position between the organic sensations, on the one hand, and those of sight and touch, on the other. They are due to the activity of the body, and hence have a purely personal reference, but they are so associated with all other senses that they take on the qualities of the latter. More especially they are the condition of our reaching any end, and hence they become associated with whatever feelings cluster about the attainment of this end. Their distinction from organic feelings as purely personal seems to be due to the fact that the latter have to do wholly with our own passive enjoyment; while the former, though originating in ourselves, are accompaniments of our *activity*, and may extend as far and wide as these activities reach in their effects. What we passively enjoy can be enjoyed by ourselves alone; what we actively enjoy may be indefinitely shared. In fact, in many cases, as when the good of some other person is the proximate end of action, there will be no pleasure in the activity to ourselves unless the other person is made happy, and thus the end of action is reached.

Use of Language

There is unconsciously embodied a great deal of psychological truth in the terms which we use to express various emotional characteristics. No matter how high these may be, their names are quite generally derived from their sensuous basis. Thus, terms which express immediate personal attraction or repulsion are derived for the most part from the senses of smell and taste. To loathe is much the same as to be nauseated at something. Dis-gust is a strong term for personal repugnance, and even its objective manifestation centres about the curl of the nostrils and of the mouth. The idea in these words seems to be that we reject the loathsome or disgusting or bitter object, as we would something offensive to stomach, taste, or smell. Agreeable things, on the other hand, are sweet, delicious, fragrant. In general, what agrees with us, or is disagreeable, is expressed in terms of the lower senses.

The Use of Language in Higher Feelings

Terms expressive of moral qualities and such as name activities are derived rather from touch and muscular activity. A person is sharp, acute, or obtuse. He has smooth, polished manners, or is rough and coarse. Character is firm or yielding. An upright man is said to be square. Some persons are called 'light, while the words of others carry weight. Dull persons are generally heavy as well; harsh people grate upon us, while fine traits attract us. Some men are slow, others fast. An act is right and of a high character, or is base and low. Good elevates a man, bad degrades him. All such adjectives show an instinctive feeling that moral qualities are connected in some way with personal activity, and that one's most striking characteristics are due to the way in which "one holds himself" towards others. Intellectual traits are designated rather by terms derived from sight, as clear, bright, sparkling, lucid; though even here terms that denote putting forth of mental activity are derived from terms of muscular action, as penetrating, incisive, etc.

Feelings of Hearing

Sensations of hearing are, for the most part, objectified, and hence lose that purely individualistic reference which constitutes their value as sensuous feelings. By the very reason of their objectification, however, they become centres for those more complex forms of feeling which cluster about objects. In especial, they constitute the sensuous basis of all the enjoyments of language and music. But such emotional effects transcend the subject we are now considering. The harmony and melody of music, however, although properly complex æsthetic effects, seem to have a sensuous aspect, in the fact that they find their basis in continued, regularly-recurrent nerve discharges. Apart from any process of development, also, slow sounds suggest sorrow, quick ones joy and mirth. Sounds get much of their emotional effect through their associations with muscular sensation, as in the march and the varied forms of the dance. Soft tones are melancholy; loud suggest impatient energy. Deep tones suggest gravity, dignity; high ones, unless so high as to be shrill, cheerful brightness or levity. Very peculiar and indescribable feelings are those due to the characteristic quality or tone-color of various instruments, as the flute, organ, violin, bagpipe. Dissonance accompanying prevailing harmony occasions a feeling of unrest and longing.

Feelings of Sight

In sight, as in hearing, there is very little of *immediate* emotional quality. This very fact, of course, indefinitely enlarges the range of emotions which visual sensations take on through their indirect connections. In particular, it is the lack of immediate reference to the organism which enables feelings of sight as well as of hearing to be the basis of æsthetic effects. We may say of feeling, as of knowledge, that the more immediate it is—that is, the less it takes us beyond what is sensuously present, the less developed it is. The more we are absorbed in the feeling as such, and the less we are absorbed in the object or activity to which the feeling clings, the more undefined and undeveloped is the emotion. Sight gives so little *direct* pleasure and pain that it is pre-eminently fitted for becoming the vehicle of higher enjoyments and sufferings.

Sensuous Characteristics

Even visual sensations are not wholly free, however, from sensuous appeal to feeling. An expanse of light gives pleasure in itself. Long-continued darkness is gloomy. A succession of cloudy days may give the blues. Black seems melancholy, or suggests earnestness; white is cheerful. The amount of white mixed with any spectral color affects its emotional tone, as may be seen in the difference between the effects of violet and lilac, blue and sea-blue, red and rose. Colors which are so mixed that the spectral colors do not stand forth at all, as gray and brown, are very properly called *neutral* colors, as they seem to be wholly indifferent to feeling. It is noticeable that, with growing civilization, there is a tendency to take less and less delight in the purely sensuous quality of colors, and to take refuge in neutral tints. Grays and browns consequently predominate in clothing, house-furnishing, etc. It is quite different with unculti-

vated taste. While a neutral tint will allow the emotional
qualities of form, design, etc., to be still more apparent, not
exciting the feelings immediately, tastes unable to appreciate the subtler enjoyments find keen delight in glaring reds
and yellows. In the spectral scale, Goethe called the colors
from red to green, *plus*, because they excite feeling; from
green to violet, *minus*, because they soothe or depress it.
Yellow seems associated with warmth, while pure blue is a
cold color. Unrefined tastes enjoy the plus and the warm
colors. There is, however, the possibility of carrying a refinement of taste to the point where it becomes fastidiousness, and ceases to find any pleasure in those colors which
normally excite a healthy enjoyment. After a period of
over-fastidiousness, taste recovers itself by having recourse
to those brighter and warmer colors which once it spurned
as barbaric and coarse.

Application of Theory

It will be seen that the discussion of sensuous feeling is in
line with our theory. Every sensation represents an activity
of the soul. It is a re-active and mechanical activity it is true,
but none the less an activity; as such, we should expect it to
give rise to pleasure and pain. As the activity of the soul in
sensation is not purely formal, or confined to one mode, but
specifies itself in the whole series of sensations differing in
quality, we should expect to find sensuous feelings highly
diversified in content. As feeling is the individual side of
consciousness, we should expect to find that the more the
sensation became objectified, the less would it appear as
immediate feeling, that is, as sensuous feeling. As knowledge is, however, one mode of the *activity* of self, we may
expect to find that what is lost in the way of direct sensuous
feeling we shall find turning up again in the form of mediate
intellectual feeling.

NOTES TO CHAPTER 11

Murray, *Handbook of Psychology*, pp. 330 - 48; Wundt, *Grundzüge der physiologischen Psychologie*, vol. i, pp. 465 - 99; Lotze,
Microcosmus, pp. 567 - 78; Laycock, *Mind and Brain*, vol. ii, pp.

274 - 93; Horwicz, *Psychologische Analysen*, vol. i, pp. 191 - 201; vol. ii, pt. 1, pp. 88 - 122; Braubach, *Psychologie des Gefühls*, pp. 12 - 39; Nahlowsky, *Das Gefühlsleben*, pp. 130 - 56; Schneider, *Der menschliche Wille*, pp. 117 - 246.

Upon the temperaments, consult Wundt (*op. cit.*), vol. ii, p. 345 ff.; George, *Lehrbuch der Psychologie*, pp. 125 - 50; Ulrici, *Der Leib und die Seele*, vol. ii, pp. 129 - 36; Braubach (*op. cit.*), pp. 112 - 40; Volkmann, *Lehrbuch der Psychologie*, vol. i, pp. 209 - 16; Fortlage, in *Acht psychologische Vorträge*; and Henle, *Anthropologische Vorträge*.

12

Formal Feeling

Distinction from Sensuous Feeling

In sensuous feeling the emotion clings to the bare presence of the sensation itself. The pleasure, indeed, that comes from the taste of an orange, the pain arising from a bruise of the finger, may become associated with the rest of our life; the pleasure of eating the orange may be enhanced by its rarity or by the thought of some one from whom it was a gift; the pain of the bruise may be increased by the reflection that it will prevent our carrying-out some cherished scheme. But the feelings in themselves, as sensuous, do not thus take us beyond their immediate presence. *Their* significance is entirely exhausted in their own intrinsic qualities. The feelings which we are now to study are those which are concerned with the connecting activity of mind. They are psychical experiences which extend beyond the intrinsic qualities of the sensation to the emotional value which it has from its connection with other experiences, past or anticipated.

Formal Feelings

Such feelings, taking us beyond what is sensuously present, may be classified under two heads. While all are due to the fact of connection, some are due to the mere *mode* of connection, with no reference to *what* is connected, while others depend not upon the mode of activity, but upon the subject-matter connected. The hearing of an unexpected remark, and the news of the death of a friend occasion feelings which in their *form* are alike. Each is due to an activity suddenly appearing which is not in harmony with that already existing. In *content*, however, the feelings may be wide-world apart; as far apart as the *quality* of that which is heard. This occasions a distinction of feelings into formal and qualitative. It is the former which we are now to consider. The formal feelings accompany, for the most part, the mechanical activities of mind which connect together the various past and present elements of psychical life; and the qualitative feelings correspond more nearly to the attentive activity which idealizes these elements and gives them their specific significance. But the correspondence is a general one and must not be pressed too far.

Feelings of Adjustment

We have to do, then, with the feelings awakened by the form of the activity without any reference to the material upon which this activity is exerted except so far as that may continue or repress the activity. Every activity may, in a certain sense, be regarded as one of *adjustment*, as it is based upon a certain stimulus, and is directed towards bringing itself into conformity with the stimulus, either by altering its own condition, or by doing away with the stimulus. There will be, accordingly, as many kinds of formal feeling as there are forms of adjustment. We recognize three general types. There is, first, the adjustment which connects or reacts against various elements in our *present* activity, corresponding, upon the whole, to simultaneous association. There is, secondly, the adjustment which brings into connection present and *past* experiences, corresponding, we may say, to successive association. And, thirdly, we have feelings depending upon the relation which present experiences bear to those anticipated in *future*, feelings which are connected with the adjusting activity of attention.

I. Feelings of Present Adjustment

1. *RELATIVE FEELINGS*

Every adjustment involves, of course, various elements. These elements stand in varying relations to each other. They may agree and allow a harmonious adjustment to occur. They may be incompatible, so that they offer some obstacle, so complete that it prevents adjustment, or of such a character that the adjusting activity must be largely expended in reconciling the opposed elements. With these variations in activity go, of course, variations in feeling. In general terms, we have feelings of *harmony*, of *conflict*, and of *reconciliation*, or harmony after conflict. When the elements are so related that they actually favor the adjusting activity, there is harmonious feeling. If the mind is stimulated at the same time in such a way that two incompatible responses are called for, there arises a sense of dis-chord, or of jar. In *form* these resulting feelings will be the same, whether the harmony or conflict be one of sense elements, of intellectual or of moral.

Varieties

While the feeling, in general, is that of the putting forth of energy so as to adjust present factors, subordinate forms must be recognized, due to the varying relations which these factors bear to each other. The student will find an advantage in analyzing these types for himself, but a few examples may be given. One of the most important feelings is that of *exercise* or the putting forth of activity. If the activity pours forth in ready and abundant measure, beating down all resistance, and making use of obstacles only to overcome them, there is a feeling of *energy*, which may amount to *triumph* or *exaltation*. If the obstacles seem too great, if the conflict results in dividing the activity so that nothing is or can be accomplished, there is a feeling of *impotence*, which may amount to *discouragement* or *depression*. If the activity appears to be rightly directed, and yet is thwarted by some circumstance which seems beyond control, there is the feeling of *impatience* passing into *discontent*, if the circumstances are continued, or *relief*, if they are removed.

Further Illustrated

There is a feeling of *clearness* when each element in the activity is appropriately directed towards its object; each part of the activity not only harmonizing with every other, but also assisting it, so that the effect of the whole is greatly heightened by this mutual furtherance. When each interferes with some other, and there is no evident way of reconciling the conflict, although this does not amount to entire opposition, there is the feeling of *confusion*. When there is conflict of various activities going on, and no resolution of them is at hand, there is the feeling of *suspense* or *uncertainty*, which enters also as one element of the feeling of confusion. At the completion of the conflict there may be the feeling of *rest* or *peace*; or the strife may have been so severe and prolonged that it is one of exhaustion.

When the conflict of activities is decided not by such a harmonizing of different elements as allows each to be included as a subordinate part in the final activity, but by the entire suppression of some one activity, there arises a very complex feeling. There is the feeling of satisfaction that the exhausting conflict is ended; there is the positive feeling of pleasure which arises from the victory of some one activity, while there is also the feeling of pain or loss which comes from the repression of some one. There is no specific name for this feeling, perhaps because it is so common; but we rarely make a decision which is not followed by a mixed feeling of content for that which is attained, and regret for that which is foregone. As already said, if the conflict is ended, not by the repression of any element, but by the harmonious inclusion of all in some comprehensive activity, there is the feeling of reconciliation, which may become *joy*.

2. FEELINGS OF EXCESS OF ACTIVITY

Feelings of present adjustment may depend not only upon the relation which various present stimuli bear to each other, but also upon the extent of the demands which these stimuli make upon the mind. The more conflict the better, provided the conflict does not become actual opposition— that is, provided all the conflicting activities are capable of being united in one whole—for such conflict only calls forth more activity and results in more complete adjustment, that is, in more complete development of the self. But the activities may be so long continued and so severe as to drain the self of its power of action. There results the feeling of *fatigue*, which may, of course, be mental in its causation, as well as physical. It is, however, more likely to accompany such activities as bear a purely external relation to the end sought. Daily manual labor is, for example, generally not sought for itself, but only for the wages which reward it. The work in itself may be repulsive and endured only for the sake of its end. This gives rise to the feeling of *drudgery*. If, on the other hand, the activity is put forth for its own sake, as in technical operations, where the working man takes pleasure in his skilful performances, or in artistic production, or in scientific research, there is a feeling of *ease*, a feeling which approaches very closely to *play* in its nature. Activities accompanied by a feeling of drudgery or lack of interest are much more apt to result in fatigue than those accompanied by a feeling of play. In fact, it may be doubted whether the latter activities, if properly alternated, can give rise to any very permanent fatigue.

3. FEELINGS OF DEFECT OF ACTIVITY

At the other end of the scale, lie those feelings resulting from lack of sufficient exercise. There is not enough stimulus to call forth activity, or else there is not enough energy in the individual to respond. In the former case, there is the feeling of *triviality*, of *insipidity*. In the latter, there is the feeling of the *blasé*. In either case, it may take the form of feeling that nothing is worth while, that all is vanity and vexation of spirit. If there is store of energy in the individual, but his surroundings are such as not to call it forth, there arises the feeling of *isolation*, of being out of joint with one's place or age. If it is hemmed in by external obstructions and allowed to find no outlet, there comes into existence the feeling of bondage, of *slavery*. Or the activities which are prevented their natural outflow may blindly react against whatever obstructs them, and there arises the feeling of *injury*, of *resentment* and destructive *anger*, which would sweep out of existence all hinderance.

II.   Feelings Due to Past Experiences

As we saw so often when studying the activities of the mind in knowing, there is no present activity which is not modified or influenced in some way by past activities. It follows that there is involved in all feelings due to the immediate exercise of energy a certain element resulting from previous exercises, and it is this element, with the various forms of feeling to which it gives rise, that we must now study. First, it may be noticed that every past experience may be more or less perfectly reconstructed in memory, and the feeling which accompanied it thereby revived, though in vaguer and slighter measure. There are the pleasu:es and the pains of *memory*. But as these are only less vivid copies of original feelings, we need not stop to consider them. The remaining feelings of this class may be classified (1) as feelings due to relative *ease of transition* from old to new experience; (2) feelings due to the relative *familiarity* or, (3) *novelty* of experience; (4) feelings of *contrast*, (5) and of *continuance*.

1. FEELINGS OF TRANSITION

Old experiences give way to new ones with various degrees of resistance. This ease of transition varies greatly in different individuals and enters largely into the determination of disposition and temperament. Where there is a disposition to cling to the line of past experience, and to resist the introduction of much novelty, there is a *firm* disposition, which in exaggerated form constitutes *obstinacy*. When but little opposition is offered to the entrance of changing experience there is a yielding, pliable, or *easy* nature, which may become *volatile*. The relative amount of resistance offered to the introduction of new experience may be an important factor in determining the will. A stable disposition may give rise to a firm will; one accessible to change to a weak will, but this by no means necessarily follows. While dispositions are different in different individuals, yet there is no one who can wholly shut himself within the old; and no one who can make himself wholly open to the new. This occasions certain varieties of feeling which are found in all.

Varieties

When past experiences tend to thrust themselves pretty constantly into the present, there arises the feeling of dwelling or lingering upon a subject, which in its extreme aspect is *brooding*. If the dwelling is upon some supposed wrong done, it takes the form of *sullenness*. If upon some past agreeable experiences in contrast with present painful ones, it is *melancholy*. "Sorrow's crown of sorrows is remembering happier things." The opposite feeling, induced by a pleasant transition, is *gladness*; while opposed to sullenness, which looks for occasion of pain, is *cheerfulness*, which is the feeling which arises from a constant tendency to find pleasure in the change of experience. The effect of increase of experience is to moderate in both directions the feelings due to change of experience. A child finds more joy in mere change of experience than an adult, while his grief at disagreeable change is much more poignant and acute, if not so enduring.

2. FEELINGS OF FAMILIARITY

Aside from the *change* which may itself give rise to feeling, we have feelings which originate in the more definite relations which past experience bears to the present. In studying association, we saw that it turns largely upon the two factors of familiarity and novelty. A feeling of familiarity, or of likeness between the present and the past experience, is pleasant because the energy which occasions it is put forth in a well-worn groove, and it requires no overcoming of obstacle and resistance. In a very general sense, it is the feeling of *comfort*; the feeling that we are "at home" in our surroundings, whether physical, intellectual, or social. On the other hand, a feeling of familiarity may be unpleasant, because the experience is so customary that it can be performed without the putting forth of much activity. A feeling may consequently arise very similar to that induced by defective activity; a feeling which takes the form of *ennui* or *monotony*, of *staleness*. We are bored instead of being comfortable.

3. FEELINGS OF NOVELTY

A feeling of novelty, on the other hand, is pleasurable in so far as it affords a new channel for the exercise of energy. It opens a fresh outlet for action. The forces which would be otherwise penned in, or only half used in repeating actions become habitual, find full scope for exercise. This feeling may take various forms. It may be one of *brightness*, or of *buoyancy*, or of *recreation*, as opposed to staleness, or ennui. If, however, the new experience is not easily reconciled with the old, if it requires a division or conflict of energy, the feeling will be painful. The feeling may be one of *strangeness*, of discomfort; or, if it is of such a nature as to reflect upon ourselves, of *rawness* and inexperience. If the new experience is accompanied with a feeling of our inability to cope with it, there is the feeling of *terror*, or *fright*.

In general, it may be said that the maximum of pleasurable feeling is occasioned by a combination of the new and the customary. Such a combination allows the mind to feel at home, as dealing with material over which it has command, while it also stimulates it to fresh and unworn activities. The pleasure derived from hearing music on its *formal* side may be considered an illustration of the advantages of a union of the recurrent and the novel. One factor satisfies the mind; the other stimulates it and keeps it on the alert. This corresponds to what is found to be the best condition of intellectual action; not bare identity nor extreme difference calls forth knowledge, but the identical in the midst of difference.

4. EFFECTS OF CONTRAST

There must be a certain amount of change, or else no activity is called forth, and where there is no activity, there is no feeling. On the other hand, there must not be complete breach of continuity, for then the energy will be expended at random and unsuccessfully. Progressive change, or contrast, is fitted to awaken pleasurable feelings. The following facts, among many which might be selected, illustrate this: When we are extremely hungry, food that would otherwise be indifferent or repulsive is very agreeable. An object which is agreeable is still more so if it finds the soul at rest, and stimulates it to some action. Moderate transitions are generally more pleasant than abrupt. The climax of a drama is not thrust upon us, but is led up to, and then the tension is gradually relieved. Unpleasant effect, however, is often best relieved by sudden contrast, so Shakespeare alternates the scenes of the fool in Lear and the grave-digger in Hamlet with those of extreme tragedy. Even in such cases, however, there is no complete breach of continuity. The character of a feeling is fixed largely by its place in the succession of ideas. A joke is not funny in the midst of exalted religious feeling; nor the sound of revelry enjoyable to one in deep mourning.

5. EFFECTS OF CONTINUANCE

On the other hand, the effect of the continuance of any feeling without the introduction of some new element deadens the feeling. This is what we should expect, for our store of activity being limited, the activity will exhaust itself if not frequently stimulated afresh. Hence pleasures of the same kind continued without interruption cease to please. Pain loses some of its painfulness if not reinforced by fresh stimuli. Only those games continue to be enjoyable which offer large opportunity for the introduction of the unexpected. Play owes much of its pleasure to the fact that it does not confine action to any definite line, but allows it constant variety. The use of artificial stimulants is constant witness to the psychological law that continuance in any state uninterruptedly is unhealthy and hence unpleasurable, and that if no natural variety offers itself, unnatural will be sought.

But, on the other hand, we must not lose sight of the fact that actions unpleasant at first, because not conducive to the welfare of the organism, may become agreeable if persisted in. The action causes a modification of the organ involved, and causes it to become finally adjusted to something originally repulsive. The finding of enjoyment in reading by one to whom books were once tedious, and the pleasures which tobacco and liquor users find in their habits equally illustrate this law. If the change of the organ is such as occasions the development of the whole organism, permanent pleasure is gained; it is possible, however, to adjust one set of organs, only upon condition that the organism as a whole is put out of healthy adjustment to its surroundings, and in such cases the temporary pleasure is necessarily followed by permanent break-down. This is true, of course, not only of physical actions, but of all coming in the moral sphere.

III. Feeling of Adjustment Directed Towards the Future

All of our activities, though based upon past experiences, have their end in the future, and there are certain feelings which arise from the relations existing between the end aimed at and the activities put forth. In a general way, the typical feeling of this class is *expectancy*, which is the feeling that accompanies the stretching forward of the mind. Its acute form is *eagerness*. If the self is much interested in the end towards which it is directed this feeling takes the form of *hope* or *anxiety*; hope if the expectation is that the result will conform to one's desires, anxiety or dread in the reverse case. *Courage* is the feeling with which one faces a future to which he feels equal; *timidity* is the feeling of inability to cope with the expected end.

Active Feelings

The activity directed towards the future may not merely passively await the expected event, but may, as it were, go forth to meet it. This in its most general form takes the form of a feeling of *pressure*, of *effort* and of *striving*. If the action is to reach the end, the feeling is one of *seeking*. If the seeking is intense it is *yearning*. If the striving is to avoid the expected end, there is a feeling of *aversion*. There is also a class of feelings which accompany the end itself. There is feeling of *success* or *failure*; of *satisfaction*, or of *disappointment*.

Summary

Feeling is an accompaniment of *activity*. It is the self finding its own nature in every activity of the soul. In each the self finds itself either hindered or furthered; either repressed or developed, and in every activity there is accordingly pleasure or pain. As no activity is entirely at random, but has certain connections and ends, feeling is an accompaniment of adjustment, of what in knowledge we learned to know as apperception. All adjustment that accomplishes itself gives rise to pleasure; all failure to adjust, or mis-adjustment, to pain. The adjusting activity is called forth by stimuli, and, under the following circumstances there is lack of adjustment or improper adjustment with consequent pain: when the stimuli relatively to the energy to be put forth are (*a*) too numerous, too conflicting or too powerful; and (*b*) too few, too much alike, or too weak (perhaps entirely absent). The right combination of unity and variety calls forth the best energy and the most successful adjustment, and hence the greatest pleasure.

NOTES TO CHAPTER 12

Murray, *Handbook of Psychology*, pp. 378 - 85; McCosh, *Emotions*, pp. 115 - 48; Bascom, *Principles of Psychology*, pp. 249 - 55; Bain, *Emotions and Will*, pp. 63 - 93, 145 - 98; Brown, *Philosophy of Mind*, vol. ii, pp. 31 - 193, 272 - 313; Braubach, *Psychologie des Gefühls*, pp. 95 - 112; Nahlowsky, *Das Gefühlsleben*, pp. 85 - 129; Ulrici, *Der Leib und die Seele*, vol. ii, pp. 182 - 99; Beneke, *Psychologische Skizzen*, vol. i, pp. 45 - 91.

13
Development of Qualitative Feelings

Distinction from Formal

We have been considering feelings so far as they are the result of the form of the activity which they accompany, without reference to the object of the activity, except so far as this influences the form. We may feel confused, or bored, or anxious about almost anything. But in thus considering feeling we have made abstraction of the fact that activities are always called forth by, and are directed towards, certain objects. There is, in a concrete sense, no such thing as a purely formal activity; there is no activity without a content. The self does not realize or develop itself in empty ways, but in specific, definite modes. Our activities are due to the objects which come within the range of our experience, and hence the feelings excited necessarily cluster about these objects. The object and the feeling cannot be separated; they are factors of the same consciousness.

Connection with Apperception

This relation of the feeling to the object is sometimes spoken of as if it were due to the law of association which connects a feeling with something which awakens the feeling. But this does not express the whole truth. The connection is not an external one of the feeling *with* the object, but an internal and intimate one; it is feeling *of* the object. The feeling loses itself in the object. Thus we say that food *is* agreeable, that light is pleasant; or on a higher plane, that the landscape *is* beautiful, or that the act is right. Certain feelings of value or worth we attribute spontaneously to the object. It is the same fact seen on the side of emotion, that we have already seen on the side of knowledge. An object becomes intellectually significant to us when the self reads its past experience into it. But as this past experience is not colorlessly intellectual, but is dyed through and through with interests, with feelings of worth, the emotional element is also read into the object, and made a constituent element of it. The object becomes saturated with the value for the self which the self puts into it. It is a universal law of the mind in apperception that it must objectify itself. The world thus comes to be a collection of objects possessing emotional worth as well as intellectual.

Mere Feeling and Interest

We may, then, distinguish between *mere* feeling and developed feeling—*interest*. Mere feeling is a mental *affection* in its isolation. A pain pricks me; a noise startles me; a picture or landscape delights me; a comprehensive philosophical or religious idea awakens me; a moral crisis arouses my whole being—in each of these cases we may consider the feeling, the pain, the alarm, the delight, etc., in itself apart from its connections. This is bare feeling. But taken concretely the feeling is integrated with the object which arouses it and with the action which accompanies it. This integration is slighter the more sensuous the feeling—as of the pin-prick—and more important the "higher" the feeling. Feeling, so far as it is taken out of its isolation and put in relation to objects of knowledge or ideals of action, is *interest*. Interest has three factors. First, as feeling, it implies a certain excitation of the self in which there is *satisfaction*. Secondly, this satisfaction is not in the mere feeling, but in some *activity* connected with the feeling. Thirdly, this activity has to do with some *object*. The mere feeling is exhausted in itself. An interest attaches to an object. We are interested in something. This necessarily, for the activity takes us beyond the feeling.

Varieties of Qualitative Feeling

It follows that there will be as many kinds of qualitative feeling as there are objects into connection with which experience has been extended. Our feeling for a broom is not the same as our feeling for a rose; our feeling for a geometrical proposition not the same as our feeling for the spectrum; our feeling for Abyssinia not the same as our feeling for our own country; our feeling for Alexander the Great not the same as our feeling for our most intimate friend. Each stands in a different relation to the self. There is, as it were, a distinct side of the self found in each, or if not a distinct side, then more of the self is projected into one than into another. There will be, therefore, as many varieties of qualitative feeling as there are objects of knowledge or ends of action.

Treatment of Qualitative Feeling

Yet it is possible to form a general classification of feelings in their quality of *interests*. Interests may be classified, first, on the basis of their connection with objects, according to the greater or less range of these objects. As our ideas come to include more and more in their scope, the feelings integrated with them get a similar extension. While the *mere* feeling is particular, because isolated, interests are *universal* through their connection with the content of ideas. Furthermore, the *mere* feeling is of necessity vague. It has no relations which define it to intelligence. But every *act* necessarily brings matters to a head, to a focus. The sight of a beautiful flower may awaken a vague shock or a diffused wave of emotion; the feelings connected with the attempt to paint it, or scientifically to analyze it, will get a limited, distinct character through this associated activity. Secondly, then, interests are *defined* feelings. We shall study the development of qualitative feeling therefore: i. As growing more universal; ii. As growing more definite. These are the lines along which feeling normally develops, but as variations arise, we have: iii. Abnormal feelings; iv. Conflict of feelings.

i.   Growth of Feeling in Universality

Our first feelings may be called *purely* personal, and personality is here confined to one's organism. Such are the feelings accompanying the various forms of bodily activity, of the appetites, of muscular action, of the eye and ear, etc. But the self is something more than a body. It enlarges itself, grows wider and deeper with every experience, and with every enlargement of the self must go a corresponding increase of the scope of feeling. We have to study a few aspects of the growth. We shall consider (1) the widening; (2) the deepening of feeling.

1. THE WIDENING OF FEELING

Our first feelings are limited, as already said, to those connected with bodily activity—to sensuous affection. The first step in the widening of feeling comes about through

1. THE TRANSFERENCE OF EMOTION. All that comes within the range of one apperceptive act will be colored by the feeling which immediately and intrinsically belongs to only one factor of the act. The pleasure, at first purely sensuous, which the child gets from his food, becomes extended to his nurse, to the utensils employed, etc., and thus becomes somewhat objectified. The pleasure is no longer *purely* personal. The child does not feel pleasure in his nurse because she is consciously recognized as the source of his pleasure in food-taking, but the feeling is instinctively transferred to her as the child's range of experience is widened to include her. There is no limit to this widening of emotion through increase of factors involved in the same act. The result, of course, may be trivial and accidental, as when the feeling relates to some memento; but if the various factors of the act have some necessary internal relation to each other, it may be important and enduring. A child's feeling for his parents, for example, is largely the result of this widening of feeling through transference. Their connection with his whole life on all its sides is so intimate that something becomes transferred to them out of almost every experience.

2. SYMBOLISM OF FEELING. Feeling is at first transferred to include that which is directly involved in the same apperceptive act with that which orginally awakens the feeling, but in its growth it is transferred to that which is also *symbolically* connected. The word "home" symbolizes great ranges of emotion. The sight of a flag calls up the deepest and most earnest feelings of patriotism; a crucifix may stir religious emotion to its very depths. In such cases there has

been no direct transference by the inclusion of the same factors in one act of *perception*. The transference is due to the idealizing action of *imagination*. Just as any intellectual conception tends to be embodied in a concrete sensuous image, so our deepest sentiments are clustered about some object which may symbolize and thus unify feeling otherwise vague and scattered. All the familiar objects of our life thus become saturated with more or less of emotional interest of which we are hardly conscious till some break in our experience causes it to discharge itself.

3. UNIVERSAL FEELINGS. Feelings originating through this operation, however, are still more or less contingent and accidental. They extend somewhat beyond the immediate self to its objective and more universal relations, yet the particular form which they take is dependent to a large degree upon unessential elements of experience. It happens that the self in its development comes in contact with objects which it thus surcharges with its own interests, but these particular forms are not absolutely necessary to the development of the self. There are some relations, however, without which the soul would remain forever undeveloped and unrealized, a mere bundle of potential capacities. There are, in other words, universal and essential realms of experience in which the self must find itself, in order to be a self at all. There thus originate classes of feeling universal in their nature.

Classes of Universal Feelings

Speaking very broadly it may be said that without relation to *things* and to *persons* the self would not be realized. It is not that the self realizes itself *by means of* these relations, but that its realization takes the form of these relations. The universe of known objects is, as we have seen, the objective side of self. But in the world of things the self does not find itself wholly manifested. They at most are but things, while it is a person. Without them it is true that there would be no development, but they cannot furnish complete development. This can occur only through personal relations. It is only in a soul that the soul finds itself completely reflected; it is only through relations to conscious individuals that one becomes himself truly a conscious individual. Since feeling is always a feeling of self, of the hinderance or furtherance of self-development through activity, and since the self is developed in virtue of its relations with things and with persons, it follows that there are two kinds of universal feeling, impersonal, and personal or social.

Divisions of Impersonal Feelings

Impersonal feelings may be subdivided into two classes. The universe of objects, through relations to which the mind is realized, may be regarded as actual or as ideal, and these originate accordingly *intellectual* and *æsthetic* feelings. There are the sentiments which spring from or answer to our desire for intellectual satisfaction; and there are those which are occasioned by our need of æsthetic gratification. Each of these classes will be considered, hereafter, and so it need now only be mentioned that these feelings do not concern two wholly different spheres, but two aspects of the same sphere. Objects may be felt as presenting meaning, and as stimulating to the search for meaning; that is, they may be felt as bearing some relation to each other. The feelings which gather about the *mutual relations of objects to each other* are intellectual. Objects may also be felt as embodying beauty and as stimuli to a search for beauty and for its creation—that is, objects may be felt to bear some relation to an *ideal*. Feelings which cluster about the *relations of objects*, not to each other, but *to an ideal*, are æsthetic.

Special Forms of Universal Feelings

The concrete forms of (*a*) intellectual, (*b*) æsthetic, and (*c*) personal feelings will be studied hereafter. Attention must now be called to the fact that they are three progressive stages of the *widening* of feeling. In intellectual feeling we get beyond the immediate presence of the sensation; we get beyond the more or less accidental relation of self to objects into which it transfers, irradiates, and reflects its own feelings; we get into those feelings which are due to the connection of objects with each other, and which have, therefore, no immediate relation to the individual self. They are the feelings which are due to the development of the universal side of self. In æsthetic feeling we advance beyond this, and feel the relation which some experience of ours bears to an ideal, which is conceived as universal, permanent, and out of the reach of individual desires and impulses. The self finds itself realized in what appears at first as not-self. It is taken beyond its limitation to its immediate sensuously-present experience, and transferred to a realm of enduring and independent relations. It marks also an advance beyond intellectual feeling, for the feeling of *worth* or value is immediately included in all æsthetic experience, as it is not in intellectual.

Social Feeling

In social feeling, we merge our private life in the wider life of the community, and, in so doing, immensely transcend our immediate self and realize our being in its widest way. In knowledge we take the universe of objects into ourselves; in æsthetic perception and creation we take the universe of ideal worths into ourselves; in social life, we make to be an element of our being the universe of personal and spiritual relations. Only thus, in any true sense, do we live the life of a developed personality at all, and thus it is that this realm of experience is the widest and most varied upon its emotional side.

Finally, feeling finds its absolutely universal expression in religious emotion, which is the finding or realization of self in a completely realized personality, which unites in itself truth, or the complete unity of the relations of all objects; beauty, or the complete unity of all ideal values; and rightness, or the complete unity of all persons. The emotion which accompanies the religious life is that which accompanies the completed activity of ourselves; the self is realized, and finds its true life in God. In sensuous feeling we find our self expressed in organic processes; in intellectual feeling we find our self expressed in the objective relations of the world; in æsthetic feeling we feel our self expressed in ideal values; in social feeling we find our self expressed in persons; in religious feeling we find our self expressed in God. We feel our self identified, one in life, with the ultimate, universal reality.

2. DEEPENING OF EMOTIONAL DISPOSITION

The second element in the universalizing of feeling is its deepening. Feeling not only widens by extension to larger ranges of experience, but it also grows more intense in itself. A child's feeling is quite fickle and superficial. It is easily excited, and as easily appeased or transformed. There is no stability of emotional life. Fixation of feeling is as foreign to a child as fixation of attention. Every adult, however, has permanent and deeply founded modes of emotional response. He has an emotional *character* as well as an intellectual. Not all objects excite feelings equally; some are relatively indifferent, and others affect him to the depths of his being. Feeling returns upon itself, and forms a disposition.

Process of Deepening

Some of the steps of the process may be considered. First there is increasing adaptation for emotion in a certain direction. Every exercise modifies the organ used in a certain way, and leaves it in a condition to act again in a similar direction more easily. The act of attention or memory, which was at first difficult, becomes easy with repetition, and the result is that feeling moves along that groove rather than elsewhere. Feeling which originally was diffused and superficial, tending to attach itself slightly everywhere, becomes concentrated and deepened. Less stimulus is henceforth required to call out the feeling in this direction. A child who constantly indulges in spiteful acts towards others, finds a constantly lessening provocation sufficient to induce anger. So with benevolence or regret, or any emotional characteristic.

Emotional Disposition

The result of this development, through repeated and frequent experiences, is that there comes to be formed certain permanent groups of emotional responses which color the person's character. Just as, in the intellectual life, the frequent occurrence of any act of apperception leads not only to an easier recurrence of the same act, but to the formation of an apperceptive organ, which tends to apprehend experiences of that nature rather than others, so channels of feeling are worn along which the emotions all tend to discharge themselves. The individual forms *dispositions*, organs of feeling. His emotional life becomes organized in certain ways. It is these emotional dispositions which, taken under the control of will and made subservient to certain lines of conduct, constitute character.

Idealization and Retention

It will be evident that the widening of feeling corresponds to the idealizing activities of apperception, while its deepening is analogous to retention. Feeling becomes wide as it extends over more comprehensive ranges of *objects* of experience; it becomes deep as it returns into the self or subject, and is organized into its very emotional structure. The two processes are also related to each other as the corresponding intellectual processes. Each requires the other for its own development. Religious and moral feelings, which are the widest of all, are also, when genuine, the deepest. Being the widest, there is no experience which does not involve them to a certain extent, and the result is that every activity performed strengthens in some way the feeling in that special direction. Where a feeling is deepened and intensified at the expense of its comprehensiveness, when a narrow feeling is dwelt upon and given prominence, the result is its isolation, a split in our nature and resulting unhealthy character and action. Healthy feeling deepens only as it widens.

II. Growth in Definiteness of Feeling

Along with the growth of feeling in comprehensiveness and in depth, goes a growth in definiteness, that is, in distinctness of content. Feeling, when undeveloped, is exceedingly vague and diffuse. But it has already been noticed that growth of feeling in definiteness depends upon its connection with the *will*, with *ends of action*. Objects are constantly becoming, through their connection with feeling, *springs to action*. This process reacts upon the feeling and makes it more definite. We have just seen how wider ranges of experience are taken into the emotional realm. We have now to see that, when so included, they render feeling specific or organized.

Illustration

A child, for example, eats an orange for the first time. This action gratifies his organic nature and occasions pleasure. This pleasure is henceforth an integral part of his conception of an orange. But this idea of the orange as agreeable now becomes a spring to future activity. The procuring and eating of oranges is now one motive to action. The result is that the organic feeling of pleasure which were otherwise exceedingly vague now becomes definite; it gathers about this special line of action. In our entire emotional life feeling is differentiating itself and becoming distinct in just this way. Nothing in our mental life is so impalpable, so hard to grasp, as feeling which has not become distinct through connection with some specific end of action.

Differentiation of Interests

There thus arises a differentiation of interests. Every object that comes within our experience gets some emotional coloring, as it helps or hinders that experience. It thus gains a special and unique interest of its own. We have already had occasion to mention what diverse forms these interests may take (page 240). It is only necessary now to mention in addition that an object, as soon as it has become interesting, becomes an *end of action in itself*. It may be food in general, or some special form of food; it may be power, physical or political; it may be knowledge, technical or of some line of science; it may be money or fame or influence. And each of these ends may thus subdivide itself into thousands of more specific forms, depending upon the individual himself. As the end becomes more specific, the feeling connected with it becomes more definite.

Two Forms of Definite Feeling

Of the feelings thus differentiated, by virtue of their association with specific ends of action, two forms may be recognized. As the feeling connected with the experience may be either pleasurable or painful, so the end may be felt as desirable or as hateful. Feeling thus specifies itself into *likes* and *dislikes*, *loves* and *hates*. Any object whatever may become an object of love or of hatred, though it is usual to restrict these terms to higher objects. The generic term expressing the relation of feeling to definite objects is *affection*. We have affection of some kind, accordingly, for every element coming within our experience. Love or liking alone is a *positive* spring to action; it tends to create or produce the object needed to satisfy the affection. Hate is destructive, and tends to put out of the way all which is felt as hindering the realization of self.

Definiteness and Universality

Aside from extrinsic and accidental sources of affection for objects of experience, it is possible to recognize certain general groups of likings, fixed by the growth of feeling in universality. Universality does not mean mere broadness; it means closer and more comprehensive relations with self. It means the enlarging of the interests of self to recognize more and more as identified with self. It is in no way opposed, therefore, to growth of definiteness of feeling. Our loves and hatreds, our affections, become more definite as our feelings correspond to wider growths of the soul. No one would speak of loving very definitely something which satisfied the narrower activities of self—the organic, as food and drink. One loves a beautiful work of art more distinctly than he does a proposition in geometry; and he loves a person more than either; while the only perfectly definite object of love can be alone the absolutely ideal self; the absolutely universalized personality, or God. It will be noticed, therefore, that definiteness of feeling must be discriminated from intensity of feeling. It often happens that the more intense a feeling is, as an appetite, the less definite it is.

Love as Completely Qualitative Feeling

It was shown, in the early part of this chapter, that qualitative feeling originates in the objectification of self; it is the internal side of this objectification. It follows that feeling must take upon itself the form of liking or love. Liking is essentially an *active* feeling; it is the outgoing of the soul to an object. It is the giving up of the immediate or personal self, and its fixation upon something which is beyond the immediate self. It is somewhat so in the lowest likings—the likings for food and drink; for these are affections for something which are necessary to *develop* the body; likings for something of which it is not immediately in possession. The fact is more clearly shown, however, as we rise in the scale of likings, and it finds its complete illustration in the fact that moral and religious love require a complete surrender of one's particular and subjective interests, with devotion to what is regarded as the permanent and universal, the thoroughly objective, self.

III. Abnormal Feelings

Before passing on to the concrete forms of qualitative feeling, we must notice the principles upon which abnormal or morbid feelings are based. All natural, healthy feeling is absorbed in the object or in the action. Healthy feeling never has an independent existence in consciousness. Even sense-feelings are absorbed. The pleasure of eating an orange seems a part of the orange. The pleasure which we derive from healthy bodily existence and activity we are not reflectively conscious of (page 221), but it is the sense of life itself. All other feelings, as we have seen, cluster about objects, and are lost in the objects; or they serve as springs to action, in the form of affections. As Mr. Martineau says, feelings are mere functions of an *integral* life, and there is an inevitable penalty attached to every attempt to detach them from this position, and live upon some particular order of feeling.

Self-conscious Feeling

Feeling is unhealthy, therefore, when set free from its absorption in the object or in the end of action, and given a separate existence in consciousness. We see this in the case of bodily disease or fatigue, when alone we are conscious of the separate existence of any organic feeling; and we see it in the higher sentiments. Feelings of knowledge are normally lost in the objects known; æsthetic feelings, in the beautiful object created or contemplated; moral feelings, in the outgoing activity which the affection for them induces. Normal feelings, in short, are regarded as real *values* in the objects which excite them, or exist only as springs to action; they subserve conduct. Cut loose from their connections, they occasion what is called "self-consciousness," in a bad sense of the term, when the individual is unduly conscious of the reference which feelings have to him as an individual. True self-consciousness, as we have learned to see, is objectified in ideas and actions; and it is only when the feelings are separated from their proper objective and volitional position, and are made independent factors in consciousness, that the "self-consciousness," which is the mark of an undue interest in some form of one's own special and peculiar characteristics, arises. There may be, of course, as many degenerate forms of feeling, that is, of "self-consciousness," as there are normal forms.

IV. Conflict of Feeling

All isolation of feeling is not only unhealthy in itself, but leads to conflict of feelings. We have already noticed some forms of conflicting feelings, so far as these are due to the form of activity (page 230). We have now to notice that there is a more or less permanent conflict of feelings resulting from the opposition of some particular individual interest to some more universal one. When we were studying the development of qualitative feeling as increasing in universality and definiteness, we were studying its *normal law*. As we have just seen, feeling may also be abnormal, that is to say, not increase in universality and definiteness. The feelings of an individual, instead of centring more and more upon objects which constitute the pain and pleasure of all, may be concentrated more and more upon such as concern his purely personal self. Instead of being made springs to actions which will take him outside of himself, he may dwell upon the feelings as states of his own private consciousness, and be led only to such actions as have reference to his own particular enjoyment. But as this individual has necessarily a universal as well as a particular side, this results in a breach of his activities, and consequent conflict of feeling.

Illustration

Take, for example, one who has what we may call an abnormal organic consciousness; one who has learned to pay attention to his own bodily feelings, and to make them the end of action, instead of regarding them as mere tokens of the well-being of his organism. Such a one has isolated these feelings, and, instead of paying attention to them so far as they relate to his own true development, he makes them an end in themselves. Such, for example, is the case with a voluptuary; such is the case with one who, for the satisfaction of his own feelings, has formed the alcoholic habit. The gratification of these interests undoubtedly results in pleasure. Pleasure always accompanies every development, every expansion of self, and such an individual is indulging the particular, private side of himself. Yet, even in purely organic matters, he has a universal side. His body should conform to *law*, and law is universal. The result of a constant neglect of this universal side is pain, disease, possibly destruction of the organism. In gratifying the purely particular side of his nature, he gets pleasure; but, as this gratification disorganizes the universal side, that which connects him with the laws of the universe, he gets ultimate pain. There is conflict of feeling.

Illustration in Social Feeling

Or, upon a higher plane, suppose that one has made the pleasures which come from money-getting an end in themselves; suppose he has isolated them from his integral being, and makes his life to consist in their gratification. From such a course, since he thus manifests and furthers one side of his being, he undoubtedly gets pleasure. Yet, in so doing, he violates the universal side of his being—the law which connects him with his fellow-men. As the well-being of his organism consists in conformity to the law of the organism, so the true well-being of his social nature consists in conformity with the law of the identification of himself and ot his interests with other men. So far as he subordinates them and their interests to his own particular wants, he is neglecting and disintegrating the universal side of himself, and the result must be pain. There is, again, necessary conflict of feeling.

Twofold Conflict

Yet it will be noticed that there is a difference in the two cases. In the first case, the individual must ultimately feel particular pains of disease, etc., just as he originally felt particular pleasures. In the latter case, unless his greed for his own private pleasures goes so far as to bring him in contact with social law which has become physical—the courts and their penalty—he may not feel any such particular pains. What he feels is rather loss, dissatisfaction, misery. His feelings of pain are rather negative than positive; he feels the loss of higher pleasure, rather than of actual pain. There may be, therefore, a conflict between particular pleasures and pains, or a conflict between pleasures and a higher general feeling of well-being, whose loss may be occasioned by the attainment of particular pleasures. This leads us to recognize a distinction between *pleasure* and *happiness*.

Pleasure and Happiness

The self is not a bare unity, but is a very complex organism, uniting physical, intellectual, æsthetic, social, moral, and religious interests. Now, in acting to gratify any one of these interests, pleasure will necessarily result, but not necessarily happiness. Pleasure will follow because the self has been expressed, has been realized in some one way. But the expression of this particular side of our nature may be in conflict with others; one physical activity may be in conflict with another, or may be in conflict with an intellectual interest. The satisfaction of one may result in lack of satisfaction, non-realization of the others. So there will be no happiness. Pleasure, in short, is transitory and relative, enduring only while some special activity endures, and having reference only to that activity. Happiness is permanent and universal. It results only when the act is such a one as will satisfy all the interests of the self concerned, or will lead to no conflict, either present or remote. Happiness is the feeling of the *whole* self, as opposed to the feeling of some one aspect of self.

Opposition of Pleasure and Happiness

There will be pleasure whenever there is any excitation which is *passively* enjoyed. A life of pleasure-seeking inevitably becomes a life of search for passive enjoyments, for *irritations*. Happiness is *active* satisfaction, or interest. Pleasure, since isolated, comes into conflict with happiness, for happiness is always built upon an active unification of various acts into a whole life. On the other hand, happiness may coexist with pain. A man who has lost money will feel pain, for he has been deprived of one mode of action; but he may continue to be happy. He may not feel the loss as a loss of *himself*. If he is thoroughly identified with more universal and permanent interests, intellectual, æsthetic, social, etc., he will not so feel it.

The Actual and the Ideal Self

So far as the more universal self has not been realized, so far as the individual has not succeeded in identifying himself thoroughly with the wider and more permanent conditions of well-being, but still finds his pleasure in activities which can relate only to particular, limited sides of his nature, the universal self remains only an ideal, and there is a conflict, a dualism between it and the actually realized self. There will also be, therefore, a conflict of feelings, so long as this ideal self is not realized. Pleasure is not a sign of well-being in itself; in an unhealthy soul, as in an unhealthy body, it may be at times a token of disorder, or of degeneration. It may signify that some organic factor is acting in accordance with its natural or acquired nature, but that this factor is isolated from the entire organism, and acting independently of it, must lead to final disintegration, or lack of harmony, unhappiness. The satisfaction of the actual self may result in loss of the ideal, the universal. Happiness, on the other hand, is at all times a sign of well-being. It is, indeed, the internal side of well-being. It is realization of one's true, permanent nature brought home to him as an individual. We have now to pass on to the treatment of the specific forms of qualitative feeling, the intellectual, the æsthetic, and the social.

NOTES TO CHAPTER 13

Upon the nature and laws of qualitative feeling in general, see Nahlowsky, *Das Gefühlsleben*, pp. 1 - 44, 68 - 81; Braubach, *Psychologie des Gefühls*, pp. 48 - 87; Horwicz, *Psychologische Analysen*, vol. ii, pt. 1, pp. 1 - 88; Lotze, *Outlines of Psychology*, pp. 73 - 82, and *Microcosmus*, pp. 240 - 48; Herbart, *Lehrbuch zur Psychologie*, pt. 2, ch. iv; Sully, *Psychology*, ch. xi; Carpenter, *Mental Physiology*, ch. vii; Maudsley, *Physiology of Mind*, ch. vi; Spencer, *Principles of Psychology*, vol. i, pp. 472 - 94; Volkmann, *Lehrbuch der Psychologie*, vol. ii, pp. 298 - 353; Drobisch, *Empirische Psychologie*, pp. 172 - 219; James, in *Mind*, vol. ix, p. 188, on "What Is an Emotion?" Mercier, in *Mind*, vol. ix, pp. 325 and 509, and vol. x, p. 1, on "Classification of Feelings." General treatises upon the emotions are: McCosh, *Emotions*; Maillet, *De l'Essence des Passions*; Maass, *Versuch über die Leidenschaften*; Kehr, *Über das Gemüth*; Jungmann, *Das Gemüth*; Krause, *Die Gesetze des menschlichen Herzens*. Special discussions upon the nature of interest are George, *Lehrbuch der Psychologie*, p. 544 ff.; Erdmann, *Psychologische Briefe*, ch. xiii; Beneke, *Erziehungslehre*, pp. 301 - 10; Bradley, in *Mind*, vol. viii, p. 573; and *passim* in Maudsley's *Pathology of Mind*. More particularly upon pleasure and pain, see Hamilton, *Metaphysics*, lects. xlii - xliv; Murray, *Handbook of Psychology*, pp. 304 - 23; Spencer (*op. cit.*), vol. i, pp. 272 - 90; Bain, *Emotions and Will*, pp. 288 - 300; Martineau, *Types of Ethical Theory*, vol. ii, pp. 297 - 307; Bradley, *Ethical Studies*, pp. 78 - 144; Green, *Prolegomena to Ethics*, pp. 233 - 55; Laurie, *Ethica*, pp. 93 - 104; Sully, *Pessimism*, ch. xi; Dumont, *Théorie Scientifique de la Sensibilité*; Delbœuf, *Théorie de la Sensibilité*; Grote, *Psychologie de la Sensibilité*; Bouillier, *Le Plaisir et la Douleur*; Schneider, *Freud und Leid*; Rolph, *Biologische Probleme*.

14
Intellectual Feelings

Definition and Treatment

Intellectual feelings are such as *accompany our apprehension of the meaning of experience*. Meaning taken by itself is universal; it is that relation of objects to each other which makes them significant of each other; but as this meaning always exists in the medium of individual consciousness, it is *felt* meaning. Objects not only signify each other, but they signify this *to us*. Experience has a meaning not only in that objects are connected with each other, but also as it is connected with ourselves. Experience is feeling, therefore, as well as knowledge; for feeling, in ultimate definition, is simply this intimate connection with self. That factor of emotional experience which has to do with the value which *relations between objects have for us* constitutes intellectual feeling. We shall take up, first, its general nature; second, intellectual feeling as an outgoing energy, a spring to action; third, the objective side of intellectual feeling, the intellectual judgment.

1. General Nature of Intellectual Feeling

Intellectual feeling is not to be considered a special form of feeling, occurring now and then in our experience. There is no experience which does not have involved in it some relation, and there is no experience, therefore, which does not involve intellectual feeling. Looked at on its internal or subjective side, our whole psychical life is a succession of intellectual feelings. Those who fail to see the objective or universal side of consciousness reduce the self, therefore, to a series of feelings. As *my* individual possession, all consciousness *is* feeling. An act of perception, an act of

256

memory, an act of imagination, an act of thinking, an act of intuition, each and all are feelings, for they are states of my unique, unsharable consciousness.

All knowledge whatever exists dissolved in the medium of feeling. Knowledge is an affair not only of objective relations, but of value for me. It bears an indescribable, absolutely personal relation to me, so that while you may know exactly the same that I know, my knowledge cannot possibly be your knowledge. The content of each consciousness may be absolutely identical, but the *form* of each, the fact that one is mine and the other yours, is absolutely distinct. Feeling, therefore, is not a psychical event appearing now and then in consciousness. It is the individual side of all consciousness. Since all consciousness has a content, that is, objective relations, all feeling must also have an intellectual element involved.

Classification of Intellectual Feelings

It is, accordingly, impossible to treat intellectual feeling at all exhaustively in this place. As its scope is as wide as that of experience, all that we can hope to do is to seek out some broad basis of division, which, however inadequate to the complexity of actual fact, will not misrepresent it. Such a division we find by classifying feelings according as they originate (1) in the acquiring of knowledge, and (2) in its possession. Such a division will be seen to correspond in a general way to the distinction made under the head of knowledge between apperception and retention. Some feelings are due to the process by which we learn to know the world; others are due to the result of this, to the organization of knowledge into the structure of our minds.

1. FEELINGS OF ACQUISITION

These correspond quite closely to the formal feelings already studied, except that we now treat them as expressing the internal side of the knowledge acquired, while formerly we treated them as the internal side of the *activity* put forth in acquiring knowledge. They may be considered as connected either with knowledge acquired through association, through dissociation, or through attention. The former are the feelings of custom; the second, the feelings of surprise; the third, the feelings of likeness and difference.

1.   The function of association being mechanical, and consisting in rendering certain combinations habitual and automatic, the feelings which accompany the acquisition of knowledge through association are those of habit and routine. A mind governed for the most part by associative processes has a dry and hard emotional life. Such minds are easy only when in old ruts, and nothing is so disagreeable as the unexpected.

2.   FEELINGS OF DISSOCIATION.   The feeling accompanying knowledge derived from the breaking-up of mechanical associations is essentially one of shock or change. Any association repeated often enough becomes fixed; it becomes part of our mental furniture. We may not *expect* that the same relation will continue forever, for expectation presupposes an active relation of the mind to experience, but we unquestionably take it for granted that it will. When any relation turns up which breaks into this order, hitherto passively acquiesced in, there is a feeling of *surprise*. Natures capable of constantly feeling surprise are much more fresh and vigorous on their emotional side than those whose sluggish associations are not easily disturbed.

Undeveloped and Abnormal Feeling

It is an observation as old as Theophrastus that a boor will not be moved to feeling by the sight of a great truth or of a beautiful statue (because he does not really see them), but that he will stand gaping for hours watching the movements of an ox. This is due to the undeveloped state of feeling. There is also an abnormal condition, not very different in practical result. This is the *nil admirari* spirit; the feeling that there is nothing in heaven or earth which can surprise one, for one has gone through it all. Such a mood results from a cessation of the healthy objectification of feelings, and from dwelling upon them as experiences of self, until the entire capacity for freshness of feeling has been destroyed.

Emotion turned inward eats up itself; and the result is either the assumption of cynicism and the *nil admirari* spirit, or the restless searching for some new thing, the latest sensation, which may stimulate the jaded and wornout emotional nature. If any one violates the law of his being by living upon his feelings, rather than upon the objects to which those feelings normally belong, his power of feeling becomes gradually exhausted, and he defeats his own end. He commits emotional suicide. There has probably never been a time when this unhealthy employment of feeling was so prevalent as it is now. The sole remedy is for the man to get outside of himself by devoting himself to some object, not for the feelings which such devotion will bring him, nor for the sake of getting outside of himself, but for the sake of the object. True feeling, as true knowledge, must be thoroughly objective and universal. There is no contradiction between this statement and the one that feeling is the internal, the subjective side of self, for the true self finds its existence in objects in the universe, not in its own private states. Although it does and must have these private states, it pays attention to them only for the sake of their universal worth. They exist not for their own sake, but as the medium through which the universe makes its significance and value apparent.

3. FEELINGS OF RELATION. The especial function of attention is to unify and discriminate. Accordingly we have the feelings accompanying the agreement or disagreement of our mental experiences. Every identification is accompanied by a peculiar thrill of satisfaction; a feeling which seems to be a combination of the feelings of harmony and of the broadening-out of the mind through the performed identification. There is a like feeling of satisfaction accompanying all clear distinction. When knowledge, previously vague and formless, becomes defined and sharply limited, there is experienced an emotion which seems to be a combination of the formal feeling of clearness hitherto spoken of, and the feeling of having reached an end. For all attention is directed towards the development of self; it has an end at which it aims, and the reaching of this end has its own peculiar

emotion of satisfaction. These feelings of relation take, of course, as many forms as there are kinds of relation. One unique feeling, however, is that of *wit*, which seems to be the feeling which arises when ideas are identified which seem wholly distinct, accompanied by a feeling of suddenness and surprise. When the identification is reached by a process of reasoning there is no feeling of wit. This must be an intuitive flash.

2. FEELINGS OF ACQUIRED KNOWLEDGE

There is not only the feeling which accompanies the acquiring of knowledge, but there is that which accompanies the possession and retention of knowledge. In its characteristic form it is a sense of ownership and of power. It may take a degenerate form, and become merely the feeling of superiority over others, of political power or social recognition which arises from the knowledge. But this occurs only when the feeling is made an end in itself. Normally, it is a feeling that we *possess ourselves*; that we have become masters of ourselves instead of being controlled by external impressions. It is a feeling of having come into possession of our own birthright. It has been said that the great advantage of education is the sense which it gives us of not being dupes. This is another way of stating the truth that the emotion which arises from the organization of knowledge into self is one of self-ownership, of freedom.

Conflict of Intellectual Feelings

As our life is one of progressive realization, not of completed development, of growth rather than of attained being, there comes to be a conflict of intellectual feelings. So far as we have mastered the relations which constitute the material of knowledge, and have organized these into our mental structure, there are the feelings of satisfaction and self-possession already spoken of. But such relations are organically connected with other relations which we have not mastered. There arise, accordingly, feelings of dissatisfaction and of limitation. Were the world divided into two parts, that is to say, were there any relations which were not necessarily connected with others, as parts of one system, such feelings would not necessarily arise. But since, as matter of fact, all relations are thus systematically connected in one whole, every relation known brings with it a dim sense of others with which it is connected, but which are not known. A feeling of knowledge is necessarily accompanied by one of ignorance, and will so continue until the whole organic system of knowledge is mastered.

Feelings of Ignorance

A feeling of ignorance is, therefore, strictly correlative to one of knowledge. A feeling of knowledge is one of the realized self; a feeling of ignorance is one of the unrealized self. One is the feeling of the objective and universal self, so far as this has been made to exist in individual form; the other is the vague and indefinite feeling of this universal self as not realized. An animal may be ignorant, for example, but we cannot conceive it to be conscious of this ignorance, unless we attribute to it a true self-consciousness. Ignorance is the feeling of the division or conflict in our nature.

A feeling of the unknown must be distinguished, therefore, from one of the unknowable. The latter would be a feeling of something utterly unrelated to self, and hence is a psychological impossibility. The feeling that something is unknown, or of ignorance, is the feeling of self, but of self as still incomplete. A feeling of the unknowable would be possible only if we could transcend wholly our own being; a feeling of the unknown is possible, if we can transcend our *present* being, and feel our true being as one which is not yet completely realized. The true function of the feeling of ignorance is, therefore, to serve as an inducement, as a spring, to further action, while a feeling of the unknowable could only paralyze all action. It leads, accordingly, by a natural transition, to our second topic.

11. Feeling as Spring to Intellectual Action

Intellectual feeling, like all feeling, takes the form of an *interest in objects*. It is directed outward; it can find its satisfaction only in an outgoing activity of self. Intellectual feeling, considered in this aspect, is *wonder*. Wonder is the attitude which the emotional nature spontaneously assumes in front of a world of objects. The feeling is utterly incomprehensible as a purely personal or selfish feeling. Wonder is the first and the final expression of the individual as it finds a universe over against it. Wonder, by false education or by selfish indulgence, may be deadened, but it is only by eliminating the very spring to all knowledge that it can be wholly annihilated. The mind cannot entirely lose the sense that it is in the presence of a universe of objects to know which is to find its own true being. Wonder is the emotional outgoing of the mind towards this universe. To lose wholly the feeling of wonder is to lose the sense of the universality and objectivity of mind; it is to sink back contented into one's own subjective possessions, and thus commit intellectual suicide.

Wonder and Surprise

It is evident that wonder is to be distinguished from surprise. Surprise is the emotion experienced when the mind finds itself confronted with an order contravening its established associations. Wonder is the emotion experienced before all objective orders whatever. We feel surprise when, expecting to find a building in a certain place, we find only a heap of smoking ruins. We feel wonder both at the presence of the building and of the ashes. We feel, that is to say, in both cases a challenge to our intelligence. We find an appeal made to our minds to discover what exists there and why it exists. It may come about that we grow so used to our customary environment that we feel wonder only when the shock of surprise strikes us, but the normal healthy attitude of the mind is wonder at all facts, familiar or novel, until it has mastered their meaning and made itself at home among them.

Wonder and Knowledge

It is not strange, therefore, that both Plato and Aristotle regarded wonder as the source of science and of philosophy, for wonder is the sole spring which can take a man beyond his subjective states, and put him in that active relation to the world which is the sole condition of getting at its meaning. But it is no less true that wonder is the cause of all growth, of all increase of knowledge. It is not only the originator, but it is the continuer of science. Ordinary minds may accept mere familiarity as sufficient credentials for a fact, but the scientific mind finds in the fact that it is familiar only additional cause for wonder. Most of us get to think that the mere fact of experience that things are such and such, is reason enough why they should be so; the scientific mind continues to wonder why they should be so, and is impelled to discover their meaning. It has been well said that there is no better test of genius than the ability to wonder at what is familiar.

Disinterestedness and Curiosity

Wonder is the simple recognition that objects have significance for us beyond the mere fact of their existence. It is accordingly the spring to that activity which shall discover their significance. A wide development of the feeling of wonder constitutes *disinterestedness*, the primary requisite for all investigation. Wonder, as the outgoing activity of mind, necessarily requires a surrender of all purely subjective and selfish interests, and the devotion of one's self to the object wholly for the sake of the latter. It is love of knowledge; and knowledge is necessarily objective and universal. It is vitiated by the presence of any merely personal interest. When the activity occurs not for the sake of the object, but for the sake of satisfying the personal emotion of wonder, we have, not disinterestedness, but *curiosity*. The feeling is separated from its connection with objects, and is given an independent existence in consciousness. This is why the term "curiosity," which might be synonymous with wonder, has come to have a bad meaning. It is wonder which has taken a personal form.

Abnormal Feelings

As such, curiosity is an abnormal feeling. It is possible, however, for intellectual feelings to assume still more unhealthy forms. Such we have when knowledge is sought for the gratification of vanity, or for the sake of show or power. A more subtle form is that distinctively nineteenth-century

disease, the love of culture, as such. When the feeling is
directed not towards objects, but towards the state of mind
induced by the knowledge of the objects, there originates a
love of knowing, for the sake of the development of the mind
itself. The knowledge is acquired because it widens and
expands self. Culture of our mental powers is made an end
in itself, and knowledge of the universe of objects is subordinated to this. The intellectual feelings are separated from
their proper place as functions of the integral life, and are
given an independent place in consciousness. Here, as in all
such cases, the attempt defeats itself. The only way to
develop self is to make it become objective; the only way to
accomplish this is to surrender the interests of the personal
self. Self-culture reverses the process, and attempts to employ self-objectification or knowledge as a mere means to the
satisfaction of these personal interests. The result is that the
individual never truly gets outside of himself.

III. Objective Side of Feeling

As this has been presupposed in what has already been
said, it may be passed over briefly here. Intellectual feeling,
in the first place, is the internal side of all knowledge; it is
objects and their relations dissolved in the medium of individual consciousness. In the second place, it is, as wonder,
the spring to intellectual activity; the source of the endeavor
to master the meaning of objects. In whatever way we look
at feeling, accordingly, we find it connected with objects.
We have now only to trace the process of its connection very
briefly.

Presentiment

All intellectual activity is directed towards an end. Yet just
what that end is we do not know; if we did, we should not be
going through the mental process of reaching it. Yet our
reaching this end depends upon directing all our thoughts
according to it; we must select and reject mental material
according to its reference to this end. The end, therefore,
exists in the mind by way of feeling. We do not know what
it is, but we dimly *feel* what it is; and we select material that

feels congruous with this end, and reject that which *feels* unharmonious. The direction of all intellectual processes by feeling is very commonly overlooked, but it is fundamental. Our knowledge consists in giving feelings definite form and in projecting them. Knowledge is the attempt on the part of feeling to give an account of itself. That aspect which guides feeling in this attempt we may call *presentiment*, using the word in a wider sense than is usual.

Intuitive Feeling

This fore-grasp of feeling upon what is not yet intellectually identified and discriminated constitutes a form of intuition. This power of intuition or of feeling in what direction truth lies, a vague power of foretelling what its general nature is and what measures must be taken to reach it, is one of the unfailing marks of intellectual genius. It is a matter which cannot be subjected to rules, and which belongs to the individual alone, since it is a matter of feeling. No mind can teach another to feel as it does. After, however, the end has been reached, it is possible for consciousness reflectively to trace the steps and formulate the process. It will be found that feeling has been controlled when it succeeds in reaching the end by certain general considerations.

Feeling and Logic

Feeling, when thus reflectively criticised and crystallized into intellectual propositions, gives rise to the rules of the logic of method. Logic, as the science of investigation, must wait upon the actual discoveries of the intellect, which are controlled by feeling. It is reflective and critical, not intuitive and creative; it, therefore, may be taught, while the actual process of discovering new truth can never be imparted. It must follow after, not precede, discovery. Logic, in short, only generalizes and crystallizes what was originally existing in the form of feeling. A judgment is the projection of a fore-feeling that things are so and so; logic can only sum up the considerations, according to which feeling works in forming these projections.

NOTES TO CHAPTER 14

Martineau, *Types of Ethical Theory*, vol. ii, pp. 141 - 54; Bain, *Emotions and Will*, pp. 199 - 209; Wundt, *Grundzüge der physiologischen Psychologie*, vol. ii, pp. 347 - 52; Nahlowsky, *Das Gefühlsleben*, pp. 157 - 62; Strümpell, *Grundriss der Psychologie*, p. 271 ff.; Beneke, *Psychologische Skizzen*, vol. i, pp. 227 - 62; Perez, *L'Éducation dès le Berceau*, pp. 35 - 72; James, in *Mind*, vol. iv, p. 317, on "Sentiment of Rationality"; Sully, *Psychology*, pp. 521 - 30.

15
Æsthetic Feeling

Definition and Mode of Treatment

Æsthetic feelings are such as *accompany the apprehension of the ideal value of experience*. They are presupposed in the intellectual emotions which are the feelings of the meaning of experience, or of the relation of objects to each other; for meaning, or relation, as we saw when studying knowledge, is a thoroughly ideal factor. We shall take up, first, the general nature of æsthetic feeling, its analysis, and various elements; second, æsthetic feeling as a spring to activity, or the fine arts; third, the objective side of æsthetic feeling, the æsthetic judgment, or taste.

1. General Nature

As just said, æsthetic feeling is that which arises from the contemplation of the ideal value of any factor of experience. This does not mean that there exists first an intellectual apprehension of certain relations, and then that this apprehension is followed by another apprehension of the congruence or incongruence of these relations to a certain ideal, accompanied by a feeling of æsthetic quality. It is meant that every element of experience stands in certain relations to the ideal of mind, and that the mind immediately responds to these relations by a feeling of beauty or ugliness. The feeling is the internal, individual side of the process; it goes before rather than follows any intellectual apprehension. We shall consider (1) the connection of the feeling of beauty with idealization; (2) the universality of the feeling; (3) the principal elements which make it.

1. IDEALIZATION AND THE ÆSTHETIC FEELING

Every content of consciousness may have an element of beauty in it, or, indeed, must have it so far as it must contain an ideal element. We speak of a beautiful landscape; a beautiful statue or musical composition; a beautiful truth, a beautiful deed or character. So the adjective ugly is applied to fact and to moral action as well as to professedly artistic creation. Yet it is not to the intellectual phase of the truth, nor to the moral aspect of the character that the æsthetic quality appertains. The truth is called beautiful because it thrills the soul with a peculiar feeling of an ideal indwelling in nature which finds an expression in this truth; the character is beautiful because of a like embodiment of an ideal. There is a sense of satisfaction felt in each, apart from any information conveyed by the truth, or any approval induced by the character. This feeling of satisfaction in the objective presentation of any harmonious ideal constitutes æsthetic sentiment.

Intellectual and Æsthetic Idealization

There is no knowledge whatever without idealization, and yet beauty is not truth, nor intellectual feeling the same as æsthetic. How this can be, the following illustration may serve to suggest. A person in knowing a locomotive goes through a process of idealization. He reads into the sensations presented to him all the relations possible and thus renders the sensations significant. Just in the degree in which he can read the results of past experience into these sensations may he be said truly to know the locomotive. Yet this process of idealization does not constitute an æsthetic quality. The idealization takes a wholly objective form. It is regarded as a property of the object. The ideal quality exists, but it is absorbed in the thing. The feelings which we have are intellectual feelings; they are feelings of the relation of the locomotive to other objects, and of its parts to each other. On the other hand, the locomotive has "beauty" so far as it is felt to be the fit and successful *embodiment of an idea in outward form.* Its inventor was an artist when he succeeded in so working out his own idea (inner at first) that it assumed the appropriate sensuous detail. Æsthetic emotion is still experienced whenever we consider not merely the parts of the machine in their reciprocal relations to one another, but the locomotive in its whole function; in its spirit or idea, its power to break down barriers of distance and bind men together in the exchange of goods and ideas. The intellectual interest has to do with the parts of a *product*; the æsthetic with the *process* of uttering an idea.

Sensuous Element in Beauty

There can be no beautiful object without the presence of the sensuous element, as there can be no object of knowledge without it. The arrangement, however, of the sensuous material is much more important from an artistic point of view than from an intellectual. When a rose is considered as an object of knowledge, it is indifferent what color it possesses. The clashing of cymbals may be made as much an object of scientific investigation as the rendering of a sonata of Beethoven. But in art, the color, even its purely sensuous qualities, and the sound, even apart from higher ideal associations, constitute much of the effect to be reached. An idea may be very beautiful in itself, but become ugly by the sensuous material used to embody it, while a comparatively mediocre conception may be rendered fairly beautiful by suitable handling of material. This increased importance of sensuous basis in art is not in contradiction to what was said in the previous paragraph regarding the greater share of idealization in art, but in confirmation of it. The sensuous material is not of greater importance in itself, but as a vehicle for presenting the ideal. In knowledge the sensation is indifferent—that is to say, any sensation is capable of conveying some information, and as mere matter of knowledge, one piece of information is as important as another; in art, the sensation is of value, because *certain* sensuous stuff serves to present the idea, while other material utterly fails.

Freedom in Art

It follows that, since in art the sensuous material is handled solely with reference to its fitness for embodying values or ideals, art appears in freer form than science. Science must conform to the relations which are found actually to exist. The freedom of art does not mean that it can deal capriciously with these actual relations or with fact. But it does mean that fact can be found to have an aspect in which it is not a constraint upon self or an external limit to self, but in which it satisfies some interest or idea of self. Art is free because it can thus handle the fact as one with self instead of as a material foreign to it. Its freedom does not lie in emancipation from law, but in the fact that the laws which it follows are laws of the self.

Idealism and Realism in Art

This enables us to decide upon the proper function of the so-called "ideal" and "real" elements in art. In strictest sense, a purely realistic, as a purely idealistic, art is impossible—that is to say, pure realism would have no meaning to appeal to the mind, for meaning is a product of idealization, and would have no interest to appeal to the emotions, for interest is a product of the putting of self into fact. And pure idealism, if interpreted to mean that sensuous material shall not be used, is impossible, for an ideal unembodied, unmanifested, would have no meaning whatever. Furthermore, all meaning is meaning *of fact*, of reality. It cannot exist in the air. The careful, minute, and faithful study of actual fact is needed, therefore, first, that one may know what the value of an experience really is; and, secondly, that one may know the concrete sensuous material which shall be used in presenting it. All art, however, is idealistic in the sense that it has for its function the appreciation of the ideal values of experience, and subordinates the treatment of its material to the conveying of this material. The material exists for the sake of the realization of the ideal.

2. THE UNIVERSALITY OF BEAUTY

This introduces us to the universal quality of æsthetic feeling. This is a necessary corollary of its ideal nature, for value, significance, is necessarily universal and cannot be confined to any one particular time or place. The form in which the idea is realized is necessarily particular; the beautiful object exists here and now; but its beauty is not a thing of time or place. An author may study a phase of society which is extremely local and transient. If his object is merely to reproduce in his pages this society, his work is not one of art, but of science. It is a study in sociology. If, however, he manages to portray through the medium of this material the ideal significance of the society, it is art. No matter how much of perishing and particular detail he may introduce, the result is universal. It is true, as we say, *to human nature*; that is, to the permanent and essential being of man, and will, therefore, always appeal to those in whom the idea of man lives. Universality does not depend upon the material employed, but upon the spirit in which it is treated. We have now to study some of the ways in which this universality of feeling appears.

(1) In the first place, the universality of æsthetic feeling necessarily precludes the lower senses from any important *rôle* in art. Tasting or smelling an object requires that it be brought into actual contact with the organism and bodily appropriated by it, either in whole or part. Such feelings may be agreeable, but they cannot be beautiful. What they convey is simply a relation of agreement between the substance and the given organism, not an agreement or harmony between the object and intelligence in general, by reason of idea symbolized by it. Such feelings are selfish; they have no universal aspect.

(2) A beautiful object must exclude the *feeling* of ownership. The beautiful *object* may be owned, but its beauty cannot be. If what one enjoys in a beautiful object is the sense of its ownership, his feeling is not an æsthetic one. So far, indeed, as any feeling enters into the experience, which is not capable of being shared by all who witness the beautiful object, the sentiment is not an æsthetic one. All enjoyment of possession, as well as of immediate physical use, must be excluded.

(3) Finally, the universality of æsthetic feeling requires that the beautiful object be not subordinated to *any* external end. There is no *separation* of use and beauty, of useful and fine art, but there is a distinction. Both kinds of art are ways of expressing an idea and thus have a common

principle. But in the *merely* useful this process of expression is simply a means to some product beyond. It has no free value, but only as leading up to the article produced. There is a divorce of the process from its product. So far as the action is useful not simply *to something else*, but in itself and to the whole self, there is beauty. A locomotive is merely "useful" if we consider it not in its relations to the idea which it actively expresses, but in relations to some external shipper or stockholder. It is "beautiful" if considered as a way of realizing social ideas and interests.

3. THE FACTORS OF ÆSTHETIC FEELING

We have already seen that the characteristics which mark æsthetic feeling are its ideality and universality; that it is characterized by great freedom, suggestiveness, and unrestrained manipulation of sensuous material to embody the ideal effect aimed at. It may be objected that these terms are all very general and vague, and that we should be able to point out just those characteristics which constitute beauty and awaken the æsthetic feeling. It is impossible to limit art in this way, however, as one of its most striking characteristics is that it cannot be defined. It is impossible to tell beforehand just what combination of qualities will appear beautiful, or how they should be arranged to excite æsthetic feeling. We can only point out the very general characteristics which all beautiful objects are found to possess.

Harmony

The most general property, constituting beauty, is *harmony*, or *variety in unity*. It is impossible to give a more definite answer, because the element of harmony may take thousands of different shapes. Art is essentially creative, and it is impossible to limit it beforehand by rules. It makes its own rules. It is impossible to tell what a beautiful object is except by creating or contemplating some particular beautiful object. We can lay down some formal considerations, but we cannot tell anything about the concrete content in any other way. We have, therefore, simply to analyze the idea of harmony.

Harmony and the Feeling of Self

Harmony is, in essence, the feeling *of the agreement of some experience with the ideal nature of the self*. This distinguishes it from the feeling of agreement or congruity which plays so important a part in intellectual feeling. That is a feeling of agreement of *relations*. Whether the feeling of beauty is excited by the perception of regular form, of a picturesque landscape, a pleasing melody, a poem, or a painting, its essence is the felt harmony of the beautiful object with our own inmost nature. We find a landscape beautiful because we find ourselves in some way reflected in it. It appeals to us. This does not mean that we have a prior conception of our nature, and, consciously finding this realized in the landscape, call the latter beautiful. Rather the landscape serves to reveal to us something hitherto unknown of our own capacities and sympathies.

Adaptation and Economy

The term adaptation also involves the idea of harmony. It has, however, two meanings. That which is merely calculated to procure some end beyond itself has an external adaptation, and is useful simply. But when many means, diverse and even opposed in themselves, are adjusted into an internal unity through some single function, purpose, or idea, which reflects itself in each detail, there is beauty. A cart-wheel has adaptation of members to an end, but the means and end are external to one another. In a living being, on the contrary, the adaptation shines through and gives meaning to each of the component members. Another term, expressing the same idea, is economy. When a result is rich and full, and is reached by a few means and these few simple and accurately fitted to the end, there is beauty. The graceful is always the economical, the awkward the wasteful and ill-adapted.

II. Æsthetic Feeling as a Spring to Action

Æsthetic feeling not only goes out into objects where it takes the form of beauty, but in its connection with these objects becomes a source of interest to the mind, and hence leads to action for the satisfaction of this interest. Æsthetic feeling, in other words, is something more than passive enjoyment of beauty; it is active delight in it, it is love for it; and love can be satisfied only with the production of that which is loved. Feeling thus becomes a spring to creative activity which in its result takes the form of the fine arts. As the intellectual feelings, as springs to action, take the form of wonder, so the æsthetic feelings take the form of *admiration*. Admiration is love of beauty, as wonder is love of knowledge.

The Fine Arts

Art is, therefore, the attempt to satisfy the æsthetic side of our nature. As the æsthetic side of our nature is the feeling of the ideal as such, it follows that art can completely satisfy admiration, only when it completely manifests the ideal— whatever that may be. And as we have seen that this ideal is the completely developed self, we may say that the end of art is to create that in which the human soul may find itself perfectly reflected. Or as the essential factor in beauty is harmony—harmony with self—we may say that the end of art is to produce a perfectly harmonized self. The various fine arts, architecture, sculpture, painting, music, and po- etry, are the successive attempts of the mind adequately to express its own ideal nature, or, more correctly stated, ade- quately to produce that which will satisfy its own demands for and love of a perfectly harmonious nature, something in which admiration may rest.

Architecture

Architecture is the beginning of this ideal creation. It is an art which appeals especially to the eye, and since its prod- ucts occupy the three dimensions of space, to touch and the muscular sense. It is the least idealized of the arts, for it depends in the largest degree upon the actual material used, and it uses this material least freely since it has to subordi- nate it to certain ends of utility. Its imposing forms, as well as its size, however, make its effects approach those of sublimity. Its æsthetic influence is one of vague, but powerful, emotion. The fact that this emotion is so akin to one of dependence and worship renders this art especially fitted for religious associations. The greatest architectural productions have always been temples and cathedrals. Another reason for this is, that a building for worship obtrudes less than any other kind its especial end of use, and so allows the artist more of that freedom of creation which is a requisite to all high art.

Sculpture and Painting

The art of sculpture appeals to the same senses as architecture, and is, indeed, generally found associated with it, all art of this kind, excepting the lower forms of domestic art, having been produced with at least a partial architectural effect in view. This art is more ideal than architecture, however, for it is less obviously subordinated to any use; its effects depend more upon the idea which is to be conveyed and less upon the material employed; and it is more intimately connected with man's own nature, for it is usually employed in constructing the human figure, and in presenting some human ideal, while architecture in itself must be confined to physical material, which is, therefore, inadequate to express man's true nature. Painting mounts a step higher. Its material is color alone, occupying two dimensions of space. It depends less upon actual objective existence (is less realistic, if one choose to use that word) than either of the preceding arts. The sensuous element in painting is nought but a certain amount of varicolored pigment laid on a surface, and, without the interpreting action of intelligence, is dead and meaningless. Painting widens the range of man's ideal expression of himself, likewise, for it represents man's passions and man's deeds, and not alone his outward figure at rest. It also brings Nature into ideal relations with man, rendering her spirit in its kinship to man's.

Music

In music the ideal factor assumes still greater prominence. The material used has no longer even an existence in space. It is rather internal in character, filling time only in the form of sounds. The æsthetic quality, or beauty, is the manifestation of man's soul through these sounds. The sounds are nothing; the indwelling idea of the artist is all. Music is not only less material than the arts already studied, but it is freer. It seems like an actual embodiment of the artist's own feelings for the beautiful. While in the other arts it is possible reflectively to trace something of the rules which the artist followed in producing, music appears like an immediate projection of a creative nature. The laws of the combination and arrangement of sounds can indeed be made out, but the laws for the selection of these arrangements remain hidden in the artist's breast. Music also reveals its higher ideal character in the part which harmony plays in it. There is harmony in architecture, but it appears as more or less external, as spatial proportion, etc.; in painting, it appears in the gradation of colors, in the massing of light and shades, in the composition of the figures; but in music, it is the very soul of the production. It is not the arrangement of the material; it is the material.

Poetry

In poetry, however, art for the first time becomes thoroughly ideal. The sensuous basis is now degraded to an arbitrary symbol having next to no value in itself. That which it possesses is musical, and has its significance only as the vehicle of ideas. Here for the first time is the content of experience adequate to the ideal form employed. That is to say, here for the first time is the subject-matter living man himself. It does not deal with his material presentment, as sculpture, nor with the shadowy representation of his form, as painting, nor with his emotions and aspirations, as music, but with his own vital personality. It is true that there is a poetry of nature, as well as of man, but nature is treated only as the reflex of man's spirit, of his hopes and fears, loves and admirations. In poetry, also, man works with even greater freedom than in music. Its material is not non-living sounds, whose freedom, after all, must be assimilated or imparted freedom, but personalities, whose action is the expression of their own inner nature. Its form is also freer, being less subject to restrictions of mathematical relations.

Forms of Poetry

Poetry may be divided into epic, lyric, and dramatic, neglecting minor subdivisions. Epic poetry treats men as, in a
certain sense, natural forces. It gives man's acts, rather than
his motives and springs to action. It shows him moved to
great deeds, in company with other men, by great external
forces, but it shows us the deeds and the company, rather
than the workings of man's heart and his individuality. It is
objective poetry. Lyric poetry, on the other hand, is little
concerned with historical happenings, or with mythical
counterfeits of history. It cares little for action and results.
It finds its field in man's inner life; it expresses his individual experiences—his loves, hates, desires, joys and sorrows.

Dramatic poetry unites many of the characteristics of
each of the two foregoing classes. It deals with men in
groups, and men in action. It shows the action, rather than
tells us of it. It does not paint life, but it sets it before us. It
shows us these acts, however, as the outcome of man's
personal motives, rather than as the result of any external
historical forces or tendencies. It shows us man, not in the
interior recesses of his own subjective nature alone, nor man
as swayed by forces beyond him to a goal of which he knows
nothing, but man as irresistibly pushing on towards an
inevitable end through his own personal desires and intentions. It shows us man's interior nature working itself out as
an objective fact. It consummates, therefore, the range of
fine arts, because in dramatic form we have the highest ideal
of self, personality displaying itself in the form of personality. The ideal and the mode of its embodiment are both
personal, and beyond this art cannot go, for in this man finds
himself expressed.

III.   The Æsthetic Judgment or Taste

Æsthetic feeling, like intellectual, has its objective side.
Beauty is a quality which we spontaneously attribute to
objects. Admiration is the energy of æsthetic feeling directed outwards. It follows that the feeling of beauty necessarily passes over into the judgment of beauty. We not only

feel a certain thrill of satisfaction, but we perform an intellectual act. We say the painting, the landscape, is beautiful; we regard the feeling not as an affection of our own subjective consciousness, but we objectify it. Feeling must express itself.

In the great artist the impulse to expression, the demand for an adequate interpretation of the feeling, is much stronger than in the ordinary individual, and so he is impelled to creation; but the impulse is strong enough in every individual, so that he *recognizes* something as beautiful. The great artists are, after all, only the interpreters of the common feelings of humanity; they but set before us, as in concrete forms of self-revealing clearness, the dim and vague feelings which surge for expression in every human being, finding no adequate outlet. Thus it is that we always find a great work of art *natural*; in its presence we do not feel ourselves before something strange, but taken deeper into ourselves, having revealed to us some of those mysteries of our own nature which we had always felt but could not express. The æsthetic judgment, in short, is implicit in all human beings. The artist helps it into light.

Taste

Just as the intellectual feelings, when precipitated in the form of judgments, are afterwards condensed in the form of logical principles and rules, so the æsthetic judgments crystallize in the form of the principles of *taste*. The "faculty" of taste is simply a generic name for the power which the individual possesses of framing judgments concerning beauty. The principles of taste are the product of the reflective analysis of the understanding as it goes over the action of æsthetic feeling, and attempts to discover the lines along which the latter spontaneously expresses itself. They are attempts to formulate the characteristics of that object which feeling, without consciousness of rules, pronounces to be beautiful. It follows that taste is something individual in its nature, depending upon the æsthetic capacity and culture of the one exercising it. It follows, also, that while the rules of taste may be imparted, the method of creating or even of appreciating beauty cannot be handed from one to another.

It is a matter of individual feeling, of æsthetic tact, and the canons of taste furnish only the dry solution of that which exists in living form in the soul of the artist. Artistic feeling is creative; taste is critical. It must follow after art, not precede it.

Function of Taste

It is with matters of beauty as Aristotle says it is with matters of right conduct; only the man of an artistic or ethical nature is a judge, in individual cases, of what is beautiful or good. Yet the formulation of the principles according to which feeling works in pronouncing anything beautiful is not useless. The attempt to say what is beautiful sets up an ideal of beauty towards which the artistic impulses may direct themselves, and which may keep them from being wasted in vain and unfertile attempts. The conscious ideal may serve as a criterion of what is produced, and as a guide of what to produce. It must not be forgotten, however, that this conscious ideal gets its definite shape only from past productions, and while new creations must be informed by this ideal, the ideal must be constantly widened to include these new developments. Every attempt to set up the ideal as *ultimate* has two evil effects. In the first place, it stifles the efforts of the individual, and substitutes for that spontaneous freedom of action which is the essence of æsthetic production a rigid obedience to externally imposed rules. In the second place, it ties the ideal down to what has already been accomplished, and thus destroys its ideal character. It fossilizes the ideal into cut-and-dried formulæ. What should be a spur to new creation becomes a burdensome command to produce nothing new.

Abnormal Æsthetic Feeling

The tendency of æsthetic feeling to get an independent existence in consciousness, and to be cultivated, not for the sake of the beautiful object, but for the sake of the personal satisfaction which it gives the one enjoying it, is great. Æsthetic feeling, in other words, degenerates into *æstheticism*. Admiration is no longer a love of beauty, an interest in whatever makes the universe lovely, but love for the pleasures of beauty; an interest in the reflex effect which the loveliness of the universe has upon the individual soul. Or a correct taste may become the object sought, rather than genuine appreciation of what gives experience its value. Instead of surrendering one's self to admiration of the beautiful object, the individual may regard admiration as a confession of weakness, and assume an attitude of superiority. He becomes a connoisseur or an amateur, and prides himself upon his fastidiousness and refinement of taste rather than loses himself in the realm of objective beauty. Feeling, in short, is shut up within itself, instead of being made the key to the unlocking of the beauty, grace, and loveliness of the universe. The penalty is inevitable—loss of freshness, of healthiness, and finally of all vitality of feeling. Feeling has to live on itself, instead of finding new food in every object of experience, and it ends by destroying itself.

NOTES TO CHAPTER 15

Allen, *Physiological Æsthetics*; Gurney, *Power of Sound*; Hamilton, *Metaphysics*, lect. xlvi; Bain, *Emotions and Will*, pp. 247 - 70; McCosh, *Emotions*, pp. 148 - 214; Sully, *Sensation and Intuition*, pp. 186 - 245, and *Psychology*, pp. 531 - 52; Murray, *Handbook of Psychology*, pp. 223 - 35, 387 - 90; Lazarus, *Das Leben der Seele*, vol. i (essay on "Humor"); vol. ii (essay on "Psychology of Fine Arts"); Strümpell, *Grundriss der Psychologie*, p. 275 ff.; Lipps, *Psychologische Studien*, fourth essay; Spencer, *Principles of Psychology*, vol. ii, pp. 627 - 48; Nahlowsky, *Das Gefühlsleben*, pp. 162 - 97; Horwicz, *Psychologische Analysen*, vol. ii, pt. 2, pp. 176 - 225; Wundt, *Grundzüge der physiologischen Psychologie*, vol. ii, pp. 179 - 94; Perez, *First Three Years of Childhood*, pp. 265 - 81; Hecker, *Die Psychologie des Lachens und des Komischen*; Siebeck, *Das Wesen der ästhetischen Anschauung*; Carriere, *Die Idee des Schönen*, and *Das Wesen und die Formen der Poesie*; Dimetresco, *Der Schönheitsbegriff*; Dreher, *Kunst in ihrer Beziehung zur Psychologie*; Hermann, *Æsthetische Farbenlehre*; Vischer, *Æsthetik*; Ulrici, *Grundzüge der praktischen Philosophie*, pp. 157 - 83; Rosenkranz, *Æsthetik des Hässlichen*; Eye, *Das Reich des Schönen*; Lotze, *Geschichte der Æsthetik*; Fechner, *Vorschule der Æsthetik*; Neudecker, *Studien* (historical); Perez, *L'Éducation dès le Berceau*, pp. 11 - 159; Joly, *Notions de Pédagogie*, p. 210 ff.; Meyer, *Aus der ästhetischen Pädagogik*; Volkmann, *Lehrbuch der Psychologie*, vol. ii, pp. 353 - 63.

16
Personal Feeling

Definition and Mode of Treatment

Personal feelings are such as *arise from the relations of self-conscious beings to each other*. All feeling is the accompaniment of self-realization. No individual can realize himself in impersonal relations—relations of things to each other or to an ideal. He can truly develop himself only in self-conscious activity, in personality, and this is impossible without relations to other persons. A person developing his personality in isolation from other persons, through contact with intellectual or æsthetic material, is impossible. It is hardly conceivable that he should ever become a being capable of knowing objects, and of enjoying beauty, without the aid and stimulus given by others; it is impossible to conceive him as developing the social side of his nature. Following the lines hitherto laid down, we shall take up: I. The general nature of personal feeling; II. Personal feeling as a spring to action, or love; III. The objective side of personal feeling, the social judgment or conscience.

I. General Nature of Personal Feeling

There are sometimes said to be two distinct *kinds* of feeling for persons; one, feelings for self, egoistic or personal feelings, properly so called; the other, feelings for others, altruistic or social feelings. This division supposes that, in the first place, feelings belong to our own limited individuality, and are considered only as they affect one's immediate self, but may afterwards be extended to include other individuals. It overlooks the necessary *reciprocal* relation of egoistic and altruistic feelings. There can be no egoistic feelings except as the self is distinguished from others and set over against them; there can be no altruistic feelings, except as others are recognized in their relations to self, and compared with it. Our first feelings are not personal, in the sense of egoistic.

They are, properly considered, not personal at all; they become personal only as they are *referred* to persons; and they cannot be referred to the *ego*, except as the *ego* is compared, consciously or unconsciously, with others, and preferred before them; they cannot become altruistic except as others are compared with the immediate claims of the *ego*. The love of property, the feeling of rivalry, of anger, of the love of approbation, the feeling of self-esteem or pride, of selfishness, may be egoistic feelings, but they are so only because of an act which recognizes, at one and the same time, self and not-self, *ego* and *alter*. The self has no meaning except as contrasted with other persons. Egoistic feelings are impossible except through a connection with altruistic feelings. "Mine" requires a contrasted "thine."

Classification of Personal Feelings

Recognizing, therefore, that personal feelings cannot be classified as egoistic and altruistic, as each necessarily involves the other, we may properly classify them, in the order of increasing universality, as social, moral, and religious. Not only are egoistic feelings *not* the original type of personal feelings, but they are not *normal* feelings at all, when egoistic is interpreted in a selfish sense. Love of property, for example, is not a selfish feeling; it is one form in which the self necessarily expands and expresses its being. It becomes selfish only when the feeling is isolated from the object, and the pleasure of property, the connection of property with one's immediate self, is made the object of contemplation or of action. Severed in this way from its connection with the object, and given independent existence in consciousness, it is, like all such feeling, abnormal.

1. SOCIAL FEELINGS

Since feelings for self are as thoroughly social in their nature as feelings for others; since, indeed, one class is not possible without the other, we recognize two forms of social feeling, of others and of self. One is the feeling of others in their relation to self; the other is the feeling of self in its relation to others. They are not feelings which can exist apart from one another; they are phases of the same feeling separable only through abstraction. Each is further resolvable into two types: feeling for others, into sympathy and antipathy; feeling for self, into humility and pride.

1. SYMPATHY AND ANTIPATHY. Both of these feelings manifest the essential unity of human nature, appearing though it does in various individuals. They are feelings *which result from the identification of one's self with another*, antipathy no less than sympathy. Were it not for the unity of one nature with another, and the possible identification resulting from this kinship, the feeling of indifference (which is properly not a feeling, but its absence) would be the only state of mind in which one person could stand towards another.

Antipathy

The special forms of antipathy are *disgust* and *indignation*. In disgust we identify the state of mind or experience of others with ourselves, and find it repulsive to our own actual state. Indignation is to be distinguished from anger and rage. The latter are more or less blind, impulsive outbursts of feeling against whatever obstructs our pleasurable activity or brings us positive pain. They may be directed against things as well as persons; it is only by experience that they come to be restricted to the latter. Indignation is a feeling that results from identifying the course of action or emotional mood of another with ourselves, when this course or mood comes short in large measure of our own ideal. Could we not identify the other person with self, and then measure both by a common ideal, the feeling of indignation would be impossible.

Sympathy

This feeling results from an identification with self of such experiences of others as are felt to be possible experiences of our own. The feeling may be unpleasant as much as that of disgust itself, but the experience which excites the latter feeling is one which we feel repulsive to our inmost self; while that awakening sympathy we feel as something common to our natures. In sympathy we take the feelings of another for our own; in disgust or indignation, we say that we would not have such feelings for our own. We generally speak of sympathizing with the griefs of others, but, of course, sympathy comprehends their joys as well. But the community of sorrow seems wider than that of gladness.

Origin of Sympathy

Sympathy has its origin in what is termed resonance or contagion of feeling. There is a psychical atmosphere as well as a physical, and one living in this atmosphere absorbs and reflects it. Laughter and crying are both "catching." We unconsciously reproduce the feelings of those about us; we take on their mood unaware. The method appears to be as follows: we see the physical sign of grief or joy. By pure reflex or imitative action our own features tend to take on this expression and induce the same feeling. There is the tendency to interpret this sign, and as the feeling can be interpreted only as it is reproduced, the person himself assumes the mood. We know what the sign of anger means only as we ourselves feel anger. These two facts combined form the psychological mechanism of the origin of sympathy.

Nature of Sympathy

But this is only the basis of the emotion. As already said, in sympathy we take the feelings of others *for our own*. The process just described only reproduces in ourselves the feelings of others; it originates certain emotions in ourselves, but that is all that it does. For sympathy, we must not only have this feeling ourselves, but we must recognize, in addition, that it is the experience of some one else. A skilful actor may, by the foregoing process, awaken in us just the emotion which he desires, but this is not necessarily sympathy. For we may recognize that it is all a "show," a make-believe, and thus, while experiencing just the same feelings as the actor, never dream of projecting them beyond ourselves, and of regarding them as the real feelings of others.

Sympathy, in short, is the reproduction of the experience of another, *accompanied by the recognition of the fact that it is his experience.*

Conditions of Sympathy

The conditions of sympathetic feeling are, therefore, first, ability to apprehend, consciously or unconsciously, the feelings of others, and to reproduce them in our minds; and, secondly, the ability to forget self, and remember that these feelings, although our own feelings, are, after all, the experience of some one else. Sympathy involves distinction as well as identification. I must not only assume into myself the experiences of a man who is suffering from poverty, in order to sympathize with him, but I must realize them as *his*; I must separate them from my own personal self, and objectify them in him.

Thus it is that many persons who are extremely sensitive to the feelings of others are quite unsympathetic. They register in their own mood each slight variation of feeling in those about them, as a barometer registers physical variations; but they have no true sympathy, for they regard these new feelings only as new experiences *of their own*; they do not project them outward. The conditions of such projection are, first, sufficient emotional experience of our own to be able to apprehend and take on those of others; second, such an *active interest* in others as will enable us to regard these experiences as truly theirs. We must not only take their life into ours, but we must put ours into them. Sympathy, as active interest, thus becomes love and a spring to action, which we will treat under the second head.

Function of Sympathy

It is impossible to over-estimate the importance of sympathy in the emotional life. It is there what attention is in the strictly intellectual department; as the latter is the sole means by which objects and relations come within the reach of our consciousness, so sympathy is the sole means by which persons come within the range of our life. It is thus an extremely universal feeling, for it takes us beyond what constitutes our immediate personality, our private interests and concerns, into what universally constitutes personality. It may be limited at first to those of our own family, our own rank in society, our own neighborhood, but this is because of a defective sympathy; it is because we have learned to sympathize only with that which is in harmony with some limited aspect of our own nature; as our nature widens and becomes developed there must be a corresponding increase of sympathy, and this increase can reach its end only in a completely developed personality, a personality which has become absolutely universal. Such a sympathy can, of course, recognize no distinction of social rank, wealth, or learning, or anything that tends to cut off one person from another.

Sympathy and Social Relations

Sympathy is the bond of union between men; it is to the social sphere what gravitation is to the physical. It is the expression of the spiritual unity of mankind. While it may, in its undeveloped condition, be confined, it is always widening to reach more men, and deepening to include more fundamental relations between men. It constitutes society an organic whole, a whole permeated by a common life, where each individual still lives his own distinct life unabsorbed in that of the community. It is possible, perhaps, to conceive of a development of sympathy such that each individual should simply take into himself the experiences of others, and not project them outward in realizing that they are the experiences of persons. Such a development would result in each living a self-absorbed life, without recognizing his relations of spiritual identity with other men. Or it is possible to conceive such a development of sympathy that each should simply project himself outward, and lose his individual life in the life of the community, becoming more and more absorbed in it. In this case a sense of separate personality would be lost. But, as matter of fact, the nature of sympathy is such that growth in individuality is a necessary accompaniment of growth of universality of feeling. Sympathy identifies others with one's self, and at the same time distinguishes them from one's self. It enables us to realize our true nature, which is universal personality, by widening our life till it becomes as comprehensive as humanity, and at the same time deepens our own distinct individuality. The growth of feeling is like the growth of knowledge—it becomes more individual through universal relations.

2. PRIDE AND HUMILITY. As sympathy and antipathy are feelings for others as connected with self, so pride and humility are feelings of self as related to others. Pride is a sense of our own worth compared with a personality not ourselves, and humility is a sense of our demerit compared with such a personality. Pride may be self-respect. As such, it is the feeling that we *are* personalities; that there is embodied in us the infinite value of a self which is worthy of respect wherever found. As such, it is not an egoistic feeling, but the obverse of sympathy. In short, it is not feeling of our particular separate qualities; it is feeling of our universal nature, that which we have in common with all personalities. When it is the feeling of some quality, acquirement, or circumstance of self, pride takes the form of self-complacency, conceit, vanity. Such feelings are egoistic, and prevent the person from getting outside of himself.

Humility

Humility is not necessarily opposed to self-respect. As self-respect is the recognition in feeling that we are persons, and, as such, cannot be put to any low use, so humility is the sense of the contrast between this personality which constitutes our real (that is, objective and universal) being, and our actual state of attainment. As such, pride and humility necessarily accompany each other. Humility may, however, be the sense of our own particular worth as compared with the particular worth of somebody else. As such it takes the form of sensitiveness, self-depreciation, perhaps even to degradation; though it may occur in the form of modesty, which, if genuine, is rather the absence of conceit than a positive form of feeling.

Complex Forms

It is not to be supposed that our analysis is able to correspond to the actual wealth of positive relations which social feelings assume; we are able only to indicate a few of the leading types. We may mention in addition certain more complex forms which result from the simple combination of these types. Antipathy combined with the egoistic form of humility, gives rise to the feeling of *envy*; sympathy, similarly combined, gives *jealousy*, for where there is jealousy there is sympathy regarding the end in view, but recognition of one's own inferiority, while envy would carp at all the attainments of another. *Malice* is the egoistic form of pride joined with antipathy; *covetousness* is the same form of feeling combined with sympathy. The student will find it an excellent psychological analysis to take the almost infinite variety of social feelings and analyze them into their elementary types.

2. *MORAL FEELINGS*

The moral feelings are based upon the social feelings, and are an outgrowth of them. We recognize moral relations to those whom we feel to be identical in nature with ourselves. The feeling of sympathy as the basis of this identification of natures is, therefore, the source of all moral feeling. Moral feelings may be extended to include all possible relations, intellectual and æsthetic, as well as the strictly social, but this only when these relations are brought into connection with personality. In studying moral feelings we have only to ascertain how they are developed out of the social feelings, and what elements, hitherto unrecognized, this development introduces.

Feelings of Rightness

As the essential characteristic of an intellectual feeling is that it is the sense of truth, or the harmony between one object and relation and the ideal unity of all relations; as the essential characteristic of an æsthetic feeling is that it is the sense of beauty, or the harmony between an object and the ideal value of all objects, so moral feeling is the sense of rightness, the feeling of the harmony existing between an act of a person and the ideal of personality. The feeling that an act is right is the feeling that in that act the ideal—that is, the perfectly objective and universal—personality is realized; the feeling of the wrongness of an act is the feeling that it does not conform to this ideal of personality, but contravenes it. Intellectual feeling deals with the relations of objects; æsthetic feeling with their ideal values; social feelings with the relations of persons; moral feelings with the ideal relations and worths of persons.

Moral Feeling is only Explicit Social Feeling

It is evident from this that moral feeling only brings into conscious recognition what is all the time *involved* in social feeling. The essence of social feeling is that in it man feels himself identified with a self more comprehensive, more permanent than his own private and particular being. He feels his true life to be that of all personalities; he feels, in short, that he cannot realize himself except in a self which will unite and harmonize all the varied experiences of humanity. It is not meant, of course, that this relation of the actual self to the ideal, universal self is consciously recognized by all to be present when they experience social feeling. It is only meant that a fair analysis reveals this relation as constituting its essence. But in moral feeling this relation is brought more explicitly into consciousness. In moral feeling man feels his true self to be one which comprehends possible relations to all men, and all acts which are necessary to bring the actual self into harmony with this true self, to make his will, in other words, conform to a universal will, he conceives as *duties*.

The Feeling of Obligation

Besides the feeling of rightness, it is evident that moral sentiment involves the feeling of obligation. In intellectual feeling, and in æsthetic feeling, there is no sense of obligation. We simply feel that the truth or the beauty is there. We feel no responsibility for its existence. If we feel any responsibility to reproduce them in ourselves, it is only because we have brought them in relation to personality, and have conceived them as elements of a completed personality —as merely intellectual and æsthetic no such responsibility is felt. But the feeling that a universal self is our own true being is necessarily accompanied by the feeling of obligation and responsibility. We feel bound to realize our own nature because it is *our* nature, and feel responsible for its non-realization, because we are not dealing with a material which seems partially external to ourselves, and hence out of our control, like the relations constituting the universe, or the ideal values which these relations express, but with our own very selves.

Reverence and Remorse

The combination of feelings of rightness and of obligation gives rise to the feeling of *reverence*. Reverence is the feeling that the object towards which it is directed is completely universal, realizing in itself the wills of all men, and hence is entirely "right" or perfect, combined with the feeling that this personality is not foreign to our nature, but is its true being, and hence is an absolute obligation upon it. The social feeling of humility becomes greatly deepened in the presence of such an ideal personality. *Remorse* is the feeling of the chasm existing between this ideal and our own actual state through some act of our own. We feel that we ought to have realized our own being, and that we could have done so, but that we have not. The feeling of this split, this dualism, in our nature constitutes remorse.

3. RELIGIOUS FEELING

Moral feeling is the outgrowth and manifestation of the true nature of social feeling; religious feeling bears a similar relation to moral. There is a conflict in moral feeling as such. Moral feeling lays hold of our own true self, as one harmonizing all elements of human character, and says that this ought to be made real, and that our actual self must be made into conformity with it. Moral feeling involves, therefore, a gulf between the actual and the ideal or universal self. Our own nature does not completely manifest itself in moral relations; it does so partly, and *ought* to do so wholly. Our nature can be completely objectified or realized only when the chasm between what is and what ought to be, between the actual and the ideal self, is overcome. Religious experience is the sphere in which this identification of one's self with the completely realized personality, or God, occurs. Religious feeling is, therefore, the completely universal feeling, and with it the progressive development of feeling ends. It brings into our experience the elements which are involved in moral and social feeling, but are not made explicit in them. We shall briefly mention some of these elements.

Feeling of Dependence

In the feeling that our actual self is not our true self there is involved the element of dependence. In social relations we feel ourselves dependent upon other personalities for our development; we feel that isolated we are deprived of most of our powers. In moral relations this dependence is consciously felt, and is expressed in the emotion of obligation. To feel that we *ought* to realize a certain personal worth is to feel our dependence upon that worth. But this feeling does not become complete. There is always our own private self which is set up over against the universal self; this private self cannot be got rid of in moral action, although we feel that it *ought* to be abolished. But in religious feeling we recognize the worthlessness, the *nullity*, of this private separate self, and surrender ourselves wholly to the perfect personality, God. We feel that there is absolutely no independent element in us. It follows, of course, that the feeling is not one of physical dependence, one upon power, but a spiritual dependence; that whatever we have and are is not of our particular selves, but from God.

Feeling of Peace

Another element of religious feeling is that of the feeling of peace. This emotion is that of complete reconciliation, of harmony. So far as we attain the moral ideal there is this feeling, for the moral ideal is simply a completely unified personality, but, as already mentioned, the moral life is one of conflict. The unity is not attained. In the religious life, however, so far as one gives up wholly his own particular self (and except as he does this, there is no religious life), and takes the life of the completely harmonious Personality for his own, he is not living a life of conflict, but of apprehending that which absolutely is. There can be no essential dualism in his life, for the only thing which is real for him is

that Being in whom personality is complete. There is, therefore, the feeling of peace.

The Feeling of Faith

Both in social and moral relations faith is involved. In moral
relations, for example, one says that something must be
realized by him which exists not as matter of fact, but as an
ideal. The moral ideal is not a mere fact in the world; it is
truly an ideal, that which ought to be actual, but is not seen
to be so. It is true that morality is not an imagination, it is
manifested in living characters in society and the state; but
these get all their moral force because they are felt to be
expressions of an ideal. This ideal, therefore, not existing as
so much fact, must be apprehended by faith. The moral life
is one of faith, for it constantly asserts that the final reality
for man is that which cannot be made out actually to exist.

The religious life only brings this element to conscious
recognition. It says that that of which alone the individual
can be sure as matter of fact, namely, his private self, is
unreal, and that the sole reality is the perfect and universal
personality, God, who cannot be immediately felt to be. It
asserts that this Personality is not only ideal, and an ideal
which *ought* to be real, as moral feeling asserts of its object,
but that it *is* perfectly real. Since the entire intellectual,
æsthetic, and moral life is one of idealization, it is evident
that the feeling of faith, which religion insists upon and
induces, is the feeling which is implicitly involved in all
experience whatever. Religious feeling, or faith, is absolutely universal, universal in its object, and universal as
coextensive with all experience.

II.   Personal Feeling as Spring to Action

Personal feeling takes the form of *interest* in persons.
It is necessarily directed outwards. It can find its satisfaction
only in the realization of that in which its interest lies.
Considered in this light, personal feeling is *love*. Love is to
persons what admiration is to ideal values, or wonder to the
objective universe. It is not a subjective sentiment, nor a
passive affection. It is active interest. It is not receptive in its

nature, but creative. It is essentially objective. We may be pleasurably affected by individuals, and may, through association, extend the pleasure we experience to these individuals; we may include them within the sphere of our personal enjoyment. But this is not love, although it is one of the means by which love comes into existence. As wonder and admiration are forgetfulness of self in the presence of the universe of objects and ideals, so love is forgetfulness of self in the presence of persons.

Love and Hate

All love is sympathy considered as spring to action, and hate is antipathy. It has been matter of discussion among psychologists whether there is any such feeling as pure hate or malevolence. Some have asserted and others denied that it is possible to assume an utterly hostile attitude towards others, and find pleasure in their loss. In one signification of the term hate, it is necessarily implied in love. As love is interest in the well-being of another for his own sake, it involves hatred for all that hinders this well-being. Since we recognize that well-being is personal and cannot be controlled by non-personal considerations, we recognize that these hinderances must be due to the person himself, and in that sense we may be said to hate him. We hate, in other words, all that prevents the realization of our love. The hatred is simply the negative side of love. Since, however, love is necessarily an emotion which finds its satisfaction in persons, hate as a feeling directed towards persons *in themselves* is a psychological impossibility. Personality is a universal characteristic, and we could not hate a person in *himself* without hating our own self.

Like and Dislike

Love, however, has an abnormal form. It is possible that the feeling should not lose itself in others, but should become turned inwards, and exist for the satisfaction of one's private self. We may regard others, in other words, only so far as they minister to our individual satisfaction. Our feeling towards them may be because they "agree" with us, or are agreeable; because they produce pleasurable emotions in us.

Such affections are "likes" rather than love. Similarly they may affect us disagreeably; they may cause us unpleasant experiences. They may do this by the possession of some quality which constantly reminds us of our own inferiority, by some quality which irritates us, or by actually injuring us. Such persons we dislike. But such feeling is an egoistic feeling, not a social one, while hate proper, since it is directed only towards that which hinders self-realization, is, in effect, a social feeling. Most of what is ordinarily called hatred is either malice or dislike.

Products of Love

Love, as interest in the well-being of personality, is necessarily creative. Wonder creates science, admiration creates the fine arts; love creates the various forms of personal relations and institutions: of these, the primary and fundamental is the family, based upon sexual, parental, and filial love. It is the most immediate and intimate form which interest in others takes. It is based in the greatest degree upon the immediate and direct demands of our nature; the demands for reproduction, for nourishment, for shelter, for protection. As, however, it is in the family that each personality most fully expresses his own nature, as the relations of persons to each other are there the most intimate, it becomes the fundamental social unit, the primary moral agency, and the ultimate source of religious education.

Other Forms

Love, however, cannot be restricted to those with whom we are in immediate natural and physical relations. Wherever there is a person, there is a possible object of personal interest. Love widens into friendship, which, taken in a comprehensive sense, is the basis of all social relations. Society, as an institution, is but the manifestation, the realization, of personal feeling as a spring to action. Personal feeling can find its goal only in relations to persons, which are permanent and universal; and all that we call society, state, and humanity are the realization of these permanent and universal relations of persons which are based upon active sympathy.

Psychologically, the bond of union in society and the state is not law in a legal or judicial sense; much less force. It is love. Law is the expression of the fact that love is not an ill-regulated gush of sentiment nor a personal indulgence, but is the universal and natural manifestation of personality. The force which society employs is the recognition by society that the universal personality is an absolute obligation upon every member of society; and that only in society can this personality be realized, and that every breach of social relations is a hinderance to the accomplishing by man of his true life. It is the manifestation by society of that *hate* which is necessarily implied in all love. The highest product of the interest of man in man is the Church. This brings into explicit consciousness the elements involved in all social organization. It *requires* love as the supreme obligation, and it brings to light the relation of this love to the perfect and universal personality, God.

III. Feeling as Social Judgment, Conscience

The feeling of rightness necessarily passes over into the judgment of rightness. We regard the feeling not as something which we subjectively experience, but as an attribute of the act of personality. We do so because we conceive that to be right which agrees with the conditions of a complete personality, and such a personality we instinctively feel to be universal and objective. The moral judgment is the explicit presence in consciousness of the objective factor involved in all personal feeling. The moral judgments, taken together, are referred to a power called conscience. Conscience is not, however, to be conceived as a special faculty of mind. As feeling, it is the emotion of rightness and obligation, together with the consequent remorse or approbation flowing from a feeling of conformity or non-conformity to the obligation. As intellectual, it is the apprehension of the content of these feelings; the apprehension of the quality of moral acts measured by the ideal of personality.

Nature of Conscience

Conscience is, therefore, intuitive. It is not such in the sense that it enunciates universal laws and principles, for it lays down no laws. Conscience is a name for the experience of personality that a given act is in harmony or in discord with a truly realized personality. It is the internal side of every personal experience. These experiences are necessarily connected with feelings of pleasure and of pain, of approbation and disapprobation. That which is felt to correspond to the perfect ideal of man is felt as harmonious, and calls forth the feeling of moral harmony which we call approbation. Conscience, like the intellectual and the æsthetic sense, is capable of development. To say this, is only to say that man's moral nature is in process of realization. With every new realization of personality comes a higher ideal of what constitutes a true man, and a keener response to relations of harmony and discord. So every degradation of manhood is accompanied by a lowering of the ideal which one can form, a blunted sense of what conforms to it, and approbation of what would otherwise flood the soul with displeasure. Conscience is, indeed, a feeling of the universal and objective worth of personal acts, but in what degree its feelings are true to fact depends upon how universal and objective is the self which feels.

Conscience and Ethics

The moral feeling, like the intellectual and æsthetic, is individual. It is the intuitive expression of the moral nature of the individual. Reason may, however, investigate the spontaneous and intuitive declarations of feeling to find the grounds upon which it works, and, having reflectively analyzed these grounds, may formulate them in the laws of conduct, as it formulates the canons of taste, and the rules of logic. It thus attempts to arrive at universal laws of action and permanent qualities of right action. It must not be forgotten, however, that a moral law is an abstraction. The concrete fact is a living personality, and what we call an ethical law is a mode of action which has been separated by reflective analysis from this personality. The moral individual does not live to realize moral law, but to realize himself, and what are termed moral laws are those modes of action which are observed to be harmoniously related to such realization. While ethics is a legitimate analysis of the moral sense, an attempt to make it render up its hidden meaning, casuistry is an abnormal manifestation of it. It is the attempt to formulate rules to decide between right and wrong action in specific cases. It thus attempts to substitute for the unconstrained freedom of the person external and foreign prescriptions. The heart of the moral life lies in the free personal determination of right and wrong. No set of rules can take the place of this personal determination without destroying the vital spring of morals.

NOTES TO CHAPTER 16

Upon social feeling we refer to the following: Sully, *Psychology*, pp. 508 - 18; Murray, *Handbook of Psychology*, pp. 360 - 77; McCosh, *Emotions*, p. 215 ff.; Bain, *Emotions and Will*, pp. 106 - 88, 210 - 27; Brown, *Philosophy of Mind*, vol. ii, pp. 206 - 53; Spencer, *Principles of Psychology*, vol. ii, pp. 558 - 77, 587 - 626; Martineau, *Types of Ethical Theory*, vol. ii, pp. 134 - 41; Laurie, *Ethica*, pp. 104 - 19; Marion, *La Solidarité Morale*, pp. 163 - 205; De Guimps, *L'Éducation*, pp. 444 - 49; Perez, *L'Éducation dès le Berceau*, pp. 224 - 64; Nahlowsky, *Das Gefühlsleben*, pp. 215 - 333; Horwicz, *Psychologische Analysen*, vol. ii, pt. 2, pp. 353 - 466, 479 - 504; Michelet, *Anthropologie und Psychologie*, pp. 474 - 85; Ulrici, *Der Leib und die Seele*, vol. ii, pp. 346 - 56; Fortlage, *Acht psychologische Vorträge* (essay on "Friendship"); Lazarus, essay on "Friendship," in *Das Leben der Seele*; Schmidt, *Über das Mitgefühl*; Duboc, *Psychologie der Liebe*. Regarding feelings of self, see Murray (*op. cit.*), pp. 356 - 60; McCosh (*op. cit.*), pp. 7 - 42; Bain (*op. cit.*), pp. 128 - 44; Stephen, *Science of Ethics*, pp. 219 - 27; Lotze, *Microcosmus*, pp. 696 - 706; Rosenkranz, *Psychologie*, pp. 143 - 56; Horwicz (*op. cit.*), vol. ii, pt. 2, pp. 232 - 301; Preyer, *Die Seele des Kindes*, pp. 392 - 406; Joly, *Notions de Pédagogie*, pp. 196 - 210. Upon moral and religious feeling, see Caird, *Philosophy of Religion*, ch. ix; Martineau (*op. cit.*), vol. ii, pp. 19 - 64; Laurie (*op. cit.*), pp. 28 - 37, 59 - 68, 148 - 55; Bain (*op. cit.*), pp. 121 - 25, 286 - 322; Abercrombie, *Philosophy of Moral Feelings;* Ulrici (*op. cit.*), vol. ii, pp. 356 - 90 (moral), pp. 418 - 53 (religious); Strümpell, *Grundriss der Psychologie*, p. 278 ff.; Nahlowsky (*op. cit.*), pp. 197 - 213; Horwicz (*op. cit.*), vol. ii, pt. 2, pp. 302 - 52, 512 - 20; Volkmann, *Lehrbuch der Psychologie*, vol. ii, pp. 363 - 73. For a pessimistic view, see Rée, *Der Ursprung der moralischen Empfindungen*, with which compare Von Hartmann, *Phänomenologie des sittlichen Bewusstseins*, pp. 163 - 322.

17

Sensuous Impulses

Nature of Will

The term will has a narrower and wider sense. In its broad sense it is synonymous with all psychical activity having a mental and not merely a physiological stimulus, and which accomplishes any result whether intended or not. In the narrower sense the word is limited to action arising from an idea and ending in making this idea real; in changing it from an idea into a presentation. In the narrower sense, there is required for will a union of feeling and knowledge in one and the same act. Will always unites *me* with some *reality*, either transforming an element of the me into objective reality, or bringing that objective reality into the sphere of my immediate feeling. It thus connects the content of knowledge with the form of feeling. Or, again, there is no knowledge without attention; but attention is simply the activity of will as it connects a universal content with an individual subject. There is also no feeling except as an accompaniment of some activity. Both knowledge and feeling, therefore, find their basis in will.

The Will and Sensuous Impulses

The will is not purely formal, but has a real content of its own. This is supplied primarily through the sensuous impulses. These do not of themselves constitute will, any more than sensations constitute knowledge. As the latter consists in relating, connecting, and systematizing sensations, in mastering and interpreting them, so will gets its existence in the co-ordination and mutual regulation of the sensuous impulses; in bringing them into harmonious relations with each other through their subordination to a common end.

We have, for example, impulses which induce us to locomotion; these impulses do not constitute a volition until they are connected with one another, and organized into a definite mode of action. The sensuous impulses, in other words, constitute the raw material, the basis of will; they must be elaborated into the actual forms of volition through a process. We shall take up, therefore, in this chapter, the raw material; shall then pass on to the processes of development of this material; and finally consider some of the results, the concrete manifestations, occasioned by the action of the processes on the sensuous impulses.

Sensuous Impulse Defined

Sensuous impulse may be defined as *the felt pressure of a state of consciousness arising from some bodily condition to express itself in producing some physical change.* It involves, therefore, some affection of the physical organism which occasions a state of consciousness; and this state of consciousness is not purely quiescent, but involves in itself, as it were, a surplus of energy which reacts against the external stimulus in some way. For example, the nervous mechanism of the eye is affected by ætheric vibration; the molecular motion conducted to the brain results there in the state of consciousness which we call the sensation of light. But there is also an affection of the self; there is a tendency either to direct the eye towards the light or away from it. The energy of this tendency or pressure towards or from a physical stimulus is sensuous impulse. The stimulus, of course, may arise from within, as in the case of hunger, where it is a condition of the organism. The sensation of hunger, so far as it gives us information of the state of our body, is the basis of knowledge; so far as it is a pleasurable or painful affection of self, it is feeling; so far as it is the tendency to react upon this feeling, and satisfy it, by bringing about some objective change, it is impulse.

Reflex Action

A sensuous impulse involves, therefore, both an internal and external side. It has, as a necessary prerequisite, a state of feeling, an affection which is agreeable or the reverse. But it has, as its necessary outcome, a tendency towards physical expression, an actual change of the body. There must be, accordingly, some mechanism to connect these two sides, to give the internal feeling its external expression. This mechanism is known as reflex action. The nerves of the cerebrospinal system of the body are either sensory or motor; that is to say, they either conduct the stimulus from a sense organ inwards, or they conduct a stimulus from a central organ to a group of muscles. These sensory and motor nerves unite in ganglia near the spinal cord. When a stimulus is transferred from a sensory nerve to a motor without the conscious intervention of the mind, we have *reflex action*.

That is to say, reflex action is *the direct and immediate deflection of a stimulus having a sense origin into a motor channel*. If something suddenly approaches the eye, the nerve stimulus is transferred to the spinal cord, and, instead of being thence continued to the brain, and giving rise to a sensation, it is discharged into a motor nerve, and the eye is immediately closed. Coughing, chewing, swallowing, etc., are other examples of reflex acts. Reflex action, as such, is a physiological process, but it is of importance here because it forms the physical basis of sensuous impulse. The reflex action, in itself, involves no consciousness, while the sensuous impulse does; but the union of sensory and motor nerves, whether in the spinal cord or brain, affords the mechanism by which any feeling may discharge itself in producing physical change, and thus relieve the pressure.

Classes of Impulses

Strictly speaking, sensuous impulses would be confined to impulses accompanying the immediate feelings which come from our senses, general and special, but, owing to their great similarity of nature, we shall treat, in connection with them, impulses of perception, imitative impulses, ideational impulses, and instinctive impulses, considering under the latter head especially those of expression.

1. GENERAL SENSE IMPULSES

Every sensation, as a concrete fact, is an impulse. In treating sensation under the head of knowledge, we spoke of it as if it were a mere state of the mind. That is only one side of it. It is also a reaction against the stimulus; it is a disturbance of the equilibrium of the organism, setting free energy which must discharge itself in producing some change. This is seen most plainly in the organic senses, where the senses appear as appetites, or as *regularly recurring tendencies to the appropriation of material external to the organism.* These demands of the sense organs may be constant, as that for air; or periodical, as those for food and drink; or irregular, like the sexual. But in all cases the sensation is not exhausted in itself, but is an impulse going out upon some foreign material. It expresses, in other words, the demand of the mind to make something outside of itself part of itself; in the given cases, part of its physical self.

2. *SPECIAL SENSE IMPULSES*

This fact is no less true of the special senses. There is a hunger of the sense of touch for bodies; of the sense of hearing for sounds; of the sense of sight for light and its colors. The contact of the hand with a body is reacted upon with an impulse to explore that body, to "feel" it. Every sound is a stimulus to the mind to observe it, to note its quality, its relations, etc. If it is particularly pleasant, the mind acts by an impulse to continue it; if disagreeable, to destroy its cause, or to take the body out of its hearing. Were not sensations something more than mere sensations, were they not impulses to action, knowledge would not originate; for there would be nothing to induce the mind to dwell upon the sensation with the accentuating action of attention; nothing to direct the mind to its qualities and relations. It follows, as a matter of course, that will would not originate, for there would be nothing to induce the mind to put forth its activities at all, much less anything to induce it to put them forth in this direction rather than in that.

3. *IMPULSES OF PERCEPTION*

The sensuous impulses just spoken of follow directly out of the state of feeling, involving no recognition of an object. There are, however, impulses which follow as directly from the perception of some object, involving *no consciousness of the end of the action*, and such we may call impulses of perception. They all come under the general head of impulses to grasp something. There seems to be a connection of some sort between the recognition of an object and a tendency to reach for and grasp it. This tendency is seen very fully developed in infants. The child soon reaches for all objects which come within the range of his vision; this impulse easily develops itself into the *play impulse*. The child grasps for objects, handles them, moves them here and there, throws his arms about, with no end in view except the expression of his own activity. It is the development of the muscular impulse in connection with the recognition of objects, and is of great importance as a stimulus to activity, and as constantly initiating new modes of activity.

4. IMPULSES TO IMITATION

Growing out of the impulses of perception, and forming a large part of the material of play, are the impulses to imitate or reproduce any perceived movement. This again is especially manifest in children, being seen both in their sports and in their relations to their elders, and is one of the most important factors in their education. A child, by pure force of imitation, takes on very largely the artistic and moral coloring of his environment. The force of the imitative impulse is seen very clearly, also, in hypnotized persons. The tendency to imitate is ordinarily checked by the presence in consciousness of other ideas and ends incompatible with the bare reproduction of something externally perceived; but when these are excluded from the sphere of consciousness, as they are in persons in a somnambulic condition, whether natural or induced, this tendency holds complete sway, and such persons often accurately reproduce every movement of the one operating upon them.

5. IDEATIONAL IMPULSES

Ideas, as well as feelings and perceptions, may be impulses to action. In ordinary life they are so only when harmonized with each other and brought into reference with some end of action, and hence are not impulses truly so called. In abnormal cases, however, the ideas seem to be freed from their co-ordination and subordination, and to work freely on their own account. In hypnotized persons, for example, any idea suggested is immediately executed, as swimming, ascending in a balloon, delivering an oration, etc.

Those having to do with persons of disordered nature recognize what they call "compulsory ideas" (*Zwangsvor-stellungen*), where the individual is impelled to the execution either of every idea that occurs to him, or of some one kind of ideas, often finding terrible expression in murder or suicide. In such cases the individual is haunted constantly by a certain idea, and finds no relief except in the performance of the corresponding act, and this although he may be suffering under no intellectual delusion whatever regarding the nature of his act.

6. INSTINCTIVE IMPULSES

In a wide sense all the impulses hitherto mentioned are instinctive. An instinctive act may be defined as *one to which an individual feels himself impelled without knowing the end to be accomplished, yet with ability to select the proper means for its attainment*. In a sense more specific, instinctive impulses may be distinguished from the forms of sensuous impulse just discussed. The ground of distinction will be the fact that the latter are reactive or reproductive only, while instinctive impulses initiate new modes of activity, having results far beyond their immediate occasion. Such, for example, is the instinctive action of a bird in building its nest. It is not only in response to the immediate stimulus, but it looks forward to a long future course of actions, in rearing the young, etc.

Instincts in Man

A complete discussion of the origin, nature, and function of instinct would take us into the realm of comparative psychology, but we have to recognize the fact that every human being performs many acts which are directly fitted to reach an end without his knowing what the end is, nor why he uses the means that he does. So far, indeed, as our intellectual, artistic, and moral activity is directly towards an end of which we have not complete consciousness, but which we yet succeed in reaching without much experimenting, it may be said that instinct enters into all the psychical life of man.

Instincts of Expression

Under the general head of instinct come those acts by which the infant takes food, by which he learns locomotion, etc. Owing to their typical character and their greater psychological importance, we shall treat briefly of the impulses which express feeling and ideas. There is a certain class of physical movements which serve to express internal states, and which do this with no intentional consciousness. Such are the cry of pain, the laugh of joy, the trembling of anger or fear, the blush of shame, the stare of astonishment, etc. They are of twofold importance: in the first place, they form the instinctive basis upon which individuals are bound together; and, in the second place, they form the material out of which are developed the higher and intentional forms of communication. The first use may be illustrated by the cry of the infant, which immediately awakens a response from its mother. The expression not only gives an outlet to the emotion, but occasions certain actions in others.

Principles of the Expressive Impulses

Every impulse is expressed by a *gesture*, using the word in the widest sense. Attempts have been made to reduce gestures to classes, and account for them on certain principles, all conventional gestures being, of course, excluded. Mr. Darwin formulated three principles: first, that of serviceable associated habits; second, of antithesis; third, that of direct action of nervous centres. By the last is meant that when the brain is strongly excited nerve force is generated in excess, and is transmitted in certain definite directions. Examples of it are found in change of color of hair from excessive grief, perspiration from great pain, the reddening of the face in rage (from disturbed heart action), etc. The principle of antithesis presupposes the prior action of other principles, and affirms that when a certain emotion expresses itself in a certain way there is a strong involuntary tendency for an opposite emotion to express itself in an opposite direction.

Thus, if feelings of fear, depression, etc., are expressed by relaxation and trembling of the muscles, feelings of strength, elation, etc., will express themselves by contraction of the muscles and a general expansion of the body.

Serviceable Associated Habits

The chief principle which Mr. Darwin relies upon is that of serviceable associated habits, in connection with the laws of heredity. This principle may be stated as follows: certain actions are now, or have been at some time, serviceable to the organism in connection with certain feelings, and have thus become associated with those feelings. Hence, when the feeling recurs, the associated movement reappears, whether or not it is serviceable in this particular case, and, indeed, even when it has become wholly useless. The expressions of extreme rage, for example, as the drawing up of the upper lip, the gnashing of the teeth, the spasmodic movements of the fingers, are relics of a time when these gestures were of use in biting, clutching, etc., that which caused the anger. So expressions of scorn, hatred, etc., are actions which were once associated with an actual attack upon an enemy, or movements which were calculated to inspire fear or submission in him.

Wundt's Principles

Wundt has supplemented these principles by two which he calls those (1) of analogous feelings and (2) of the relations of movement to sense-ideas. By the latter principle is meant that when we speak of persons or objects which are present we point to them; if absent, in their direction; that we unconsciously imitate their shape, measure their size, etc., by movements of the hands. The principle of the association of analogous feelings states the law that feelings of a similar emotional tone are easily connected, and that when connected the *expression* of one is transferred to the other. For example, there is a certain expression following the tasting of sweet substances, another of bitter, etc. Now all experiences, however ideal in their nature, which are agreeable possess a tone analogous to that of the sweet taste, and hence they naturally express themselves by the same external signs. Such are the principles recognized by the chief authorities, but the matter cannot be regarded as scientifically settled yet.

Expressive Impulses and Language

Those physical changes which express emotions serve as signs to others of our own state, and thus form the basis of communication. By language, however, we mean, in addition, the expression of thoughts, involving also the idea that the expression is with the conscious purpose of sharing our experience with others. But as these signs come under the general definition of gesture, they may be very briefly noticed here. They all come originally under the second principle of Wundt. He recognizes two sorts of signs of this class—the demonstrative, which point towards the object, and the plastic, which imitate some of its salient features. These gestures, by a sort of reflex action, are accompanied by sounds which aid in expressing the emotion awakened, and which, by the principle of association of analogous feelings, react upon and strengthen the dumb gestures. Thus the sound becomes in time the sign of the object. The sounds, in short, have certain likenesses in emotional tone to the feelings awakened by objects, and this likeness enables them to symbolize the object to the mind. This forms the sensuous basis of speech. It must be recognized, however, that the sound must be used with the intention of its serving as a sign, must be recognized by others as a sign, and must be adopted by the community before it becomes language proper. And not all authorities agree with Wundt in his account of the origin of vocal gesture, or speech. This question opens up the whole wide field of the psychology of language, into which we cannot go.

NOTES TO CHAPTER 17

Upon reflex action and motor impulse, see Ferrier, *Functions of Brain*, ch. ii; Bain, *Senses and Intellect*, pp. 46 - 53, 262 - 76, and *Emotions and Will*, pp. 351 - 87; Preyer, *Die Seele des Kindes*, pp. 157 - 215; Volkmann, *Lehrbuch der Psychologie*, vol. i, pp. 321 - 38; vol. ii, pp. 437 - 51; Lotze, *Microcosmus*, pp. 254 - 61; Wundt, in *Mind*, vol. i, p. 161 ff., on "Central Innervation and Consciousness";

Lazarus, *Über die Reize des Spiels*; and especially for the whole subject of impulse, Schneider, *Der thierische Wille*, pp. 95 - 418. Upon impulses of expression, see Darwin, *Expression of Emotions*; Spencer, *Principles of Psychology*, vol. ii, pp. 539 - 57; Sully, *Sensation and Intuition*, pp. 23 - 37; Ferrier (*op. cit.*), p. 67 ff.; Wundt, *Grundzüge der physiologischen Psychologie*, vol. ii, pp. 418 - 27; Michelet, *Anthropologie und Psychologie*, pp. 215 - 34; Schneider, *Der menschliche Wille*, pp. 453 - 88; Rosenkranz, *Psychologie*, pp. 163 - 84.

Upon instinct, in addition to references in Appendix B, see Spencer (*op. cit.*), vol. i, pp. 432 - 43; chapter on instinct in Darwin's *Origin of Species*; Bascom's *Comparative Psychology*, pp. 147 - 78; Perez, *First Three Years of Childhood*, pp. 44 - 59; Joly, *L'Instinct*; Preyer (*op. cit.*), pp. 174 - 207; Wundt (*op. cit.*), vol. ii, pp. 327 - 44; Schneider (*op. cit.*), pp. 55 - 84; George, *Lehrbuch der Psychologie*, pp. 169 - 204.

18
Development of Volition

Impulses and Volition

The sensuous impulses form the basis, the material, the *sine qua non* of volition, but they do not constitute it. Volition is *regulated, harmonized impulse*. It involves a double process: first, the various impulses must be co-ordinated with each other; secondly, they must all be brought into harmonious relations with an end, must be subordinated to one principle. *Volition is impulse consciously directed towards the attainment of a recognized end which is felt as desirable.*

Elements of Volition

A volition or act of will involves, therefore, over and above the impulse, knowledge and feeling. There must be knowledge of the end of action; there must be knowledge of the relations of this end to the means by which it is to be attained; and this end must awaken a pleasurable or painful feeling in the mind; it must possess an interesting quality, or be felt to be in immediate subjective relation to the self. The impulses furnish the moving force by which the end whose quality is recognized, and whose necessity for the happiness of self is felt, is actually brought about. It is the energy which furnishes its actual accomplishment, directed along the channels laid down by the intellect for the satisfaction of feeling. Feeling, in other words, determines the position of the lever; knowledge furnishes the fulcrum for its use; the impulse applies the force. Each of these elements is an abstraction arrived at by analysis from the concrete whole—a volition.

Development of Volition

We have, therefore, to study the process by which the concrete forms of volition are built up from the crude material of impulse. The successive steps of the process may be formulated as follows: First, there is awakened the state of mind known as *desire*; there is then a conflict of desires; this is concluded by the process of deliberation and *choice*; these result in the formation of an end of action which serves as the purpose or *motive* of action; this purpose is then, through the medium of its felt desirability, handed over, as it were, to the realm of the impulses, which realize it.

1. DESIRE

We begin with Desire, and shall study its (1) origin, (2) object, and (3) development.

1. ORIGIN.   Impulse does not constitute desire. Impulse goes straight and blindly at an end, but it does not know this end, nor does it feel that there will be pleasure in reaching it. A bird in building its nest has no thought of the purpose which the nest is to subserve, nor does it feel that any pleasure is to be gained by building it. It builds to satisfy the felt *pressure* from within. The internal force of feeling constrains it to act in a certain way. When, however, an act has been once or oftener performed through impulse, and a certain end is reached which is discovered to be pleasurable or painful, there arises the state of mind known as *desire* or as *aversion*.

Example

The child, for example, impelled by a perceptive impulse, grasps for an object. He reaches it, we will say, and it proves soft and pleasure-giving to touch and possibly to the palate. Now, by the laws of apperception, this pleasure and this object are associated together as parts of one experience. Or, it is felt as rough; perhaps it burns; at all events, it occasions pain. This pain and its object are associated. Now this object stands in a certain definite relation to experience, and a relation which is brought, according to the theory of pleasure previously explained (page 248), into intimate and personal connection with the self. The object now has an interest, and becomes a spring to action. This objective interest constitutes desire. Impulse occurs no longer blindly, but with reference to that object which satisfies itself, this satisfaction being made known to us through pleasure. Desire and aversion are impulse *plus* respectively the idea of an object which satisfies or thwarts the impulse, as revealed to us by pleasure or pain.

2. OBJECT OF DESIRE.   It has been held that what we desire is in all cases pleasure, what we are averse to is pain. For example, a child desires an apple. It is said that the true object towards which the desire is directed is the pleasure which comes of eating the apple. If a man desires to resist temptation and tell the truth, his real object of desire is the pleasure which results from the act. But it is evident that this view overlooks two facts. First, the pleasure is a mere abstraction; the concrete existence is the object which gives the pleasure. It is quite true that no object would be desired unless it were in that relation to self which we call feeling, that is, pleasure or happiness; but it is just as true that what is desired is not the pleasure, but the object which affords pleasure. The other fact which is overlooked is that we do not desire the object *because* it gives us pleasure; but that it gives us pleasure because it satisfies the impulse which, in connection with the idea of the object, constitutes the desire. The child desires the apple, for he has the idea of the apple as satisfying his impulse. Only for this reason does he conceive it as pleasure-giving. Pleasure follows after the desire, rather than determines it.

And this is not in contradiction to what has been said regarding the origin of desire. Desire is the impulse plus the feeling of satisfaction got in its realization. But impulse is always towards an end, and the satisfaction is because this end has been reached. Desire merely adds the knowledge or feeling of that line of conduct or of that object in which the impulse will fulfil itself. Desire is the impulse in its known objective connection. The pleasure is one element in it, and an element subordinated to the objective experience.

Desire and the Self

While in a proximate way it is true that the object as satisfying impulse, and therefore giving pleasure, is the end of desire, in ultimate reference the truth is that a certain conceived state of the self is the object of desire. What the child concretely desires is himself in possession of the apple; what the man desires is himself in conformity with a certain idea of himself—himself as truth-telling. The object which satisfies the impulse is only the *means* through which the desire is realized. It is desired only because it is felt to be necessary to the satisfaction of self. Pleasure, as we have so often seen, is the accompaniment of the activity, or development of the self. It has no existence except as the internal side of this activity. When it is said that the object of desire is pleasure, this can be interpreted to mean only that what is desired is a certain activity or realization of self, which is anticipated as pleasurable, *since* it is a realization.

3. DEVELOPMENT OF DESIRE.   The development of desire is constituted by the progressive objectification of impulse. As sensation becomes knowledge when it is distinguished, and thus ceases to be a mere state or affection of self, so impulse becomes desire when it ceases to be a mere outgoing towards something which is not consciously presented to the mind, and becomes distinguished from the self as a possible end of action. Desire implies a consciousness which can distinguish between its actual state and a possible future state, and is aware of the means by which this future state can be brought into existence. It involves a permanent self which regards itself both as a present and future self, and acts with reference to their connection. It involves, in short, a self which can project or objectify itself. It not only *has* impulse, but it knows that it has; it sets before itself the satisfaction of impulse as the form which action may take. The development of desire will consist, accordingly, in the increasing separation of the impulse as an immediate affection from the self, and its objectification into a possible end of action. The impulse for food develops into the desire for it when the condition of want is recognized and distinguished from the present self; when, in short, it is objectified.

System of Desires

All desires form a system, that is, have an internal connection with each other. There is no such thing as an isolated desire, a desire which does not get its quality fixed by its reference to other desires. The self forms a necessary bond of union between them. When desire for food and drink ceases to be a blind impulse, it is put in possible relation to all the acts of the man. The man's desire for food has reference to his desire to live and perform certain acts; to support his family, to gain a recognized position, to contribute to society. It is a pure abstraction apart from such reference. Even the desire for intoxicating liquor implies such a reference, unless it is blind impulse. It implies love of companionship, desire to drown sorrow, to escape from pressure of physical irritation or of circumstance, etc. The child's desire to eat an orange may be in relation with a desire to obey a command, a desire to put off the pleasure to some other time, a desire to be generous, etc. Just in the degree in which desire is developed, it is brought into relation with a larger and larger sphere of desires. Desire must be as universal as the self is. The development of desire being through the objectification of self and the recognition in feeling of the distinction between the actual and the unrealized self, it follows that as desire is developed, each desire is brought into wider relations with self, and hence with other desires.

The Conflict of Desires

Because no desire is isolated, but each is in potential relation to every other, through its connection with self, it follows that desires may conflict with each other. The desire to work and to support a family may conflict with desire for personal ease or indulgence; the desire to tell the truth with that to gain some personal advantage or avoid harm; the desire to eat an orange with the desire to give it away. That is to say, the person may regard himself as satisfied in various modes of action which are incompatible with each other. The self projects itself or imagines itself realized in these various forms; since the actual realization in one, however, precludes that in another, there arises strife. It is important to notice that it is a strife or conflict which goes on in the man himself; *it is a conflict of himself with himself*; it is not a conflict of himself with something external to him, nor of

one impulse with another impulse, he meanwhile remaining
a passive spectator awaiting the conclusion of the struggle.
What gives the conflict of desires its whole meaning is that
it represents the man at strife with himself. He is the oppos-
ing contestants as well as the battle-field.

2. CHOICE

The recognition of the conflict of desires leads us to the
discussion of the mode in which it is settled—the fact of
choice. The conflict arises because the self is capable of
feeling itself satisfied in various modes of action or being,
only one of which can actually be brought about. The process of choice is that process by which some one of
the conflicting desires is first isolated and then identified
with the self to the exclusion of others. This process
may be longer or shorter, automatic or a painful deliberation.

Automatic Choice and Deliberation

In perhaps the larger number of cases in adult life the conflict is settled so directly and immediately that it hardly
appears in consciousness. Choice is the identification with
self of a certain desire; when the desire is in accord with
the direction in which the self habitually works, this identification takes place almost automatically. For example, a
merchant can hardly be said to choose to go to his business
in the morning. The desires which conflict with this deed are
generally so transient, compared with the fixed routine, that
the man instinctively, as we say, goes to his work. In other
words, his self has become so organized in one direction
through past acts of choice, it has become so stable and set,
that it identifies itself with this act at once. If, on the other
hand, the question is as to some new venture in trade, there
is no such organized self to fall back upon. The desire of
new gain, the aversion to possible loss, the desire to continue
in old lines, and to get the better of a competitor, struggle
with each other; probabilities upon this side and that must
be weighed, and it is only at the end of a process of *deliberation* that a choice is made, or one line of conduct identified
with self. Deliberation is the comparison of desires, their

mutual reference to each other; choice is the decision in favor of one.

3. THE END OF ACTION OR MOTIVE

A desire when chosen becomes a *motive*. We often speak of a conflict of motives, but in strict use this is improper. There is a conflict of desires, but the formation of a motive is the cessation of the conflict by settling the self upon some one motive. A motive is sometimes spoken of as the strongest desire. This may be either false or a mere truism. It is not true if it is meant to imply that the desires carry on a conflict with each other till all but the strongest is exhausted, and this survives by sheer preponderance of force. No such conflict goes on. The conflict of desires is the conflict of self with self. The conflict of desires ends when the self reconciles or concludes this internal struggle by setting itself in some one direction, by choosing to realize itself in the line laid down by some one desire. This desire is then the strongest, because the whole force of the self is thrown into it. This desire, in short, is nothing but the self having formed a definite purpose. It is now a motive or spring to action; it is the end of action. The action is only the reaching of this end, the execution of the motive. It gives us no new information to say that the act is determined by the motive, for the motive is the act which the self chooses to perform.

Motive and Ideal

It is only necessary to notice in addition that the motive to action, the end of action, is always *ideal*. It makes no difference how apparently material it is. Suppose it be a desire for food. The food, it is true, may already exist; but it is not the existence which is desired. What is desired is the eating of food, and this does not exist as matter of fact, but only *in idea*, or ideally. We never choose what exists already as matter of fact for us; we only choose that which has no objective being for us. Choice, in fact, is the declaration of self that a certain ideal shall be realized. The motive is another word for the ideal. The motive to getting food is the idea of satisfying one's self in the food. Since the object of desire is always the *self* in a certain state or act, it may be said that choice is the declaration by self that a certain ideal of self shall be realized.

Choice and the Intellectual Processes

It will be seen that the act of choice brings explicitly into consciousness what is involved in all intellectual acts. There is possible no knowledge without attention. Attention involves the discrimination of sensations from each other, and the identification of some one group of these sensations with self—in short, an act of choice. Furthermore, knowledge, as will, works towards an end, which is ideal, and has to select and arrange means for reaching this end. The process of knowledge is a process of volition. In studying knowledge, we simply neglect the process in behalf of the *product*. Knowledge was finally seen (page 134) to mean the realization of an ideal self; in studying volition we see whence this ideal comes, that it is the objectification of self by self, and whence come the means by which the end is reached, the ideal accomplished.

4. REALIZATION OF THE MOTIVE

We have now studied the method by which an impulse, when combined with the idea of a self satisfied through this impulse, gives rise to desire; and have seen that this desire when identified with the self becomes a motive or end of action. But this motive is ideal; it exists only in idea. It is something that should or ought to be, not that actually is. We have now to notice briefly the process by which the end is attained, the motive realized.

Dissatisfaction

The first element involved is the pain which arises from a feeling of the difference between the actual state of self and that ideal state which is the motive to action. The self has identified itself in choice with a certain mode of being or action. Yet this mode with which it feels itself identified is not actual. The self is not that which it has said it is; it involves a contradiction in itself, and the feeling of this disparity is necessarily one of pain. This feeling of pain, or dissatisfaction with what is, serves as a stimulus to go beyond that which is actual and realize the end. No matter how strongly a certain thing is desired, nor how firmly it has been chosen, unless the contemplation of the choice awakens a feeling of dissatisfaction with what actually is, no volition will ever result. The ideal will remain existing in idea only. As a representation held before the mind, it has no moving power. It is a motive *to action*, but not a motor force *of action*.

Action of Impulses

The pain thus awakened serves as stimulus to cancel the contradiction in the self between its actual and its represented state, and thus to experience real satisfaction. Actually to do this, to realize the chosen end, impulses must be called in. It should not be forgotten that our mode of exposition is necessarily one of abstraction, in which we isolate one factor after another. In isolating the factors of choice, motive, etc., we have neglected that from which we originally started, impulse. We must now return to this, for it is the *impulsive* character of that which has been desired and chosen that insures its actual realization. The end can be brought about only by surrendering it to the realm of the impulses, which possess the necessary outgoing force. More properly, we reach an end by allowing the impulsive force of the desire which was checked during the process of deliberation to express itself through the act of choice. It is always a physical impulse of some sort or other which furnishes the force which realizes the end, thus changing the motive into a deed.

Action of Intellect

But the impulses will not reach the end working blindly. They must be directed along certain channels by the intellect. The mind, in other words, must not only have an end before it, must not only have the sensuous impulse with which to reach this end, but must also have a conception of the *means* to the end, the paths which the impulse must follow. These means, however, are not intrinsically distinct from the end. They are only proximate ends; they are the

end analyzed into its constituent factors. For example, the
end of volition is the construction of a house. The means are
the plans, the brick and mortar, the arrangement of these by
the workmen, etc. It is evident that the end is not something
intrinsically different from the means; it is the means taken
as a harmoniously manifested whole. The means, on the
other hand, are something more than precedents to an end.
The first means, the plans, are only the end in its simplest,
most immediate form, and the next means are an expansion
of this, while the final means are identical with the end.
When we look at the act as a realized whole, we call it end;
when we look at it in process of realization, partially made
out, we call it *means*. But the action of the intellect is
requisite to analyze the end, the whole, into its means, the
component factors.

The System of Ends

It is evident, from what has been said, that ultimately there
can be only one end to human action. All other ends are
proximate ends; absolutely they are means, though also,
relatively, ends when looked at in their connection with
other acts. The house has its end in sheltering the family, in
manifesting artistic taste, etc. The sheltering of the family
has still another end, the preservation and development of
life, individual and social. Each end is referable to a higher
end, which, stated in most general form, is self-realization.
All acts are means to self for its own realization; yet it must
be remembered that this self-realization is not a last term
over and beyond the means, but is only the organized harmonious system of the means. It is the means taken in their
wholeness.

Desire, Choice, and the Self

We arrive at this same result when we consider the nature
of desire and of choice. What is desired is always the self in
some act or state. Choice is only the explicit identification of
this act or state with the self. The end of every desire and
choice, in other words, is the self. The self constitutes the
one end of every volition. Yet what is desired is not the self
in general; it is some specific self, the self doing or experi-

encing this or that. The self, in other words, has a content. It cannot be realized by some one act; it can be realized only by realizing every possible legitimate desire; that is, every desire whose realization does not preclude the realization of some other. We realize the self only by satisfying it in the infinite variety of concrete ways. These are means, because they are partial manifestations; the self is the end, because it is the organic unity of these various aspects of self-realization.

The Goal of Will

It is evident, therefore, that will can find its goal only in the completely realized self. It can find its goal, in other words, only in itself. Till the will is completely real, that is, until the whole self has become objective and universal, will must have an end towards which it cannot cease striving. It can find its goal only when the actual and the ideal self are at one. Till this point is reached there is a dualism in the self; always a conflict. The will is in itself universal, and this presence of the universal element must prevent the self resting in any realized attainment. It must form the spring to renewed action. It is the essence of the will to objectify or realize itself. It always holds up its objective or real self, therefore, as the end of all action, into which the given self must be transformed.

Form and Content of Will

This real self, which the will by its very nature, as self-objectifying, holds before itself, is originally a bare form, an empty ideal without content. We only know *that* it is, and that it is the real. *What* it is, what are the various forms which reality assumes, this we do not know. But this empty form is constantly assuming to itself a filling; as realized it gets a content. Through this content we know *what* the true self is, as well as that it is. It is so in knowledge; it is so in artistic production; it is so in practical action. A man feels there is truth and the feeling impels him to its discovery. What actually constitutes truth he knows only as he finds it. A man feels there is beauty and is impelled to its creation; when he has created, the idea of beauty has taken unto itself a definite content. A man feels there is some end advantageous for him or obligatory upon him; what this is in its fullness he knows only as he grasps it and makes it real for himself. The will, as self-objectifying, is at once the source of the empty form, which is the moving spring to realization, and of the process by which it is reached, and the form and content made one.

Stages of Realization

Ultimately, there is but one end, the self; all other ends are means. But there are degrees of subordination. In our treatment of will, we shall begin with the lowest group of ends, that which has the element of means in it to the greatest extent, and work upward. We begin, then, with physical volition, control of the body; go on to prudential volition, control of purposes for an end recognized to be advantageous; and finally treat moral volition, or the control of the will for itself as the absolutely obligatory end. It alone is absolute end. Every other group is also means.

NOTES TO CHAPTER 18

Spencer, *Principles of Psychology*, vol. i, pp. 495 - 504; Sully, *Psychology*, pp. 522 - 93; Perez, *First Three Years of Childhood*, pp. 99 - 109; Maudsley, *Physiology of Mind*, ch. vii; Drobisch, *Empirische Psychologie*, §99; Radestock, *Habit in Education*, pp. 49 - 62; George, *Lehrbuch der Psychologie*, pp. 552 - 71; Schneider, *Der menschliche Wille*, pp. 260 - 359; Erdmann, *Psychologische Briefe*, ch. xvii; Wundt, in *Philosophische Studien*, vol. i, p. 337 ff., "Zur Lehre vom Willen"; and *Grundzüge der physiologischen Psychologie*, vol. ii, pp. 383 - 95. For disorders of will, see Maudsley, *Body and Will*, pt. 3, and Ribot, *Diseases of Will*. Particularly upon desire, choice, and motive, see Bascom, *Principles of Psychology*, pp. 300 - 16; Sully (*op. cit.*), pp. 626 - 46; Murray, *Handbook of Psychology*, pp. 398 - 405; Bain, *Emotions and Will*, pp. 420 - 98; Brown, *Philosophy of Mind*, vol. iii, pp. 324 - 473; Volkmann, *Lehrbuch der Psychologie*, vol. ii, pp. 397 - 437; George (*op. cit.*), p. 548 ff.; Rosenkranz, *Psychologie*, pp. 323 - 30; Ulrici, *Der Leib und die Seele*, vol. ii, pp. 322 - 45; Drobisch (*op. cit.*), pp. 220 - 39; Tappan, *The Will*, pp. 331 - 51; Laurie, *Ethica*, pp. 37 - 48; Sidgwick, *Method of Ethics*, pp. 34 - 47; Beneke, *Erziehungslehre*, pp. 219 - 81.

19
Physical Control

Problem

We need, in adult life, only intend a certain movement to have that movement follow. The will to walk is followed by the act of locomotion; the desire of uttering some word leads to just that word being pronounced. We take a pen in hand, and express our thoughts by a series of muscular movements directed to that end. We will to move the head, and do it; or we select the motion of some one finger. The problem which we have to solve is how the idea of a certain movement occasions that exceedingly complex adjustment of muscles which produces the movement. We have to see how it is that our movements cease to be purely impulsive and become directed to reaching an end which is present in idea to the mind—how they become voluntary.

Basis of Solution

We have, of course, prior to experience no knowledge of the relations of means to the end; we have no idea of what movements must be performed in order to do a given act, say walk. Nor do we, after experience, have any *direct* knowledge of the relations of means to end. That is to say, all our movements are performed by certain arrangements of muscles, but of these muscles and of the mode in which they act we know nothing. Even if we study anatomy and learn the arrangement and action of our muscular system, this gives us no aid in performing any definite movement. It does not help us, in playing the piano, to know just what muscles are brought into requisition for the performance of the act. We fix our attention upon the end to be reached, and let the direct means, the muscles, take care of themselves. The basis of solution, therefore, cannot be found in any knowledge of the muscular system. It is found, however, in the *sensations* which accompany all muscular action.

Nature of Solution

Every change of every voluntary muscle is accompanied by a sensation, and this, of course, whether the change occurs impulsively or through conscious volition. The result is that this sensation becomes to us a sign or symbol of the movement. The will, it must be remembered, does not have to originate the muscular impulse; it has only to direct the outgoing force in such a way that it shall subserve a required end. Now the muscular sensations constantly report to consciousness the state of the body, and of the muscles which make it up. Prior to experience we do not know what these reports signify; we do not know, in short, what change corresponds to a given sensation. Our experience consists in learning to interpret these sensations; in seeing what acts they stand for. Having learned this, knowing that a certain sensation means a certain movement, we control the movements by controlling the sensations. We learn, in other words, not only the meaning of a sensation, but the connection of the various sensations, and in what order sensations must be arranged in order to occasion other sensations.

Process of Physical Control

In studying, accordingly, the process by which we learn to govern our bodily impulses, and direct them to an end, we have to study the process by which we learn how to interpret any muscular sensation, see what movement it stands for; and the process by which we are enabled to connect these sensations together, so that a group of sensations comes to mean a certain complex act, made up either of simultaneous or of successive movements. We not only learn the meaning of each isolated sensation, but we learn how it must be combined with others to reach a certain result. The process is similar to that of attention, where we select and combine certain sensations, and neglect others, in order to reach the intellectual end we have in view; except that in the present case the sensations are selected and connected with reference to a practical end rather than to an intellectual. The end in one case is producing some external change; in the other, of some internal change, some new combination of ideas; but the process is identical in both. Psychologically, the end is identical in each, for we know nothing of the muscular change to be effected, but only of the sensations which accompany this change.

Mode of Treatment

We shall take up, first, the process by which we come to know what act each muscular sensation represents—the process by which muscular sensation becomes *definite*, and movements *specific*; and, secondly, the process by which muscular sensation becomes more *comprehensive*, and movements *harmonized* with each other—the process by which we connect muscular sensations with each other, either simultaneously or successively.

1. The Differentiation of Motor Impulses

Originally all motor impulses, except such as are, by instinct or through heredity, adjusted to some specific though unconscious end, are vague, undefined, and diffused through the whole system. The motor impulse for food is adjusted in the infant to just the acts which are necessary to get food, those of sucking, and so with some other impulses which we have studied. But the vast majority of muscular impulses have no such definite adjustment. They originally spend themselves in spreading through the whole system, according to their intensity, accomplishing no definite result. There is an impulse to locomotion, but this impulse does not instinctively seek the precise channels which will accomplish the end. It loses itself in undefined movements of the whole body; so also do the impulses to speak, to write, etc. We have first to study the process by which the impulse becomes definite or limited to producing a certain number of movements.

Process of Experimenting

This is by a process of experimentation. It may be illustrated by the way in which a child learns to reach for and handle an object. This has its basis, as already explained, in a reflex impulse of grasping. The child sees, we will say, a brightly colored ball. This awakens in him a purely instinctive impulse to grasp it. He may fail, because it is out of his reach. From this failure, however, he learns something. He learns that a certain visual sensation is connected with a distance of an object longer than the reach of his arm. By repeated failure, there is set up a distinct association in his consciousness of certain visual sensations with the muscular feelings due to the movements of his arm and body. He may, however, grasp the object. If so, there is formed an association between this distance and the muscular sensation accompanying the successful movement. This association becomes solidified by repeated experience. The process of learning to reach the object consists, accordingly, in forming the association between the visual sensation, which means distance, and the muscular sensation, which means movement.

Further Illustration

Imagine a child learning to talk. Our starting-point here is the reflex impulse to utter sounds; the problem is to control these impulses in such a way that intelligent articulate speech shall result. The child hears a certain sound applied to objects. His business now is to make some one of his reflex sounds—the raw material which he has in stock—correspond to the sound—reproduce it. His attempts are partial failures, but each of these failures allows him to eliminate certain sounds. His feeling of non-success leads him successively to discard many of them; while each attempt that is successful forms an association between the auditory sensation which is the sign of an object, and the muscular sensation which is the sign of that movement which occasions this sound. He learns to interpret auditory sensations in terms of muscular, and *vice versa*. This process of experimentation has three results:

(1) It leaves in consciousness a distinct idea of the end to be reached. We must not conceive the problem as if the child has originally a distinct notion in consciousness of the end he has to reach, and needs only to learn the means of

reaching it. The child has only a very indefinite idea of what constitutes the act of reaching an object or of pronouncing a word before he has actually accomplished it. *It is only when he has reached the end that he knows what the end is.* He begins with a vague consciousness that there is an end to be reached, and the result of his experimentation is that he knows *what* this end is. His vague impulse has now taken definite form in the distinct idea of some act which he performs.

(2) The movement becomes localized just in the degree in which the idea of the act becomes definite. The original movement is vague and diffuse, like the idea of it. A child in learning to walk moves his whole body. In learning to write the motor impulse is expended through the arm, the head, the mouth, and tongue; probably more or less through the whole body. Similarly with learning to play the piano. But the result of his experimentation is that the motor impulse becomes differentiated. It does not seek an outlet indifferently through any and every muscle of the body, but is confined to certain channels. The movement, in short, becomes specialized.

(3) Less and less stimulus is required in order to set up the movement. This follows directly from the restriction of the impulse to a definite channel. So long as the force is expended in moving the whole body, a large amount is required, most of which is wasted; only that being economically used which is actually employed in that one part of the movement which is necessary to the result. With every localization of movement comes a saving of the stimulus, until, when just the proper channel alone is employed, one hundredth of the original force may suffice. The result is that a less violent and more internal stimulus serves to occasion the action.

Degrees of Stimulus Required

The original stimulus is, in all probability, the demand of the whole organism for food. Nothing less than a disturbance of the equilibrium of the entire organism suffices. In the next stage a sudden and violent affection of one of the senses serves—a sudden pain, a bright light. Then, as the force becomes more and more utilized as it is properly directed, the performance of an act by another person occasions enough disturbance to impel us to it. As the process advances it is no longer necessary to have the action presented to us through our sensations as a stimulus; the request or suggestion of another suffices. Then comes the last and final development, when an idea of the action originating from within serves to occasion the act. A stimulus which is wholly ideal is all that is necessary to occasion the discharge of superfluous nervous force into just its proper channel. The mind has no longer to oversee the whole expenditure of the energy; it has, as it were, only to open the valve which liberates the force, and by its own self-executing mechanism directs it. An *idea* of the end is stimulus enough to open the valve.

II.   The Combination of Motor Impulses

All physical control involves co-ordination and mutual connection of the motor impulses. In order to walk it is not enough that there should be a definite idea of the end, and the localization of each movement necessary. There must also be an idea of the successive and simultaneous steps of the process; the various movements must be harmonized. This comes about also through a process of experimentation, by which the child learns not only to associate some muscular sensation with a given tactual or visual sensation, but also learns to associate various muscular sensations with each other. Suppose the attempt is to utter a certain sentence. In addition to the process just described, there will be an association of all the muscular sensations accompanying the successive sounds. In playing the piano there will be also simultaneous associations added. The principles of successive and simultaneous association, in short, are sufficient to account for the various phenomena of the combination of motor impulses. The associated sensations become signs of the associated movements. Three effects of this process of association may be noticed.

(1) The idea of the movement to be performed becomes more complex. The infant begins with a very simple

and immediate idea. His first voluntary efforts are limited to movements containing very few elements, and the end of which is directly present. The consciousness of an end which is remote, and which can be reached only by the systematic regulation of a large number of acts, cannot be formed until the combination of motor impulses has realized some such end. Then there exists in consciousness the idea of an end comparatively remote in time, and comprehending many minor acts. The man lives in the future, and with the consciousness that his present acts do not exhaust themselves in themselves, but have reference to this future. Take, for example, the consciousness of one learning a trade. He must put before himself the idea of an accomplishment which cannot be reached for years, and must recognize the subordinate relation which his movements through these years bear to the end willed. The idea in consciousness becomes ever more complex and further projected in time.

(2) Along with this goes an extension in the range of movements. The original movements are isolated. Each has no meaning beyond itself. With growth of consciousness of a comprehensive end, this isolation ceases. Each is considered only in its reference to others with which it is combined, while all are subordinated to a common end. In an adult of pretty complete volitional control, almost all movements, whether of recreation or of business, are connected together through their reference to some unity, some final purpose which the man intends. There is involved first a process of *inhibition*, by which all movements not calculated to reach the end are suppressed; second, *co-ordination*, by which the remaining movements are brought into harmonious relations with each other; and, third, *accommodation*, by which they are all adjusted to the end present in consciousness.

(3) There is also a deepening of the control. The movements become organized, as it were, into the very structure of the body. The body becomes a tool more and more under command, a mechanism better fitted for its end, and also more responsive to the touch. Isolated acts become *capacity* for action. That which has been laboriously acquired becomes spontaneous function. There result a num-

ber of *abilities* to act in this way or that—abilities to walk, to talk, to read, to write, to labor at the trade. Acquisition becomes function; control becomes skill. These capacities are also *tendencies*. They constitute not only a machine capable of action in a given way at direction, but an automatic machine, which, when consciousness does not put an end before it, acts for itself. It is this deepening of control which constitutes what we call *habit*.

The Nature of the Will

In studying this process of physical control, we have been studying in a concrete way, the nature of the will itself. The will is sometimes spoken of as if it were a force outside of the rest of our nature: sometimes a legislative force, laying down rules for the feelings and impulses; sometimes an executive force, carrying out the decrees of the intellect upon the impulses. Then the will is spoken of as directing the body to do this or that, and there arises the insoluble problem of how a spiritual force like the will can operate upon a material substance like the body. But these views are based upon an inadequate conception of volition. As we have seen, it is not the will standing outside of the body, which directs the body to perform some movement. The performance of the action is the existence of the will. The will is the concrete unity of feeling and intellect; the feeling carries us to a certain result, the intellect takes cognizance of this result, the end, and of the means to it, and now places this as a conscious motive or end in the feelings, and controls them thereby. The whole process is will. The intellectual operation of representing the means and end, and the feeling which impels us to the end, have no separate existence.

Illustrations

Let the process, for example, be that of learning to walk. Where does the will come in? In the first place, we have the more or less unconscious operation of feeling; the craving of the muscular system for exercise, and the tendency of this feeling to impel itself along certain lines and produce locomotion. That this is the end in view and how it is to be reached, there is, of course, no knowledge. But the impulses bring about certain actions. By the child's instinct and more especially by the aid of other wills, some of these are seen to be useless, *without an end*, and are inhibited; others are successful. From those which are successful, the idea of an end is consciously framed by the intellect; there now exists the *idea* of walking and of the means which constitute it. This end, however, is simply the due localization and combination of the various motor impulses by which it is reached. The impulses are now controlled. We may say, if we wish, that they are controlled by the will; more properly, however, their control, the union of impulse and intellect, feeling and end, *is* the will. The process is the same, if one takes the example of the acquisition of a foreign language by an adult, except that the adult does not have to rely so much on the unconscious experimentation of his feelings as they work to the end, which they finally hit upon; for through the greater development of his intellect he appropriates the results of the acquirements of others. Conscious imitation, in short, plays a larger part than unconscious feeling towards an end. The volitional element is the same. It is the co-ordination of impulses for an end recognized by the intellect.

Body and Will

The will is not, therefore, a force outside of the body. The will (so far as physical control is concerned) is *the body, so far as this is organized so as to be capable of performing certain specific and complex acts.* The will has given itself concrete existence by constituting the body its mechanism, its expression. In other words, the defining and combining of motor impulses so that they bear a harmonious relation to each other is the existence of the will, so far as physical control is concerned. The end is only another name for the harmony. The will is not formal, but has a real content.

Twofold Nature of Will

The will, therefore, gets concrete existence only so far as the soul, through its experimentation with the motor impulses, reaches an end, which is the intelligent, harmonious relation of these impulses. But why do the feelings tend to project themselves towards an end? Why does the self experiment with the feelings? Why does it inhibit or reject some as useless? Why does it employ others? The answer to these latter questions is because it feels pain in the one and satisfaction in the other. But why should it? These questions lead us to recognize that the soul through its impulses is already feeling towards an end, and that it is guided constantly by the feeling which its acts bear to this end as shown by the accompanying satisfaction and dissatisfaction. What the actual reaching of this end does, is to make the will articulate, body it forth in definite shape.

We must recognize, therefore, that the will has a two-fold nature. On the one hand, it sets up (originally, no doubt, in the form of feeling) an end, and guides the impulses towards this end; as such it is the source, the spring to all realization of self. On the other hand, will is the actual reaching of this end; it is the definite harmonizing of the impulses. As such it is realized self. In the latter form only is the will a definite, concrete existence. Yet the unconscious projection of the self in the form of impulses, and the sequent experimentation with them till they are harmonized, are the sources of this definite realization of will. Will is the cause of itself, in other words. The process of our actual life is simply that by which will gives itself definite manifestation, bodies itself forth in objective form. Just what will is, we can tell only so far as it has thus realized itself; but will is never exhausted in any such realization, and its continued action in the form of impulse towards an end as yet not formulated is the source of all change, all growth in psychical life.

Dependence of Will

In addition, it needs to be noted that the possibility of physical control depends upon the connection of the individual will with other wills. In its lower forms, as locomotion, it is dependent upon these other wills for guidance, encouragement, and approval, as well as largely for models of imitation. Were the infant left to himself, it is safe to say that either he would never accomplish the act, or that it would take a much longer time, and be very clumsily done. In the higher forms, as talking, writing, etc., there is not only dependence of the foregoing kind, but of the material also, for the content of the will is due to other wills. In learning to speak, the individual merely appropriates the product of the wills of the community in which he lives. In learning to walk, indeed, he does not create. He merely reproduces by his will, under the direction of the wills of others, certain physical relations. In learning to speak, he reproduces under the direction of other wills, and reproduces that which owes its existence to these wills; he reproduces social relations through physical processes.

NOTES TO CHAPTER 19

Carpenter, *Mental Physiology*, pp. 209 - 18, 279 - 315, 376 - 86, and in *Contemporary Review*, vol. xvii, p. 192 ff.; Calderwood, *Relations of Mind and Brain*, ch. v; Lotze, *Outlines of Psychology*, pp. 83 - 88; Lazarus, *Das Leben der Seele*, vol. ii, pp. 59 - 71; Ulrici, *Der Leib und die Seele*, vol. ii, pp. 301 - 21; Schneider, *Der menschliche Wille*, pp. 407 - 52; Steinthal, *Einleitung in die Psychologie und Sprachwissenschaft*, pp. 263 - 89; Hoppe, *Das Auswendiglernen*.

20
Prudential Control

Relation to Physical

Physical control forms in a twofold way the basis of the higher developments of will. In the first place, the body is the mechanism by which all changes in the world must be brought about. Thinking involves the use of speech and the control of the brain; moral purpose involves in its execution movements, etc. Physical control is a necessary precondition of all more developed forms. Secondly it develops the same factors of will that are involved in the complex modes of control. Regulation of motor impulses so that they conform to an end involves the choice of an end, the apt selection of means, fixed resolution, and determined adherence to a course of action. All the elements constituting will are thus brought into play.

Prudential Control

It is distinguished from physical by the fact that the co-ordination and regulation of movements is now only a means, not an end in itself. It includes all *actions in which the impulses are directed towards an end which is regarded as advantageous, or away from an end which is considered harmful.* The word *"prudential,"* therefore, is used in a very wide sense *to express all actions dictated by motives of anticipated gain or loss.* It is further distinguished from physical control by the fact that the latter is not directed by any conscious representation of future benefit, but rather by instinctive feeling; and from moral control by the fact that the latter occurs to fulfil obligation, not to reap advantage. The same act may illustrate each kind of control. A child, for example, learning a foreign language does not do it with any motive of the advantages that are to accrue to him from it; a youth may set about learning the language because he sees it is necessary to his business success; furthermore, if the business success is necessary in order that he may support a dependent mother, the act becomes also moral.

Analysis of Prudential Act

The various factors of an act of the prudential class may be shown from the example just given. The first element is the creation and development of the desire, of the want. There must be produced the conscious want of succeeding in business. This is something over and above any sensuous impulse; it arises only when the sensuous impulses are associated with wider ranges of experience. We have to study, first, the process by which the desires for whose satisfaction prudential action occurs are developed. This desire is then constituted an end or motive of action, and those means are selected which are best fitted to reach the end. It involves, secondly, the development of intelligent selection and adaptation of means to result; which will vary, thirdly, according as this end is purely practical, is intellectual, or is emotional.

1. Development of Desires

As already said, sensuous impulse, as for food, does not constitute the desire for food. Desire involves at least three additional elements. In the first place, there must have been experience of something which satisfied the impulse. The impulse must have become associated with the act in which it resulted, and also of the pleasure which accompanied this act. In the second place, there must be explicit recognition of the fact that the impulse is not at the present time satisfied. There must be recognition of lack. The individual must feel that the act, with its pleasure, which was his once is not his now. And, in the third place, there must be conscious recognition that this experience which formerly satisfied the impulse will do so again. Desire implies *recognition of present non-satisfaction; remembrance of past satisfaction, and anticipation of future satisfaction through a similar experience*. The development of desire will be, of course, merely the process by which these three elements are brought into existence.

Illustration

It follows that every new experience may result in the creation of a desire. Every experience may bring about such
measure of self-satisfaction as will cause that experience,
when it is re-presented in consciousness and compared with
the present experience, to be an object desired. For example,
a child performs some act, say, doing an errand, which is
rewarded with money. Money is now an object of desire. It
constitutes a possible motive of action, as it could not do
before experience of it. With this money he purchases, perhaps, toys, which give him new satisfaction, and form a new
object of desire. These toys he may share with his play-
mates, and thus gain their approbation, which in turn affords a new source of desire. To this process there is no
conceivable end. It is also evident that the process of development *widens* desires and renders them *definite*. The range
of things wanted is constantly enlarged; the idea of that
which is wanted, that which will satisfy need, becomes more
precise and accurate.

Imagination and Desire

With the development of imagination, especially of constructive imagination as opposed to reproductive, desire
somewhat changes its character. All desire, as requiring
anticipation of a future state, involves imagination. With
growth of imagination desire gets to be more comprehensive
and more distinct. As imagination becomes plastic, shaping
old material into new forms, desire is no longer limited to
experiences precisely similar to those already experienced.
Imagination creates ideals towards which desire projects
itself. It constructs conceptions of honor, of wealth, of fame,
which are no less real for desire than the experiences of
every-day life.

Imagination not only extends desire to ideal embodi-
ments, but it determines largely the channels which desire
shall follow. Every imagination of anything is the idea of it
as real, and is, in so far, desire. There is no surer way of
strengthening desire than allowing the imagination to dwell
upon some conception. The idea of a thing is the projection

of the mind towards it. So the objects, the kinds of objects, upon which imagination dwells decide what desires, what class of desires, are of most importance for an individual. A merchant's desires are not as an artist's; a scholar's not like an artisan's; and the difference of the desires is largely due to the fact that the habitual mental areas upon which the mind dwells are so different. The close relation between desire and imagination is nowhere better illustrated than in the artist. Here this imagination, the ideal bodying forth of beautiful objects, becomes a desire so strong for the actual existence of these objects that one is instinctively led to create them. The relation exists no less in the mercantile and practical spheres. The man who lets his thoughts run constantly on money and the advantages to be gained from it is the man of strongest desire for it. So far is it from being true that the man of imagination and the man of action are opposed that it should rather be said that only the man of vivid and close imagination can be a man of action. Dreamy action is the result of dreamy, that is, vague and scattering, imagination.

II. Choice of Ends and Means

With every extension of experience and every new development of imagination there arises, therefore, a growth of desire in distinctness and in range of comprehensiveness. All objects and all ideals become saturated with that close connection with the experiences of the self that constitutes them desirable. As such they come into constant contact and conflict with each other. There are all degrees of relationship existing between them. Some are directly in line with each other and mutually strengthen each other, as, say, desire for wealth and for social recognition. Others, though not opposed in themselves, may necessitate choice of opposed means, as desire for increase of learning and for social enjoyment. Others may be directly incompatible with each other, as desires for the approval of others and for personal self-indulgence. This conflict of ends and means requires that some one be chosen and the conflict ended.

Grounds of Choice

The nature of choice we have studied previously. It is the selection of some one desire, its identification with self, and consequent objectification as an end of action. The chosen desire becomes the motive. We have now only to study the grounds of choice. Why is one desire selected and decided upon as an end of action while another is rejected? The desire which is chosen becomes the motive, but what is the motive to choice? In prudential action the general answer is, that desire is chosen whose satisfaction is conceived to result in the most advantage. Of all possible ends that is made the actual end whose realization affords the most benefit. Superior advantage of result is the motive in all prudential action. But what are the factors which decide what will be regarded as most advantageous, and hence be made the motive?

1. CHOICE DEPENDS ON INDIVIDUAL CHARACTER-ISTICS

That which appears of most worth to one will not to another. The factors which are, for the individual, accidental will decide largely where choice falls. The hereditary influences, the early home life, the circumstances of education and of surroundings all enter in to fix what one considers to be of the higher advantage to himself. A savage's idea of what is most desirable differs from that of the civilized man, and that of the ancient Greek from that of the modern Briton. Every choice which renders a desire a motive reflects also the past experience of the person. He will not be apt to choose that which has not been in intimate connection with his former doings. The channels along which he has habitually directed his imagination, the fancies he has indulged in, will also be determining factors.

2. CHOICE DEPENDS UPON KNOWLEDGE

But supposing that the individuals who choose are alike in other respects, their choice of an end will depend upon their knowledge. Just in proportion as one's knowledge in a given direction is comprehensive and definite will he be able to tell which of many possible ends is the most advantageous. One may choose, for example, to engage in a certain business as the best of many alternatives, and this may turn out about the most harmful, because of influences which his limitation of knowledge would not allow him to take into account—the character of his business associates, a financial crisis, perils by fire and water, etc. To sum up, we may say, the person makes that an end which he regards as productive of most advantage; what he regards as most advantageous depends upon the accidents of his birth, surroundings, and past experiences, and upon the extent of his knowledge in enabling him to determine that whose selection will prove of greatest profit.

Choice of Means

Along with the choice of end goes the choice of means to reach the end. In a general way it may be said that the choice of the end *is* the choice of means. In choosing an end one must choose whatever is necessary to it. But many different ways of accomplishing the one end may present themselves, out of which some one must be selected. Aside from personal idiosyncracy, the essential factor in deciding is the range of knowledge. The means at hand will be compared by the intellect; the mind will calculate so far as it may the consequences of choice in either direction, will weigh the resulting advantages and disadvantages of each, and then strike the balance in favor of the side upon which most advantage lies, so far as knowledge will allow it to be calculated.

III. Forms of Prudential Control

These are three, practical, intellectual, and emotional.

1. PRACTICAL CONTROL

This includes all actions externally directed with a view to reaching some advantage. It involves, in the first place, the checking or *inhibition* of some action. A child, for example, sees some sweetmeats, and is impelled to eat them by the idea of the satisfaction they will give him. There then occurs another thought—the representation of his mother's displeasure or of possible sickness. These originate an aversion to the sweetmeats, and an action away from them. This conflict will result in the checking of one or the other of the actions. The fact that all volitional action implies some degree of possible conflict shows that the first step in control is inhibition. The next is *postponement*. That is to say, the child acts with reference to more remote ends. He undergoes some present painful operation in consideration of some future good, the recovery of health. Or he abstains from present pleasurable indulgence, thinking of some future pain. Or he goes through some operation, in itself perhaps a matter neither of desire nor of aversion, because he sees it to be a necessary condition of something that is desired. Postponement becomes connection of acts. As inhibition leads him to refer one present act to another and consider them in their relations to each other, so the postponement of action leads him to connect his acts serially, and make successive acts mutually tributary to one another.

Enlargement of Scope

The third and final step is that the actions occur with reference, not only to more remote ends, but to more *inclusive* ones. The child acts with reference to health as a comprehensive, permanent end. He so acts with reference to the approval of others, to the attainment of a mastery of some trade, etc. Then he may form a most comprehensive end, say happiness, which shall include all these, and act with reference to that. So far as he does thus act with reference to some one comprehensive end, he has himself in perfect prudential, practical self-control, for this comprehensive end will lead him to inhibit all acts which are not in accordance with it, and to connect all successive acts so as to lead up to it.

Results

As the result of this increasing control, action becomes more reasoned or *deliberate*; evincing more pertinacity or *perseverance*, and being more resolute or *determined*. The deliberateness of an act is opposed to its impulsiveness. If we bring reason to bear upon an impulse, the result is that we do not act immediately, but from the consequences which reason shows as likely to flow from the act. Early impulses are also easily turned aside. The occurrence of some other impulse leads the child to forget the act upon which he is engaged, and diverts his energies into the new channel. The setting-up of a more remote end towards which all mediate acts must be organized, changes this. Will becomes persevering. It recognizes that action must persist in one choice to accomplish anything. Uniting the qualities of deliberation and perseverance, together with a firm grasp upon the end of action, is *resolute* will. A child may persevere to the attainment of some chosen end, but his will cannot be called determined or resolute unless he is conscious of what the end is, how it is related to other ends, and has consciously subordinated them to it; unless, in short, he has formed an end which is comprehensive. A firm or controlled will is deliberate in making its choice, tenacious to this choice, and resolute in making use of whatever means will realize it.

2. INTELLECTUAL CONTROL

To go exhaustively into the subject of intellectual control would be simply to repeat what has already been said concerning attention. This, indeed, has been defined as inner will. The study of its mode of action is merely the study of the way in which the mind masters and controls its thoughts, directing them to some end. It may be recalled here that attention involves an inhibiting activity. In giving attention even to the least complex presentation the attracting force of all other presentations must be disregarded. The positive development of intellectual control, on the other hand, is seen in increased ability to fix the mind upon some one subject—*concentration*—and in the ability to pursue longer and longer courses of subordinate mental processes, all leading up to a final goal. In memory we manifest intellectual control in the process of recollection, where we fixate attention upon some element and thereby greatly increase its power to redintegrate what we are seeking for. Thinking is an example, on a large scale, of intellectual control; for here we consciously adjust our conceptions with a view of bringing about a certain mental result.

3. EMOTIONAL CONTROL

Here, as in the other forms, the first step is a negative one, to restrain the feeling. This is chiefly brought about indirectly by the control of the muscular system. In studying the sensuous impulses, we saw that emotions tend to manifest themselves in movements. It follows that if we can control these movements, by the process studied in the last chapter, we also control the emotions. In controlling feelings like anger, for example, the first thing to be done is to repress its outward manifestation. But this may simply turn the feeling into another channel. If it is repressed from any external motive, it is almost sure to do so. In this case anger turns into sullen brooding or a desire for revenge. It is evident that there must be some further method of checking feeling. This is again indirect through control of our thoughts. That is to say, if anger is the feeling to be inhibited, the thoughts must be kept away from the person who has inflicted the injury and from the injury itself, and directed towards any benefits that may have been derived from the person, or towards any subject that will arouse pleasurable feeling. This suggests the most efficient method of repressing any feeling, namely, calling up an opposed emotion which will expel it. In general, it may be said that it is not the way to get rid of a feeling to destroy it, leaving a vacuum. This is impossible. It can be done only by introducing a stronger opposed feeling.

Positive Control

Many psychologists have treated the subject of control of feeling as if it were exhausted when it is shown how feeling is repressed. But this is a one-sided view. Feeling is a normal factor of our psychical life, and involves, therefore, as much as any other factor, regulated development towards a certain end. The inhibition of feeling is not an end in itself, but merely a necessary means in order that the feelings which are not inhibited may be duly developed. Anger is repressed only that benevolence or some other emotion may express itself. Were feeling really suppressed, all action would be suppressed also, for no desire, no motive to act, would remain.

The positive control of feeling consists in so directing it that it becomes a stimulus to knowledge or to action. The emotion of indignation, for example, is controlled, not when it is obliterated, but when it is so directed that it does not expend itself in vague or violent reaction, but quickens thought and spurs to action. Many of the world's greatest orations, as well as deeds of valor, are so many illustrations of controlled indignation. Feeling that merely expresses *itself* is uncontrolled; feeling that subserves the intellect or the will is controlled. Feeling does not cease to be feeling in becoming thus subservient; on the contrary, it becomes more susceptible, readier, and deeper.

NOTES TO CHAPTER 20

Martineau, *Types of Ethical Theory*, vol. ii, pp. 65 - 74; Bain, *Emotions and Will*, pp. 399 - 419; Carpenter, *Mental Physiology*, pp. 386 - 428; George, *Lehrbuch der Psychologie*, p. 576 ff.; Volkmann, *Lehrbuch der Psychologie*, vol. ii, pp. 463 - 89.

21

Moral Control

Relation to Prudential

Prudential action is not in itself moral action, yet there is no prudential action which is not potentially in the ethical sphere, and hence either moral or immoral. Actions may be directed, for example, so as to preserve health, and carry on a business which it is supposed will lead to wealth. So far they are only prudential. But as soon as the preservation of health is seen to be a duty (and so, in many cases, with the securing of a certain competency), the acts become moral action. Or if the securing wealth will necessitate the non-securing of some other end, which is recognized to be higher, or will necessitate certain means, as dishonesty or lying, the act becomes immoral. The terms "prudential" and "moral" do not refer, therefore, to two kinds of acts, for the same act may be either or both. What is the distinction?

Distinction of Moral from Prudential

In brief, the difference is that a prudential act is measured by the *result*; the moral, by the *motive*. A man may *intend*, for example, to gain a certain advantage for himself by embarking in a certain line of action, but his knowledge is limited. New circumstances occur, and his purpose is thwarted. The action turns out to be a disadvantageous or *imprudent* one. But if a man *intends* a moral action the result cannot be immoral, however unforeseen or deplorable it may be. On the other hand, an act which appears rash at the time may, by lucky and opportune happenings, result in gain. But an act whose *purpose* is immoral cannot result in morality, no matter how beneficial to any one it may be. If a surgeon intends to save a man's life, and performs an act with that motive solely, and the result is the man's death, the result is deplorable, but it is not wrong. If a man intends to kill another, but, failing, unwittingly does the man a great benefit, the *result* is a desirable one, but the action is immoral. *Actions, in short, that are judged from their motives alone are acts lying in the moral sphere.*

Analysis of Moral Action

Why do we make this distinction? Why do some acts get their character established by their results, and others by their motives? This question is an ethical question, if we inquire into the ultimate ground of the distinction; it is a psychological question when we ask through what conditions it originates as a fact in psychical life. It is a psychical fact that we do judge some acts by their motives and others by their results, and this difference must have its origin in some psychical processes. We have only to inquire what, as matter of fact, these processes are. This brings us to the analysis of a moral action, to see what constitutes it.

Responsibility

Before answering directly the question why we estimate the quality of some acts by their results and that of others by their intention, we must recognize a further difference between prudential and moral acts. The doer recognizes his personal responsibility for the act in the latter case, while in the former he does not. The person may regret the result of a course of action undertaken to derive some benefit, if it turns out hurtfully, or if the disadvantages outweigh the accruing gains, but he does not *blame* himself for this result. This gives us the added fact that an individual does not hold himself responsible for the result of his actions, but only for their motives. When the result is the direct outcome of the motive, responsibility is extended, of course, to the former.

Basis of Distinction

It is easy to see why a man does not hold himself responsible for the result of an action, except so far as that result is the legitimate effect of his motive in action. *It is because the result is beyond his control.* The commencement of the action may lie with him; its issue does not. The final outcome is determined by a multitude of causes of which the

THE EARLY WORKS OF JOHN DEWEY

one acting can foresee only a few. It is impossible, in originating an action, to tell how many forces, hitherto unno-
ticed, may be set in motion; it is impossible to tell how many
forces independently set in operation by others may cross the
workings of these forces, sometimes reinforcing them, sometimes nullifying them. Or, as was said before, the ground of
decision in prudential action is the surroundings and knowledge of the one deciding. Whether the result is reached or
not depends upon the extent and limitations of these decisive
factors. For these limitations one does not hold himself responsible, and, because he does not, he does not hold himself
responsible for the result.

Actions in the Moral Sphere

On the other hand, if some acts are judged by their motives,
and if the actor holds himself responsible for these motives,
it follows that he must regard these motives as *within his
control*. For example, the surgeon, taking measures to perform an operation, which finally results fatally, judges his
act to be unsuccessful from the prudential point of view, but
not to be immoral. He did the best he knew how. The issue
lay with forces of nature. Suppose, however, that from a
motive of indifference, of love of ease, or of love of speedy
fame, he has not gained some information which he might
have acquired regarding the state of his patient, and which
would have induced him to act otherwise. In such a case he
blames himself for the result, that is, he judges it from the
moral point of view. He estimates his act from the quality of
its motive, and he does so because he recognizes that, while
he does not make the result, he does make the motive.

Moral Action and Personality

The fact that we estimate the quality of some acts as successful or non-successful according to their outcome, while
we estimate that of others as moral or immoral according to
their motive, is, therefore, due to the fact that the latter are
determined by *personality* alone, while the former are determined by some accident or *contingency*, as it were, of personality. Some actions affect the man, what he *is* in himself;
others affect the circumstances of the man, what he *has*

about him. A man's wealth, his health, his knowledge, his general prosperity are not himself; they are what the man has or would have. A man's will is himself. Every act that arises from will or personality, but has its result in something external to that will, something which the will *has*, is a prudential act. Every act that both arises from and affects the will, the being of a man, is in the moral sphere.

The wealth a man possesses, the esteem in which he is held, the degree of bodily well-being which characterizes him, are circumstances of the man; they are not the man. All acts which aim at these external circumstances are estimated by the extent to which they realize these circumstances; by their results. Where a man wills to tell the truth he wills *to be* something; and even if what he says is false by reason of the limitation of his knowledge, *he* is still true. The fact about which he makes his statement is external, and his knowledge of it is decided by facts external to him. His motive to tell the truth is internal to him, and is decided by himself, and cannot be changed by the contingency of the result. If his motive is truth, he cannot be false, no matter how false the actual result may be.

Prudential Actions become Moral

None the less actions directed towards the attainment of wealth, of health, of knowledge, of esteem, etc., are, as matter of fact, in the moral sphere, and form, indeed, the content of most moral actions. How can we reconcile this statement with the one previously made that they are external to personality, circumstances *of* it? The reconciliation lies in the fact that while health, knowledge, etc., do not in themselves constitute personality, or will, they may be *necessary conditions of its realization*. A man cannot be the *person* he otherwise would be, if he is ignorant, sickly, and so poor as not to be able properly to support his family. So far as these circumstances are necessary to the realization of personality, they become themselves moral ends, and constitute acts which are judged by their motives. Taken by themselves, or in abstraction from the realization of personality, they are not such; taken as ends in opposition to the realization of personality they become immoral.

Summary

It is evident from what has been said that moral action only brings into explicit consciousness that which is virtually contained in prudential action. All prudential action must have its end ultimately in its effect upon the person willing; health, knowledge, etc., cannot be ultimate ends. They are ends only *because* in them the personality reaches its end and becomes itself. When we treat them as if they were ends in themselves, we are simply neglecting or abstracting from their effect on the will itself. When we complete our account by taking this into consideration, we are in the realm of moral action. When we do take personality into account we judge the act from its motive; for while the result is external to the personality, the motive is internal to it and reveals what the personality is and would be.

The actual will to *be* something, not the mere desire or longing for it, but the resolute choice to be it, constitute the being it. The will *to have* it does not constitute the having it. A man who wills to be good will be good. A man who wills to be learned, to be a statesman, etc., is not necessarily such, because, after all, these are circumstances which he may have, not the personality which he is. The man also holds himself responsible for the moral action, because his personality constitutes the motive; it is not constituted by anything external to him. The recognition of personality as constituting the essence of moral action enables us, therefore, to account for its two distinguishing features—that it is measured by its motive, and that responsibility for it is recognized.

Treatment of Subject

Having analyzed moral action, we have now to consider (1) the process of the development of ethical desires, whether moral or immoral; (2) the nature of ethical choice; (3) the result of moral control, formation of character, etc. The caution already mentioned must be kept in mind; though we are dealing with ethical material, we are dealing with it only as a matter of psychological experience.

I. Development of Ethical Desires

Ethical desires, whether moral or immoral, arise when any action is to be performed whose result is seen to affect personality itself, and not any of its possessions or circumstances. As matter of historic development, they probably consciously arise in the conflict between *having* something and *being* something. The child, for example, has been told not to touch some sweetmeats, and is very desirous of eating them. Now the desire of eating them is not in itself, of course, immoral, but it conflicts with the desire to be in harmony with his mother's wishes and the worthy recipient of her love. The child does not reason the matter out, but he feels that if he yields to his desire he will have come short of that which he should be. This consciousness of coming short of his own true being is, without doubt, a reflex one and not a direct one; that is to say, he feels himself measured by a standard of himself which his mother holds up, and not by a standard which he consciously holds before himself; but the psychological essence of the act remains unchanged. He feels that the desire is immoral, because its gratification will lead to a lowering of himself. He will *have* more immediate pleasure, but *he* will be less. The desire to obey he feels to be moral, for the opposite reason.

Extension of Desire in the Ethical Sphere

The process roughly sketched here constantly widens the range of feelings and desires which are felt to have moral bearings. At the beginning, in many, perhaps all cases, the child feels the ethical bearing only of such acts as are directly commanded or are forbidden; acts which are accompanied also by pleasures and pains as their rewards and penalties. Only such acts are seen to have any relation to his own personal worth. But as his experiences widen and his feelings come in contact with more objects his desires increase, and more and more of these desires are seen to have direct bearing upon the inner core of his own being, as distinct from the circumstances of his life. The widening extends also in another direction. Not only does he recognize that each desire has, if realized, some connection with himself, but he recognizes also that each will is a personality as much as himself. He sees that while he may *have* more or less than other persons, he can be a person or will no more and no less than they. The claims of their personality are equal to the claims of his. This gradually extends his desires to include the welfare of those in the same family with him. No end can be set to the process in either direction. There is no desire which does not have a possible bearing upon the realization of himself; there is no person who does not have a possible relation to him which may become the source of a desire for the realization of that personality. Of course, the desire may tend the other way; it may be towards such a gratification of himself as will thwart his own realization or that of some other person.

Conflict of Desires

The same processes that originate desires bring them into opposition with each other. The difference between the conflict of desires in the ethical and in the prudential sphere is, that since in the latter acts are judged by their results, desires range themselves along a scale, and the question is simply concerning which desire to gratify in order to get the most advantage; in the ethical sphere, since actions are judged by their motives, the conflict is between two desires, which represent not a possible more or less, but an actual opposition. The conflict is between desires for qualitatively opposed ends. In other words, the conflict is always between desire for an end which is felt to be good, and desire for an end which is felt to be wrong. The desire, as said before, is not wrong in itself, but its satisfaction is felt to be wrong, because it is incompatible with the realization of the good. In ethical matters the lesser good is felt to be the bad.

II. Ethical Choice

This conflict of desires is settled, as are all similar conflicts, by the act of choice or decision, which is that identification by self of itself with one of the desires which renders it the motive to action. The act of choice selects some desire, and says that that one shall be realized. The object of any desire is ideal, for it has no existence as yet; choice changes the mere longing for its reality into the assertion that it shall be made real. Choice is practical judgment. Judgment (page 186) asserts that some reality is possessed of some ideal quality, or that some ideal quality is real. Choice asserts that this ideal quality *shall be* real. Judgment as theoretical is about things as they are; judgment as practical is about things as the self will have them to be.

Grounds of Choice

Any desire becomes a motive because it is chosen. Why is it chosen? Why does the self reject one desire which is competing for its identification with self and select another? To answer this question we must distinguish between the *content* and the *form* of what is chosen. In prudential choice the form is identical in all acts; for it is the advantage to be gained by that act. The content is the specific advantage sought for—health, public reputation, place. And the ground of choice is, that content is chosen *which seems to the chooser* to correspond most closely with the form under which it is subsumed—advantage. In moral actions, on the other hand, there are two forms, not one, possible, and the choice is primarily not about the content to be included under the form, but about the form itself. The form is good or bad. The question which content shall be willed, whether truth, temperance, courage, patience, purity—which, in short, of the virtues, is a subordinate question, as is the one regarding any content of bad action or a vice. To answer the question regarding the grounds of choice, we must ask separately regarding the content and the form.

Choice of Content

Why is this or that special kind of good action chosen rather than another? Or, to put the question more correctly, why does one regard one course of action as the good, while to another the good content is something else? Such, of course, is the fact. A South Sea Islander's idea of what actually constitutes good is hardly the same as that of a civilized

man. The occupant of a crowded tenement-house in a large
city, surrounded from birth by almost every variety of evil,
can hardly have the same ideas of what constitutes the
content of good and of bad as one educated in a refined
family and subject from the first to the most elevated and
purifying influences. The ideal, the standard, of one varies
from that of another; that is to say, the content which is
conceived as coming under the form of good or bad varies.

Reason for This

In stating that this difference exists we have virtually shown
why it exists. The reason that one chooses one content as
good while to another the same content appears as unwor-
thy, or even positively bad, is the relative limitation and
extent of the circumstances of each, which cause the knowledge or conception of each to take the form that it does. The
grounds for the choice of a given content in moral action are
precisely what they are in prudential action. The choice in
each case is limited by the man's birth, early training,
surroundings, and resulting knowledge. The good to one
man may be to abstain from stealing a loaf of bread, to keep
himself free from the influences of intoxicating liquors; to
another man it will be to devote his life to the elevation of
humanity through great self-sacrifice. Each comes under the
form of good; but the content which is given this form is the
result of the *circumstances* of the person, using that word in
its widest sense.

Choice of Form

But there is another question yet to be answered: why does
the will choose good in preference to bad, or *vice versa?* We
have seen why it chooses the special good that it does, but
why should it choose good at all? What are the grounds of
this choice? It is evident from what has been said that the
grounds of this choice cannot be external to the will, but
must be in the will itself. The moral worth of the act is
constituted by its motive, and not by its result; and the
motive is constituted by the will itself, by the personality.
The answer to the question why one man chooses truth as a
good under certain circumstances while another chooses

kindness could be found in the antecedents and circumstances of the chooser if our knowledge were sufficiently
extended. Why he chooses a good at all rather than a wrong
finds its answer only in the will of the man himself. He will
have himself good. The reason that he will is, that he will.
Only the ideal of himself as good will satisfy him. If we ask
why this ideal alone is satisfactory we can get no other
answer than this: he wills to be satisfied in that, and in that
alone. It is willed because it is satisfactory; it is satisfactory
because it is willed as that the man would be.

Meaning of this Circle

In other words, we here reach an ultimate fact in the psychological constitution of man. *He has the power of determining
himself.* He has the power of setting up an ideal of what he
would have himself be, and this ideal in form depends only
upon himself. If one man chooses moral evil under certain
circumstances, and another man chooses moral good, the
sole answer to the question why each acts as he does is that
one man *will* have *himself* good, the other bad. Each wills a
certain ideal of himself, and according to the ideal willed so
is he. In moral matters a man *is* what he would have himself
be. The will to be good is the being good. In moral action, in
other words, the action is measured by the motive, and the
motive is decided by what a man's ideal of himself is; by his
conception of what would realize his nature. This ideal of
self-realization depends *for its form* upon the self and upon
that alone. For its content, for its specific and concrete filling
up it depends, as previously shown, upon his education,
surroundings, etc. But the man's own will, the core of his
personality, decides what he would have himself be, and this
decision decides what he is. Man determines himself by
setting up either good or evil as a motive to himself, and he
sets up either as he *will* have himself be.

Summary

Just that specific act which a man chooses as good or bad
depends upon circumstances external to himself. For it, in
other words, he is not responsible. He is responsible only for
his motive. If his motive is good he is not responsible for the

special direction which the act takes unless this is the result of some previous choice of his own. In moral matters, as in prudential, a man can do only the best that he knows. But a man in willing the good at all does not merely will the best that he knows, or that his circumstances permit of, but he wills the best absolutely, the best that the universe permits of. The concrete content of the good action, the virtues, depend upon social development; the good depends upon the will only. The good is the will to be good.

III.   The Result of Moral Action

The result of moral control is the formation of character. Each act as it is performed has, if it is a moral act, its effect upon personality. It organizes it in a certain direction. It gives it a specific set or bent. Moral action results from the ideal which a man forms of himself, and occurs in order that he may realize himself. This realization of the moral self constitutes character. A man begins with that whole complex of feelings and desires which are given him by nature and his social surroundings, and with the capacity of choosing from these, and constituting some one, that is, some anticipated state or activity of himself, an end of action. Each action, as it takes place, gives his will a definite content. It changes the capacity to choose into something actually chosen. It furnishes the will with certain specific concrete organs. This furnishing is what we call character.

Nature of Character

Character is the will changed from a capacity into an actuality. The will is the power to realize self morally. Character is the self realized. It is still will, but it is will made organic and real. From this fundamental nature of character flow certain subordinate results, which may be summed up as follows: first, the formation of generic volition as opposed to particular; second, the regulation of desires; third, more accurate and intuitive choice; fourth, more effective execution.

1. GENERIC VOLITION

By this term is meant a volition that covers a large number of subordinate specific volitions. The result, for example, of a general tendency to perform acts from virtuous motives, that is, from the will to realize the good, is the generic volition of goodness. When a strong temptation is presented to a child, it is conceivable that he has to stop, as it were, and execute a specific volition "to be good" in this especial case. If, under similar circumstances, he acts in a similar way habitually, it is evident that his character finally gives rise to a general intention or purpose "to be good," and each special right act is simply the manifestation of this governing purpose of the life. Another name given to this same fact is that of "immanent preference." This phrase brings out the additional fact that the generic volition continues in action even when there is no overt occasion for its manifestation. A man's will to be temperate does not cease when he happens not to be eating or drinking, or satisfying any appetite. It is still immanent in his being, and serves unconsciously to direct the course of his actions.

2. REGULATION OF DESIRES

Original impulses are natural in the sense that they spring from the physical and psychical constitution of man. As such, they are no more under his control directly than are any forces of nature. But desire originates only when these impulses are satisfied, and there arises the intellectual representation of that act which satisfies them. Up to a certain point the formation of desires is a spontaneous, natural process. But we have already learned that it is the will, the man himself, who decides which of these desires shall be realized. The satisfaction of any desire strengthens it, for it adds to it a new representation of the act, and of the pleasure which necessarily accompanies the act. Refusal to make the desire a motive or end of action not only represses this particular desire, but weakens all desires similar to it. A desire never satisfied would finally die of inanition. It is evident, therefore, that every choice strengthens some desires and weakens others. It controls them. Still more is this the case when the choice has become a generic or immanent one. This encourages the growth of all desires in harmony with itself, and serves as a check upon all others by the very fact of its existence. The formation of a settled character finally decides what a man's desires shall be. It strangles all opposite ones at the moment of their birth.

3. ACCURATE AND INTUITIVE CHOICE

It is evident that this control of desires exercises great influence upon every *future specific choice*. Where there is no desire there can be no motive. Where the desires are all, or almost all, along one line they reinforce each other, and the specific act of choice follows almost as a matter of course, after next to no conflict. With the formation of an organized character, choice becomes speedy. It follows from the same line of reasoning that it becomes more and more intuitive or spontaneous. Where no character has been formed moral action requires considerable hesitation and a process of deliberation. Without stopping to discuss whether or not our ideas of duty are intuitive, it is evident that it is not always intuitive just *what* is our duty in a specific case where there is a conflict of claims upon us. Just in the degree, however, in which acts, whether vicious or virtuous, have reacted upon the will, and have been organized into its structure, does the will act spontaneously. It is conceivable that a child, in the process of forming a character, may often hesitate long. It is not conceivable that a very good or a very wicked man should; that is, about the nature of the act; there may be hesitation concerning results. The same process renders choice more definite and less vague. At the beginning one does not know just what he is choosing. As character is formed the nature of the motive is better and better estimated.

4. EFFECTIVE EXECUTION

The moral act, as we have seen, does not depend upon its character for its execution. The will to execute is *morally* its execution. This presupposes, of course, that there be a real act of choice, and that there are no "mental reservations." Nothing is commoner than for a man to make up his mind in a certain way upon its surface, while underneath the will has set itself in an opposite direction. It requires a well-formed character for truth not to deceive one's self in this way. But objectively considered, the execution of the act is highly important. For *other men* there is no way of judging a motive except by its result. If the motive is thwarted in its execution the actor does not feel remorse, but he cannot help feeling regret. From the standpoint of the world the important thing is to get the right thing done, and no man can consider himself an effective power whose ability to execute his intentions does not bear a commensurate ratio to his intentions. The sole condition of effective execution is an organized character, and for two reasons.

(1) Character constitutes a reservoir of energy which may be drawn upon to bring about the end willed. In character there are conserved the results of all previous acts. Each has lent some of its own strength to the will. Character is multiplied volition; it is will which has ceased to be isolated, and which has concentrated itself. It is will which is no longer sporadic, but has turned its force in one direction. The man with character, whether good or bad, is not easily daunted. He does not recognize obstacles. His eye is upon the end, and upon that alone. Weakness means instability, and instability is lack of character.

(2) Another reason for the practical efficiency of character is suggested by Aristotle when he says that the man who rejoices in abstinence is temperate; the man who abstains but is grieved thereby is still intemperate. We have already seen that the force which carries out any choice is the impulsive action of *feeling*. Intellect proposes the end; this is chosen, and the propulsive tendency of feeling realizes it. Now only the man with fixed character takes a great and, what is more, an enduring pleasure in the anticipation of a certain end. Only the man of truthful character can be said to rejoice in the truth for its own sake. Only he, therefore, is likely to have that supply of propulsive feeling which will see to it that the truth is actually told, no matter what the difficulty. Love is the only motive which can be relied upon for efficient and sure action; and only the man of character has fixed love of a thing for its own sake; and

that which is sought for anything but itself is not a moral end.

NOTES TO CHAPTER 21

Murray, *Handbook of Psychology*, pp. 235 - 40; Sully, *Psychology*, pp. 649 - 80; Radestock, *Habit in Education*, pp. 81 - 86; Volkmann, *Lehrbuch der Psychologie*, vol. ii, pp. 489 - 513; Herbart, *Lehrbuch zur Psychologie*, pt. 3, ch. v; Strümpell, *Grundriss der Psychologie*, pp. 283 - 93; Fortlage, *Acht psychologische Vorträge* (essay on "Character"); Marion, *La Solidarité Morale*, pp. 108 - 45; Hagemann, *Was ist Charakter?* De Guimps, *L'Éducation*, pp. 431 - 43; Perez, *L'Éducation dès le Berceau*, pp. 265 - 300; Joly, *Notions de Pédagogie*, pp. 164 - 96; Beneke, *Erziehungslehre*, pp. 310 - 43; Dittes, *Naturlehre der moralischen Erziehung;* Wendt, *Die Willensbildung*; Habel, *Entwickelungsgeschichte des Willens*; Grube, *Von der sittlichen Bildung der Jugend*; Wiese, *Die Bildung des Willens*; Hall, *Princeton Review* for 1882, articles on "Moral Training of Children," and "Education of Will."

22

Will as the Source of Ideals and of Their Realization

Will is Self

We have now finished our study of the various factors of the self. It is now necessary very briefly to notice their relation to each other. The unity of the self is the will. The will is the man, psychologically speaking. Knowledge we have seen to be in its essence a process of the realization of the universal self-consciousness; feeling to be the accompaniment of self-realization; and its specific quality to be dependent upon the definite form of self-realization accomplished. Will we have just seen to be the self realizing itself. This is involved throughout in physical and prudential control, and it is explicitly developed when we study moral control. Here the will is seen to be self-determination. The will, in short, constitutes the meaning of knowledge and of feeling; and moral will constitutes the meaning of will.

Will, Knowledge, Feeling

Knowledge is the objectification of feeling or sensation by the will, in the process of apperception. Sensation or feeling is itself meaningless, except in its relation to sensuous impulse, which constitutes the raw material of the will. Sensuous impulse is the will in the process of becoming. It is the will before it has obtained the control of itself; before it is self-determined. The construction of knowledge out of sensuous impulse, or out of sensation, by the apperceptive process is simply one aspect of the will obtaining control of itself. It is the will determining itself to an objective and universal form. The varieties of qualitative feeling, on the other hand, are the accompaniments of the self-determination of the will. They accompany either the outgoing action of the will or its action as it takes some objective content and dissolves it in the medium of the individual. Knowledge, in short, is the objective universal aspect of will; feeling is its subjective individual aspect. Will, as the process which includes and unites both, is the self.

Twofold Nature of Will

There is involved in the will and hence in the self a twofold mode of action. The will is the source, the origin of ideals, and also of their realization. The will is always holding itself before itself. The self has always presented to its actual condition the vague ideal of a completely universal self, by which it measures itself and feels its own limitations. The self, in its true nature, is universal and objective. The actual self is largely particular and unrealized. The self always confronts itself, therefore, with the conception of a universal or completed will towards which it must strive. What this will or self as complete is, it does not know. It only feels that there is such a goal, and that it is only as it attains it that it experiences any abiding satisfaction; that is to say, happiness. This will or self which the will sets before itself is its ideal.

Function of the Ideal Will

This ideal will serves as a spur to the actual self to realize itself. It leads to discontent with every accomplished result, and urges on to new and more complete action. It serves also to measure all accomplishments; it serves as the criterion by which to judge them. The feeling of harmony, which is the mind's ultimate test of intellectual truth, æsthetic beauty, and moral rightness, is simply the feeling of the accord between the accomplished act and the completed activity which is the ideal.

The Realizing Activity of Will

But the will does more than set up this ideal of absolute truth, absolute beauty, and absolute goodness. The will is the activity which realizes this ideal and makes it a fact of recognized validity in life. It gives this form, its content; it specifies it and makes it definite. Intellectual life consists not only of the goal of truth towards which intelligence is striving, but also of truth attained. Æsthetic life finds its motive power in the working within it of an ideal of beauty; but this ideal has also worked itself out in some degree, and created specific beautiful forms. The moral life has its motive in a perfect will, a will absolutely at harmony with itself, and this ideal has manifested itself in social institutions and in personal character. It is not one self or will which is the ideal, and another will which is the source of its attainment; but the ideal will has been a constant motive power, which has energized in bringing forth the concrete attainments in knowledge, beauty, and rightness.

The Moral Ideal in Particular

The ethical will brings clearly to light what is implicitly contained in the intellectual and emotional processes. We have in these latter the feeling of perfect or completely harmonized truth and beauty as constituting the reality of the psychical life; but we do not have the conscious *recognition* that this ideal is the true self to which the actual must be made to conform. In moral will there is this recognition: the good self or will is felt to be absolutely obligatory, and its realization not a matter of advantage or even of mere growth or development. It is a matter of *rightness*, for the coming short of which there is the feeling of guilt.

We also see the closer identification in the ethical realm of the will as ideal and the will as realizing power in the fact that here motive and act are one. The will to know the truth or to create beauty does not constitute the willed result. There is a gap between the motive and the attained end. The realization of the motive depends upon conditions more or less external. But in ethical matters it is not so. As we have repeatedly noticed, the choice of the motive constitutes, for ethical purposes, the attainment of the end. The will to be good is the good. In moral will, therefore, the ideal will is recognized as the ground of the actual self. The obligation of the perfect upon the actual imperfect self is the conscious manifestation of this fact. Furthermore, the unity of the ideal will as the goal, with the will which reaches this goal, the unity *involved* in all volition, is explicitly developed. Moral will makes definite and clear the meaning of intellectual and æsthetic action. Were it not for what we find manifested in moral will, the action of the intellect in searching for truth, and the creative activity of the æsthetic imagination, would remain ultimately incomprehensible.

Remaining Dualism in the Moral Will

The moral will, however, does not entirely overcome that dualism between the actual and the ideal selves which is involved in the other two spheres of action. The moral will is incomplete or partial in its action. The acting from a good motive in a given case constitutes being good in that case. This choice sufficiently repeated results in the formation of a good character. Yet this character never gets so formed that it can dispense with the repeated act of choice whenever there is conflict of good and bad desires. The choice may grow more rapid, accurate, and intuitive, but the act of choice remains necessary. To say that it remains necessary is to say that the will as ideal and the will as actual have not been truly unified. Were they once truly unified there would be no need of the repetition of the act of their identification. Each act would flow naturally and spontaneously from their complete unity.

Religious Will

Moral action, in short, is particular in its nature. It may cover a multitude of cases, but it is not universal in itself. It is religious will which performs the act of identification once for all. The will, as religious, declares that the perfect ideal will is the only reality; it declares that it is the only reality in the universe, and that it is the only reality in the individual life. It makes it a motive, once for all, of action; and not of this or that action, but of life, and of life generically and absolutely. Religious will declares that the perfect will is the only source of activity and of reality, and that it is in itself perfect activity and perfect reality. It is the completely self-determined. In it realization and the ideal are one. There is no longer any dualism between the will as it is and the will as it ought to be.

Religious Action

As religious will makes this declaration, so religious action is the continuous appropriation of the truth asserted by it. The religious will declares that God, as the perfect Personality or Will, is the only Reality, and the Source of all activity. It is therefore the source of all activity of the individual personality. The Perfect Will is the motive, source, and the realization of the life of the individual. He has renounced his own particular life as an unreality; he has asserted that the sole reality is the Universal Will, and in that reality all his actions take place. In other words, the source of his concrete actions is no longer the will that the ideal and actual *ought to be* one, and that in this specific case they shall be, but it is the will that they *are* one; and this specific case, as well as all others, is the manifestation of this unity. In short, while moral action is action directed to render the actual *conformable* to the ideal, religious action is action directed to the embodiment of the ideal in the actual.

Faith

This will that the real and the perfect Will or Personality are one constitutes the essence of the religious act known as *faith*. It transcends knowledge, for knowledge, while always the realization of a complete self, is never its *complete* realization. There is always a chasm between actual knowledge and absolute truth. There can be no knowledge beyond the ground that knowledge actually covers. There cannot be knowledge that the true reality for the individual self is the universal self, for knowledge has not in the individual compassed the universal. But this will or faith, while transcending knowledge, is yet implied in all knowledge. The motive to knowledge and the energy of its realization is the *belief* that there is truth, and that every act of intellect, legitimately performed, leads to truth. In knowledge there is no ultimate justification for this belief. It finds its validity and the revelation of its meaning only in the will that the real and the ideal of truth are one in a perfect personality—God. This act of faith also precedes and transcends *feeling*. There is, in the feeling of *harmony*, the feeling of unity, but this feeling accompanies will. It is the internal side of the universal or objective unity realized through the will. Without this act of will, all feeling is that of discord, of incongruence.

Summary

We find the unity of the psychical processes already studied, and therefore their ultimate explanation, in the fact that man is a self; that the essence of self is the self-determining activity of will; that this will is an objectifying activity, and that, in objectifying itself, it renders itself universal. The result of this activity is *knowledge*. The objectified will is science; the objectifying activity is the intellect. This will or activity also renders an account *to itself* of its own doings. It is internal to itself. The objective universal result is at one and the same time existent in the medium of the individual's consciousness. This subjective aspect of the activity is *feeling*. As expressing the furtherance or hinderance of the activity, it is pleasure or pain; as an accompaniment of an actual realization, it possesses content and is qualitative.

The activity which is both subjective and objective, which unites the individual and the universe, which finds its motive in feeling and its result in knowledge, and at the same time changes this known object into the felt subject is the will, the unity of psychical life. But the activity of the will is not exhausted in these realizations of itself through knowledge and feeling; the will *is* universal in its nature, and therefore must always hold before itself its own universal nature. This universal nature of will with which the will confronts itself constitutes what we call ideals. According as it takes the nature of a universal harmony of truths it is the intellectual ideal; as the universal harmony of feelings, it is the æsthetic; as the universal harmony of volitions, it is the moral.

Moral will is the conscious realization by man that the real and the ideal *ought* to be one, and the resulting attempt to make them one in specific acts and in the formation of character. Religious will is conscious realization that they are one because man is a self-determining power. It is the realization that a perfect will is reality. It is the realization of freedom through the realization of the union of finite and the infinite Personality. It is only when we recognize this latter activity of will that we are able really to comprehend the previous forms of activity. Without it there remains a contradiction in them. Without it knowledge is only of that which has been individually objectified; the universal which is its goal remains a blind postulate, impossible to account for. Without it feeling can be only dissatisfaction, for it must reveal discord between what is and what is felt after, its goal of happiness. With it all psychical life may be indifferently described as the progressive realization by the will of its ideal self, or as the progressive idealization of the actual through the ultimate, absolute reality. In either case is it progressive appropriation of that self in which real and ideal are one; in which truth, happiness, and rightness are united in one Personality.

Appendix A

Since every psychological treatise is influenced largely by its philosophical basis, a brief characterization of the standpoint of the principal writers referred to in the body of the work will not be amiss. Brown, Hamilton, and McCosh belong, of course, to the Scotch school. With the same school, but influenced more by German philosophy, Porter may be classed. Murray has connections with the same school, but his point of view is rather that of the Post-Kantian movement. Mill is of the traditional English (or associational) line. Of the same school are Lewes, but affected by the physiological development of the sciences, and Spencer, influenced in the same way and also by the theory of evolution. Lewes also shows the influence of the German "Völkerpsychologie" school. Sully has his standpoint fixed by the same fundamental metaphysical principles, but is influenced largely by the later experimental treatment of the science. Bain has given the most thorough and detailed exposition of the special questions of psychology to be found in English from the standpoint of the English school modified by physiological considerations. In Germany Herbart's influence has been, upon the whole, dominant in psychology, and Volkmann, Waitz, Strümpell, Schilling, Glogau, Drobisch all build upon his foundation in a more or less independent way. Steinthal and Lazarus cannot be classed as Herbartians, but they reflect more of Herbart, perhaps, than of any other one man. The same may be said of Morell in English, while Ward shows decided traces of his influence. Lotze is difficult to class, having, upon the whole, an independent basis; he is indebted to Kant and to Herbart in about equal measures, while he is everywhere influenced by the physiological aspects of the science. Much the same may be said of Ulrici, although the latter was not an independent investigator in experimental psychology. Other Herbartians not referred to in the preceding pages are Lindner, Stoy, and Ballauf. Erdmann, Rosenkranz, and Michelet are all Hegelians, as is George, upon a more independent basis. Rosenkranz has written upon pedagogy from this standpoint, and Thaulow's *Hegels Ansichten über Erziehung und Unterricht* belongs here. Ostermann's *Pädagogische Psychologie* follows Lotze. Beneke, Dittes, Schrader, and Kern reflect Herbart in their educational treatises. Stoy's *Encyclopädie der Pädagogik* contains a bibliography, as do also the works of Fröhlich and Joly, referred to in the body of this work. Every educationalist is acquainted, of course, with Diesterweg's *Wegweiser*, with its valuable references.

Appendix B

We add the following references upon psycho-physics: Fechner, *Elemente der Psychophysik*, *In Sachen der Psychophysik*, and *Revision der Hauptpunkte der Psychophysik*; Müller, *Zur Grundlegung der Psychophysik*; F. A. Müller, *Das Axiom der Psychophysik*; Delbœuf, *Éléments de Psychophysique*; Ribot, ch. vii of *Contemporary German Psychology*; *Philosophische Studien*, vol. i, p. 556; vol. ii, p. 1, and p. 655; Ward, in *Mind*, vol. i, p. 452; Langer, *Die Grundlagen der Psychophysik*.

Upon comparative psychology the following works may be consulted: Romanes, *Animal Intelligence*, and *Mental Evolution in Animals*; Lubbock, *Ants, Bees, and Wasps*; Lindsay, *Mind in Lower Animals*; Houzeau, *Étude sur les Facultés Mentales des Animaux*; Blanchard, *Les Metamorphoses, les Mœurs et les Instincts des Insectes*; Bourbon del Monte, *L'Homme et les Animaux*; Fournié, *La Bête et l'Homme*; Joly, *Psychologie Comparée: L'Homme et l'Animal*; Espinas, *Des Sociétés Animales*; Carus, *Vergleichende Psychologie*; Bastian, *Beiträge zur vergleichenden Psychologie*; and Perty, Flügel, and Gleisberg upon *Das Seelenleben der Thiere*.

Upon genetic psychology see: Preyer, *Die Seele des Kindes*; Perez, *First Three Years of Childhood*, and *La Psychologie de l'Enfant*; Kussmaul, *Untersuchungen über das Seelenleben des neugeborenen Menschen*; Egger, *Sur le Développement de l'Intelligence et du Langage*; Löbisch, *Die Seele des Kindes*; Schultze, *Die Sprache des Kindes*; Taine, in *Revue Philosophique*, for Jan., 1876; Darwin, in *Mind*, vol. ii, p. 285 ff.; Pollock, in *Mind*, for July, 1878; Genzmer, *Die Sinneswahrnehmungen des neugeborenen Menschen*.

Checklist of references

To make completely accurate all Dewey's references in the notes sections following the chapters of *Psychology* and in the appendices, it was necessary to compile a checklist of the books and articles mentioned. That list is included in the present edition so that modern readers can make fullest use of the references.

Most of the works referred to in *Psychology* are now difficult or impossible to locate. When the editors did not have access to the book itself, available sources were searched exhaustively to verify all information. Sources used to ascertain bibliographic data are included at the end of the checklist. In addition to the sources listed, none of the numerous others consulted gave any clues as to the details of the two items which remain incomplete: Habel, *Entwickelungsgeschichte des Willens*; and Schnell, *Die Anschauung*. General references to several names have not been expanded for similar lack of information: Ballauf, Kern, Lindner, Max Müller, and Schrader.

For this edition, we have listed the edition of each work which seems most likely to have been the one used by Dewey, by reason of the work's publication date, evidence from correspondence or other sources, the particular translator, or general accessibility at the time *Psychology* was written. It should be mentioned that in the notes to Chapter 1 (17.36 - 42) and Chapter 3 (74.13 - 19) sections were added for the 1891 revision which include references published after 1887.

Corrections and expansions in titles, authors' names, etc., have been made silently and conform to those in the original works. Corresponding corrections which became necessary in the notes and appendices appear in the List of Emendations in Notes and Appendices.

Abbott, Thomas Kingsmill. *Sight and Touch*. London: Longman, Green, Longman, Roberts and Green, 1864.

Abercrombie, John. *The Philosophy of the Moral Feelings*. New York: Harper and Brothers, 1836.

Adamson, Robert. Review of *A Handbook of Psychology* by J. Clark Murray, *Mind*, XI (Apr. 1886), 252 - 56.

———. Review of *Outlines of Psychology* by James Sully, *Mind*, IX (July 1884), 427 - 39.

Allen, Charles Grant Blairfindie. *The Colour-Sense: Its Origin and Development*. London: Trübner and Co., 1879.

———. *Physiological Æsthetics*. London: H. S. King and Co., 1877.

Autenrieth, Hermann Friedrich. *Rede über das Gedächtniss*. Tübingen: Fues, 1847.

Bain, Alexander. *The Emotions and the Will*. 3d ed. London: Longmans, Green, Reader and Dyer, 1875.

———. *The Senses and the Intellect*. London: J. W. Parker and Son, 1855.

Bascom, John. *Comparative Psychology, or the Growth and Grades of Intelligence*. New York: G. P. Putnam's Sons, 1878.

———. *The Principles of Psychology*. New York: G. P. Putnam's Sons, 1869.

Bastian, Adolf. *Beiträge zur vergleichenden Psychologie: Die Seele und ihre Erscheinungweisen in der Ethnographie*. Berlin: F. Dümmler, 1868.

Bastian, Henry Charlton. *Brain as Organ of Mind*. London: Kegan Paul and Co., 1880.

Beneke, Friedrich Eduard. *Erziehungs- und Unterrichtslehre*. Vol. I: *Erziehungslehre*; Vol. II: *Unterrichtslehre*. Berlin: E. S. Mittlcr, 1835 - 36.

———. *Psychologische Skizzen*. Vol. I: *Skizzen zur Naturlehre der Gefühle, in Verbindung mit einer erläuterten Abhandlung über die Bewusstwerdung der Seelenthätigkeiten*; Vol. II: *Über das Vermögen der menschlichen Seele und deren allmähliche Ausbildung*. Göttingen: Vandenhöck und Ruprecht, 1825 - 27.

Bergmann, Julius. *Grundlinien einer Theorie des Bewusstseins*. Berlin: Loewenstein, 1870.

Berkeley, George. "An Essay Towards a New Theory of Vision," *The Works of George Berkeley*, ed. Alexander Campbell Fraser (Oxford: Clarendon Press, 1871), I, 93 - 205.

Bernstein, Julius. *The Five Senses of Man*. New York: D. Appleton and Co.; London: H. S. King and Co., 1876.

Bertrand, Alexis. *L'Aperception du corps humain par la conscience*. Paris: Germer-Baillière, 1881.

Binz, Carl. *Über den Traum* (Nach einem 1876 gehaltenen öffentlichen Vortrag). Bonn: A. Marcus, 1878.

Blanchard, Émile. *Metamorphoses, mœurs et instincts des insectes*. Paris: Germer-Baillière, 1868.

Bleuler, Eugen, and Lehmann, Karl. *Zwangsmässige Lichtempfindungen durch Schall und verwandte Erscheinungen auf dem Gebiete der andern Sinnesempfindungen*. Leipzig: Fues, 1881.

Bouillier, Francisque. *Du plaisir et de la douleur*. Paris: Germer-Baillière, 1865.

Bourbon del Monte, J. B. François. *L'Homme et les animaux: Essai de psychologie positive*. Paris: Germer-Baillière, 1877.

Bowne, Borden Parker. *Introduction to Psychological Theory*. New York: Harper and Brothers, 1887.

Bradley, Francis Herbert. *Ethical Studies*. London: H. S. King and Co., 1876.

———. *The Principles of Logic*. London: K. Paul, Trench and Co., 1883.

———. "Is There Any Special Activity of Attention?" *Mind*, XI (July 1886), 305 - 23.

———. "Sympathy and Interest," *Mind*, VIII (Oct. 1883), 573 - 75.

Braubach, Wilhelm. *Zur Fundamentallehre der Pädagogik als strenger Wissenschaft*. Also published under the title: *Psychologie des Gefühls als Bewegung des geistigen Lebens*. Wetzlar: Rathgeber, 1847.

Brown, Thomas. *Lectures on the Philosophy of the Human Mind*. 4 vols. Edinburgh: A. and C. Black, 1824.

Butler, Samuel. *Unconscious Memory*. London: D. Bogue, 1880.

Cabot, J. E. "The Spatial Quale," *Journal of Speculative Philosophy*, XIII (Apr. 1879), 199 - 204.

Caird, Edward. "Metaphysic," *Encyclopædia Britannica* (9th ed.), XVI, 79 - 102.

Caird, John. *An Introduction to the Philosophy of Religion*. Glasgow: Maclehose, 1880.

Calderwood, Henry. *The Relations of Mind and Brain*. London: Macmillan and Co., 1879.

Carpenter, William Benjamin. *Principles of Mental Physiology*. London: H. S. King and Co., 1874.

———. "Physiology of Will," *Contemporary Review*, XVII (May 1871), 192 - 217.

Carriere, Moriz. *Æsthetik: Die Idee des Schönen und ihre Verwirklichung im Leben und in der Kunst*. 2 vols. Leipzig: Brockhaus, 1885.

———. *Die Poesie: Ihr Wesen und ihre Formen mit Grundzügen der vergleichenden Literaturgeschichte*. Leipzig: Brockhaus, 1884.

Carus, Friedrich August. *Geschichte der Psychologie*. Vol. III of *Nachgelassene Werke*. Leipzig: J. A. Barth und P. G. Kummer, 1808.

Carus, Karl Gustav. *Vergleichende Psychologie, oder Geschichte der Seele in der Reihenfolge der Thierwelt*. Vienna: Braumüller, 1866.

Cattell, James McKeen. "Über die Zeit der Erkennung und Benennung von Schriftzeichen, Bildern und Farben," *Philosophische Studien*, II (1885), 635 - 50.

Clarke, Edward H. *Visions: A Study of False Sight*. Boston: Houghton, Osgood and Co., 1878.

Classen, August. *Physiologie des Gesichtssinnes zum ersten Mal begründet auf Kants Theorie der Erfahrung*. Braunschweig: Vieweg und Sohn, 1876.

———. *Über das Schlussverfahren des Sehactes*. Rostock: Leopold, 1863.

Cobbe, Francis Power. *Darwinism in Morals, and other Essays*. London: Williams and Norgate, 1872.

Cohen, Hermann. *Die dichterische Phantasie und der Mechanismus des Bewusstseins*. Berlin: F. Dümmler, 1869.

Cornelius, Carl Sebastian. *Die Theorie des Sehens und räumlichen Vorstellens*. Halle: Schmidt, 1861.

Czermak, Johannes N. *Über das Ohr und das Hören*. Berlin: C. Habel, 1873.

Darwin, Charles Robert. *The Expression of the Emotions in Man and Animals*. London: J. Murray, 1872.

———. *On the Origin of the Species by Means of Natural Selection*. London: J. Murray, 1859.

———. "A Biographical Sketch of an Infant," *Mind*, II (July 1877), 285 - 94.

Day, Henry Noble. *Elements of Psychology*. New York: G. P. Putnam's Sons, 1876.

Delbœuf, Joseph-Rémi-Léopold. *Éléments de psychophysique générale et spéciale*. Paris: Germer-Baillière, 1883.

———. *Le sommeil et les rêves*. Paris: F. Alcan, 1885.

"Le sommeil et les rêves," *Revue philosophique*, VIII (Oct. 1879), 329 - 56; *ibid.*, VIII (Nov. 1879), 494 - 520; *ibid.*, IX (Feb. 1880), 129 - 69; *ibid.*, IX (Apr. 1880), 413 - 37; *ibid.*, IX (June 1880), 632 - 47.

———. *Théorie générale de la sensibilité*. Brussels: F. Hayez, 1876.

Delhez, Constantin. *Gymnastik der Sinne für die erste Erziehung des Kindes*. Vienna: Lechner, 1876.

Delon, Charles, and Delon, Fanny. *Méthode intuitive: Excercices et travaux pour les enfants selon la méthode et les procédés de Pestalozzi et de Froebel*. Paris: Hachette, 1873.

Dewey, John. "The New Psychology," *Andover Review*, II (Sept. 1884), 278 - 89.

———. "The Psychological Standpoint," *Mind*, XI (Jan. 1886), 1 - 19.

———. "Psychology and Philosophic Method," *Mind*, XI (Apr. 1886), 153 - 73.

Diesterweg, Friedrich A. W. *Wegweiser zur Bildung für deutsche Lehrer*. 3 vols. Essen: G. D. Bädeker, 1850, 1851, 1877.

Dimetresco, Constantin D. *Der Schönheitsbegriff: Eine ästhetisch-psychologische Studie.* Leipzig: Matthes, 1877.

Dittes, Friedrich. *Naturlehre des Moralischen und Kunstlehre der moralischen Erziehung.* Leipzig: Mayer, 1856.

Donaldson, Henry Herbert. "On the Temperature-Sense," *Mind,* X (July 1885), 399 - 416.

————, and Hall, G. Stanley. "Motor Sensations on the Skin," *Mind,* X (Oct. 1885), 557 - 72.

Dörpfeld, Friedrich Wilhelm. *Beiträge zur pädagogischen Psychologie.* Gütersloh: Bertelsmann, 1886.

Dreher, Eugen. *Die Kunst in ihrer Beziehung zur Psychologie und zur Naturwissenschaft.* Berlin: Hempel, 1878.

Drobisch, Moritz Wilhelm. *Empirische Psychologie nach naturwissenschaftlicher Methode.* Hamburg: Voss, 1842.

————. *Erste Grundlehren der mathematischen Psychologie.* Leipzig: Voss, 1850.

Duboc, Julius. *Die Psychologie der Liebe.* Hannover, Leipzig: Rümpler, 1874.

Dumont, Léon A. *Théorie scientifique de la sensibilité: Le plaisir et la peine.* 2d ed. Paris: Germer-Baillière, 1875.

Ebbinghaus, Hermann. *Über das Gedächtniss: Untersuchungen zur experimentellen Psychologie.* Leipzig: Duncker und Humblot, 1885.

Egger, A. Émile. *Observations et réflexions sur le développement de l'intelligence et du langage chez les enfants.* Paris: Picard, 1879.

Erdmann, Johann Eduard. *Psychologische Briefe.* Leipzig: G. Geibel, 1856.

Espinas, Alfred. *Des sociétés animales: Études de psychologie comparée.* 2d ed. Paris: Germer-Baillière, 1878.

Estel, Volkmar. "Neue Versuche über den Zeitsinn," *Philosophische Studien,* II (1885), 37 - 65.

Eye, August von. *Das Reich des Schönen.* Berlin: E. Wasmuth, 1878.

Fechner, Gustav Theodor. *Elemente der Psychophysik.* 2 vols. Leipzig: Breitkopf und Härtel, 1860.

————. *In Sachen der Psychophysik.* Leipzig: Breitkopf und Härtel, 1877.

————. *Revision der Hauptpunkte der Psychophysik.* Leipzig: Breitkopf und Härtel, 1882.

————. *Vorschule der Æsthetik.* 2 pts. in 1 vol. Leipzig: Breitkopf und Härtel, 1876.

Ferri, Luigi. *La psychologie de l'association depuis Hobbes jusqu'à nos jours (histoire et critique).* Paris: Germer-Baillière, 1883.

Ferrier, David. *The Functions of the Brain.* London: Smith, Elder and Co., 1876; New York: G. P. Putnam's Sons, 1886.

Flügel, Otto. *Das Seelenleben der Thiere.* 2d ed. Langensalza: Beyer und Söhne, 1886.

Fortlage, Carl. *Acht psychologische Vorträge.* Jena: Maufe, 1869.

Foster, Sir Michael. *A Text-book of Physiology.* Philadelphia: H. C. Lea's Son and Co., 1881.

Fournié, Edouard. *Essai de psychologie: La bête et l'homme.* Paris: Didier, 1877.

Frensberg, [———]. "Schlaf und Traum" (Vortrag gehalten im April 1883), *Sammlung gemeinverständlicher wissenschaftlicher Vorträge,* eds. R. Virchow und Fr. von Holtzendorff. Hamburg: J. F. Richter, 1885.

Friedrich, Max. "Zur Methodik der Apperceptionsversuche," *Philosophische Studien,* II (1885), 66 - 72.

Fröhlich, Gustav. *Die wissenschaftliche Pädagogik.* Vienna: Pichlers Witwe und Sohn, 1883.

Frohschammer, Jacob. *Über die Principien der Aristotelischen Philosophie und die Bedeutung der Phantasie in derselben.* Munich: A. Ackermann, 1881.

Galton, Francis. *Inquiries into Human Faculty and its Development.* London: Macmillan and Co., 1883.

———. "Statistics of Mental Imagery," *Mind,* V (July 1880), 301 - 18.

Geiger, Lazarus. *Ursprung und Entwickelung der menschlichen Sprache und Vernunft.* 2 vols. Stuttgart: J. G. Cotta, 1868, 1872.

Genzmer, Alfred. *Untersuchungen über die Sinneswahrnehmungen des neugeborenen Menschen.* Halle: M. Niemeyer, 1882.

George, Leopold. *Die fünf Sinne.* Berlin: G. Reimer, 1846.

———. *Lehrbuch der Psychologie.* Berlin: G. Reimer, 1854.

Gerber, Gustav. *Die Sprache und das Erkennen.* Berlin: Gaertner, 1884.

Gladstone, W. E. "The Colour-Sense," *Nineteenth Century,* II (Oct. 1877), 366 - 88.

Gleisberg, Johannes Paul. *Instinkt und freier Wille, oder das Seelenleben der Thiere und des Menschen.* Leipzig: D. Wigand, 1861.

Glogau, Gustav August. *Grundriss der Psychologie.* Breslau: Koebner, 1884.

Goethe, Johann Wolfgang von. *Theory of Colors.* Trans. with notes by Charles Lock Eastlake. London: J. Murray, 1840.

Graber, Veit. *Grundlinien zur Erforschung des Helligkeits- und Farbensinnes der Thiere.* Prague: Tempsky; Leipzig: Freytag, 1884.

Green, Thomas Hill. *Prolegomena to Ethics*. Ed. A. C. Bradley. Oxford: Clarendon Press, 1883.

Grote, Nicolas (Grot, Nicolaï). *Psychologie de la sensibilité dans son histoire et ses fondements* (*Psychologiia Tchouvstvovaniy v yeia Itorii i Glavnyh Osnovah*. St. Petersburg: Imperial Academy of Science, 1879 - 80). [Reviewed in *Revue philosophique*, X (Oct. 1880), 441 - 43.]

Grube, August Wilhelm. *Von der sittlichen Bildung der Jugend im ersten Jahrzehend des Lebens*. Leipzig: F. Brandstetter, 1855.

Guillaume, Jean-Marie-Amédée. *Nouveau traité des sensations*. 2 vols. Paris: Germer-Baillière, 1876.

Guimps, Baron Charles-Frédéric-Louis-Roger de. *La philosophie et la pratique de l'éducation*. Paris: A. Durand, 1860.

Gurney, Edmund. *The Power of Sound*. London: Smith, Elder and Co., 1880.

Habel, [————]. *Entwickelungsgeschichte des Willens*.

Hagemann, August. *Was ist Charakter und wie kann er durch die Erziehung gebildet werden?* Dorpat: Krüger, 1881.

Hall, G. Stanley. "The Education of the Will," *Princeton Review*, X (Nov. 1882), 306 - 25.

————. "The Moral and Religious Training of Children," *Princeton Review*, IX (Jan. 1882), 26 - 48.

————. "The Muscular Perception of Space," *Mind*, III (Oct. 1878), 433 - 50.

————. "The New Psychology," *Andover Review*, III (Feb. 1885), 120 - 35; *ibid.*, III (Mar. 1885), 239 - 48.

————. "Studies of Rhythm," *Mind*, XI (Jan. 1886), 55 - 62.

————, and Donaldson, Henry Herbert. "Motor Sensations on the Skin," *Mind*, X (Oct. 1885), 557 - 72.

Hamilton, Sir William. *Lectures on Metaphysics and Logic*. Vols. I and II: *Metaphysics*; Vols. III and IV: *Logic*. Edinburgh: W. Blackwood, 1859 - 60. 2d ed. London: W. Blackwood, 1861 - 66.

Harms, Friedrich. *Die Philosophie in ihrer Geschichte*. Vol. I: *Geschichte der Psychologie*. Berlin: T. Grieben, 1878.

Hartley, David. *Conjecturæ quædam de sensu, motu et idearum generatione*. Tract 3 of *Metaphysical Tracts by English Philosophers of the Eighteenth Century*. Ed. Samuel Parr. London: E. Lumley, 1837.

Hartmann, Eduard von. *Phänomenologie des sittlichen Bewusstseins*. Berlin: C. Duncker, 1879.

————. *Philosophy of the Unconscious*. Trans. William Chatterton Coupland. 3 vols. London: Trübner and Co., 1884.

Hecker, Ewald. *Die Physiologie und Psychologie des Lachens und des Komischen*. Berlin: F. Dümmler, 1873.

Heine, Gerhard. *Die pädagogische Seelenlehre als Grundlage für die Erziehungs- und allgemeine Unterrichtslehre.* Cöthen: Schettler, 1879.

Helmholtz, Hermann Ludwig Ferdinand von. *On the Sensations of Tone as a Physiological Basis for the Theory of Music.* Trans. Alexander J. Ellis. London: Longmans, Green, Reader and Dyer, 1875.

———. *Optique physiologique.* Trans. Émile Javal and N.-Th. Klein. Paris: V. Masson et fils, 1867.

———. *Popular Lectures on Scientific Subjects.* Trans. E. Atkinson. London: Longmans, Green, Reader and Dyer, 1873.

———. *Die Thatsachen in der Wahrnehmung.* Berlin: A. Hirschwald, 1879.

———. "Physiologische Optik," *Wissenschaftliche Abhandlungen* (Leipzig: J. A. Barth, 1883), II, 229 - 500.

———. "Schallbewegung," *Wissenschaftliche Abhandlungen* (Leipzig: J. A. Barth, 1882), I, 223 - 426.

———. "Über die Mechanik der Gehörknöchelchen," *Wissenschaftliche Abhandlungen* (Leipzig: J. A. Barth, 1883), II, 503 - 88.

———. "Über die Natur der menschlichen Sinnesempfindungen," *Wissenschaftliche Abhandlungen* (Leipzig: J. A. Barth, 1883), II, 591 - 609.

Henle, Friedrich Gustav Jacob. *Anthropologische Vorträge.* 2 vols. Braunschweig: Vieweg und Sohn, 1876, 1880.

Hensen, Victor. *Über das Gedächtniss.* Kiel: Universitätsbuchhandlung, 1877.

Herbart, Johann Friedrich. *Johann Friedrich Herbarts sämmtliche Werke.* Ed. G. Hartenstein. 12 vols. Leipzig: Voss, 1850 - 52.

———. *Lehrbuch zur Psychologie.* Ed. G. Hartenstein. Hamburg: Voss, 1882.

Hering, Ewald. *Beiträge zur Physiologie.* Leipzig: Engelmann, 1861 - 64.

———. *Über das Gedächtniss als allgemeine Function der organisierten Materie.* 2d ed. Vienna: C. Gerolds Söhne, 1876.

Hermann, Conrad. *Æsthetische Farbenlehre.* Leipzig: M. Schäfer, 1876.

Hermann, Ludimar, ed. *Handbuch der Physiologie.* Vol. III, in 2 pts.: *Handbuch der Physiologie der Sinnesorgane.* Leipzig: F. C. W. Vogel, 1879 - 80.

Hochegger, Rudolph. *Die geschichtliche Entwickelung des Farbensinnes.* Innsbruck: Wagner, 1884.

Hodgson, Shadworth Holloway. *The Philosophy of Reflection.* 2 vols. London: Longmans, Green, Reader and Dyer, 1878.

———. *Time and Space: A Metaphysical Essay.* London: Longman,

Green, Longman, Roberts and Green, 1865.

Höffding, Harald. *Outlines of Psychology.* Trans. Mary E. Lowndes. London: Macmillan and Co., 1891.

Hoppe, Janus. *Das Auswendiglernen und Auswendighersagen in physiopsychologischer, pädagogischer und sprachlicher Hinsicht.* Hamburg, Leipzig: Voss, 1883.

Horwicz, Adolf. *Psychologische Analysen auf physiologischer Grundlage.* 3 pts. in 2 vols. Halle: C. E. M. Pfeffer, 1872 - 78.

Hostinský, Otakar. *Die Lehre von den musikalischen Klängen.* Prague: H. Dominicus, 1879.

Houzeau, Jean Charles. *Étude sur les facultés mentales des animaux comparées à celles de l'homme par un voyageur naturaliste.* 2 vols. Mons: H. Manceaux, 1872.

Huber, Johann. *Das Gedächtniss.* Pt. 2 of *Psychologische Studien.* Munich: T. Ackermann, 1878. [Pt. 1 published later.]

Jäger, August. *Die Entdeckung der Seele.* 3d enl. ed. 2 vols. Leipzig: E: Günther, 1883 - 85.

Jahn, Max. *Psychologie als Grundwissenschaft der Pädagogik.* Leipzig. Frohberg, 1883.

James, William. *Feeling of Effort.* Boston: Society of Natural History, 1880.

———. *The Principles of Psychology.* New York: Henry Holt and Co., 1890.

———. "The Association of Ideas," *Popular Science Monthly,* XVI (Mar. 1880), 577 - 93.

———. "Brute and Human Intellect," *Journal of Speculative Philosophy,* XII (July 1878), 236 - 76.

———. "The Sentiment of Rationality," *Mind,* IV (July 1879), 317 - 46.

———. "The Spatial Quale," *Journal of Speculative Philosophy,* XIII (Jan. 1879), 64 - 87.

———. "What Is an Emotion?" *Mind,* IX (Apr. 1884), 188 - 205.

Jardine, Robert. *The Elements of the Psychology of Cognition.* London: Macmillan and Co., 1874.

Jeanmaire, Charles. *L'Idée de la personnalité dans la psychologie moderne.* Toulouse: Douladoure-Privat, 1882.

Jeffries, Benjamin Joy. *Color Blindness: Its Dangers and its Detection.* Boston: Houghton, Osgood and Co., 1879.

Joly, Henri. *L'Imagination.* Paris: Hachette, 1877.

———. *L'Instinct: Ses rapports avec la vie et avec l'intelligence.* Paris: E. Thorin, 1869.

———. *Notions de pédagogie.* Paris: Delala'n Frères, 1884.

———. *Psychologie comparée: L'Homme et l'animal.* Paris: Hachette, 1877.

Jungmann, Joseph. *Das Gemüth und das Gefühlsvermögen der neueren Psychologie*. 2d ed. Freiburg: Herder, 1885.

Kehr, Carl. *Über das Gemüth und seine Bildung*. Gotha: Thienemann, 1879.

Kollert, Julius. "Untersuchungen über den Zeitsinn," *Philosophische Studien*, I (1883), 78 - 89.

Krause, Albrecht. *Die Gesetze des menschlichen Herzens*. Lahr: Schauenburg, 1876.

Kussmaul, Adolf. *Die Störungen der Sprache*. Leipzig: F. C. W. Vogel, 1885.

———. *Untersuchungen über das Seelenleben des neugeborenen Menschen*. Leipzig: C. F. Winter, 1859. 2d ed. Tübingen: Moser, 1884.

Ladd, George Trumbull. *Elements of Physiological Psychology*. New York: Charles Scribner's Sons, 1887.

———. *Introduction to Philosophy*. New York: Charles Scribner's Sons, 1890.

———. *Outlines of Physiological Psychology*. London: Longmans, Green and Co., 1891. [Recast form of *Elements of Physiological Psychology*.]

Lange, Karl. *Über Apperzeption: Eine psychologisch-pädagogische Monographie*. Plauen: F. E. Neupert, 1879.

Langer, Paul. *Die Grundlagen der Psychophysik*. Jena: Dufft, 1876.

Laurie, Simon Somerville (Scotus Novanticus). *Ethica: or, the Ethics of Reason*. London: Williams and Norgate, 1885.

———. *Metaphysica nova et vetusta: A Return to Dualism*. London: Williams and Norgate, 1884.

Laycock, Thomas. *Mind and Brain*. 2 vols. Edinburgh: Sutherland and Knox, 1860.

Lazarus, Moritz. *Das Leben der Seele*. 2d enl. ed. 3 vols. Berlin: F. Dümmler, 1876 - 82.

———. *Über die Reize des Spiels*. Berlin: F. Dümmler, 1883.

Le Conte, Joseph. *Sight: An Exposition of the Principles of Monocular and Binocular Vision*. New York: D. Appleton and Co.; London: Kegan Paul and Co., 1881.

Lederer, A. *Die Methodik der Gewöhnung*. Vienna: Pichlers Witwe und Sohn, 1879.

Lehmann, Karl, and Bleuler, Eugen. *Zwangsmässige Lichtempfindungen durch Schall und verwandte Erscheinungen auf dem Gebiete der andern Sinnesempfindungen*. Leipzig: Fues, 1881.

Lewes, George Henry. *Problems of Life and Mind*. First Series: *The Foundations of a Creed*. 2 vols. London: Trübner and Co., 1874 - 75.

————. *Problems of Life and Mind.* Third Series, Problem First: *The Study of Psychology, its Object, Scope, and Method.* London: Trübner and Co., 1879. [This part of the Third Series of *Problems of Life and Mind* was published separately at the request of the author.] Problem Second: Mind as a Function of Organism; Problem Third: The Sphere of Sense and the Logic of Feeling; Problem Fourth: The Sphere of Intellect and Logic of Signs. London: Trübner and Co., 1879.

Lindsay, William Lauder. *Mind in Lower Animals in Health and Disease.* 2 vols. London: Kegan Paul and Co., 1879.

Lipps, Theodor. *Psychologische Studien.* Heidelberg: Weiss, 1885.

Löbisch, J. E. *Entwickelungsgeschichte der Seele des Kindes.* Vienna: Haas, 1851.

Lorenz, Gustav. "Berichtigungen zu dem Aufsatze über die Methode der richtigen und falschen Fälle, etc.," *Philosophische Studien,* II (1885), 655 - 57.

Lotze, Hermann. *Geschichte der Æsthetik in Deutschland.* Munich: J. G. Cotta, 1868.

————. *Grundzüge der Psychologie.* Leipzig: S. Hirzel, 1881.

     Outlines of Psychology. Trans. and ed. George Trumbull Ladd. Boston: Ginn and Co., 1886.

————. *Logik.* Leipzig: Weidmann, 1843.

     Logic. Trans. Bernard Bosanquet. Oxford: Clarendon Press, 1884.

————. *Medicinische Psychologie, oder Physiologie der Seele.* Leipzig: Weidmann, 1852.

     Principes généraux de psychologie physiologique. Trans. A. Penjon. 2d ed. Paris: Germer-Baillière, 1881.

————. *Metaphysic.* Trans. Bernard Bosanquet. Oxford: Clarendon Press, 1884.

     Metaphysik. Leipzig: Weidmann, 1841.

     Métaphysique. Trans. A. Duval. Paris: Firmin-Didot, 1883.

————. *Microcosmus: An Essay Concerning Man and His Relation to the World.* Trans. Elizabeth Hamilton and E. E. Constance Jones. 2 vols. Edinburgh: T. and T. Clark, 1885.

————. "De la formation de la notion d'espace: La théorie des signes locaux," *Revue philosophique,* IV (Oct. 1877), 345 - 65.

Lubbock, Sir John. *Ants, Bees, and Wasps: A Record of Observations on the Habits of the Social Hymenoptera.* 3d ed. London: Kegan Paul and Co., 1882.

Maass, Johann Gebhard Ehrenreich. *Versuch über die Leidenschaften.* 2 vols. Halle, Leipzig: Russ, 1805.

Mach, Ernst. *Grundlinien der Lehre von den Bewegungsemp-*

findungen. Leipzig: Engelmann, 1875.

Magnus, Hugo Friedrich. *Die Entwickelung des Farbensinnes.* First Series, Pt. 9 of *Physiologische Abhandlungen.* Jena: Fischer, 1877.

Mahaffy, John Pentland. *Kant's Critical Philosophy for English Readers.* Vol. I: *The Æsthetic and Analytic;* Vol. III: *Kant's Prolegomena to any Future Metaphysic.* London: Longmans, Green, Reader and Dyer, 1872 - 74. [Vol. II was not published. Vol. III becomes Vol. II in subsequent editions.]

Maillet, Émile. *De l'essence des passions: Étude psychologique et morale.* Paris: Hachette, 1877.

Marion, Henri. *De la solidarité morale: Essai de psychologie appliquée.* Paris: Germer-Baillière, 1880.

Märkel, Gustav. *Über die Einbildungskraft und ihre Bedeutung für Unterricht und Erziehung.* Döbeln: Schmidt, 1878.

Martineau, James. *Types of Ethical Theory.* 2 vols. Oxford: Clarendon Press, 1885.

Marty, Anton. *Die Frage nach der geschichtlichen Entwickelung des Farbensinnes.* Vienna: C. Gerolds Söhne, 1879.

Maudsley, Henry. *Body and Will.* London: K. Paul, Trench and Co., 1883; New York: D. Appleton and Co., 1884.

———. *The Pathology of Mind* [3d ed. of second part of *Physiology and Pathology of Mind,* recast, enlarged, and rewritten]. New York: D. Appleton and Co., 1880.

———. *The Physiology of Mind* [3d ed. of first part of *Physiology and Pathology of Mind,* recast, enlarged, and rewritten]. London: Macmillan and Co., 1876; New York: D. Appleton and Co., 1878.

McCosh, James. *The Emotions.* New York: Charles Scribner's Sons; London: Macmillan and Co., 1880.

Mehner, Emil Max. "Zur Lehre vom Zeitsinn," *Philosophische Studien,* II (1885), 546 - 602.

Mercier, Charles. "A Classification of Feelings," *Mind,* IX (July 1884), 325 - 48; *ibid.,* IX (Oct. 1884), 509 - 30; *ibid.,* X (Jan. 1885), 1 - 26.

Meyer, Bruno. *Aus der ästhetischen Pädagogik.* Berlin: Gebrüder Paetel, 1873.

Michaut, Narcisse. *De l'imagination: Étude psychologique.* Paris: Germer-Baillière, 1876.

Michelet, Karl Ludwig. *Anthropologie und Psychologie, oder die Philosophie des subjectiven Geistes.* Berlin: Sander, 1840.

Miquel, F. W. *Beiträge zu einer pädagogisch-psychologischen Lehre vom Gedächtniss.* Hannover: Rümpler, 1850.

Mill, John Stuart. *Dissertations and Discussions: Political, Philo-*

sophical, and Historical. 4 vols. Boston: W. V. Spencer, 1865 - 68.

——. *An Examination of Sir William Hamilton's Philosophy and of the Principal Philosophical Questions Discussed in his Writings.* London: Longman, Green, Longman, Roberts and Green, 1865.

Monck, William Henry Stanley. *Space and Vision.* Dublin: W. McGee, 1872.

Montgomery, Edmund. "Space and Touch," *Mind,* X (Apr. 1885), 227 - 44; *ibid.,* X (July 1885), 377 - 98; *ibid.,* X (Oct. 1885), 512 - 31.

Morell, John Daniel. *Elements of Psychology.* London: W. Pickering, 1853.

Müller, Ferdinand August. *Das Axiom der Psychophysik.* Marburg: R. Friedrich, 1881.

Müller, Georg Elias. *Zur Grundlegung der Psychophysik: Kritische Beiträge.* Berlin: T. Grieben, 1878.

Murphy, Joseph John. *Habit and Intelligence: A Series of Essays on the Laws of Life and Mind.* 2d rev. ed. London: Macmillan and Co., 1879.

Murray, John Clark. *A Handbook of Psychology.* London: A. Gardner; Montreal: Dawson Brothers, 1885.

Nagel, Albrecht. *Das Sehen mit zwei Augen und die Lehre von den identischen Netzhautstellen.* Leipzig: C. F. Winter, 1861.

Nahlowsky, Joseph W. *Das Gefühlsleben.* Leipzig: Pernitzsch, 1862.

Neudecker, Georg. *Studien zur Geschichte der deutschen Æsthetik seit Kant.* Würzburg: Stahel'sche Buch- und Kunsthandlung, 1878.

Ostermann, W. *Die Grundlehren der pädagogischen Psychologie.* Oldenburg: Schulze, 1880.

Panum, Peter Ludwig. *Physiologische Untersuchungen über das Sehen mit zwei Augen.* Kiel: Schwers, 1858.

Pape-Carpantier, Marie Olinde. *Notice sur l'éducation des sens et quelques instruments pédagogiques.* Paris: C. Delagrave, 1878, 1881.

Perez, Bernard. *L'Éducation dès le berceau: Essai de pédagogie expérimentale.* Paris: Germer-Baillière, 1880.

——. *The First Three Years of Childhood.* Ed. and trans. Alice M. Christie, with an introd. by James Sully. Chicago: A. N. Marquis and Co.; London: W. Swan Sonnenschein, 1885.

——. *La psychologie de l'enfant: L'Enfant de trois à sept ans.* Paris: F. Alcan, 1886.

Perty, Maximilian von. *Über das Seelenleben der Thiere: Thatsachen und Betrachtungen.* Leipzig, Heidelberg: C. F. Winter, 1865.

Pflüger, Eduard Friedrich Wilhelm, ed. *Archiv für die gesamte Physiologie des Menschen und der Thiere.* Bonn: Cohen und Söhne, 1868 - 1910.

Philosophische Studien.
     Vol. I, see: Kollert, Staude, Tischer, Trautscholdt, Wundt.
     Vol. II, see: Cattell, Estel, Friedrich, Lorenz, Mehner, Tchisch, Wundt.

Pollock, Frederick. "An Infant's Progress in Language," *Mind,* III (July 1878), 392 - 401.

Porter, Noah, *The Human Intellect* (with an "Introduction upon Psychology and the Soul"). New York: Charles Scribner and Co., 1868.

Preyer, William. *Die Seele des Kindes.* Leipzig: T. Grieben, 1884.

Radestock, Paul. *Habit and its Importance in Education: An Essay in Pedagogical Psychology.* Trans. F. A. Caspari. Boston: D. C. Heath and Co., 1886.

———. *Schlaf und Traum: Eine physiologisch-psychologische Untersuchung.* Leipzig: Breitkopf und Härtel, 1879.

Rée, Paul. *Der Ursprung der moralischen Empfindungen.* Chemnitz: Schmeitzner, 1877.

Ribot, Théodule Armand. *Diseases of Memory: An Essay in the Positive Psychology.* Trans. William Huntington Smith. New York: D. Appleton and Co., 1882.

———. *The Diseases of the Will.* Trans. J. Fitzgerald. New York: J. Fitzgerald, 1884.

———. *Les maladies de la personnalité.* Paris: F. Alcan, 1885.

———. *La psychologie allemande contemporaine (école expérimentale).* Paris: Germer-Baillière, 1879.
     German Psychology of To-day, the Empirical School. Trans. James Mark Baldwin. New York: Charles Scribner's Sons, 1886.

———. Les théories allemandes sur l'espace tactile," *Revue philosophique,* VI (Aug. 1878), 130 - 45.

Riemann, Carl Wilhelm Julius Hugo. *Über das musikalische Hören.* Leipzig, Göttingen: Vandenhöck und Ruprecht, 1874.

Robertson, George Croom. "Association of Ideas," *Encyclopædia Britannica* (9th ed.), VII, 730.

———. "Psychology and Philosophy," *Mind,* VIII (Jan. 1883), 1 - 21.

Rolph, W. H. *Biologische Probleme zugleich als Versuch zur Entwicklung einer rationellen Ethik.* 2d enl. ed. Leipzig: Engelmann, 1884.

Romanes, George John. *Animal Intelligence.* London: Kegan Paul and Co., 1882; New York: D. Appleton and Co., 1883.

————. *Mental Evolution in Animals* (with a posthumous essay on instinct [by] Charles Darwin). New York: D. Appleton and Co.; London: K. Paul, Trench and Co., 1884.

————. "Consciousness of Time," *Mind*, III (July 1878), 297 - 303.

Rosenkranz, Johann Karl Friedrich. *Æsthetik des Hässlichen.* Königsberg: Gebrüder Bornträger, 1853.

————. *Psychologie, oder die Wissenschaft vom subjectiven Geist.* Königsberg: Gebrüder Bornträger, 1837.

Rubinstein, Susanna. *Psychologisch-ästhetische Essays.* Heidelberg: C. F. Winter, 1884.

Sanford, Edmund C. "A Laboratory Course in Physiological Psychology," *American Journal of Psychology*, IV (Apr. 1891), 141 - 55.

Scherner, Karl Albert. *Entdeckungen auf dem Gebiete der Seele.* First book also published under the title: *Das Leben des Traums.* Berlin: Schindler, 1861.

Schilling, Gustav. *Lehrbuch der Psychologie.* Leipzig: F. Fleischer, 1851.

Schleiden, Matthias Jacob. *Zur Theorie des Erkennens durch den Gesichtssinn.* Leipzig: Engelmann, 1861.

Schmidt, Eduard. *Über das Mitgefühl.* Pt. 1 of *Psychologische Skizzen.* Rostock: Deberg, 1837.

Schneider, Georg Heinrich. *Freud und Leid des Menschengeschlechts.* Stuttgart: Schweizerbart, 1883.

————. *Der menschliche Wille vom Standpunkte der neueren Entwickelungstheorien.* Berlin: F. Dümmler, 1882.

————. *Der thierische Wille.* Leipzig: Gebrüder Abel, 1880.

————. *Die Unterscheidung.* Zürich: Schmidt, 1877.

Schnell, [————]. *Die Anschauung.*

Schnell, C. Ferdinand. *Der Lernakt.* Langensalza: Comptoir, 1867.

Schopenhauer, Arthur. "Über das Sehen und die Farben," Pt. 2 of *Schriften zur Erkenntnisslehre, sämmtliche Werke*, Vol. I. Ed. Julius Trauenstädt. Leipzig: Brockhaus, 1873 - 74.

Schumann, Johann Christian Gottlob. *Kleinere Schriften über pädagogische und kulturgeschichtliche Fragen.* 2d ed. Pts. 1 - 3. Hannover: Meyer, 1878 - 79.

Schultze, Carl August Julius Fritz. *Die Sprache des Kindes.* Leipzig: E. Günther, 1880.

Sergi, Giuseppe. *Teoria fisiologica della percezione.* Milan: Fratelli Dumolard, 1881.

Seth, Andrew. "Philosophy," *Encyclopædia Britannica* (9th ed.), XVIII, 791 - 96.

Sidgwick, Henry. *The Method of Ethics.* London: Macmillan and Co., 1877.

Siebeck, Hermann. *Geschichte der Psychologie.* 2 vols. Gotha: F. A. Perthes, 1880 - 84.

———. *Das Wesen der ästhetischen Anschauung: Psychologische Untersuchungen zur Theorie des Schönen und der Kunst.* Berlin: F. Dümmler, 1875.

Sigwart, Christoph von. *Logik.* Vol. I: *Die Lehre vom Urtheil, vom Begriff und vom Schluss*; Vol. II: *Die Methodenlehre.* Tübingen: H. Laupp, 1873 - 78.

Spencer, Herbert. *The Principles of Psychology.* 2d ed. 2 vols. New York: D. Appleton and Co., 1877.

Spitta, Heinrich Theodor Johannes. *Die Schlaf- und Traumzustände der menschlichen Seele.* 2d ed. Tübingen: Fues, 1882.

Staude, Otto. "Der Begriff der Apperception in der neueren Psychologie," *Philosophische Studien*, I (1883), 149 - 212.

Stein, Karl Heinrich von. *Über Wahrnehmung.* Berlin: C. Duncker, 1877.

Steinthal, Heymann. *Abriss der Sprachwissenschaft.* Pt. 1: *Die Sprache im Allgemeinen, Einleitung in die Psychologie und Sprachwissenschaft.* Berlin: F. Dümmler, 1871.

Stephen, Leslie. *The Science of Ethics.* London: Smith, Elder and Co., 1882.

Stoy, Karl Volkmar. *Encyclopädie, Methodologie und Literatur der Pädagogik.* Leipzig: Engelmann, 1878.

Stricker, Salomon. *Studien über die Association der Vorstellungen.* Vienna: Braumüller, 1883.

———. *Studien über das Bewusstsein.* Vienna: Braumüller, 1879.

———. *Studien über die Sprachvorstellungen.* Vienna: Braumüller, 1880.

Strümpell, Ludwig Heinrich. *Grundriss der Psychologie, oder der Lehre und der Ermittlung des Seelenlebens im Menschen.* Leipzig: Böhme, 1884.

———. *Die Natur und Entstehung der Träume.* Leipzig: Veit, 1874.

Stumpf, Carl. *Tonpsychologie.* Vol. I. Leipzig: S. Hirzel, 1883.

———. *Über den psychologischen Ursprung der Raumvorstellung.* Leipzig: S. Hirzel, 1873.

Sully, James. *Illusions: A Psychological Study.* London: Kegan Paul and Co., 1881.

———. *Outlines of Psychology, with Special Reference to the Theory of Education.* London: Longmans, Green, Reader and Dyer, 1884.

———. *Pessimism: A History and Criticism.* London: H. S. King and Co., 1877.

———. *Sensation and Intuition: Studies in Psychology and Æsthetics.* London: H. S. King and Co., 1874.

———. "Comparison," *Mind*, X (Oct. 1885), 489 - 511.

———. "Dream," *Encyclopædia Britannica* (9th ed.), VII, 452 - 59.

———. "The Question of Visual Perception in Germany," *Mind*, III (Jan. 1878), 1 - 23; *ibid.*, III (Apr. 1878), 167 - 95.

Taine, Hippolyte Adolphe. *On Intelligence.* Trans. T. D. Haye. New York: Holt and Williams, 1872.

———. "M. Taine on the Acquisition of Language by Children," *Mind*, II (Apr. 1877), 252 - 59. ["M. Taine contributed to the *Revue Philosophique*, No. 1. (January 1876) a remarkable series of observations on the development of language in a young child, which are here made accessible by translation to English readers."]

Tappan, Henry Philip. *A Treatise on the Will.* Glasgow: Lang, Adamson and Co., 1857.

Tchisch, Waldemar von. "Über die Zeitverhältnisse der Apperception einfacher und zusammengesetzter Vorstellungen untersucht mit Hülfe der Complicationsmethode," *Philosophische Studien*, II (1885), 603 - 34.

Thaulow, Gustav Ferdinand. *Hegels Ansichten über Erziehung und Unterricht.* Kiel: Akademische Buchhandlung, 1853 - 54.

Thring, Edward. *Theory and Practice of Teaching.* Cambridge: The University Press, 1883.

Tischer, Ernst. "Über die Unterscheidung von Schallstärken," *Philosophische Studien*, I (1883), 495 - 542.

Trautscholdt, Martin. "Experimentelle Untersuchungen über die Association der Vorstellungen," *Philosophische Studien*, I (1883), 213 - 50.

Treuge, Julius. *Der Anschauungsunterricht.* Münster: Coppenrath, 1885.

Überhorst, Carl. *Die Entstehung der Gesichtswahrnehmung.* Göttingen: Vandenhöck und Ruprecht, 1876.

Ulrici, Hermann. *Grundzüge der praktischen Philosophie.* Pt. 2 of *Gott und der Mensch.* Leipzig: T. D. Weigel, 1874.

———. *Der Leib und die Seele.* Pt. 1, in 2 vols., of *Gott und der Mensch.* Leipzig: T. D. Weigel, 1873.

Vierordt, Karl von. *Der Zeitsinn nach Versuchen.* Tübingen: H. Laupp, 1868.

Vischer, Friedrich Theodor von. *Æsthetik, oder Wissenschaft des Schönen.* 3 vols. Reutlingen, Leipzig: C. Mäcken, 1846 - 57.

Volkmann, A. W. "Sehen," *Handwörterbuch der Physiologie*, ed. Rudolph Wagner (Braunschweig: Vieweg und Sohn, 1846), III, Pt. 1, 265 - 351.

Volkmann, Wilhelm. *Lehrbuch der Psychologie vom Standpunkte des Realismus und nach genetischer Methode.* 2 vols. Cöthen: Schulze, 1884 - 85.

Waitz, Theodor. *Grundlegung der Psychologie, nebst einer Anwendung auf das Seelenleben der Thiere, besonders die Instincterscheinungen.* Hamburg: F. A. Perthes, 1846.

———. *Lehrbuch der Psychologie als Naturwissenschaft.* Braunschweig: Vieweg und Sohn, 1849.

Walsemann, A. *Das Interesse: Sein Wesen und seine Bedeutung für den Unterricht.* Hannover: C. Meyer, 1884.

Ward, James. "An Attempt to Interpret Fechner's Law," *Mind,* I (Oct. 1876), 452 - 66.

———. "Psychological Principles," *Mind,* VIII (Apr. 1883), 153 - 69; *ibid.,* VIII (Oct. 1883), 465 - 86.

———. "Psychology," *Encyclopædia Britannica* (9th ed.), XX, 37 - 85.

Weber, Ernst Heinrich. "Der Tastsinn und das Gemeingefühl," *Handwörterbuch der Physiologie,* ed. Rudolph Wagner (Braunschweig: Vieweg und Sohn, 1846), III, Pt. 2, 481 - 588.

———. "Über den Raumsinn und die Empfindungskreise in der Haut und dem Auge," *Berichte über die Verhandlungen der königlich Sächsischen Gesellschaft der Wissenschaften zu Leipzig, mathematisch-physikalische Klasse* (Leipzig: S. Hirzel, 1852), pp. 85 - 154.

> [Now under the title: *Sächsische Akademie der Wissenschaften Leipzig, math.-naturwissenschaftliche Klasse. Berichte.* (1852).]

Wendt, Ferdinand Maria. *Die Willensbildung vom psychologischen Standpunkte.* First Series, Pt. 3 of *Pädagogische Sammelmappe.* Leipzig: Siegismund und Bolkening, 1875.

Wiese, Ludwig Adolf. *Die Bildung des Willens: Eine historische Betrachtung zur Geschichte der deutschen Pädagogik.* 4th ed. Berlin: Wiegandt und Grieben, 1879.

Wundt, Wilhelm Max. *Beiträge zur Theorie der Sinneswahrnehmung.* Leipzig, Heidelberg: C. F. Winter, 1862.

———. *Grundzüge der physiologischen Psychologie.* 2d ed. 2 vols. Leipzig: Engelmann, 1880.

———. *Logik: Ein Untersuchung der Principien der Erkenntniss und der Methoden wissenschaftlicher Forschung.* Vol. I: *Erkenntnisslehre;* Vol. II: *Methodenlehre.* Stuttgart: F. Enke, 1880 - 83.

———. *Vorlesungen über die Menschen- und Thierseele.* 2 vols. Leipzig: Voss, 1863.

———. "Central Innervation and Consciousness," *Mind,* I (Apr. 1876), 161 - 78.

————. "Sur la théorie des signes locaux," *Revue philosophique*, VI (Sept. 1878), 217 - 31.

————. "Über das Weber'sche Gesetz," *Philosophische Studien*, II (1885), 1 - 36.

————. "Über die Methode der Minimaländerungen," *Philosophische Studien*, I (1883), 556 - 72.

————. "Über psychologische Methoden," *Philosophische Studien*, I (1883), 1 - 38.

————. "Weitere Bemerkungen über psychische Messung," *Philosophische Studien*, I (1883), 463 - 71.

————. "Zur Geschichte und Theorie der abstracten Begriffe," *Philosophische Studien*, II (1885), 161 - 93.

————. "Zur Lehre vom Willen," *Philosophische Studien*, I (1883), 337 - 78.

Ziller, Tuiskon. *Vorlesungen über allgemeine Pädagogik*. Leipzig: Matthes, 1876.

SOURCES OF BIBLIOGRAPHICAL INFORMATION IN CHECKLIST OF REFERENCES

Bayerische Staatsbibliothek, Munich, Germany.

Bibliographie der deutschen Zeitschriften-literatur, Ergänzungsband, Vols. XI - XII, XIV - XVIII.

Boring, Edwin G. *A History of Experimental Psychology*. New York: Appleton-Century-Crofts, Inc., 1950.

————. *The Physical Dimensions of Consciousness*. New York, London: The Century Co., 1933.

————. *Sensation and Perception in the History of Experimental Psychology*. New York, London: D. Appleton-Century Co., 1942.

British Museum Catalogue of Printed Books. Ann Arbor: J. W. Edwards, 1946.

British Museum General Catalogue of Printed Books. London: The Trustees of the British Museum, 1960 - 65.

Bücher-Lexicon. Leipzig: Ludwig Schumann, 1834 - 52; T. D. Weigel, 1853 - 86.

Catalogue général des livres imprimés de la bibliothèque nationale. Paris: Imprimerie nationale, 1897 - 1964.

Dictionary of Philosophy and Psychology. Ed. Mark Baldwin. Vol. III, Pts. 1 and 2. New York: Peter Smith, 1949.

Handwörterbuch der Physiologie. Ed. Rudolph Wagner. Vols. I - IV. Braunschweig: Vieweg und Sohn, 1842 - 53.

Helmholtz, Hermann von. *Wissenschaftliche Abhandlungen.* Vols. I - III. Leipzig: J. A. Barth, 1882 - 83, 1895.

Höffding, Harald. *A History of Modern Philosophy.* Trans. B. E. Meyer. 2 vols. New York: Dover Publications, Inc., 1955.

J. C. Poggendorffs biographisch-literarisches Handwörterbuch zur Geschichte der exacten Wissenschaften. Ed. A. J. von Oettingen. Vols. III - IV. Leipzig: Johann Ambrosius Barth, 1898 - 1904.

Journal of Speculative Philosophy. Ed. William T. Harris. Vols. XVII - XX. New York: D. Appleton and Co., 1882 - 86.

Library of Congress Catalog Printed Cards. Ann Arbor, Michigan: Edwards Brothers, Inc., 1946; *Supplement, ibid.,* J. W. Edwards, 1948.

Mind. Ed. George Croom Robertson. Vols. I - XIII. London, Edinburgh: Williams and Norgate, 1876 - 88.

Müller, Johannes. *Die wissenschaftliche Vereine und Gesellschaften Deutschlands im neunzehnten Jahrhundert.* Berlin: Behrend and Co., 1917.

Philosophische Studien. Ed. Wilhelm Wundt. Vols. I - II. Leipzig: Engelmann, 1881/85.

Revue philosophique de la France et de l'étranger. Ed. Th. Ribot. Vols. IV and VI. Paris: Germer-Baillière, 1877, 1878.

Staatsbibliothek der Stiftung Preussischer Kulturbesitz, Marburg, Germany.

University of Pennsylvania Library, Catalog, Programmschriften Collection.

Windelband, Wilhelm. *A History of Philosophy.* Trans. James H. Tufts. 2 vols. New York, Evanston: Harper and Row, 1958.

A note on the text

The text for Dewey's *Psychology* was first set in type, electroplated, and printed in 1886, though issued with an 1887 date on the title page. The original plates were used—with repairs, resetting, and various kinds of modification—throughout the book's history of twenty-six printings.

The long publishing history of *Psychology* can be divided into two periods: the first, from 1886 to 1899, associated with Harper and Brothers; and the second, from 1900 to 1946, associated with the American Book Company. During the first period, Dewey made two extensive sets of revisions in the text, and type was reset for a number of pages and parts of pages. During the second period, no revisions were made and the plates were repaired and mechanically adjusted only as absolutely necessary. The final printing of the text[1] shows clear evidence of plate wear throughout—e.g., in blurred type and in many missing or broken letters, numbers, and punctuation marks.

Psychology was Dewey's first book. As late as February 1886 he wrote that he wondered whether he would succeed in getting it published,[2] but within three months he had signed a contract with Harper and Brothers.[3] Harper's published 1500 copies of the book with a copyright dated 4 November 1886 (Copyright registry #24897), and followed the standard practice of the time in putting the following year's date, 1887, on the title page. Both deposit copies received by the Copyright Office in the Library of Congress on 22 November 1886 have been lost.[4]

[1]   Preserved in the offices of the Dewey Project, Southern Illinois University, Carbondale, Illinois, gift of the American Book Co., 55 Fifth Ave., New York City.
[2]   Letter to H. A. P. Torrey, 16 Feb. 1886, quoted by George Dykhuizen, "John Dewey and the University of Michigan," *Journal of the History of Ideas*, XXIII (Oct.–Dec. 1962), 516.
[3]   Original draft of contract preserved by Harper and Row, 49 E. 33rd St., New York City.
[4]   Letter from Waldo H. Moore, Chief, Reference Division, Copyright Office, Library of Congress, 13 May 1966. Preserved by Dewey Project, Southern Illinois University, Carbondale, Illinois. The copyright law in effect in 1886 provided that before publication a printed copy of the title of the book should be sent to the Librarian of Congress and that within ten days from publication two copies of the book itself should be delivered.

Seven copies of the first printing were collated on the Hinman Machine to determine whether the 1886 (1887) text was printed more than one time. The seven were found to be identical in every respect and one of these copies (see page lviii) was used as copy-text for the present edition.[5]

In 1888 Dewey submitted revisions for the text estimated to cost $41.[6] The changes required the resetting of type and preparation of new plates for seven complete pages and the modification of plates for 134 additional pages. Although there was significant revision of content for this version, many of the changes can properly be called corrections, and few corrections or changes in accidentals were necessary after this revision. No reset type appears except in those pages which had changes. Harper and Brothers registered a second copyright on this "new and revised edition" on 16 January 1889 (#2093), but the Copyright Office has no record of deposit copies being received, nor was the 1889 copyright notice carried in any printing. In a "Note to the Second Edition" Dewey mentioned his "hope that the changes made in this edition will be found to make the book conform more nearly to the purpose as stated" (in the "Preface" of the 1887 printing). He made no attempt to list such changes specifically by page numbers as he did later in the "Third Revised Edition".

The 1889 printing, often referred to as the "second edition" because of the "Note to the Second Edition" which appeared on the verso of the title page, was reprinted only once, the following year. The only change made for this exact reprinting was in the title-page date, which became 1890.

Further revisory changes in content and some corrections were made in the text in the summer of 1891. For this, Dewey's final revision of the text, fifteen pages were completely reset and new plates prepared. Forty-seven more pages show modification of the plates with some type reset and extensive patchwork. A

The Copyright Office preserves the Harper printed form dated 3 Nov. 1886 requesting copyright of *Psychology* (along with "*The Mikado's Empire*. By W. E. Griffin. New Edition."). Accompanying, on a single leaf, is the printed title of *Psychology* dated 1886. Examination of this deposit title against the title of the book as issued reveals that the plate was altered to substitute "7" for the original "6". This change was made, as customarily with books published late in one year, in order to give them currency in the following year, the period of their anticipated greatest sale.

[5]   The steps used in determining the choice of copy-text are more fully described in Textual Principles and Procedures, pp. xi–xv.

[6]   Harper and Brothers manufacturing notations, 15 Oct. 1888. Courtesy of the publisher.

third copyright on *Psychology* was registered by Harper and Brothers on 20 August 1891 (#29768), and two deposit copies were received 30 September of the same year. Harper's called this the "Third Revised Edition", a designation that appeared on the title page for the rest of the book's life. In a "Note to the Third Edition", Dewey wrote, "Many of the changes in this edition are in statement of particular facts where the science has advanced since the book was first written." This statement is followed in the same "Note" by a listing of pages on which there were changes of "a paragraph or more". The ambiguity of these references to changes, coupled with the lack of specific identification of changes in the 1889 version, led to the erroneous assumption that the "Third Revised Edition" accounted for most of the changes from the original text. As indicated above, however, a significant amount of alteration was made for the 1889 printing. Collation on the Hinman Machine reveals that, of the total of 203 pages which had some or all of the type reset to make corrections or changes during the Harper and Brothers period, considerably more than half, 141, of these plate changes were made for the 1889 version. It is also significant to note the length of the changes in each of the two revisions. Of the 206 changes made for the 1889 printing, 194 were less than a sentence, 6 were of one or more complete sentences but less than a paragraph, 2 were of a paragraph or more but less than a page, and 4 were a page or more in length. In the total of 56 revisions made for the 1891 printing, 38 were less than a sentence, 8 were of one or more sentences but less than a paragraph, 4 of one or more paragraphs but not a full page, and 6 were of one or more pages.

The various emendations lists in the present edition have been designed to provide the complete history of the text with all its variants, both substantive and accidental. The lists include not only the approved emended reading and the copy-text reading, but also the intermediate readings from the 1889 and 1890 printings, making it possible to follow in minute detail the changes in Dewey's thought during this brief but revolutionary period in his development, approximately 1886 to 1891.

The remaining years of the Harper and Brothers period of the text, from 1892 to 1899, were characterized by yearly reprintings of the "Third Revised Edition", with no changes of any kind save the date on the title page. Despite the fact that Dewey moved from the University of Michigan to the University of Chicago in 1894, his title appeared on the title page of each of these printings as "Professor of Philosophy in Michigan University".

These were, however, also the years when five large publishers[7] put together their textbook lists to form the American
Book Company. By the end of the century, Harper and Brothers
was ready to assign its contract for *Psychology* to this offspring;
formal transfer of the book was made on 17 January 1900.[8]

The American Book Company's period of publishing the
text extended from 1900 to 1946, when the book went out of
print entirely, although the last of the fourteen printings by this
publisher was probably made in 1930. The publisher provided
the editors of the present edition with the "Marked Copy" used to
prepare the first American Book Company printing in 1900,[9]
and this proved to be the 1899 Harper and Brothers printing
with changes dated February and June 1900 pasted in. The
modifications were limited to the changed imprint and to Dewey's
title, which became for the 1900 printing "Head Professor of
Philosophy in the University of Chicago". The new 1900 title
page, without a date, was used in all the remaining printings of
the book, even though Dewey became Professor of Philosophy at
Columbia University in 1904.

The lack of a date on the title page of the American Book
Company printings, and the Harper and Brothers 1891 copyright notice on the verso of the title page, together caused all
American Book Company printings to be listed by scholars and
by libraries as "[c1891]". This widespread practice caused a
great deal of confusion about the chronology of the various
printings of the "Third Revised Edition", since it falsely suggested that several Harper and Brothers printings post-dated
those of the American Book Company. The publishing history
presented here shows clearly that such confusion is unnecessary.
Although there are no dates on the title page of the American
Book Company printings, and complete manufacturing records
no longer exist, it is possible to fix the date of each printing with
reasonable accuracy from records of plate repair and correspondence in the publisher's files. On the verso of the title page of
the American Book Company printings, there is a code consisting
of small capital letters "w. p." with an arabic number identifying each of fourteen printings made between 1900 and 1930. This
code refers to the Washington Press, at first located on Washington Square in New York City and later at Bloomfield, New

---

[7]   A. S. Barnes and Co.; Ivison, Blakeman, Taylor and Co.; Appleton
and Co.; Van Antwerp, Bragg and Co.; and Harper. See Helmut Lehmann-
Haupt, *The Book in America* (New York: Bowker, 1951), pp. 260 ff., for
a fuller discussion of this period.
[8]   Contract as transferred preserved by American Book Co.
[9]   Copy preserved by American Book Co.

Jersey. The records still available would indicate that the book was probably reprinted each year or every other year from 1900 to 1911. Reprinting then seems to have been sporadic—1914, 1915, 1920, 1925, with the final reprinting made in 1930. In 1942, Dewey gave his permission for the plates to be sold as old metal, in compliance with an order of the War Production Board.[10] As sales of the book had dwindled to practically nothing,[11] the publisher let it go out of print entirely in 1946 and Dewey assigned all rights to the American Book Company on 15 August 1946.[12]

The amount of plate repair and resetting of type during the American Book Company period was minimal for fourteen reprintings extending over a period of thirty years. The number of plates repaired or replaced for eight of the last nine reprintings was: 1907, 10; 1908, 2; 1909, 11; 1911, 8; 1914, 31; 1915, 17; 1925, 13; 1930, 17. Collation on the Hinman Machine of the first and last printings by this company, and of various intervening printings, reveals only two changes in the modified plates—one a correction[13] and the second an error.[14]

Complete information on the collation and the preparation of the present text is given in the lists that follow. With this information, the student can reconstruct Dewey's original text, trace changes he made in content, and evaluate editorial decisions made in preparing the present text. Each section has a brief introductory statement to explain its use more fully.

To summarize the steps taken to develop the present critical text, a total of 395 alterations were made in the 1886 (1887) Harper and Brothers first printing which was used as the copy-text. In the text itself a total of 226 changes were made; of this number, only 28 were editorial. Eight of these were changes in substantives and 20 in accidentals (7 spelling changes, 3 in hyphenation, and 10 changes from italic to roman type for reasons of syntax). Except for those spelling and hyphenation changes clearly required by Dewey's customary usage (13.34–35, 35.21, 67.34, 76.34, 89.26, 160.5, 264.5, 301.7), the editorial emendations are discussed in the Textual Notes that follow the List of Emendations in the Copy-Text. In the sections of notes following each chapter, and in the appendices, 100 changes were

10   Handwritten note on letter of W. W. Livengood to John Dewey, 10 Dec. 1942.
11   Letter from Mauck Brammer, Managing Editor, American Book Co., 26 Apr. 1965.
12   Contract preserved by American Book Co.
13   69.22 "cocoaine" corrected to "cocaine".
14   153.16 "on" for correct reading "of".

made; 87 of these were editorial and necessary for corrections. The changes in these sections are detailed in the list of Emendations in Notes and Appendices. In the revised system of headings used in the present text, 69 changes were adopted, 38 of which can be classified as editorial—all typographical.

This brief tabulation thus serves to indicate that most of the emendations made throughout the copy-text were authoritative revisions made by Dewey and incorporated in the present edited text as his final intentions.

Jo Ann Boydston

1 July 1967

List of symbols

B. Other Designations

Page-line number at left is from present edition. All lines of print except running heads and chapter titles are counted.

Reading preceding bracket is from present edition.

Square bracket signals end of reading from present edition, followed by the symbol [I^{1-26} or W] identifying first appearance of reading.

"W" means "Works", the present edition, and is used for emendations made here for the first time.

The superior plus mark $^+$ is used with a printing number to mean all printings following the one listed. I^{4+} means 1891 printing and all that follow, or I^{4-26}.

The asterisk indicates that a textual note on that emendation follows the list of emendations.

For emendations restricted to punctuation, the wavy dash $\sim$ means the same word as before the bracket, and the caret $_\wedge$ indicates the absence of a punctuation mark.

The word "*stet*" with a printing number indicates a reading retained from an edition subsequently revised; the rejected variant follows the semicolon.

A dagger † in the left margin is used to signal a short intermediate variant included within a longer section subsequently revised.

Emendations in the copy-text

The single edition of *Psychology* (I) was printed twenty-six times, the first twelve by Harper and Brothers and the last fourteen by the American Book Company. The dates of these printings appear in the List of Symbols. Dates of the American Book Company printings were approximated from records of plate maintenance and repair and from the publisher's correspondence.

Copies of the printings collated by sight and by machine are listed below with their present location and marks of identification. Those owned by the Dewey Project, Southern Illinois University, Carbondale, Illinois, are designated "D.P." and numbered; unless noted, there are no other identifying marks in these copies.

1887   (I^1) D.P. 1 (1062443); D.P. 2 (Evans); D.P. 3 (Abbott); University of Michigan Library (Gift of the children of Robert Mark Wenley); University of Michigan Library (Gift of Dean A. S. Whitney); Library of Congress (no perforations on title page or page 99, penciled BF131D5, 7-1-58, on title page); Library of Congress, copy 2, 1930B1, M25 43, with perforations on title page and page 99.

1889   (I^2) New York State Library (1117915)

1890   (I^3) D.P. 1(Collection of George E. Axtelle); D.P. 2(Amélie Devergie)

1891   (I^4) Library of Congress, copy 2, copyright deposit stamp 29768W2

1892   (I^5) University of Pennsylvania Library (Alice M. Smith Collection, Book No. 258)

1893   (I^6) University of Michigan Library (Gift of Miss Beulah Whiteset)

1894   (I^7) Southern Illinois University, Morris Library (74326)

1895   (I^8) University of Chicago Library (506495)

1896   (I^9) Oberlin College Library (164898)

1897   (I^{10}) Wesleyan University (Ohio) (26969)

1898   (I^{11}) New Hampshire State Library (59044)

1899   (I^{12}) American Book Company, "Marked Copy"

w.p. 1   (I^{13}) D.P.

W.P. 3   (I^{15}) D.P.; Cincinnati University Library (57773)
W.P. 4   (I^{16}) Ohio University Library (130.D51, copy 1)
W.P. 6   (I^{18}) D.P.; New York Public Library (589213)
W.P. 7   (I^{19}) D.P.
W.P. 8   (I^{20}) D.P.
W.P. 10   (I^{22}) University of Michigan Library (2883313)
W.P. 12   (I^{24}) American Book Company
W.P. 14   (I^{26}) D.P. (Gift of American Book Company)

Neither of the copyright deposit copies of I^1 is still in existence.[1] Machine collation of the seven copies of the first printing, listed above, revealed no variants, substantiating the publisher's indication that the original printing of 1500 copies was the only printing of the 1887 text.[2] The D.P. 1 (1062443) was used in subsequent collation and as copy-text for the present edition.

One copy of I^2 (1117915) was compared on the Hinman Machine with the copy of I^1 described above and pages with reset type revealed by that collation were sight collated. Machine collation of the two D.P. copies of I^3 against I^2 showed the 1890 text to be an exact reprinting of the so-called "second edition." The authenticated first printing (29768W2) of I^4 was machine collated against I^1 to identify reset pages which were in turn collated by sight to isolate variants. All revised, rewritten, and reset passages of I^2 and I^4 were similarly compared against one another.

One copy each of I^{5-12} was collated against I^1 and against I^4. One copy of I^{13} (D.P.) was compared by machine with one copy of I^{26} (D.P.); pages with reset type identified in this collation were then spot-checked in I^{15} (57773 and D.P.), I^{16}(130.D51), I^{18} (589213 and D.P.), I^{19} (D.P.), I^{20} (D.P.), I^{22} (2883313), and I^{24} (on loan from American Book Company).

The list below includes all changes in both substantives and accidentals in all printings of the text of *Psychology* collated for this edition, except those made silently and described in the Textual Principles and Procedures and in the introductions to the various emendations lists. All variants in authoritative printings collated are listed and identified as to source, even though rejected by the editors. The list thus provides a complete record of the changes in the text throughout its history.

J.A.B.

---

[1]   Letter from Waldo H. Moore, Chief, Reference Division, Copyright Office, Library of Congress, 13 May 1966. Preserved at the Dewey Project Office, Carbondale, Illinois.

[2]   Letter from Eugene Exman, 16 June 1965. Preserved at Dewey Project Office.

LIST OF EMENDATIONS IN COPY-TEXT

3.27   it is] I²⁺; is it I¹
4.24   will] I²⁺; shall I¹
7.16   namely, facts of nature] I²⁺; which exist externally I¹
7.25   may know] I²⁺; it knows I¹
8.22   refer to the individual] I²⁺; are individual facts I¹
*10.14   minds] W; mind I¹⁺
10.16   *knower*] I²⁺; *form* I¹
10.16   *the known*] I²⁺; its *content* I¹
11.27   psychology] I²⁺; philosophy I¹
12.11–13.23 *Difficulties of Introspection* . . . physical facts.] I⁴⁺;

      Defects of Introspection.—Introspection can never become *scientific* observation, however, for the latter means the direction of attention to certain facts according to some end or purpose. In observation of physical phenomena the things attended to remain entirely indifferent to and unchanged by the process of observation. In psychical events this is not so. The very act of attending to a psychical state changes its character, so that we observe, not what we meant to observe, but a comparatively artificial product. Since the mind's supply of energy is limited, it may often occur that the very effort of attention will absorb most of it, and the facts which we wished to observe will vanish, and nothing remain but the tension of the mind. The rule for introspection must be, therefore, to use for the most part only accidental phenomena, such as are not expected, but are noticed in an incidental way. It follows, therefore, that memory must be utilized rather than direct conscious perception; this remove from direct knowledge, however, renders the results subject to all the uncertainties of memory. It follows, also, that the most voluntary and distinct facts
† of mind will be most [more I²⁻³] open to introspection, and that the more subtle and involuntary phenomena will necessarily either escape it or be transformed.

      Failure as Explanatory Method.—So far we have dealt with introspection merely as giving us the *facts* of the science, and have seen that even here it fails. But its most conspicuous failure as method is when it is employed to account for or explain these facts. The facts can be explained only as they are related to each other, or reduced to more fundamental unities. Now, introspection cannot show us these relations or unities. It is necessarily limited to certain changing, extremely transitory phenomena, a succession of perceptions, ideas, desires, emotions, etc. The laws under which these facts come, the more fundamental activities which connect them, cannot be immediately perceived. Introspection will not even enable us to *classify* facts of consciousness. To classify them we must go beyond the present observed state and compare it with others which are no longer actually present. We do not gain much if we merely add memory to direct observation, and then compare; for classification requires a principle for its basis, and neither observation nor memory can supply this. Introspection, as a method of classification and explanation, has been noted rather as a source of illusions and deceptions in psychology than as the source of scientific comprehension. Introspection must, therefore, be carefully distinguished from self-knowledge. Knowledge of self is the whole sphere of intelligence or mind; introspection is the direction of mind in one limited channel, to the observation of particular states. I[1-3]

13.34–35 sense organs] W;   sense-organs I[1+]

13.37–14.1   The method . . . uses physiological] I[2+];   This is the department of psycho-physics. It differs from physiology in that the latter investigates only the physical processes of life, while psycho-physics makes use of these I[1]

13.39   psychical] I[4+];   psychica- I[2-3]

14.1   *physio-|logical*] I[4+];   *physial|logical* I[2-3]

14.11–12 nerve and cerebral physiology cannot of themselves] I[2+]; what is ordinarily called physiological psychology cannot I[1]

16.24   imagination,] I[2+];   imagination, at least, I[1]

*19.19   the] W;   a I[1+]

19.27   involves] I[2+];   is an act of I[1]

19.27   since] I[2+];   whether it be I[1]

19.27–28 tree, in the] I[2+];   tree, the I[1]

19.28   or in] I[2+];   or I[1]

20.32   act] I[2+];   item I[1]

24.22   is potentially] I[2+];   is I[1]

26.6   topics] I[2+];   heads I[1]

26.22–23 successive stages] I[2+];   concrete forms I[1]

29.2–12 *Sensation Identified* . . . eye, etc.] I[4+];

            Definition.—The elements of intelligence which, through their combinations, constitute knowledge are termed sensations. Sentience is the term used to express the capability of the mind for sensations, while the specific organs which realize this capacity are called sensory, or simply the senses. A sensation may be generically defined as *any consciousness arising in the self through some bodily occasion.* More specifically, it is the *elementary consciousness which arises from the reaction of the soul upon a nervous impulse conducted to the brain from the affection of some sensory nerve-ending by a physical stimulus.* I^{1-3}

31.21–22 nineteen] I^{4+}; fourteen I^{2-3}; twenty I^1

31.26–27 whizzing] I^{2+}; whirring I^1

31.28 three hundred and ninety-two] I^{4+}; four hundred and fifty-one I^{1-3}

31.31 finishes] I^{4+}; appears I^{1-3}

31.34 effects most largely] I^{4+}; effects below warmth I^{2-3}; effects I^1

32.21–22 the stimulus without chemical change] I^{4+}; the sound stimulus in vibratory form I^{1-3}

34.24–37.18 *Erroneous Theory . . .* psychical condition.] I^{4+};

Double Meaning of Term Sensation.—The term "sensation" is ambiguous. It may refer either to an event in mental life or to the significance of this event. In referring, for example, to a sensation of red we may mean either a mental affection or the quality suggested by this affection. The sensation, as an occurrence or excitation, may occur without any relation to anything else, as when one, in the midst of silence, is affected by a loud noise. The excitation, as a new event in consciousness, comes in abruptly and without connection with other experiences. But the quality of the sensation, the recognition of the sound and of its various characteristics, is not thus a new and original state. Recognition of quality requires comparison and association. The significance of the sensation cannot be known excepting through activity of intelligence, bringing it into complex relations. On the two points immediately following we are to speak of sensation simply as excitation, or mental affection. So considered,

1. *It is an Elementary Consciousness.*—One object of every science is to analyze or decompose complex phenomena into their simpler constituent elements. Thus the chemist attempts to account for the phenomena of the reaction of bodies upon each other by the supposition that there are certain primordial, unanalyzable atoms from whose composition and ways of acting the more complex

facts result. So the physicist finds himself compelled, for the sake of simplicity of explanation, to suppose the existence of a physically unanalyzable unit, the molecule. The psychologist finds himself, in a similar way, confronted with facts which are indefinitely more complex than those of chemistry or physics. He finds himself forced, accordingly, to the supposition of a psychical unit beyond further analysis, and forming the basis and material out of which the concrete forms of knowledge are built up by means of certain processes and laws to be hereafter studied. This elementary unit he calls a sensation.

2. *It is a Subjective Consciousness.*—This term, subjective, does not mean simply that sensation is a psychical, not a physical, state; that it exists for the self, and is not a bare existing fact. This is true of all the phenomena of consciousness. It is here used to distinguish sensations from those facts of psychical life which have an *objective reference.* Such facts tell us about things and events that exist independently of ourselves, about something which is really there, as we say. They enable us to appreciate or apprehend something objective. Thus I know 'that this paper is white, the ink is black, etc. I do not mean that there is a feeling in my mind of white paper or of black ink, but that the real paper is really white, etc. Such states of mind evidently go beyond themselves, and tell us of something objective. It is not so with sensations. They have no reference to things really there. They tell of nothing beyond their own existence. They do not tell us what some *thing is;* they only report how the *subject* is *excited.*

Sensations not Actual Knowledge.—Hence sensations are not, *as excitations*, knowledge. They are the necessary conditions or raw material of knowledge. Knowledge always refers to an object, and to get this reference to an object the sensation must be elaborated and transformed and made to point to something beyond itself. The means by which the objective reference is got will be studied under the head of the processes of knowledge. It is sufficient to notice now that sensations become knowledge only as they are related to each other in certain definite ways. To know is not merely to have a sensation, but to refer this sensation either to an external object, as the thing having a quality corresponding to the sensation, or to ourselves.

Properties of Sensation.—These may be reduced to

four: *duration, quality, intensity,* and *extensity.* All psychical states occupy a certain time, have a certain characteristic content all their own, fill consciousness with a certain
force, and occupy, as it were, a certain area. These properties cannot, strictly speaking, be described or defined any
more than what color is can be told to a blind man. But
each one knows for himself that a sound, for example,
occupies a certain length of time in his consciousness; that
it is something peculiar to itself, not to be confounded or
compared with a color or a taste; and that it is either weak
as a whisper or strong as the sound of a cannon. By extensity is meant a certain massiveness or voluminousness
in sensation, illustrated by the difference between, say, the
squeak of a slate-pencil and the reverberations of thunder,
or between a drop of rain and a plunge into water.

4. *Sensations may be Classified.*—Each quality or
modality forms a class by itself. As already pointed out
(page 31), the soul answers to the stimulus originating in
all nerve organs with a characteristic response, and hence
there will be as many classes of sensations as there are
kinds of organs. As almost every nerve structure in the
body may, under appropriate conditions, occasion sensations, it would follow that we may have an indefinitely
large number of classes of sensation. But, fortunately, certain general features are found which broadly mark off
these organs from each other. Some of these organs are
found to be specifically formed for giving rise to sensations
—as the eye for light, the ear for sound; while nerves connected with other organs—as the stomach, the lungs—have
as their main business the regulation of some bodily function—as digestion, respiration—and only secondarily and
incidentally occasion conscious states. This leads to the
broad division of sensations into specific, and organic or
general. I²⁻³;

1. *It is an Elementary Consciousness.*—One object of
every science is to analyze or decompose complex phenomena into their simpler constituent elements. Thus the
chemist attempts to account for the phenomena of the
reaction of bodies upon each other by the supposition that
there are certain primordial, unanalyzable atoms from
whose composition and ways of acting the more complex
facts result. So the physicist finds himself compelled, for
the sake of simplicity of explanation, to suppose the existence of a physically unanalyzable unit, the molecule. The

psychologist finds himself, in a similar way, confronted with facts which are indefinitely more complex than those of chemistry or physics. He finds himself forced, accordingly, to the supposition of a psychical unit beyond further analysis, and forming the basis and material out of which the concrete forms of knowledge are built up by means of certain processes and laws to be hereafter studied.

Nature of Sensation.—This elementary unit he calls a sensation. The sensation is not a fact immediately present in consciousness. We do not have direct knowledge of it any more than we do of the atom or molecule. Actual mental life is concrete, not made up of isolated atomic sensations. It is thoroughly complex, and no simple element can be immediately laid hold of. In fact, knowledge always consists in *relation*—in the connection of elements, and their mutual reference to each other—and so no isolated, unrelated sensation, such as we suppose forms the material of knowledge, could possibly be immediately known. Sensations are known, then, only as the result of a process of abstraction and analysis, and their existence is supposed only because, without them, it would be impossible to account for the complex phenomena which are directly present in consciousness.

2. *It is a Subjective Consciousness.*—This term, subjective, does not mean simply that sensation is a psychical, not a physical, state; that it exists for the self, and is not a bare existing fact. This is true of all the phenomena of consciousness. It is here used to distinguish sensations from those facts of psychical life which have an *objective reference.* Such facts tell us about things and events that exist independently of ourselves, about something which is really there, as we say. They enable us to appreciate or apprehend something objective. Thus I know that this paper is white, the ink is black, etc. I do not mean that there is a feeling in my mind of white paper or of black ink, but that the real paper is really white, etc. Such states of mind evidently go beyond themselves, and tell us of something objective. It is not so with sensations. They have no reference to things really there. They tell of nothing beyond their own existence. They do not tell us what some *thing is;* they only report how the *subject* is *affected.*

Sensations not Actual Knowledge.—Hence sensations are not, *of themselves*, knowledge. They are the necessary conditions or raw material of knowledge. Knowledge always refers to existence, and to get this reference to existence the sensation must be elaborated and transformed and made to point to something beyond itself. The means by which the objective reference is got will be studied under the head of the processes of knowledge. It is sufficient to notice now that sensations become knowledge only as they are related to each other in certain definite ways. To know is not merely to have a sensation, but to refer this sensation either to an external object, as the thing having a quality corresponding to the sensation, or to ourselves. This analysis of complex forms of knowledge into simple units, which are not by themselves knowledge, but only the raw material of knowledge, however hard to make at first, is one necessary for any comprehension of the facts of cognition.

    3. *The Elementary Subjective Conditions of Knowledge Possess certain Original Properties.*—These may be reduced to three: *duration, quality,* and *intensity.* All psychical states occupy a certain time, have a certain characteristic content all their own, and fill consciousness with a certain force. These properties cannot, strictly speaking, be described or defined any more than what color is can be told to a blind man. But each one knows for himself that a sound, for example, occupies a certain length of time in his consciousness; that it is something peculiar to itself, not to be confounded or compared with a color or a taste; and that it is either weak as a whisper or strong as the sound of a cannon. It is to the characteristic difference between a taste and a smell that the term quality or modality applies, while intensity signifies the difference between, say, a dim and a bright light.

    4. *Sensations may be Classified.*—Each quality or modality forms a class by itself. As already pointed out (page 31), the soul answers to the stimulus originating in all nerve organs with a characteristic response, and hence there will be as many classes of sensations as there are kinds of organs. As almost every nerve structure in the body may, under appropriate conditions, occasion sensations, it would follow that we may have an indefinitely large number of classes of sensation. But, fortunately, certain general features are found which broadly mark off these organs from each other. Some of these organs are found to be specifically formed for giving rise to sensations—as the eye for light, the ear for sound; while nerves connected with other organs—as the stomach, the

lungs—have as their main business the regulation of some
bodily function—as digestion, respiration—and only secondarily and incidentally occasion conscious states. This leads
to the broad division of sensations into specific, and organic
or general. I[1]

35.21   sense organs] W;   sense-|organs I[4+]
40.7   *quantitative*] I[2+];   complete I[1]
43.28   psychical.] I[2+];   psychical. This is seen in two ways: I[1]
43.29–45.10   (2) Sensation is . . . to existence.] I[2+];

(1.) *From the Two Elements Involved in Sensation.*—
There is no sensation without both the physical action of
the body in the shape of motion, and psychical action in
the way of the soul's response to it. Attempts to do away
with either of these elements are equally futile. Thus, on
one side, the soul *completes* nature. What significance or
value would nature have for us were it nought but a never-
ending, monotonous series of motions? All the variety of
nature as it appears to us, all that gives it interest, the
infinite difference in colors and sounds, in shapes and
forms, etc.—all this is due to the response of the soul to
simple motions.

Sensations not Subjective States Alone.—Sensations,
accordingly, are not mere subjective states of our own
absolutely separated from nature. As Lotze says: "Sound
and color are no worse because they are simply *our* sensations. They constitute, in fact, the exact end which nature
was aiming at with its waves of ether and light, but which
it could not accomplish by itself alone. To reach this end
it needed soul, so that there might be realized through the
action of the soul in sensation the beauty of shimmering
light and of ringing sound." As the soul is the completion
of nature, so nature in the form of physical motions is
necessary to the activity of the soul. Were it not stimulated
by them, it would remain an eternal blank, never revealing
itself in the endless riches of manifestation which it now
shows forth.

(2.) *From the Two Principles Involved in Sensation.*
—On the one hand, there is the *psychical* principle by
which the soul develops an utterly new state, something
which can be accounted for only by attributing to the soul
original and unique powers, transcending the highest
principle of physical action—that of the correlation of
energy. But, on the other hand, there is the *mechanical*
principle. The physical stimulus is necessary, and, once

given, the soul reacts upon it with a necessity and invariability comparable only to the mechanical processes of nature. It is not left to the soul to say whether there shall be a sensation or not, nor of what kind it will please to have it. The fact of the order, constancy, and certainty of sensations requires the mechanical principle for their comprehension, as much as the fact that they are states of consciousness requires the psychical.

2. *Sensations as Raw Material of Knowledge.*—Out of the stuff of sensations, upon them as data, are built both the world as known and the self as existing. There is no need of dwelling upon this here, as the whole subject of knowledge will but illustrate the means by which this raw material of sensation is worked up into the concrete forms of knowledge. The existence of sensation is equally necessary on both subjective and objective sides. Without it the self would remain forever unrealized, a mere bundle of capacities, and the world would remain forever unidealized or unknown, a mere blank. From the sensations of various kinds, through their elaboration by processes hereafter to be studied, are built up the concrete forms of the world as it exists for our knowledge, and are constructed those definite ways of knowing which make the soul, on its intellectual side, a reality.

We have now to study these various kinds of sensations, having determined the nature of sensation in general. I¹

45.12–47.35   *The Original Sensation . . . of vibration.*] I⁴⁺;

Kinds of Sensations.—Sensations are classified, as already stated, into specific and general: those originating through organs especially adapted for their production, and those which are occasioned incidentally through organs whose main function is the regulation of some organic activity. Both of these orders of sensations are subdivided into classes. Lest it may be thought from this that they have no likeness in kind, it may be well to precede their particular study by a few remarks regarding touch, as the connecting link of the various classes of sensation.

Touch, as Fundamental Sense.—Whether we study this sense from its physiological side, the organ through which it is realized, or from the psychological side, the conscious states in which it is expressed, we are led to the conclusion that touch is the fundamental sense.

1. *Physiological.*—If we consider the organism pos-

sessing the lowest form of nervous apparatus, we find it to be capable of responding to stimuli of immediate contact only. Yet there is evidence that these organisms appreciate stimuli which we cannot appreciate through the sense of touch. Differences of color, for example, call forth various actions on the part of the organism; there is no evidence to show that this is appreciated as difference of color, but it is felt in some way, so as to call forth different actions. This gives us reason for believing that originally the organs of touch serve in an undifferentiated way for the reception of all stimuli whatever. This conclusion is strengthened when we find that, as we advance in the animal scale, each new sensory organ is developed out of the same layer of the body that contains the touch organs; and these new organs seem to be but higher developments of portions serving previously to discriminate sensations of contact.

2. *Psychological.*—This is the result which we should have been led to expect, looking at the matter psychologically. Motion is, as we have seen, the sole stimulus of sensation; and motion can affect the body only by actual contact with it. The various sense organs are thus organs differentiated for the reception of various modes of motion, *i.e.*, for various kinds of contact. Touch, as we know it, is immediate contact; hearing, receiving waves of some ponderable medium, brings us in contact, as it were, with bodies at a distance; while the eye, sensible to etheric vibrations, extends the range of contact indefinitely. As long ago as the times of the Greek Democritus, it was remarked that all the senses are reducible to touch. There are also other striking psychological peculiarities of touch.

(1.) *It Forms the Connection between the General and the Special Senses.*—(i.) It is like general sensation, since it has no especially differentiated organ, but is distributed by means of the skin over the whole body. It is like the special senses, since this organ gives rise to contact sensations, specifically, not incidentally. (ii.) It passes by gentle gradations into each. Sensations of tickling, tingling, and pricking, with those of heat and cold, scattered over the whole body, connect touch with organic sensation. Such facts as that vibrations between about thirty and forty thousand per second are felt as sound, while below thirty they seem to be actual jars, and above forty thousand whirs in the body itself, and that in the blind and deaf touch serves for eye and ear, show the affinity of touch with the special senses. (*iii.*) It stands midway between general and specific sensation with reference to feeling or emotional tone. In organic sensations the factor of feeling predominates above the cognitive aspect. Such sensations serve rather to tell us whether the organism is affected pleasantly or the reverse, than to give us knowledge about objects. The reverse is the case with specific sensation. In touch it is difficult to tell which element predominates. That contact sensations are the basis of a large store of knowledge cannot be denied, while the importance of their emotional side is shown by the fact that in ordinary language to *feel* anything is to touch it.

(2.) *Touch also Occupies a Unique Psychological Position, by Virtue of its Connection with the Muscular System.*—No nerve organ can be purely passive, even physically speaking, in sensation. It must adjust itself to the stimulus. The mouth must secrete saliva and move the sapid substance about. We must sniff with the nostrils. The tympanum of the ear must be stretched; the eye-lenses must be accommodated, and the two eyes converged, and each must have muscular connections. But the connection of contact sensations with muscular sensations is still more

† intimate. They are inextricably united [Normally they are
† inextricably united. I^{2-3}]. It is only in cases of [It is only in I^{2-3}] disease that we ever have one without the other. Thus the activities of our own body and those of external bodies are indissolubly associated from the first. The whole importance of this we shall learn hereafter.

(3.) *Touch is the Test Sense*, as well as the source of the others. They return to it, as well as proceed from it. It is the gold basis from which the other senses issue promises to pay. We may have sensations of light which are produced within the organism itself; noises may be subjective "roarings;" smells and tastes, etc., may arise from a disordered organism. The test of whether something exists corresponding to the sensation is always an appeal to touch, with its associated muscular activity. We are sure the object is really there when we can *get hold of it*. The sparks we see when we fall we know to belong to ourselves, and not to the object, because they are not associated with some constant touch sensation; they change position with every change of position of the body. I^{1-3}

48.29 although their stimulation is not always] I^{2+}; the stimulation of which appears to be I^1

49.2–5 These are (1) sensations . . . place sensations.] I^{4+}; Two kinds are recognized: (1), pressure sensations, due to the weight of the affecting body; (2), place sensations, due to the position of the body affected. I$^{1-3}$

49.13 thirteenth] I^{4+}; third I$^{1-3}$

49.15 1/13] I^{4+}; 1/3 I$^{1-3}$

49.17 30] I^{4+}; 10 I$^{1-3}$

49.17 2⅓] I^{4+}; 3⅓ I$^{1-3}$

49.21 13:14] I^{4+}; 3:4 I$^{1-3}$

49.36 1/13] I^{4+}; 1/3 I$^{1-3}$

49.37 1/19] I^{4+}; 1/16 I$^{1-3}$

50.1 1/19] I^{4+}; 1/16 I$^{1-3}$

51.20–21 a distinction between . . . of it: that is, we] I^{2+}; that it simply expresses a universal law of psychical judgment: that we I^{1}

52.9–26 *Discriminating Power* . . . other hand.] I^{4+};

Sensory Circles.—That portion of the skin which has a local sign of its own is known as a sensory circle, and the skin is regarded as made up of a myriad of these circles. They differ much in size in various parts of the body, as is shown by the following simple experiment. The dulled points of a pair of compasses are placed upon the skin, separated from each other a certain distance, and the person touched tells whether he feels two points or one. The spatial separation of the two points necessary for the recognition of two distinct sensations measures the diameter of that portion of the body which has one and the same local sign; that is, the sensory circle. The discriminative sensibility is greatest upon the tongue. There two separate sensations are recognized when the points are 1/24 of an inch apart. Upon the tip of the fingers the distance discriminated is 1/12 of an inch, while upon the middle of the back the points must be separated at least 1½ inches. I$^{1-3}$

53.2–55.12 *Meaning of Muscular Sensation* . . . for them.] I^{4+};

1. *Physical Stimulus.*—This is broadly marked off from that of the other senses in arising from an activity originated by the organism itself, not by an external affection. It stands opposed to the other senses as active to passive. As long as the muscle is merely affected by strain or pressure from without there is contact sensation alone. Muscular sensation arises only when the organism *reacts* against the pressure. It is due to the body's own exertion.

2. *Organ.*—There are three theories regarding the physiological process which ultimately results in sensation.

(1.) One theory holds that there are specific sensory nerves which end with certain organs in the muscles, and that the muscular sensations take their rise there, just as visual sensations do in the retina of the eye.

(2.) Another theory holds that there are no specific
† muscular nerve organs [sensations I²⁻³], but that the so-
† called muscular sensations [those so-called I²⁻³] are in reality produced by the tension, the push and pull, of the muscles against the skin, ligaments, joints, etc.

(3.) The third theory is known as the innervation theory, and holds that the sensation is of central, not peripheral *origin*, and is a feeling of effort or *expended energy*. It originates in the brain and is transmitted
† [*energy*, originating in the brain and transmitted out I²⁻³] along the motor nerves. It is probable that while each of these theories may have an element of truth within it, the second approaches nearest to the real state of the case.

3. *The Sensations.*—These are most conveniently divided into sensations of (1) movement, or unhindered effort, and those of (2) strain, or impeded effort. The muscles may contract freely without experiencing external resistance, or they meet external obstruction. The sweep of the arm through the air illustrates the first; the pushing of a box the second. Sensations of movement vary with the *direction* of the movement, whether it be up or down, right or left, and with its *duration*, whether it be performed swiftly or slowly. Sensations of resistance vary in *intensity* according to the amount of resistance which has to be overcome.

Psychological Importance.—The muscular sensations are exceedingly important, both in themselves and in their combination with other classes.

(*i*.) *In Themselves.*—The sensations of duration and direction of movement, combined with that of force exerted, enable us to get a very accurate knowledge of the position and tension of various muscles, and thus forms the basis of our knowledge of our own body, and gives us the basis for discriminating our own body from extra-organic bodies. Furthermore, since knowledge of the position of the body and of its various parts is the necessary condition of performing any intentional movement, the

muscular sensations are as important for volition as for
knowledge. The muscular sensation constantly reports to
consciousness the exact condition of the position and tension
of all voluntary muscles, and thus enables the mind to
control old movements and instigate new ones.

(*ii.*) *In Connection with Other Senses.*—Of the union
of muscular sensation with that of touch we shall presently
speak. With reference to vision, it may be noticed that the
eye is liberally supplied with a complex and carefully
adjusted system of muscles, which makes it the easiest
moved and most discriminating in its movements of all
the organs of the body. The muscles also are so arranged
that the mechanism of each eye is internally regulated,
and the two eyes always act in unison. For hearing,
muscular sensations are important in three ways. First,
they enable the mechanism of the ear to be so arranged
that the ear is adjusted to the greatest possible range of
sounds, and to the most delicate discrimination of any
sound. Secondly, they form the connection between the
organs of speech and hearing, and thus render it possible
to reproduce, voluntarily, tones and noises. Thirdly, they
form the connection between sounds and certain regular
movements—those of marching, dancing, etc.—and thus
greatly sharpen, if they do not actually incite, the sense of
rhythm. In the sense of taste, the muscles serve to keep
the food in motion, thus varying the sensation and bringing it in contact with the most sensitive parts; while in
smell it is found that, without constant motion of the
odorous gas, occasioned by sniffing, there is no sensation
of odor produced. I[1-3]

55.25   ⅟₁₉] I[4+];   ⅟₁₆ I[1-3]
55.26   ⅟₁₃] I[4+];   ⅓ I[1-3]
58.18   taste-buds] I[2+];   papillæ I[1]
59.20-21 from, say, twenty] I[4+];   from fourteen I[2-3];   from eighteen
         I[1]
59.23   vibration of the amplitude] I[4+];   wave width I[2-3];   wave
         length I[1]
59.24   has] I[4+];   possesses I[1-3]
59.26   of] I[4+];   to I[1-3]
59.34   *basilar*] I[4+];   *basilear* I[1-3]
60.16   tone-color] I[2+];   tone, color I[1]
61.11   whizzing] I[2+];   whirring I[1]
61.16   occasions] I[2+];   occasion I[1]
62.20-34 *Musical Tones . . . combinations.*] I[4+];

> *Physical Basis.*—Vibrations, as already said, differ in form. One is elliptic, another perpendicular, another of a third form, etc., as the vibrations of a pendulum, a trip-hammer, a cord, a membrane. Now, it is discovered that of these only that of a pendulum or tuning-fork is simple; all others may be regarded as complex, composed of the union of a number of these simple vibratory units. These bear certain definite numerical ratios to each other. All beside the simple one are in integral multiple ratio to the simple; that is, their *rates* are to the rate of the simple vibration as 1, 2, 3, 4, etc., are to one. The vibrations of a piano will have one set and combination of these ratios, that of an organ another, and this property is the physical basis of tone quality. I^{1-3}

64.2–3   three hundred and ninety-two] I^{4+};   four hundred and fifty-one I^{1-3}

64.6   indirectly.] I^{4+};   indirectly through the so-called actinic effect. I^{1-3}

65.29–30 and that the retinal elements stimulated are a mosaic-work.] I^{4+};   interrupted by the blind spot, and, in general a mosaic-work. I^{1-3}

66.22–23 in the daytime we do not see the light of the stars in addition to that of the sun] I^{4+};   we do not see the stars in the daytime I^{1-3}

67.34   millimetre] W;   millimeter I^{1+}

69.2   barely sensitive of] I^{2+};   sensitive to no kind of I^{1}

69.18–19 Again the heat and cold spots do not] I^{2+};   Neither do the heat and cold spots I^{1}

69.22   cocaine] I^{19+};   cocoaine I^{1-18}

75.21–76.1 By an object . . . it is felt.] I^{4+};   This characteristic presents a double contrast to the properties of sensations.

†   (1.) Sensations, [— I^{2-3}] smells, tastes, etc., [— I^{2-3}] are purely subjective. They exist only as affections of the mind. What we know is objective. It exists as a reality beyond the bodily organism. It follows from this that while sensations are necessarily transitory, passing away as they are experienced, the objects known are permanent, existing whether they occasion sensations or not. (2.) The sensations are not, as such, connected or related with one another. Each is itself separate and distinct from every other. I^{1-3}

76.34   coexistence] W;   co-existence I^{1+}

*78.10   is] W;   *is* I^{1+}

78.22   whatever] I^{2+};   and which I^{1}

79.7   existence] I^{2+};   existences I^{1}

*79.22   relations] W;   relation I^{1+}

79.23–25 Such relations . . . life] I^{2+}; If ideas are related both to those existing *simultaneously* and *successively*, all elements are connected, and our mental life, both as a whole and in its particulars, I^1

79.37 each other] I^{2+}; each I^1

79.38 a] I^{2+}; one I^1

81.28–32 that activity . . . felt.] I^{4+}; the relating activity which combines the various sensuous elements presented to the mind at one time into a whole, and which unites these wholes, occurring at successive times, into a continuous mental life, thereby rendering psychical life intelligent. I^{1-3}

*81.29   through] W; though I^{4+}

84.4 43] W; 44 I^{4+}; 45 I^{1-3}

85.3–88.10 The mind binds . . . or end.] I^{4+}; These are either *simultaneous* or *successive*. To state the law in amplified form: The mind combines into a whole all sensations occurring at the same time, and connects successively all ideas thus formed.

  I. *Simultaneous Association.*—The law of simultaneous association is that *whenever any associating activity occurs for the first time, all elements present are fused into one whole.* This is as necessary for knowledge as the presence of the sensations. It is this fusion which insures that sensory elements do not remain so many isolated atoms, but combine with each other into definite forms. Two varieties of fusion may be recognized: (1) that in which the elements combined are those of the same sense; (2) that in which they are of different senses.

  1. Under this head comes, first, the summation of the various minute stimuli necessary to occasion a state of consciousness. Not every stimulus is felt, but the stimuli must reach a certain number per second, varying with each sense organ, before feeling results. Were not they [they not I^{2-3}] associated as they occurred, no cumulation would occur. But other forms of fusion occur. The tone which we hear, for example, is always composite, though it may seem to consciousness ultimate and unanalyzable. There must be first, as just stated, cumulation of at least eighteen stimuli per second, and then the tone will have a definite quality due to the presence of partial tones along with the fundamental. Any of our ordinary color sensations is a fused product also. It is made up of three elementary sensations, of red, green, and violet. Even that sensation which we ordinarily call red is not saturated red, but has some trace

of green and violet in it, as may be shown by tiring the nerves which respond to green and violet, when the isolated red stands out much deeper than before. This fusion is shown also in the phenomena of color blindness.

2. *Sensations Occurring through Various Organs are also Fused.*—Flavor, for example, is a combination of tactile, gustatory, and odoriferous elements. The association of muscular sensations with those of the other senses has already been noticed. In ordinary optical sensation there is at least a triple association. There is, first, the color or visual sensation proper, itself compound, as just explained; there is, secondly, the muscular sensation, itself the fused result of the sensations coming from all the muscles of both eyes; and there is, thirdly, the local sign, due to the part of the retina affected. This may serve as an example of the amount of fusion involved in an apparently simple sensation.

Transition from Simultaneous to Successive Associa-tion.—It is evident that the same activity may occur twice. The mind which exerts the activity is the same; the elements upon which it is put forth may not vary. I saw the color, red, yesterday; and I see it again to-day. That is, the same self performs the same associating activity resulting in the apperception of red. Now, if the associating activity were always thus identical, in all its members, we should never know that there was more than one activity, and hence succession would never arise in our conscious life. This would remain simultaneous, that is, without connection of different ideas.

Introduction of Differential Elements.—But this con-dition of complete identity is not fulfilled. There are variable elements introduced, due either to change in the mind exercising the activity, or in the elements associated. The self which exists to-day is indeed the same self which acted yesterday, but it is the same self with a difference. The self which has once apperceived red is not quite the same that it was before, and the further apperception of blue will still further alter it, and so on. The self, in its *specific* character, in short, is changed by every experience through which it passes. On the other hand, the elements combined are con-stantly changing. I do not always see red, nor even red and blue. Novel sensations are constantly presenting themselves. Now this double variation necessitates a variation in the *activity*. If neither the mind acting, nor the elements acted upon, are quite the same, the resulting act must differ. It is this change in activity which brings the successive element into our experience, and which breaks up the dull monotone of simultaneity of psychical life into the rich, variegated succession which actually characterizes it.

II. *Successive Association.*—The law of successive association is as follows: *When any associating activity recurs, all elements which have been previously involved in it, recur also.* Successive association is, therefore, based on simultaneous. It takes place only when some activity *recurs*, and recurrence implies previous occurrence. It may be called *connective* association, as simultaneous association is fusion. In this connection, neither of the two factors of identity and difference may be left out of the account. On one hand, were there no point of identity between the present activity and some previous one, there would be no succession, for there would be no continuous mental life. There would be a new psychical life, which would no more enter into succession with my past life than any other life does with mine now. On the other hand, if there were no element of difference in the midst of identity, there would be no succession, because there would be no change.

Redintegration.—Connective association presents the following features: An associative activity which occurs is, partially at least, a recurrence of some previous activity; that is, has some elements the same. Consequently, according to the law, all the elements of this original association recur also. Were they wholly like they would be immediately fused in the present. But certain elements of the one are unlike those of the other, and this offers an obstacle to their fusion. This different element will accordingly stand out separately, or get an independent existence. This element is thus at the same time called up because of its presence in the same activity formerly, and repelled from fusion in the present activity because of its incongruity with it. Being present in consciousness, and, at the same time, repelled from the existent consciousness, it must follow upon it. This is the essence of successive association, or, as it is sometimes called, *re-presentation.* It is also known as *redintegration.* The original fusion, uniting various sensory elements into one whole, may be termed integration. In redintegration an activity, on recurring, completes itself by restoring all elements which were previously involved in it, although they are not now sensuously present. They are re-presented. I[1-3]

*86.34   a] W;   *omitted* I⁴⁺
88.18   difference. At some time,] I²⁺;   difference at some time. I¹
88.30   the idea either] I²⁺;   either the idea I¹
89.7–8   (2) By similarity, together with their laws and sub-varie-
           ties.] I²⁺;   2. By similarity; 3. The function of association
           in the psychical life. I¹
89.26   coexisting] W;   co-existing I¹⁺
93.25   write] I²⁺;   unite I¹
*96.10   accompanies] W;   accompany I¹⁺
105.22–23 at some time] I²⁺;   sometimes I¹
106.10   In the integrated totality] I⁴⁺;   As already noticed I¹⁻³
108.12   dissociation] I²⁺;   association I¹
*115.19   for] W;   *for* I¹⁺
118.34   reference] I²⁺;   deference I¹
124.3   perform adjustment] I²⁺;   perform definite adjustment I¹
124.4   be decided] I²⁺;   be I¹
124.11   only in] I²⁺;   in his I¹
129.10   of] I²⁺;   the I¹
129.11   not interested] I²⁺;   interested I¹
133.34–135.2   *Retention is not . . .* former motions.] I²⁺;

Retention and Idealization.—Another reason for calling
the process of retention organization is the fact that the
elements retained become organically united with the self,
that is, become factors of the self, or ideal. Retention is the
process by which external, actually-existing material is
wrought over into the activities of self, and thus rendered
internal or ideal. It is a process by which existence is trans-
muted into significance; the not self into the self; bare fact
or data into intelligence. The sensuous existence has gone;
what remains is the ideal meaning, the value of the sensuous
datum for intelligence. The process of retention taken with
that of apperception is the means by which the universal
content, which is one side of the subject-matter of psychology, becomes wrought over into the individual self, which
is the other side (page 9). The reality of bare objective existence is lost in the ideal reality of existence in and for the
self. The process can have no end until the individual self
has become thoroughly organized, that is, until all possible
objects, events, and relations have been apperceived and
retained in the living unity of the self; until, in other words,
all possible facts have become idealized by being given
relation to the self.

The Process of Knowledge.—Retention and apperception are two sides of the process of knowledge. In appercep-

tion the universe, the world of things, events, and relations, comes to exist *for us*, that is, in conscious intelligence. This process occurs just to the extent to which we can idealize it by putting the self into it. In retention the self comes to exist as real; the mind realizes or objectifies itself just to the extent to which the world is apprehended and taken into self. Apperception occurs through the self; retention through the universe. Each process necessitates the other. The universe gets conscious existence for us as the individual self is read into it; the individual self becomes real as it finds itself in this universe. One side of the process of knowledge makes the universe individual by giving it its conscious unified existence in the self; the other makes the individual self universal by realizing its capacities in concrete forms of knowledge. Psychologically speaking, the world is objectified self; the self is subjectified world. In knowledge the world is taken into the mind and gets ideal meaning, and at the same time the self grows into likeness with the world, as the latter is taken into it and organically connected with it. Having studied the various activities of knowledge, we have now to study the forms in which it appears, or the stages of this development of world and of self. I[1]

137.2–138.7   We have finished . . . *Process*] I[2+];

KNOWLEDGE is, therefore, a self-developing process, one side of which results in the existence for consciousness of a world of things, events, and relations, while the other side results in the organized or realized existence of mind. The world known is the externalized self; the self existing is the known, or internalized world. Knowledge, accordingly, is not a purely individual process, which each carries on for himself, independently of all other intelligence. It is universal, as manifested by the fact that it consists in the development of a known universe, and by the fact that even the individual self which knows gets reality only as this universe is constructed in knowledge.

Knowledge not Arbitrary or Unreal.—The statement that knowledge is the construction by the mind of a universe must not be thought to mean that knowledge is arbitrary, or the universe a product of imagination, or of the processes of individual minds. It means that mind or intelligence is necessarily universal in its nature, and that the construction of the universe of knowledge is the necessary manifestation of this universal character of intelligence. Since the mind is universal, the world exists in the same universal or real

sense with it; it is a permanent objective reality, because
intelligence is a permanent objectifying activity. The knowledge of the finite individual is the process by which the
individual reproduces the universal mind, and hence makes
real for himself the universe, which is eternally real for
the complete, absolutely universal intelligence, since involved in its self-objectifying activity of knowledge. The
student will thus see more clearly what is meant by defining
psychology as the science of the reproduction of the universe
in and by the individual than he could when the definition
was made.

   Knowledge a Progressive Process.—Knowledge is,
therefore, in the individual, the gradual process by which
he realizes his selfhood, or the universal objective character
of intelligence. It is the process by which the individual is
lifted into universality of intelligence, as he constructs the
world which he knows. I¹

138.28–139.2   active integration . . . completing it.] I⁴⁺;   constructive, interpreting, idealizing activity of intelligence. The
particular objects of perception get their existence, as
known, through their relations to self. It follows from this,
secondly, that the other activities of mind do not bring
about a departure from reality, as they go beyond the
particular things to universal relations, but a nearer approach to it. The realities known in perception are not
realities *per se*, but only through their relation to the constructive activity of intelligence; and the other activities of
mind consist simply in developing these relations to intelligence, and thus coming more and more to consciousness
of the ultimate reality, intelligence itself. They, in short, are
necessary to the complete development of perception itself.
I¹⁻³

*139.7   as] W;   *as* I¹⁺
151.29   should] I²⁺;   would I¹
158.27   are] I²⁺;   is I¹
160.5   associative] W;   asso-|ative I¹⁺
160.17   given] I²⁺;   other I¹
164.5   arsis] I²⁺;   arthis I¹
168.25   are] I²⁺;   is I¹
169.30–31   attention] I²⁺;   apperception I¹
169.33   attention] I²⁺;   apperception I¹
169.36   dissociation] I²⁺;   association I¹
170.28   higher] I²⁺;   highest I¹
*170.34   subtle] W;   subtile I¹⁺

171.33   idealized element] I^{2+}; idealizing process I^1
171.35   actual existence] I^{2+}; direct presence I^1
172.29   weaning] I^{2+}; weaving I^1
173.6   that] I^{2+}; the I^1
173.8   explicitly freed] I^{2+}; freed I^1
173.10   Imagination] I^{2+}; The imagination I^1
174.3   side] I^{2+}; self I^1
174.10   unified life] I^{2+}; universal self I^1
*177.3   as] W; *as* I^{1+}
179.7–180.9 Every mental state . . . of production.] I^{4+}; Con-
          ception is, as the name implies, taking together into one
          idea the element of meaning common to a number of ob-
          jects and things. It is, as the German word (Begriff) sug-
          gests, the begrasping into one thought of the idea present
          in a plurality of objects. Conception is, in short, the simplest
          act of thinking; it is the apprehension of the universal, as
          perception is the apperception of the particular. We perceive
          this man; we conceive *man*. The perception of man is re-
          ferred to some present sensation; it is the idealization of
          this sensation, so that it symbolizes a present reality. The
          conception of man is not tied down to any particular ob-
          ject; the sensation which is its basis is idealized so that it
          symbolizes any and every man. It does not refer to all men,
          because it has part of the perception of every possible man
          in it as an existence; it refers to all men because it *means*
          all men; it is universal through its ideal element, or what it
          points to, not from its existence.

†   *The Existence of a Conception* [*Concept* I^{2-3}] *is Par-*
†   *ticular.*—The conception [concept I^{2-3}], like every other
†   mental content, is particular in its existence [*existence* I^{2-3}].
†   It occurs at a [definite I^{2-3}] given time in the psychical life,
†   and has sensuous basis and detail. The conception [concept
          I^{2-3}] of rose, of book, of gravitation, of law, is always, as
          to its existence, some particular image. It is only its mean-
          ing that is universal. This particular image *symbolizes* all
          objects of the kind. Between the image and the concept
          there is, as to mode of existence, no essential difference. The
          difference is in the laying of stress, of accent. In the image
          all emphasis is laid upon the concrete sensuous embodiment
          of the idea; in the concept the particular nature; the exist-
          ence, of the image, is entirely neglected. Let any one think
          of a locomotive, and he will find in his mind an image
          which is particular, an image which will differ, in different
          minds, from a vague outline to a pretty complete picture;

but this imagery, whether schematic or complete, is neglected in thinking the locomotive. Probably no one would be conscious of the existence of this definite image if he did not purposely look for it. What is experienced is only the symbolic quality of the image; its power of signifying the essential property, the *idea* of a locomotive. This applies to all locomotives, for without this idea, this meaning, no presentation would be interpreted as a locomotive. I$^{1-3}$

*179.11   fantasy] W;   phantasy I^{4+}

183.19   concept] I^{2+};   conception I^1

187.25   apperception consists] I^{2+};   they always consist I^1

188.11   should] I^{2+};   would I^1

188.24–25   Judgment is at one time synthetic, at another, analytic.] I^{2+};   Every judgment is at once analytic and synthetic. I^1

190.9–18 *Test of Truth* . . . be false.] I^{2+};

        Truth and Intelligence.—It is evident from this that truth is but another name for intelligence. Every act of intelligence is a relating act. Complete intelligence is completeness of relations; the perfect harmony of all relations with each other. From this standpoint it may be said that intelligence regards as false all that contradicts its own nature, and as true all that is in harmony with it. Truth, in short, is harmony with universal intelligence; this means not only harmony with all intelligences, but harmony with the universal workings of one's own intelligence. I^1

190.25   or the acquired system of relations] I^{2+};   which also constitutes intelligence I^1

192.16   the mediate factor.] I^{2+};   meaning, the *idea.* I^1

193.32   is dependent] I^{2+};   depends I^1

*194.23–24   of extension] I^{2+};   extension I^1

194.25   is to] I^{2+};   to I^1

*195.19–27   For example, . . . the event.] I^{2+};   One may say that *a posteriori* knowledge is based on *a priori*, for there would be no experience were it not for the presence of relation, of reason; or he may say that *a priori* is based on *a posteriori*, for it is but the complete development of experience; the development of experience to the point where it recognizes its own rational character, its meaning, which is always universal. I^1

198.28–29   Sensation, as mere psychical existence, does not constitute fact.] I^{2+};   Sensation does not constitute fact, as opposed to the activity of mind. I^1

216.13   *activity*] I^{2+};   an *activity* I^1

217.36–37   Qualitative feelings,] I^{2+};   feelings which cling to the

content experienced—Qualitative feelings. Then we have
(IV.) the Complex feelings, arising from a union of all
sources—the sentiments— I[1]

220.3   Connected with] I[2+];   One element of I[1]

220.3   may] I[2+];   must I[1]

220.33   Sensations] I[2+];   Feelings I[1]

226.6   excite] I[2+];   excited I[1]

233.11–13 *familiarity or*, (3) *novelty* of experience; (4) feelings of
contrast, (5) and of *continuance*.] I[2+];   *novelty or familiarity* of experience; (3) feelings of *contrast* and *continuance*. I[1]

*233.12   or] W;   *or* I[1+]

240.9–31 *Mere Feeling . . . the feeling.*] I[4+];

Connection with Self-realization.—Put from the side of
the self, the process is as follows: All feeling is an accompaniment of self-activity. The soul realizes itself partially in the body through organic processes, and this occasions sensuous feeling. It realizes itself also in the various
modes of activity by which it connects its present, past,
and future activities together. This occasions *formal* feeling.
But it realizes itself most adequately through the sphere of
objective relations. Without the psychical construction of
the various forms of knowledge and of volitional action, the
self would remain for the most part a bundle of undeveloped,
unrealized capacities. As we saw in studying knowledge
(page 153), the world of known objects and the self knowing are in reality two phases of the same process. The development of each depends upon the development of the
other. Relation to objects is more than a *means* of self-
development; it *is* the development of the self. Whatever
feeling accompanies self-development must, therefore, necessarily accompany this sphere of objective relation, and
vice versa. Feeling objectifies itself, for all activity of the
self results in objectification, and feeling is the accompaniment of the activity. I[1-3]

241.11–25 in their quality . . . *defined* feelings.] I[4+];   Feeling, like
knowledge, proceeds from the indefinite and particular to
the definite and universal. The growth of feeling towards
the *universal* occurs on the basis of its connection with the
objects of knowledge. As our cognitive life widens, our
emotional becomes more comprehensive. The growth of feeling towards the *definite* is due to its connection with the
ends of action. A feeling once associated with an object becomes a spring to action in a given direction, and as feeling
gets whatever universality the object possesses, so it as-

sumes whatever definiteness the action has. The actions, for
example, which are directed simply to the maintenance of
life in general are accompanied by vague, though intense,
feelings; those which aim to support it by some given line
of action, as a trade, will have the concomitant feelings cor-
respondingly specific, varying indeed with the especial trade
adopted, as carpentry or blacksmithing. I¹⁻³

244.26–27 *relations of objects*] I²⁺; felt relations of objects I¹
244.27 but] I²⁺; *but* I¹
251.5 real *values* in] I⁴⁺; properties of I¹⁻³
251.6 excite] I⁴⁺; excited I¹⁻³
251.11–12 objectified in ideas and actions] I⁴⁺; thoroughly objective and universal I¹⁻³
252.12–13 a voluptuary] I²⁺; every voluptuary I¹
252.15 results] I²⁺; result I¹
252.19 should] I²⁺; must I¹
254.5–11 There will be . . . a whole life.] I⁴⁺; It often occurs, therefore, that pleasure may be in opposition to happiness. The
satisfaction of some special interest may result in loss of
well-being; the exercise of some particular activity may
destroy the harmony of the various elements of the self.
And happiness is simply the feeling of well-being; of complete harmony of all interests and activities. I¹⁻³
262.9–10 to know which] I²⁺; which to know I¹
264.5 because] W; becauses I¹⁺
*264.35 according] W; accordingly I¹⁺
*267.2 as] W; *as* I¹⁺
268.35–269.8 the locomotive has . . . an idea.] I⁴⁺; it is beautiful
only so far as it is felt as embodying an idea in the harmonious relations of its factors. Its original constructor may
well have experienced æsthetic emotion when he saw before
him, in realized form, his own ideal plan. The conformity
between the idea and the existence would occasion æsthetic
satisfaction. In other words, there is idealization in knowledge, but it is unrecognized, only the objective relations
being felt. In the perception of beauty the ideal quality is
not only there, but it is felt to be there, and hence an
intimate connection with the perceiving subject is recognized. A personal value is always attributed to an æsthetic
object as it is not to an intellectual. I¹⁻³
269.34–35 material utterly fails.] I²⁺; utterly fails. I¹
269.37 that,] I²⁺; ∼ ∧ I¹
270.1 art] I²⁺; that art I¹
270.3–11 The freedom . . . the self.] I⁴⁺; It must regulate itself by

the actual; art by the ideal. The latter need conform only to the ideal, and to the necessity of so handling the sensuous form that it shall fitly express the ideal. Science reproduces by the understanding; art creates by the imagination. Art may not confine itself to a detailed portrayal of fact, but must depict the value, the significance for the self, of the fact. The obligations which rest upon it are that it shall faithfully get at this value or ideal, and with right feeling select and manipulate the form which is to embody it. I$^{1-3}$

271.19   into] I^{2+};   in I^1

271.38–272.10   There is no . . . and interests.] I^{4+};   Not only must it be kept free from all subordination to any person's private ends, but it must be freed from all subservience to anything outside itself. Any too open appearance of utility detracts from beauty. Too open appearance of any didactic or moral end detracts also. A work of art may instruct, but so far as it aims at instruction, it fails in beauty. It may elevate the character, but so far as its construction is made subservient to teaching a moral lesson, it is unbeautiful. Since the time

†   of Schelling [Schiller I$^{2-3}$] it has been recognized that æsthetic activity partakes of the nature of play. It has its end in its own free manifestation. Beauty exists for its own sake, and æsthetic feeling owes much of its quality to its being a feeling of spontaneous unconstrained action. I$^{1-3}$

272.13   ideality and universality;] I^{2+};   ideal and universal character; I^1

272.14   characterized] I^{2+};   marked I^1

272.27   The] I^{2+};   This I^1

273.17–33   *Adaptation and Economy* . . . and ill-adapted.] I^{2+};

We do not measure the beautiful object by our conception of self, but we realize the self through the perception of the object, and this act of realization of the ideal self, this embodying, in definite form, of the ideal hitherto vague and undeveloped, is accompanied by the thrill of harmony. It is not the harmony, the regularity, the proportion as objective, that is, as congruous relation of parts, which excites the feeling. The objective harmony would have no interest for us, that is, would awaken no feeling, were it not felt as manifesting or developing our nature into greater harmony. The harmony may be either universal or particular, that is to say, it may be in harmony with the universal ideal of human nature, or it may be in harmony with the particular ideal of itself which a given individual or generation has unconsciously before it. In

this connection what was said, in treating imagination, of
the pathetic fallacy may be referred to. I¹

275.23–24 two dimensions] I²⁺; one dimension I¹
275.24 actual] I²⁺; the actual I¹
282.38 others] I²⁺; self I¹
282.38 self] I²⁺; others I¹
283.34–36 identification with self of . . . own.] I²⁺; identification
of . . . own with self. I¹
283.36–37 of disgust itself,] I²⁺; which excites disgust, I¹
287.2 knowledge—it] I²⁺; knowledge. It I¹
288.1 types] I²⁺; tpye I¹
288.21 the strictly] I²⁺; strictly I¹
288.22 only] I²⁺; is only I¹
291.12 and] I²⁺; as I¹
295.10 to] I²⁺; of I¹
296.26 feeling] I²⁺; judgment I¹
299.2–10 The term . . . same act.] I²⁺; knowledge is the universal
aspect of consciousness; feeling, its individual. These two
aspects find their unity in will. Knowledge is that side of
consciousness which reports to us something that is; feeling that side which reports it *to me* or *to thee*. Every given
consciousness is both knowledge and feeling; it is feeling,
for it is mine; it is knowledge, for it has a content of significance. But a union of feeling and knowledge in one and
the same act is what we know generally as will. I¹
*300.13 as] W; *as* I¹⁺
300.26 energy] I²⁺; feeling I¹
300.32 self, it is] I²⁺; self, is I¹
300.32–33 the tendency to react upon this feeling] I²⁺; this feeling
plus the tendency to react upon it I¹
301.7 sense organ] W; sense-organ I¹⁺
301.9–10 unite in ganglia near] I²⁺; have points of meeting in I¹
301.29 impulses] I²⁺; those I¹
301.35 especially those of expression] I²⁺; those of expression
especially I¹
*302.6 as] W; *as* I¹⁺
302.11 going out] I²⁺; outgoing I¹
304.6 persons] I²⁺; those I¹
*304.27 its] *stet* I¹; his I²⁺
304.36 his knowing] I²⁺; knowing I¹
*304.36 nor] *stet* I¹; or I²⁺
305.23 is expressed by] I²⁺; of expression is I¹
305.28 third, that of] I²⁺; third, of I¹
305.29 last] I²⁺; latter I¹

307.14   point] I²⁺; points I¹
307.15   imitate] I²⁺; imitates I¹
*309.3   is] W; *is* I¹⁺
310.34   connection] I²⁺; relations I¹
314.7   desires] I²⁺; motives I¹
317.3   nor] I²⁺; and I¹
320.18   absolute end. Every] I²⁺; end. Each I¹
323.1–2   of some] I²⁺; some I¹
323.3   both] I²⁺; each I¹
323.21   the] I²⁺; those I¹
323.22   those] I²⁺; the act I¹
328.30   separate] I²⁺; separated I¹
328.38   reached,] I²⁺; ∼ — I¹
*329.24   is] W; *is* I¹⁺
332.8   Secondly it] I²⁺; But it also I¹
332.9   that] I²⁺; which I¹
337.31   externally] I²⁺; which are *externally* I¹
*338.34   result] W; results I¹⁺
344.21   lay] I²⁺; lies I¹
345.27–28   made . . . it] I²⁺; made (. . . it) I¹
348.14   will] I²⁺; shall I¹
350.12   the] I²⁺; that I¹
350.14   cause] I²⁺; causes I¹
362.15–16   *feeling*] I²⁺; feeling I¹

TEXTUAL NOTES

10.14   minds] The reading "mind" in all previous printings seems to be an original printer's error never recognized until the present edition. With "the thing known is such for all mind whatever", one may compare the almost exact parallel in 9.10–11, "facts presented *to* the selves or minds which know them". In the passage in question "minds" seems to be equated with the plural "intelligences", as also in 10.7–8 "it is open to *all* intelligences". Although "mind" in the singular can be a philosophical concept, Dewey is here appealing to specific and concrete "minds" or "intelligences" as representative of a group of thinking, intelligent persons.

19.19–20   the death] Although "a death of a friend" is not necessarily an error, the invariable phrase "the death of a friend", as in 18.24, 19.28, 19.33, 25.7 suggests that "a death" is the compositor's memorial anticipation that was never detected.

78.10 is] The setting of this word in italic in I^{1+} seems to be a simple compositorial confusion. On such analogies as 78.8, Dewey's definition, given in italic, would not include the purely syntactical "is" that introduces the definition.

79.22 relations] The plural form is required by the heading and the content of the paragraph, especially 79.23.

81.29 through] The omitted "r" in "through", overlooked in all previous printings (I^{1-26}), is supplied here as clearly required by the sense of the sentence.

86.34 a] In revising this section for I^4 where it first appeared, the author or the editor inadvertently omitted the article, and the error was not corrected in subsequent printings. The editors have supplied the article for the present edition.

96.10 accompanies] The accidental combination of a collective singular but a plural verb escaped correction in all printings (I^{1-26}). The editors here correct it for the first time.

115.19 for] See note at 78.10.

139.7 as] See note at 78.10.

170.34 subtle] The reading "subtile" in all printings need not imply a distinction between "subtle" and "subtile" in the modern manner, which Dewey seems never to have made. Instead, "subtile" is merely an acceptable nineteenth-century spelling for "subtle"; but since Dewey seems not to have employed this old-fashioned spelling, the natural inference here is that a compositorial form has crept into the text.

177.3 as] See note at 78.10.

179.11 fantasy] Dewey's characteristic spelling "fantasy", as at 170.28, appears as "phantasy" in this section written for I^4 and continued in all subsequent printings. It is changed here to conform to the author's usual style.

194.14–195.27 The order of the two paragraphs between 194.14 and 195.27 was reversed in I^2. One internal change in heading at 194.14 is listed in the Special List of Emendations in Headings. Substantive changes within the reversed paragraphs appear in the List of Emendations in the Copy-Text.

233.12 or] See note at 78.10.

264.35 according] The context makes it sufficiently clear that "accordingly", the reading of all printings, is a simple error.

267.2 as] See note at 78.10.

300.13 as] See note at 78.10.

302.6 as] See note at 78.10.

304.27   its]   That the change from the I¹ "bird in building its nest" was intentional in I² to "his nest" is shown by the resetting of the type and its substitution in the plate. Moreover, no evidence exists that the type was reset in order to repair an accident to the plate, the error being inadvertently made in the process. The change of "its" to "his" must be taken as a conscious alteration. On the other hand, to accept the change as intentional is not necessarily to associate it with Dewey's known revisions in I². The probable cause for the error in I² is very likely to be found in a correction or revision nine lines below in the original in which the word "his" is inserted in I² before "knowing" in the phrase of I¹, "end without knowing what the end is". It seems probable that in some manner the printer in charge of bringing the plate for I² into conformity with a marked copy of I¹ mistook the direction and in addition to the insertion of "his", also in error substituted "his" for "its". Elsewhere Dewey refers to a bird building *its* nest, as in 310.14–15, "A bird in building its nest", and 310.17, "It builds".

304.36   nor]   The I² change to "or" of I¹ "nor" is quite certainly unauthoritative, the result of an alteration in the plate a few words earlier in the line in order to add the authoritative "his" after "without". The printer was short of space because of the addition and therefore omitted the "n" as a means of better justifying his new and crowded line. Dewey's customary idiom calls for the "nor": see "I do not always see red, nor even red and blue" I¹⁻³ 95.11–12; "The world of strict perception has no past nor future" I¹⁺ 154.6–7; "there exists no consciousness of the process involved, nor of the relation of the means" I¹⁺ 101.28–29. One should notice, also, that in I² 317.3 Dewey altered the "and" of I¹ to "nor": "No matter how strongly a certain thing is desired, and [I²⁺ nor] how firmly it has been chosen".

†

309.3   is]   See note at 78.10.

329.24   is]   See note at 78.10.

338.34   result]   The context requires correction of the overlooked error "results" found in all printings.

Emendations in notes and appendices

In the notes following each chapter and in the two appendices, A and B, of *Psychology*, Dewey listed a total of some 250 books and well over 50 articles for readers who wanted further information on the subjects discussed in the text. These references are chiefly in German and English, but there are also a number of titles in French, Italian, and Latin. This extensive use of works in other languages was the source of a number of spelling, punctuation, and substantive errors in the original printings of the reference notes and the appendices.

Additional difficulties in using these sections were caused by abbreviations of book titles and by the inconsistent and indiscriminate use of "*op. cit.*" When several works by the same author were mentioned, the "*op. cit.*" became practically valueless for the reader. In fact, this abbreviation was occasionally used when no prior reference to that author had occurred.

These problems were complicated by the fact that only the surnames of authors were used. There were several authors with the same surname as well as instances of misspelled names serious enough to lead to confusion between authors.

For the present edition, an exhaustive supplementary checklist of references has been prepared and appears immediately after the text of *Psychology*. This list has the author's full name, complete title of the work, and publication information. It can be used in conjunction with the reference notes and the appendices to identify any of the works to which Dewey referred.

No useful purpose would have been served by reproducing the notes and the appendices in their original form. To make these sections useful for the modern student, a number of editorial emendations in mechanical and punctuation matters were made silently. Each book title is listed the first time it appears in any section so that there is no "*op. cit.*" reference to the notes of any preceding chapter. If more than one work by an author is mentioned in a section, "*op. cit.*" refers only to his work last mentioned previously in that particular section. Each notes section and the appendices can thus be read independently of the preceding ones.

Other kinds of changes made silently were the following:

1. Commas were added where appropriate after such abbreviations as "*ibid.*"
2. Semicolons were consistently put outside quotation marks.
3. The period was deleted after small roman numerals referring to chapters, volumes, etc.
4. Accent marks were supplied on capital letters in German and French titles.
5. Abbreviations were regularized in "ch.", "introd.", "lect.", "bk."
6. The use of numbers with abbreviations was made consistent as follows: "ch.", small romans; "pt.", arabic; "vol.", small romans; "Series", spelled out, as in "Third Series".
7. Latin abbreviations were italicized: *ibid.*, *op. cit.*, *passim.*
8. Titles of books and periodicals were put in italics rather than double quotation marks.

All other changes made in the notes and the appendices as they appeared in the copy-text are listed below:

17.3   "Metaphysic"] W; "Metaphysics" I[1+]
17.6   Principles," by Ward;] W; Principles;" I[1+]
17.6–7   "The Psychological Standpoint," and "Psychology as Philosophic Method,"] W; "The Psychological Standpoint,ᴧ and ᴧ Psychology as Philosophic Method," I[1+]
17.23   1885] I[4+]; 1886 I[1-3]
17.24   and by] I[2+]; and I[1]
17.28   Harms's] W; Harm's I[1+]
17.36–42 Höffding . . . philosophy.] I[4+]; *omitted* I[1-3]
26.n5   introd., p. iii] W; introd. iii I[1+]
27.2   *zur*] W; der I[1+]
27.5   *Microcosmus*] W; Microscosmus I[1+]
27.7–8   *Sprach-|wissenschaft*] W; Sprachwissen-|schaft I[2+]; Sprachswissen-|schaft I[1]
27.10   *Pédagogie*] W; Pedagogie I[1+]
72.n4   *Idearum*] W; Ideorum I[1+]
72.n11   Guillaume] W; Gillaume I[1+]
*72.n12   *Outlines*] W; Elements I[1+]
*72.n12   27] W; 28 I[1+]
*72.n21   *Wissenschaftliche*] W; Philosophische I[1+]
*72.n31   *Sinnesorgane*] W; Sinnesorganen I[1+]
72.n31   pt. 2] W; vol. ii I[1+]
73.9   *L'Aperception*] W; L'Apperception I[1+]
73.9   *la*] W; le I[1+]
73.10   pt. 2] W; vol. ii I[1+]

73.16   pt. 2] W;   vol. ii I¹⁺
73.24   pt. 2] W;   vol. ii I¹⁺
73.25–26 *Tone Sensations*] W;   "Theory of Tone Sensations" I¹⁺
73.27   426, and] W;   428; I¹⁺
73.28   88] W;   90 I¹⁺
73.30   pt. 1] W;   vol. i I¹⁺
73.33   463] W;   453 I¹⁺
73.34   Hostinský] W;   Hostinsky I¹⁺
73.38   *Colour-Sense*] W;   Color Sense I¹⁺
73.40–41 *Hel-|ligkeits-*] W;   Helligskeits- I¹⁺
73.41   *Farbensinn*] W;   Farbensinn I²⁺;   Farbensinnes I¹
73.42   *Optique Physiologique*] W;   "Physiologique Optique" I¹⁺
74.1   pt. 1] W;   vol. i I¹⁺
74.6   pt. 2] W;   vol. ii I¹⁺
74.13–19 On the senses, . . . April, 1891.] I⁴⁺;   *omitted* I¹⁻³
135.n4   Hume,] I²⁺;   ~ ∧ I¹
135.n9   *Senses and Intellect*] W;   "Sense and Intellect" I¹⁺
135.n13 Murray,] W;   ~ ∧ I¹⁺
135.n21 *zur*] W;   der I¹⁺
*135.n26 *Outlines*] W;   Elements I¹⁺
*135.n26 39] W;   40 I¹⁺
135.n26 and] W;   *omitted* I¹⁺
135.n32 and] W;   *omitted* I¹⁺
*136.1–2 *Out-|lines*] W;   Elements I¹⁺
*136.2   46] W;   47 I¹⁺
136.2   and] W;   *omitted* I¹⁺
136.10   –90, and] W;   290; I¹⁺
136.14   Friedrich] W;   Fredrich I¹⁺
136.17   *Apperzeption*] W;   Apperception I¹⁺
136.21   *Teaching*] W;   Education I¹⁺
136.22–23 Fröh-|lich] W;   Frohlich I¹⁺
*152.9–10 Jardine, *The Elements of the Psychology of Cognition*]
         W;   Jardine (*op. cit.*) I¹⁺
152.n12 *Teoria*] W;   Theoria I¹⁺
152.n29 963), and] W;   963); I¹⁺
152.n30 500] W;   502 I¹⁺
152.n32 and] W;   *omitted* I¹⁺
153.1   pt. 1] W;   vol. i I¹⁺
153.4   *Gesichtssinnes*] W;   Gesichtsinnes I¹⁺
153.7   *Gesichtssinn*] W;   Gesichtsinn I¹⁺
153.16   and] W;   *omitted* I¹⁺
*153.16 *Outlines*] W;   Elements I¹⁺
153.16   *of*] W;   of I¹⁻²²;   on I²⁴⁺
*153.16 65] W;   66 I¹⁺

153.20   James and Cabot] W; Cabot and James I[1+]
153.24   vol. ii] I[2+]; *omitted* I[1]
166.n8   *the*] W; *omitted* I[1+]
167.15   *Lernakt*] W; Lernact I[1+]
167.16   Schumann] W; Schuhmann I[1+]
167.18   Miquel] W; Miguél I[1+]
176.11   Cobbe] W; Cobbes I[1+]
176.14   *Traums*] W; Traumes I[1+]
213.n10   *L'Idée*] W; L'Idee I[1+]
*255.n5   *Outlines*] W; Elements I[1+]
*255.n5–6 82, and] W; 83; I[1+]
255.n11   Is] W; is I[1+]
255.n15   *Leidenschaften*] W; Liedenschaften I[1+]
255.n27   *Delbœuf*] W; Delbouef I[1+]
255.n27   *Théorie*] W; Theorie I[1+]
280.n5   245, and] W; 245; I[1+]
280.n15   *Schönen, and*] W; Schönen;" I[1+]
297.n17   Stephen] W; Stephens I[1+]
307.n3   276, and] W; 276; I[1+]
320.n2   504] I[2+]; 506 I[1]
320.n8   "Zur] I[2+]; on "Zur I[1]
320.n10   –95] W; 395 I[2+]; 394 I[1]
*331.n4   *Outlines*] W; Elements I[1+]
*331.n5   88] W; 91 I[1+]
365.6   Thaulow's] I[2+]; Thalow's I[1]
365.6   *Hegels*] W; Hegel's I[1+]
366.2   *Sachen*] W; Sachen I[2+]; Lachen I[1]
366.7   556] W; 566 I[1+]
366.11   *Intelligence,*] W; ~∧ I[1+]
366.12   *in Animals*] W; *omitted* I[1+]
366.15–16 Bourbon del Monte] W; Bourdon de Monte I[1+]
366.17–18 *Psychologie Comparée: L'Homme et L'Animal*] W;
          "Psychologie Comparée" and "L'Homme et l'Animal" I[1+]
366.18   *Sociétés*] W; Sociétes I[1+]
366.19–20 *vergleichen-|den*] W; vergleichende I[1+]
366.26   *Développement*] W; Developpement I[1+]
366.26   Löbisch] W; Lobisch I[1+]

TEXTUAL NOTES

72.n12   Dewey referred to a translation of *Elements of Psychology*
          six times [72.n12, 135.n26, 136.1–2, 153.16, 255.n5, 331.n4].
          Each of the references is actually to *Outlines of Psy-*

chology, the first English version of Lotze's *Grundzüge der Psychologie*, based on the third German edition of 1884 and translated by George T. Ladd. The source is verified both by the subject matter of all the references and by the beginning page number of each. Ending page numbers have been made accurate at 72.n12, 135.n26, 136.2, 153.16, 255.n5, 331.n5. We can only speculate that Dewey's familiarity with the German version, his translation for his own use of "*Grundzüge*", and his acquaintance with Ladd's work *Elements of Physiological Psychology* combined in some fashion to cause the mistaken reference to *Elements* rather than the correct *Outlines*.

72.n21   The article to which Dewey clearly intended to refer was "Über die Natur der Menschlichen Sinnesempfindungen," vol. ii, pp. 591–609, of Helmholtz's *Wissenschaftliche Abhandlungen*.

72.n31   The correction in spelling was made here in this edition at first reference to the work where also the full title *Handbuch der Physiologie der Sinnesorgane* was substituted for the copy-text reading "(*op. cit.*)".

152.n9–10   The title of the work has been supplied. Even though the copy-text uses "(*op. cit.*)" at this point, no title of any work by Jardine is listed before this reference nor in the references which follow.

SPECIAL LIST OF EMENDATIONS IN HEADINGS

No doubt to enhance the book's usefulness to students, an elaborate system of headings in *Psychology* categorizes the contents in such detail that no index was provided. Whether Dewey himself wrote the headings or whether they were supplied by the publisher is not known, but the system is easily the most complicated to be found in his works. Unfortunately, in the original version it was also inconsistent in the typographical distinction of the different levels, and occasionally misleading in the order of subordination. The second and fourth printings altered some headings to conform to the added or substituted subject matter but did comparatively little to revise the standing system.

Because there is no evidence that Dewey disapproved of the headings structure, it must be considered sufficiently authoritative to be retained with a minimum of editorial intervention. Hence except

for the silent elimination of periods and dashes, all changes are listed
below for the record, whether editorial or drawn from the revised
printings I² and I⁴. The one exception to be noted is that substantive
changes of headings made by Dewey as a part of and within passages
revised in I² and I⁴ properly appear in the List of Emendations in
the Copy-Text in the context of the rewritten passages.

Editorial emendation has aimed at reducing the inconsistency to
some order both in subordination and in typography. In addition, the
editors have chosen to eliminate a confusing seventh level of heading
that occurs only in Chapters 3 and 4.

8.18   *as*] I²⁺; *or* I¹
14.3   *Physiological Psychology*] I²⁺; *Experimental Method* I¹
32.9   2. *THE PHYSIOLOGICAL STIMULUS*] I²⁺; II. THE
          PHYSIOLOGICAL STIMULUS I¹
34.11   II] I²⁺; III I¹
34.12   *as*] I²⁺; *or* I¹
37.19   III] I²⁺; IV I¹
40.16   (1)] W; (*i.*) I¹⁺
41.2–3   (2) Materialism fails to throw any light upon the specific
          facts of sensation.] W; (*ii.*) *Materialism Fails to Throw
          any Light upon the Specific Facts of Sensation.* I¹⁺
43.17   IV] I²⁺; V I¹
45.11   DEVELOPMENT OF SENSATION] I⁴⁺; *Special Senses*
          I¹⁻³
46.9–10   (1) The development is from emotional to intellectual.] W;
          1. *The Development is from Emotional to Intellectual.* I⁴⁺
46.24–25 (2) The development is from the vague to the definite.] W;
          2. *The Development is from the Vague to the Definite.* I⁴⁺
47.4–5   (3) The development involves increased differentiation and
          mobility of sense organs.] W; *The Development Involves
          Increased Differentiation and Mobility of Sense Organs.* I⁴⁺
49.1   *SENSATIONS*] I⁴⁺; *Sensation* I¹⁻³
51.1   *i.*] W; (*a.*) I¹⁺
51.7   *ii.*] W; (*b.*) I¹⁺
51.17   *iii.*] W; (*c.*) I¹⁺
53.1   II. Muscular Sensation] *stet* I¹⁻³; *omitted* I⁴⁺
68.34   I.] W; *omitted* I¹⁺
69.8   II.] W; *omitted* I¹⁺
69.25   III.] W; *omitted* I¹⁺
75.19–20 (1) Actual knowledge is concerned with a world of related

objects] W; 1. *Actual Knowledge is Concerned with a World of Related Objects* I^{1+}

76.10–11 (2) Actual knowledge is concerned with relations.] W; 2. *Actual Knowledge is Concerned with Relations.* I^{1+}

77.5–6 (3) Actual knowledge is concerned with ideal elements.] W; 3. *Actual Knowledge is Concerned with Ideal Elements.* I^{1+}

78.17 I] W; A I^{1+}

81.27 II] W; B I^{1+}

83.2 I] W; A I^{1+}

83.7 1] W; I I^{1+}

83.28 2] W; II I^{1+}

85.1 ·II] W; B I^{1+}

91.4 i.] W; (a.) I^{1+}

92.6 ii.] W; (b.) I^{1+}

94.15 i.] W; (a.) I^{1+}

95.19 ii.] W; (b.) I^{1+}

97.8 i.] W; (a.) I^{1+}

98.28 ii.] W; (b.) I^{1+}

99.6 iii.] W; (c.) I^{1+}

100.1 III] W; C I^{1+}

115.33 1.] W; (1.) I^{1+}

116.16 2.] W; (2.) I^{1+}

172.10 *Universalizing Activity of Imagination*] I^{2+}; *Imagination a Universalizing Activity* I^1

178.36 *Aspects*] I^{2+}; *Aspect* I^1

193.31 *Reasoning*] I^{2+}; *all Reasoning* I^1

*194.14 *Particular*] I^{2+}; *The Particular* I^1

216.24 *The Source of Qualitative Feelings*] I^{2+}; *The Self a Real, not Formal, Activity* I^1

234.14 3.] I^{2+}; *omitted* I^1

235.23 4.] I^{2+}; 3. I^1

236.7 5. *EFFECTS*] I^{2+}; *Effect* I^1

249.14 *Definiteness and Universality*] I^{2+}; *Various Forms of Likings* I^1

301.36 1.] I^{2+}; *omitted* I^1

302.15 2.] I^{2+}; *omitted* I^1

302.34 3.] I^{2+}; *omitted* I^1

303.15 4.] I^{2+}; *omitted* I^1

303.33 5.] I^{2+}; *omitted* I^1

304.16 6.] I^{2+}; *omitted* I^1

315.3 3.] I^{2+}; *omitted* I^1

316.20 4.] I^{2+}; 3. I^1

323.16 DIFFERENTIATION] I^{2+}; *Localization* I^1

324.36–37 (1) It leaves in consciousness a distinct idea of the end to be reached.] W; 1. *It Leaves in Consciousness a Distinct Idea of the End to be Reached.* I¹⁺

325.10–11 (2) The movement becomes localized just in the degree in which the act becomes definite.] W; 2. *The Movement becomes Localized . . . definite.* I²⁺; 2. Just in the degree in which the act becomes definite *the movement becomes localized.* I¹

325.22–23 (3) Less and less stimulus is required in order to set up the movement.] W; 3. *Less and less Stimulus is Required in Order to Set up the Movement.* I¹⁺

326.37–38 (1) The idea of the movement to be performed becomes more complex.] W; 1. *The Idea of the Movement to be Performed becomes more Complex.* I¹⁺

327.18–19 (2) Along . . . an extension in the range of movements.] W; 2. Along . . . *an Extension in the Range of Movements.* I²⁺; 2. Along . . . *an extension in the range of movements.* I¹

327.34 (3) There is also a deepening of the control.] W; 3. *There is also a Deepening of the Control.* I¹⁺

337.30 *PRACTICAL CONTROL*] I²⁺; *Practical* I¹

355.14 (1)] W; (1.) I¹⁺

355.25 (2)] W; (2.) I¹⁺

359.12 *Ideal*ʌ] I²⁺; ~, I¹

*   See textual note for 194.14–195.27, p. lxxxvii.

Word-division list

Word-division at the end of a line in the copy-text may present something of a problem for editorial decision whether Dewey's own general custom (insofar as it coincides with the style of the copy-text itself) requires certain words to be treated as hyphenated or as un-hyphenated compounds. The editors have decided the form of clear-cut cases silently. However, all doubtful examples, or examples that need emphasis, have been listed here, according to the formula

106.36   tread-mill

The reader should observe that in the present edition (W), all end-of-the-line hyphenations are the modern printer's unless specific record is made of those hyphenated compounds within the line in the copy-text that are ambiguously broken and hyphenated at the end of the line by W, which are recorded as in the formula

62.14   tuning-|fork] tuning-fork I^{1+}

There are no instances of possible compounds hyphenated at the end of the line in both the copy-text and W.

I. Compounds broken at the end of the line in the copy-text, I^1, or in emended passages adopted from I^2 and I^4, occurring internally in W:

24.9   in-coming
47.12   eye-lenses
63.33   eye-ball
67.14   blue-green
78.25   subject-matter
102.14   all-important
106.36   tread-mill
108.36   well-known
121.16   internally-initiated
147.17   so-called
149.23   head-light
150.15   not-self
190.7   standpoint

206.19	self-related
215.23	selfhood
225.20	pre-eminently
232.28	outflow
242.18	food-taking
252.35	fellow-men
261.17	self-consciousness
278.13	self-revealing
285.31	over-estimate
286.27	self-absorbed
290.23	outgrowth
294.12	well-being
327.29	*co-ordination*
332.7	precondition
344.32	non-successful

II. Compounds that are broken and hyphenated at the end of the line in W but appear as hyphenated compounds within the line in the copy-text, I[1], or in emended passages:

9.15	subject-|matter] subject-matter I[1+]
16.31	self-|consciousness] self-consciousness I[1+]
25.33	self-|sufficient] self-sufficient I[1+]
37.2	re-|connecting] re-connecting I[1+]
42.18	intra-|organic] intra-organic I[1+]
43.6	self-|originated] self-originated I[1+]
44.18	subject-|matter] subject-matter I[1+]
50.37	psycho-|physically] psycho-physically I[1+]
62.14	tuning-|fork] tuning-fork I[1+]
89.7	sub-|varieties] sub-varieties I[2+]
104.7	re-|presentation] re-presentation I[1+]
118.13	self-|development] self-development I[1+]
126.7	self-|knowledge] self-knowledge I[1+]
126.8	ready-|made] ready-made I[1+]
127.13	apple-|blossom] apple-blossom I[1+]
130.24	self-|developing] self-developing I[1+]
151.4	self-|externalization] self-externalization I[1+]
152.n25	*Text-|book]* Text-book I[1+]
161.20	well-|trained] well-trained I[1+]
164.37	not-|self] not-self I[1+]
191.26	self-|contradictory] self-contradictory I[1+]
205.7	actually-|performed] actually-performed I[1+]
212.8	self-|related] self-related I[1+]

217.19   self-|realization]   self-realization I[1+]
224.31   regularly-|recurrent]   regularly-recurrent I[1+]
237.36   mis-|adjustment]   mis-adjustment I[1+]
240.20   pin-|prick]   pin-prick I[1+]
250.20   sense-|feelings]   sense-feelings I[1+]
281.6   self-|conscious]   self-conscious I[1+]
284.35   make-|believe]   make-believe I[1+]
287.17   self-|complacency]   self-complacency I[1+]
287.21   self-|respect]   self-respect I[1+]
301.5   cerebro-|spinal]   cerebro-spinal I[1+]
319.8   self-|realization]   self-realization I[1+]
319.26   self-|objectifying]   self-objectifying I[1+]
332.16   co-|ordination]   co-ordination I[1+]
342.10   non-|securing]   non-securing I[1+]
357.7   self-|realization]   self-realization I[1+]
364.8   Post-|Kantian]   Post-Kantian I[1+]

Index

Index

Abstraction: as process of conception, 180–81; selecting activity of attention in, 181

Accidentals: xii; concept capitalization, xii–xiii, xvii; authority of, xiv; treatment of, xv

Action, ethical, 349–52

Action, moral: analysis of, 343; responsibility in, 343–44; and personality, 344–45; and will, 345; as prudential action, 345–46; results of, 352–56. *See also* Character; Control, moral

Action, prudential: becomes moral, 345–46

Action, religious, 361

American Book Company, xi, xlix, lii

Apperception: defined, 78; problem of, 78–81; stages of, 81–82; organs of, 112; dependent on adjustment, 123–25; relation to retention, 130–32; as memory, 133; and conception, 180; connection with qualitative feeling, 239–40

Architecture, 274–75

Art: freedom in, 269–70; realism in, 270; idealism in, 270; end of, 274

Arts, the fine: 274; architecture, 274–75; painting, 275; sculpture, 275; music, 275–76; poetry, 276–77

Association: law of, 83; conditions of, 83–84; transition to higher forms, 84; and dissociation, 84, 106–7; representative, 85, 87–88, 104; presentative, 85–87; forms of, 85–99; by similarity, 88–89; by contiguity, 88–93; in psychical life, 101–3; unconscious cerebration in, 104; simultaneous, 106; successive, 106–7; and attention, 117; of ideas in memory, 156; in recollection, 159–60; in intellectual feeling, 258; effects in motor impulses, 326–28

Attention: and association, 117; and consciousness, 117; defined, 118; as selecting activity, 118, 181; distinction from dissociation, 118–19; nature of, 119, 129–30; selection in, 119–21; as adjusting activity, 122–26; as relating activity, 126–30; unifying activity in, 127–28; growth of, 128; distinguishing activity of, 128–29; distinction in, 128–29; difference in, 128–29; unification in, 129–30; separation in, 129–30

Beauty: sensuous element in, 269; universality of, 270–72; and economy, 273; and harmony, 273

Berkeley, Bishop: theory of spatial relations, 144–45

Bibliographical terms: as used in present edition, ix*n*; impression, ix; edition, ix; printing, ix

Caird, Edward: mentioned, xxiii

Character: nature of, 352; results of, 353–56

Choice: in volition, 314–15, 316; in prudential control, 335–37; ethical, 348–52; result of character, 354

ciii

edition," l; copies collated, li, lvii–lviii; "third edition," lii; copy-text, liii, liv, lviii; critical text, liii–liv; system of headings in, xciii–xciv; word-division in, xcvii

Reasoning: defined, 192–93; explicit, 193; implicit, 193; universal element in, 193–94; particular element in, 194; *a priori*, 194–95; *a posteriori*, 194–95; inductive and deductive, 195, 196–98; fact and law in, 198–99; and judgment, 199–200; and conception, 199–200; and systematization, 201

Redintegration. *See* Association

Retention: defined, 78, 130; and apperception, 130–31, 132; nature of, 132–33; as organization, 133; distinguished from memory, 133; of ideas, 133–34; form of, 134; synonyms for, 134–35; and qualitative feeling, 247

Revisions: authorial, x, xi, xii, xiii; in *Psychology*, xi, xxiv–xxv, xxvi, xlix, l, 5; of accidentals, xii, xiv; of substantives, xii, xiv; in various impressions, xiii; unauthoritative, xiii, xiv, xvi; evidence of, xiv; recording of, xvi–xvii

Rhythm: in psychical life, 161–62; nature of, 162; and time perception, 162–63; not confined to art, 163

Science: psychology as, 3, 9; physical, 11; nature of, 76–77; philosophy as, 202

Self: as consciousness, 7–8; as individual, 8; individuality of, 8; as subject of psychology, 9; and feeling, 21–22, 216, 254–55; as knowing, 77; growth of, 77, 78; in adjustment, 125–26; and perception of objects, 150–51; and memory, 164–65; connection with space and time, 166; and intuition, 206, 209–11;

actual and ideal, 254; and harmony, 273; and volition, 311–12, 318–19; as will, 357

Self-consciousness, 16

Sensation: defined, 29; elements of, 29; external stimuli to, 30–32; characteristics of, 31; physiological stimuli, 32–34; as element in consciousness, 34–37; continuum, 35–37; connection with stimuli, 37–43; functions of, 43–45; quality in, 44–45; differentiation of, 45–47; of pressure, 49; of place, 51–52; muscular, 53–55, 142, 143; of smell, 56–57; of taste, 58–59; of hearing, 59–63; of sight, 63–68; of temperature, 68–70; organic, 70–72; interest in, 109–10; of touch, 144. *See also* Feeling

Seth, Andrew: mentioned, xxiii

Sight: physical stimulus, 63–64; organ of, 64; blind spot, 64; muscular mechanism of, 64–65; as sensation, 65–67; muscular sensations in, 67; in color distinction, 67–68; muscular activity in, 68; feelings of, 225–26

Signs, local, 52, 142, 143–44

Size, perception of, 149–50

Smell: organ of, 56; physical stimulus, 56; and appetite, 57; and organic feelings, 57; and taste, 59, 221–22

Sounds: intensity of, 60; pitch in, 61–62; timbre of, 62; musical, 62–63

Stimuli: extra-organic, 31–32, 33; in sensation, 32, 37–43; physiological, 32–34; in smell, 56; in taste, 58; in hearing, 59; in sight, 63–64; in feeling, 219–20; in motor impulses, 325–26

Substantives: xii; authority of, xiv

Sympathy: and antipathy, 283; defined, 283–84; origin, 284; nature of, 284–85; conditions of, 285; function, 285–86; and social relations, 286–87

Systematization: defined, 201; and reasoning, 201; process, 201